Form and Surprise
in Composition

Form and Surprise in Composition

Writing and Thinking Across the Curriculum

John C. Bean   John D. Ramage

Montana State University

Macmillan Publishing Company

New York

Macmillan Publishing Company
866 Third Avenue, New York, New York 10022

Library of Congress Cataloging-in-Publication Data

Bean, John C.
   Form and surprise in composition.

   Includes index.
   1. English language—Rhetoric.   2. Interdisciplinary
approach in education.   I. Ramage, John D.   II. Title.
PE1408.B468   1986   808'.042   85-11472
ISBN 0-02-307470-1

Printing: 5 6 7 8   Year: 8 9 0 1 2 3 4

ISBN 0-02-307470-1

Preface

In composing *Form and Surprise in Composition: Writing and Thinking Across the Curriculum*, we have had three aims. First, we wanted *Form and Surprise* to be a book about writing as process, informed throughout by the assumption that through language humans make meaning, just as through drafting and revising writers come to discover what they know. Second, we wanted our text to help students develop generic thinking skills essential for success in all disciplines: the ability to ask questions and pose problems, to conduct dialectic inquiry, to generate ideas, to create hierarchical structures of thought, and to argue logically and humanely. Finally, that *Form and Surprise* serve as an introductory freshman composition text particularly suited for institutions emphasizing writing-across-the-curriculum.

WRITING-ACROSS-THE-CURRICULUM

To appreciate the design of our text, readers should know something about our vision of writing-across-the-curriculum. In such a program, we believe, instructors across campus would require some writing in all their courses, and this writing itself would be regarded both as a process and as a mode of learning. The aim of writing-across-the-curriculum, as the faculty of Beaver College put it so well, is to enable students to join the ongoing conversation that characterizes an academic discipline. To enter this conversation, students need the ability to pose questions within the discipline and to conduct the kind of reasoned inquiry that the discipline demands.

To this end, *Form and Surprise* focuses on what educational psychologist William Perry calls the growth from dualistic "right answer" thinking toward more relativistic "issue-oriented" thinking. Our purpose in this text, therefore, is not to teach the styles and formats appropriate for different disciplines but to show that at the core of all disciplines is a body of problems and issues that generates ongoing discussions. The text attempts to address two kinds of thinking problems common to most beginning college students: the problem of thinking of something to say, known variously as the problem of invention, discovery, or creativity; and the problem of organizing ideas into a structured discourse of generals and specifics.

These two thinking problems are reflected in our title *Form and Surprise*. By "form" we mean an essay's shape or organization; by "surprise" we mean its inventiveness, its newness, its capacity for disturbing or bringing pleasure. Of course, form and surprise are not separable qualities that can exist independently. But the habits of seeking form and surprise can be developed through the kinds of writing assignments contained in the text.

Based on our experiences in helping to direct the Montana State University Thinking Skills and Writing Project, funded in part by a grant from the Fund for the Improvement of Postsecondary Education, we believe a writing-across-the-curriculum text should prepare students for the kinds of writing tasks they are apt to be given at an institution where writing is a mode of learning. Here are four expectations common at our own university:

1. *Ungraded writing*, particularly short in-class freewrites or journals. Wary of open-ended response journals popular in the sixties, some of our faculty have preferred guided journals in which students respond to daily writing tasks developed in advance by the instructor and aimed at increasing learning of course content as well as thinking skills. The guided journal sequences in our text introduce students to this kind of daily exploratory writing, enabling them to learn the value of "writing for self" as a means of discovery and clarification.

2. *Short essays*, usually two to three pages long but sometimes as short as a single paragraph (at our institution we call one- or two-paragraph essays "microthemes"), that have come to replace longer term papers for most classes at the lower division level. Instructors design the assignments to promote the kinds of learning and thinking valued in the course. Instructors can grade short essays rapidly, thus enabling them to assign more writing. Moreover, if all students are writing on the same topic, instructors can provide "models feedback" by discussing representative essays in class.

3. *Group collaboration*, wherein small groups of students work together on a research or problem-solving project, sometimes producing individual essays based on common research but often producing a single group report. Since group or committee writing is common in business and professional life, some instructors across the curriculum believe that undergraduates should experience the successes and frustrations of group writing. This text provides guidance for students asked to work together on writing projects.

4. *Peer review* at all stages of the writing process. Ideally, every essay submitted as final copy to an instructor, no matter what discipline, should have been read in various draft stages by fellow students. A freshman writing course must therefore train students not only to be writers but also to be courteous and helpful readers of their classmates' works-in-progress. Our text encourages a small group workshop approach to writing and provides specific guidance for peer-reviewing of drafts. The accompanying *Instructor's Manual with Sample Student Essays*, available to all instructors, provides considerable guidance in teaching students how to critique each other's work.

THE WRITING ASSIGNMENTS

The formal writing assignments that comprise the core of our text are aimed at developing patterns of thought useful for college writers. Appropriately for an introductory writing course, students are encouraged to write about personal experience; but they are also encouraged to regard their experiences from a "problematic" point of view that can be transferred to their academic course work. The main writing assignments for the text occur in Chapters 8, 12, and 13. They are arranged progressively in three categories: problem-solution essays (roughly equivalent to exposition), issue-defense essays (roughly equivalent to persuasion), and story-based essays (roughly equivalent to description and narration but composed in what James Britton has referred to as the "poetic mode").

The general logic of *Form and Surprise* can be seen in the text's sequence of ten formal assignments:

1. A short essay that proposes a solution to a problem (Chapter 8).
2. An essay that explains two or more alternative solutions to a problem (Chapter 8).
3. An essay that poses a problem, gives an expected solution, and then shifts to an unexpected solution (Chapter 8).
4. An essay that explains a contradiction or quandary that leaves the writer puzzled (Chapter 8).
5. An analytical essay that presents the writer's answer to a puzzling question about topics selected from different disciplines (Chapter 8).
6. An essay that sets forth reasons in support of a position (Chapter 12).
7. An essay that summarizes an opposing position and then shows weaknesses in that position (Chapter 12).
8. An essay that supports a position through the use of a Rogerian "listening" strategy (Chapter 12).
9. A longer argumentation essay that uses a combination of strategies (Chapter 12).

10. A story-based essay that uses narration and description to convey its "truth" poetically rather than transactionally (Chapter 13).

These assignments are supplemented by a series of short "microthemes" (Chapter 6) aimed at helping students understand principles of form. The microtheme assignments guide students to produce short essays that shift back and forth among several levels of generality. Students who warm up on a few of the microtheme tasks will usually develop the organizational skills needed for success in the longer essays.

A distinguishing feature of our text is the way it helps students discover ideas for their essays. In this text "invention" is more than "pre-writing." Rather, invention is a fresh way of regarding the world, a habit of problematizing experience, a predisposition to ask questions and find contraries. To this end the text emphasizes James Britton's "expressive" writing as a means of puzzling and exploring. The heart of invention in this text is the guided journal, which encourages students to develop new habits of thought. The four guided journal sequences are designed to make students more aware of their writing and thinking processes at a personal level.

Our emphasis on journal writing follows from our belief, derived in part from Michael Polanyi, that all knowledge, even the most abstruse and abstract knowledge, is ultimately personal. Either a person understands a concept in his or her own language or parrots it in another's. The journal sequences serve as self-instructional guides to a variety of discovery strategies ranging from freewriting to formal heuristics, from idea-mapping to Peter Elbow's believing and doubting game.

A COMPREHENSIVE RHETORIC

As a comprehensive rhetoric, the text also contains explanatory chapters aimed at providing theoretical background for the assignments as well as instruction in skills and concepts (exclusive of sentence-level skills normally treated in handbooks). Included within each chapter are ample "For Class Discussion" exercises suitable either for small group problem-solving tasks or for general class discussion. The major parts of the text can be briefly summarized.

Part I, "Some Basic Principles and Skills," explains the theory of language and cognition underlying the text, including composing as a recursive process, the advantage to writers of "problematizing experience," the way effective writing converts information into meaning, and various principles for achieving form and surprise in an essay. Part II, "Problem-Solution Essays," includes an extensive discussion of question-asking, both as an introduction to problem-solution essays and as a way of encouraging students to view themselves as active learners. Part III, "Issue-Defense

Essays," contains a discussion of argumentation that goes beyond both formal logic and Toulmin logic in its system for helping students generate arguments. Part IV, "Story-Based Essays," explains our view of narrative and descriptive writing as a way of creating story, the language where all disciplines converge. Part V, "Readings about Thinking, Writing, and Learning," provides a short anthology of readings related to thinking, writing, and learning. From these readings we have drawn much of the illustrative and problem-posing materials used in Part I. Finally, the book concludes with an appendix about working in groups that offers a rationale for using small groups and offers advice to students for making their small groups work.

THE INSTRUCTOR'S MANUAL WITH SAMPLE STUDENT ESSAYS

The text is supplemented with a comprehensive Instructor's Manual derived from the pooled experiences of more than a dozen teachers who have used the text in various draft forms over a three-year period. The Instructor's Manual also contains representative sample essays for many of the text's assignments. These essays—both weak and strong—can be reproduced for use in class discussions and "norming" sessions of the kind explained in the Appendix to the text.

BACKGROUND AND ACKNOWLEDGMENTS

The approach taken in this text to the teaching of writing has grown out of a major writing-across-the-curriculum project at Montana State University known as the "MSU Thinking Skills and Writing Project." Through interaction with faculty from across campus, aided by such influential workshop leaders as Ken Bruffee of Brooklyn College, Harvey Wiener of La Guardia Community College, John R. Hayes of Carnegie-Mellon University, Karen Spear of the University of Utah, Joanne Kurfiss of Weber State College and Will Pitkin of Utah State University, our vision of writing-across-the-curriculum has grown and changed. An early draft of the book was used in an experimental section of freshman writing in 1983, and over the next two years the 2,000 or so students who have used evolving versions of the text have had the greatest influence on its shape.

As those familiar with recent pedagogy will recognize, our book owes much to the ideas of many scholars. We would like to single out for special appreciation several major figures who have most influenced our thinking: Kenneth Bruffee, whose work in the philosophy of collaborative learning redirected our whole approach to composition; Ann Berthoff, whose NEH Summer Seminar in Philosophy and Composition introduced coauthor John Ramage to the rich body of scholarship relating language to thought; Toby

Fulwiler and Randall Freisinger, whose work at Michigan Technological University has done much to promote the value of expressive writing in the academic disciplines; Andrea Lunsford, whose research into the cognitive strategies of beginning writers has influenced our sense of assignment design; and Peter Elbow, who taught us the believing and doubting game.

We would also like to offer thanks and appreciation to the following people who contributed so much to the development of our text: to Stuart Knapp, Academic Vice-President of Montana State University, who has unflaggingly supported writing at our institution and who had the political courage to establish the university's Teaching/Learning Program, which has generously funded a whole series of pilot projects in writing-across-the-curriculum; to the Fund for the Improvement of Postsecondary Education for its major institutional grant creating the MSU Thinking Skills and Writing Project; to Jack Folsom, the director of the MSU Thinking Skills and Writing Project, and to our colleague from the School of Business, Dean Drenk, our copartner in the project, who is among the most influential voices for writing-across-the-curriculum on our campus; to Cheryl Roller, Adele Pittendrigh, Kathy Ramage, Carol Haviland, and Judy Keeler, the composition professionals who piloted our text in its earliest versions and gave us invaluable suggestions for revisions; to those faculty from Beaver College, SUNY-Binghamton, and Georgia State University who participated with us in a FIPSE-supported consortium on thinking skills; to Bob Morasky, Shannon Taylor, Paula Petrik, Glenn Lehrer, Ron Mussulman, Rita Flaningam, Nat Owings, Dick McConnen, Larry Kirkpatrick, Denny Lee, Steve Custer, Ken Weaver, Shirley Cudney, and other faculty from MSU who have been leaders in the writing-across-the-curriculum movement; to Paul Ferlazzo, the former head of MSU's English Department, for his understanding and generous encouragement; to the following external reviewers who gave us timely and often biting criticism of our early drafts—Roger J. Bresnahan (Michigan State University), Toby Fulwiler (University of Vermont), C. W. Griffin (Virginia Commonwealth University), David A. Jolliffe (University of Illinois at Chicago), Becky Kirschner (Michigan State University, Institute for Research on Teaching), Andrea Lunsford (University of British Columbia), and William E. Smith (Utah State University); to the following students who have provided the examples of student writing used throughout the text—Bonnie Abbott, Molly Weaver, Jeff Pentel, Tracy Williams, Catherine Clarke, Anita Foster, Judy Gehman, Marvin Drake, Mark Babb, Barbara Moore, and Wendy Foster; to Susan Didriksen, for whom we first began our work at Macmillan, and to Eben W. Ludlow, who well deserves his reputation as one of the best editors in the business; and finally to our families who put up with us throughout the ordeal of writing—Kit, Matt, Andrew, Stephen, and Sarah Bean; Kathy, Laura, and Chris Ramage.

Brief Contents

Detailed Contents

PART III

ISSUE-DEFENSE ESSAYS   255

PART IV

STORY-BASED ESSAYS   353

* Includes a 3–4 hour group project: Defining "Good Writing," pp. 439–448.

CHAPTER 1

The Writing Process: An Introduction to the Text

This book is about the writing process, even though no two people ever go through the process in the same way. Many students, however, don't realize that writing is a process at all. They believe that experienced writers sit down at their desks and compose a finished essay on the first try. But the truth is that most serious writers write slowly and laboriously, throwing away a dozen sentences for every sentence they keep, writing and crossing out, concentrating heroically for brief spurts of productive writing and then entering long minutes of drought punctuated by trips to the coffee pot and the bathroom. The page from the draft of an engineering professor's article on engineering education (Figure 1-1) shows the kinds of changes writers typically make on their drafts.

THE WRITING PROCESSES USED BY EXPERIENCED WRITERS

We said at the outset that no two people go through exactly the same writing process. How experienced writers set about their own writing is as individual as their fingerprints. When co-author John Bean sat down to write the first draft of this present chapter, he had no outline, just the memory of an school year. ~~A~~ The major ~~conclusion of our report~~ assumption of our program is that

improvement of students' communication skills will not be

possible unless students are required to do written and oral work

--and receive appropriate feedback--regularly throughout the

four years of their engineering curriculum. This goal can be

best achieved if faculty learn to design short, focused writing

or speaking assignments, ~~in addition to the~~ as well as longer technical

reports that we would like to require of our students prior to

graduation. ~~These more numerous short, focused writing or~~ Once the instructor sees the value of short writing and

~~speaking assignments should~~ speaking assignments focused on the master of engineering concepts, they build coherently on each other

can then cooperate to design sequences of assignments that

according to a consistant theory of cognitive development. ~~and if~~ What follows

are some examples of writing and speaking assignments that have recently

~~faculty can increase their efficiency in providing effective~~

been used in our department

~~feedback without an unexceptably large increase in workload our~~

~~goal to improve the students communication skills should be~~

~~achieved. Our philosophy is that no one has to do a lot if~~

~~everyone does a little.~~

Strategy of Using Communications Assignments to Support

Engineering Learning

Written Examples

~~First~~ Since, we use writing and oral communications as a mode of

learning, ~~by~~ we design~~ing~~ assignments that develop mastery of

engineering concepts and principles. For example: in an

introductory sophomore statics course taught to construction

engineering technologists, the concept of force, moment and

couple is often confusing. If ~~this~~ these concept~~s~~ ~~is~~ are not clarified ~~near~~

~~the beginning of the quarter~~ early, the students have ~~a difficult time~~ difficulty

~~understanding how these three concepts are interrelated and how~~

FIGURE 1-1   Page from the Draft of an Engineering Professor's Essay

hour's discussion with John Ramage the day before. A year before that, Ramage had written another version of Chapter 1—a version that had long been discarded, although its ideas had shaped many parts of the book. Like Bean, Ramage doesn't work from an outline. Unlike Bean, however, Ramage has before him dozens of pages of chaotic scribblings, each one an exploration of an idea that might fit somewhere in some part of a chapter. His first draft is an attempt to put together pieces of ideas scattered throughout dozens of sheets of scratch paper. Bean, on the other hand, tends to work from condensed "idea notes," each one a line or two of cryptic phrases that trigger ideas that make sense only to him. When Bean starts writing, he imagines an initial sequence of ideas in his head and starts putting words on paper. Whenever he sees better ways to organize his material, he makes notes to himself in the margins of the draft. The only thing Bean and Ramage have in common at this point is that neither knows for sure where his ideas will lead until he begins to write. (More on this later.)

Our friends and acquaintances who write regularly—experienced students, fellow professors, attorneys, journalists, business people, engineers, military officers—all have their individual approaches to writing. One of our colleagues writes an incredibly messy rough draft and then types out a completely revised finished copy on the next draft, working painfully over each emerging paragraph, doing ten minutes of silent mental manipulations of language for each minute of typing. A much larger percentage of writers, however, reach a finished draft by going progressively through four or five intermediate drafts—revising them until they are too messy to read any more, then retyping them for another round of revisions. The more experienced the writer, the more likely that a fresh draft early in the writing process will be radically different from the previous one. These writers, in fact, almost completely dismantle their first constructions, like a child knocking over a block house, and start fresh, building on what was learned the first time to create a more appropriate structure the second time.

Along the way writers have a fascinating number of neuroses and fetishes. Some write first drafts in pencil and then switch to a typewriter or computer. Some must have exactly the right kind of writing implement and paper. Some write double or triple spaced and make elaborate changes between the lines, including cuttings and pastings to move parts around. Some compose at the typewriter; some can only compose with the solid feel of pen or pencil between thumb and forefinger. The development of word processors only adds to the variety. Some people compose and revise directly at the terminal, their essays going through all the transformations of the writing process without ink ever touching paper. Others use the computer like a secretary who types out a succession of fresh drafts, each one to be revised the old-fashioned way—with pen and ink. But whatever the process, they all share a sense of exploration and discovery as they grope their way toward a final product that eventually captures "what they want to say."

There are two categories of writers, however, who do not, as a rule, go through the writing process as we have described it. It will be instructive to look at both of these categories as a way of understanding the writing process more thoroughly.

The first class includes those who routinely write under intense time pressure, for example, journalists or business people who must churn out several dozen important business letters a day. These people sometimes get angry at the way composition teachers stress the slowness of the writing process. "If I had to go through six rough drafts for every letter I write," one business executive once told us at a workshop, "I would have been fired my first month on the job." Similarly, journalists covering a late-breaking story to be reported in the next morning's early edition haven't time to worry about drafts.

But further examination of these people's writing process actually confirms rather than denies the importance of the writing process as we have described it. For example, business people often develop formulas for their letters that allow them to plug information into standard formats, and frequently business letters are short, cutting down on elaborate decisions about organization. Moreover, most business people know exactly whom they are writing to and why they are writing when they set out to compose a letter or memo. These features make extensive drafting less necessary. But when the same business people have to prepare major reports to the corporate board, complete with important recommendations defended with supporting data, they once again revert to the writing process we have described—a much slower, evolutionary sequence of drafts. Of course, some people, by training or by unusual genes, can do preliminary drafting "in their heads" and turn out highly respectable writing quickly. But these people, like sword-swallowers or double-jointed jugglers, are the exceptions, not the rule.

There is, however, another class of writers who really do *not* go through the writing process as we have described it. These writers really do turn out finished copy the first time; they see revision not as radical "re-seeing" of the ideas discovered in the first draft but mainly as correcting a few superficial errors in spelling or grammar and recopying for neatness. These writers, by and large, are the vast majority of students who sign up for freshman English courses throughout the country. Extensive research by composition specialists, ranging from interviews with beginning writers to actual observation of their process as they compose, has confirmed this phenomenon again and again. Inexperienced writers tend to be satisfied with their first drafts and turn them in as finished copy, as if a perfectly respectable caterpillar could pass for a butterfly. For some reason, they do not seem obsessed by the need to write successive drafts. Why is this so?

Inexperienced writers, we believe, don't go through the writing process because they haven't learned to pose for themselves the same kinds of problems that experienced writers pose. To use a term that we will define more fully in the next chapter, they haven't learned how to "problematize" their experience, to see how essays arise out of contradictory views of the world. For experienced writers, essays are attempts to make readers understand something in a new way, just as we are now trying to make you understand our view of why beginning writers don't go through the writing process. The best way for you to appreciate the kinds of problems that experienced writers face is for us to ask the converse questions, "Why is it that experienced writers *do* go through the writing process? Why do they write so many drafts? Why can't they get it right the first time?"

WHY EXPERIENCED WRITERS NEED A SUCCESSION OF DRAFTS

We will suggest three inter-related reasons, each of which you might find surprising.

Writing to Discover Meaning

Reason One: At the outset, experienced writers don't really know what they want to say. Inexperienced writers often misunderstand the relationship between language and thought. They believe that thinking is done invisibly in the brain in a mysterious process without language. Then, after the ideas are all clear, the thinker somehow packages them up in language to deliver to someone else. This misconception—that thinking occurs separately from language—prevents beginning writers from appreciating what happens when an experienced writer constructs a draft. As we will explain more fully later, writers use language to explore and make meanings. In arranging words on a page, a writer is not so much trying to say clearly what he already knows as to *discover* what he knows, or even actually to *make* what he knows.

Let's construct a simple analogy from the world of architecture to help clarify the concept. Suppose you come suddenly into wealth and decide, for some strange reason, to remodel the kitchen in your house. You want to tear out all the old fixtures and cabinets and start over again, allowing yourself the option of adding windows, moving doors, or even building an addition. At the outset you aren't sure what you want. What size room do you want? How much counter space? Where do you want doors and windows? What kind of appliances? What size and color? Where should they be located in relation to windows and doors? What kind of floor covering and style of cabinets? What about lighting?

You check out some "do-it-yourself" books from the library, and they all suggest that you draw scale models of various floor plans and then cut out little cardboard figures to represent counters and appliances. You move these around on your floor space until you *discover what you like.* In other words, you don't begin knowing what you want; you only discover what you want in the act of arranging cardboard symbols, of making your ideas visible. Moreover, as you arrange and rearrange your symbols your design problems become increasingly complex. Although you want the sink under a window, putting it there leaves no room for the refrigerator. The problems become even more complex as you begin actual construction because what looked good at the planning stage looks awful when you really build it. Although you liked the early American cabinet style when you saw it in the catalog, those cabinets now look cheap in your kitchen. Moreover, they clash with the futuristic wallpaper you chose. You decide to return the cabinets and wallpaper to the store and start over. As you try out these various "rough drafts" of your new kitchen, you realize how impossible it is for the mind to imagine the whole kitchen at once; its design grows through trial and error with lots of backtracking.

This analogy may help illuminate the writing process. Instead of cardboard figures, however, words become the symbols you manipulate, and your successive drafts become attempts to discover what you are struggling to say. Just as you discard a dozen possible ways to organize your kitchen in choosing the one you want, so you discard numerous "tries" at an idea in your search for the language patterns that convey the meanings that you are simultaneously seeking and making.

Let's now move from an analogy to an example. Several physics teachers at our university use short writing assignments to help their students learn physics, based on the assumption that you don't really understand something until you can explain it to someone else. Figure 1-2 shows a typical writing assignment from a course in introductory physics.

We've interviewed many students about their experiences in writing these assignments. Students often tell us that they "thought" they understood the concept until they tried explaining it. Suddenly the concept started getting cloudy. They reread the text; they began discussing the problem with classmates; they began seeing the problem suddenly as a *real* problem. Their first drafts became only approximations of what they were trying to say, a painful way of forcing themselves to think more clearly. Significantly, the more the instructor demanded that the essay explain the solution to another student *who didn't already understand the physics concepts involved*, the more the writers became dissatisfied with early drafts and rewrote them. During their first drafts they tried to get the ideas clear *for themselves*; then in later drafts they tried to make these ideas clear to their readers. These students' experiences illustrate clearly that writers often don't start off knowing what they want to say. They go through the writing

Suppose you put a big block of ice in a bucket and then fill the bucket with water until the water level is exactly even with the edge of the bucket. (The ice, of course, is now floating in the water.)

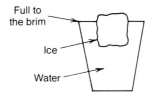

Full to the brim

Ice

Water

Now we will wait for several hours for the ice to melt. Which of the following will happen? (Neglect evaporation)

a. The water level in the bucket will remain exactly the same.
b. The water level in the bucket will drop.
c. Some water will overflow the sides of the bucket.

Your task: After deciding upon your answer, explain it in writing. Imagine that you are writing to a classmate who doesn't yet understand flotation and who is arguing for what you consider the wrong answer. Your task is to explain your reasoning so clearly that your essay serves as a little textbook, *teaching* your classmate the physics principles involved. Thus, your essay will be judged *not simply* on whether or not you figure out the correct answer but on whether or not you can write clearly enough to *teach* a fellow classmate.

FIGURE 1-2   A Short Writing Assignment in Physics

process to discover what they know. For them the writing process truly began once they posed for themselves a significant problem—both the problem of understanding the physics concept and the problem of explaining it to someone else.

Writing to Discover Audience

Reason Two: *At the outset experienced writers don't know their audience.* Besides not knowing what they want to say, experienced writers often don't start out knowing for sure who their readers are. To return to our kitchen analogy, suppose now that you are a business person who buys old houses and remodels them for resale. You've recently bought two houses—a '50s style tract house in a working-class suburb and an old brownstone in a newly fashionable urban neighborhood where upscale professionals are moving back into the city. Now you aren't designing kitchens for yourself but for others, in this case, for two different kinds of buyers whose tastes in kitchens are probably as different as potato chips from brie or a pickup camper from a Saab. What kinds of kitchens would be appropriate for each house?

The writer's problem is similar, only more complex. Who will read your essay? Why might they want to read it? What do they already know about your topic? What do you know about your topic that they don't already know? What interests them? What bores them?

A typical school setting is an artificial and potentially damaging environment for beginning writers because students become used to thinking of their teachers as their audience—single individuals who, by job description, have to read what students write because they assigned it. In real life, however, readers read essays because they want to, and unless you imagine your essays as bringing some sort of benefit or pleasure to persons other than your teacher, you won't be setting for yourself the same sort of writing problem that experienced writers set.

One reason, then, that experienced writers go through so many drafts is that they are seeking to clarify their sense of audience. The engineering professor we mentioned at the beginning of this chapter was troubled throughout his drafting process by his unclear sense of an audience. Although he knew he was writing about education to a group of civil engineering professors, he couldn't decide how much they knew or didn't know about his topic, which concerned strategies for designing writing assignments in engineering courses. How much did these professors know about recent theories that link writing to thinking and learning? If they didn't know about it, how much space should he take to summarize it? Would they be naturally interested in this background or would he have to figure out a way to make it interesting for them? If they already knew about it, would this section insult their intelligence or otherwise bore them? The only way he could proceed was to write a draft and then get feedback from those engineering colleagues he could rope into reading his draft. (Incidentally, he got contradictory advice, complicating even more his sense of audience!)

Throughout this text we will be asking you to imagine audiences different from your teacher, audiences that you must somehow reach and influence. Unless otherwise specified, your audience will be your fellow classmates, but your sense of who these classmates are and what they need won't be clear at the outset. You will discover, in fact, that your readers' needs and wants will change with every topic you might choose so that you can clarify your sense of an audience only by discussing your drafts with your classmates.

Writing to Discover Purpose

Reason Three: *At the outset experienced writers don't know their purpose in writing.* By *purpose* we mean the writer's stance toward her topic and her audience. If you ask beginning writers in the middle of their drafts why they are writing an essay, they are apt to say, "Because my teacher assigned it." Experienced writers, however, express purpose in terms of the impact they want their essays to have on their audience. Do you want your audience to learn something? To experience or feel something? To become aware of something they were previously unaware of? To change their minds about something? To do something?

Again, our civil engineering friend had a major problem discovering his purpose. Did his audience already believe in giving writing assignments in engineering courses but not know how to go about it? If so, then his essay would have to include lots of how-to information and examples. Or was his audience skeptical about using writing assignments, believing that teaching writing was the job of the English Department? If so, then his essay would have to persuade readers that writing assignments could actually help students learn engineering. He would have to reduce his "how-to" examples and include instead a lengthier discussion of theory and some testimonial success stories. In short, what you put into an essay depends on why you are writing it as well as to whom you are writing it.

We have now tried to show you that experienced writers are propelled through the writing process in order to make discoveries for themselves about what they want to say, whom they want to say it to, and why they want to say it. This is one dimension of the "problem" they pose for themselves in setting out to write. The other dimension of the "problem" involves the content of the essay itself: essays generally exist in order to answer a question. The writer, of course, must understand that readers will be testing the writer's answer against other possible answers. The questions themselves exist because we live in an imperfectly understood world where every person's view of the world differs in certain features from everyone else's. Essays are attempts to communicate to each other across these gaps, to bring world views somewhat closer together.

BEGINNING WRITERS AND THE PROBLEM OF ALIENATION

Let's return now to our original question: "Why don't beginning writers go through the writing process as we have been describing it?" So far we have explained that beginning writers don't pose for themselves the same problems that experienced writers pose. But there is another reason also, one that we might call "alienation," that is, a sense that school assignments are somehow a pointless game governed by arbitrary rules.

Earlier we likened the writing process to the process of designing a kitchen. We can imagine, however, a school setting in which students would quickly shut down the "kitchen-designing" process. Suppose teachers required students to draw designs for buildings instead of to write essays as regular homework (after all, to many students both tasks might seem like equally pointless busywork). Imagine the following conversation in which Pete discusses an assignment with Jane:

Pete: What are you doing in Smith's class these days?
Jane: We had to draw another floor plan last week. We had to design a plan for remodeling a kitchen.
Pete: Was it hard?
Jane: No, I wrote out my design in about twenty minutes. It was no sweat.
Pete: What did you get on it?
Jane: I got a C−. I didn't make my lines neat enough. Smith really knocks your grade if you don't use a ruler. I also didn't put in a microwave oven.
Pete: What?
Jane: Jefferson's brother had Smith a year ago. He says Smith only gives out A's if you put in a microwave oven. I wish I'd known that ahead of time.
Pete: Oh, well, it's all stupid anyway.

Why didn't Jane go through the "kitchen-designing process" as we described it earlier? In what ways does this dialogue between Pete and Jane reveal some truths about writing in a school setting? Contrast this dialogue with a dialogue you can imagine between a professional kitchen designer and a friend discussing work she'd just done for a big client. Our point, of course, is that you won't go through the writing process unless you really *want* to communicate ideas that are important to you. In short, if you are going to go through the writing process, you've got to turn a school assignment into something that matters to you.

TWO METAPHORS FOR DESCRIBING THE WRITING PROCESS

In order to describe the writing process, teachers are often tempted to break it down into stages such as "pre-writing, writing, and re-writing" or "invention, shaping, and editing." These terms can often be helpful because writers clearly do operate in stages—sometimes placing words for the first time on blank sheets of paper, at other times revising and editing passages that are already written. The problem, however, is that the stages always overlap. For example, late in the writing process, at a stage where you could be expected to be worrying mainly about sentence structure or spelling, you might suddenly decide that your essay would be improved if you changed its purpose somewhat. This decision forces you to revise your entire essay, writing a new introduction and reshaping your paragraphs to meet the new purpose. The writing process is thus too recursive, too full of starts and stops and loops backward, to break into clearly distinguished stages.

Instead, we will now attempt to describe the writing process by using two kinds of metaphors—the metaphor of the developing embryo and the metaphor of the cabinetmaker building a piece of furniture.

The Embryo

The embryo metaphor emphasizes the growth of an idea from infancy to maturity and the extensive modification that takes place during that process. The butterfly embryo, developing from fertilized cell into caterpillar into butterfly, is the most startling example of transformation, and is an especially useful analogy for a writer, whose ugly caterpillar draft can be transformed into a butterfly essay if the writer can get a coherent vision of content, audience, and purpose by the end of the writing process.

The embryo metaphor can help you appreciate how unfortunate the assigning of grades can be in a school setting if, for example, the criteria for a finished essay are applied too early to a perfectly healthy intermediate draft. We tell our students that a "C" essay is often an "A" essay turned in too soon. Just as a caterpillar is not a "C" butterfly, many essays receiving "C's" or "D's" in college are actually promising drafts that aren't yet finished. And just as a butterfly cannot come into existence without first being a caterpillar, an "A" essay cannot come into existence without first being a "C" draft as measured by the criteria of a finished essay. Thus an "A" writer is apt to turn out first an "F" draft (again measured by the criteria of a finished product) and then revise that into a "D" draft, then into a "C" draft, and so on until it matures into an "A" draft. Inexperienced writers, however, are apt to turn in their "C" drafts as finished products and forever after think of themselves as "C" writers.

The Cabinetmaker

But the embryo metaphor, as helpful as it is, is also misleading because it doesn't indicate the role of a guiding intellect that makes choices and shapes the process. (A caterpillar turns naturally into a butterfly, but essays don't write themselves naturally.) The cabinetmaker metaphor, on the other hand, lets us imagine the role of an artist constructing a work of art. The cabinetmaker begins first by drawing a series of sketches for the design of, say, a desk (roughly equivalent to notes, doodles, and early drafts of an essay); then the cabinetmaker produces a meticulous design plan with attention to measurements and angles (roughly equivalent to the shaping or outlining stage of writing). At this point the cabinetmaker cuts and shapes the separate pieces for the desk and assembles them (equivalent to writing a late draft). Finally the cabinetmaker finishes the piece, sanding it again and again and applying coats of varnish—a process that often takes as long as the whole design and building stages combined (roughly equivalent to editing, where the writer worries about graceful sentence structure and correctness).

But this metaphor too is misleading because wood is objective and static while words are almost infinitely fluid and can be shaped to create an infinite number of meanings, none of which exists in a concrete way like wood. In some sense essays really do develop like embryos, taking on a life of their own and growing with an independence that the writer succumbs to rather than controls, as if a table leg talked back to the cabinetmaker, insisting on becoming the rung of a chair instead. What we must admit, finally, is that the writing process is too complicated to describe, too elusive even to fully understand. What goes on when writers write is at the very center of intelligence itself, at the core of the mystery of being human instead of a genetically wired animal or a silicon chip. We can all, however, become more conscious of our own writing processes and can make changes in the process which result in better writing.

For Class Discussion

1. What follows are two drafts of a student's essay about the dilemma of conducting medical research on animals—an early "discovery" draft and a final draft. The essay was written in response to the "contradiction–quandary assignment" in Chapter 8, pages 228–236. Discuss the changes that occurred between the initial draft and the final one and try to account for them in terms of the writer's changing perception of content, audience, and purpose.

Early "Discovery" Draft

Do you think it is right to experiment on animals? This is a controversy that has caused a lot of arguments and disagreements for many years. The fight between the opposing sides has generated much publicity and legislation. The Animal Welfare Act was drawn up in an attempt to create a balance between animal welfare and animal research. The passage in 1966 did little to stop the dispute. Is this a good bill?

Animal research is good. A large percentage of all advancements in medical science have been advanced upon knowledge gained through animal-based research. There was a case of two young boys that had been in an automobile accident who had received severe burns. In the past they would have had no hope for their survival, but today, thanks to the extensive research done in this area on pigs, their lives were saved. Because of the great importance of animals to research institutions nationwide, there is great care put into housing and feeding them. Right here at Montana State University, construction has taken place in Lewis Hall, a new facility, strictly for housing laboratory animals. These animals, usually from animal shelters, get better treatment than most house pets. A veterinarian is at hand at all times, and their nutritive intake monitored constantly. They take good care of these animals because the Animal Welfare Act made laws saying they had to. Without these laws maybe our scientists wouldn't take good care of the animals.

But animal research is bad. Animals are virtually dependent upon humans and should not be taken advantage of. By manipulating animals and administering unusual treatments upon them, we are cruelly violating their rights. We, as humans, have no right to decide how much pain should be inflicted upon an animal or how and when it will die. A greatly publicized issue that demonstrates this is the case of "Baby Faye." In this case, an infant was born with a defective heart. The doctors, in an attempt to save the infant, sacrificed a baby baboon and transplanted its heart into a human infant. This caused an uproar in the Animal Rights groups nationwide. They argued that the doctors were overstepping their ethical bounds and trying to "play God." They had no right to eliminate the life of the baboon, especially with no guarantee that it would benefit the human.

The pros and cons of this argument have been and will be debated for a long time. It is a situation in which we, personally, must decide upon. I am still wondering if the research is worth it. Is it most advantageous to use animals as human substitutes, or is this a selfish act on the part of the humans and a violation of the animal's rights. I guess every person has to decide this issue for himself or herself.

Final Draft

A Cruel Dilemma

The young lab assistant gave the monkey a last affectionate pat before snapping shut his cage door. She had become so attached to the small, homely animal in the last three weeks, she would miss him. But Cindy knew from the beginning that the animals she cared for were being raised for the purpose of animal-based research, so she had taken special care not to develop too much of a liking for any of them. The exception was the monkey. When he was shipped in, she just couldn't resist his sad brown eyes and humanlike gestures. As the date for the experiment involving the monkey drew closer, Cindy felt confused and pressured. She knew very little about the research being done on the monkey, but she suspected it was important. Even so, she wasn't sure if she agreed with the use of animals in experiments. Is it right to use animals in medical research? Does the long-range benefit to humans outweigh the torture we impose on defenseless, pain-feeling creatures?

The animal lovers of the world speak in a strong, loud voice against the use of animals in research. They argue that most of the information scientists get from animal research could be obtained in other ways. They also argue that animals have rights just as much as human minorities; if it is wrong to do medical experiments on prisoners or mentally retarded people, it is wrong to do them on other of God's creatures also. They point to the excruciating pain that test animals often have to endure. A recent issue of *Newsweek* brought this point home clearly. It showed animals in various states of mutilation—rabbits with huge pussy eyes being eaten away by toxic chemicals, dogs with cancerous growths all over their bodies, monkeys strapped motionless to boards, their bodies covered with wires attached to monitoring devices. Although scientists are supposed to give test animals painkillers, many times they don't, and often the painkillers wear off weeks before the animals mercifully die.

The many people supporting animal-based research would retaliate against the views expressed in the preceding paragraph by pointing out the large number of life-saving advancements in medicine that result from experiments involving animals. A specific example of this is improvement in the field of burn therapy. In Oregon, there was a case of two young boys who had been involved in a fiery automobile wreck. Both boys received severe third degree burns over 97 percent of their bodies. In the past, neither would have had any chance for survival. But today, thanks to the extensive research done in this area on pigs, their lives were able to be saved. Supporters of animal research also insist that, by and large, animal research is done as humanely as possible. New federal regulations govern any research institution's use of animals. Great care is taken when deciding the relevancy of the experiments the animals are used in. Biannual inspection of facilities and extensive paperwork serve the purpose of insuring that no mistreatment is taking place.

Both sides in this issue have presented strong cases, and neither shows signs of giving up on what they believe in. What makes the dilemma so troubling for me is that both arguments seem equally strong. When I think of the need for cancer research and other kinds of new medical knowledge, I acknowledge that we have to experiment on animals. When I am in this mood, I say that humans and animals are not equal in the great scheme of things and that indeed the life of a human is more important than the life of a test monkey. But when I think of Cindy and her little monkey friend and when I look at those horrible pictures in *Newsweek*, I think that humans have no right to inflict this pain on fellow creatures. At this point I think that humans are arrogant to declare their superiority in the great scheme of things. American Indians call the animals their brothers. Is scientific progress worth harming a brother? I don't know, so I am left with a dilemma.

2. We claimed early in this chapter that most college freshmen, whom we have classified as inexperienced writers, do not go through the writing process as we have described it. Is our claim true for you? How would you

describe the process you go through when assigned an essay to write? Decide through small group or class discussions to what extent our observations about student writers seem true for the majority of students in your class at this time.

THE WRITING PROCESS AND THE SIGNIFICANCE OF OUR TITLE: *FORM AND SURPRISE*

Another way of thinking about the writing process is to think of it in terms of one's final goals. Thinking about writing in this way is helpful primarily because it simplifies the task a good deal. As we've seen, there isn't any single writing process that we can point to as being definitive. There are almost as many writing processes, it seems, as there are writers. Additionally, research into the processes of individual writers suggests that they move back and forth between different stages of the process so rapidly that it's almost impossible to follow, let alone map, any particular process. But if we can think of the process in terms of the shift back and forth between two major goals, we can see that the writing processes of all experienced writers have an underlying similarity.

We call these two goals "form" and "surprise." What we mean by these two terms will become gradually clearer as you read Part I of this text. For now, though, a preliminary explanation will be useful.

We should note at the start that the terms are not exactly parallel: *form* is a property of the written text; *surprise* is a response inside the reader's mind. If we were to create pairs of parallel terms we would call them something like "form and disorder" or "predictability and surprise." But it is precisely because form and surprise are not parallel that they are useful terms. Indeed, writers find themselves constantly pulled in opposite directions toward one or the other of these sometimes complementary and sometimes competing goals of writing. For example, you may find yourself writing along, explaining some concept in laborious detail, clarifying, connecting, forming your thoughts, when you suddenly realize, "but my audience already knows all that." Hence you force yourself to start over again. Your revision is a reaction to your sense that there has to be an active tension between order and newness, form and surprise.

By way of further clarification of these two central terms, let's consider them in light of the two different words we use to label the sort of writing you do in college: "composition" and "essay." As we shall show, the concern for form is implicit in the root meaning of the word "composition," and the concern for surprise is implicit in the root meaning of the word "essay."

Form

The word *composition* derives from *compose*, which means to put conflicting elements together in peace and harmony. The *com* of *compose* is the same *com* as in *community* or *communion* and suggests a coming together, an establishing of relationship. Our term *form* refers to the "relatedness" of a composition, that is, to its shape or organization. As will be explained in detail later in the text, form derives from the relationship of the parts to the whole. Form is created when you weave back and forth between generalizations and the specific details that support those generalizations. To describe form, teachers use such terms as "unity" and "cohesion" and refer to "thesis statements," "topic sentences," and "transitions." Since all these terms will be defined in due course, what you need to understand now is that compositions, like other works of art, have structures with identifiable parts arranged into a whole. This pattern, or shape, is what we mean by "form."

Surprise

The other word commonly used for a piece of writing is *essay*, which derives from a word meaning *attempt* as you might know from taking French or Spanish where the verb for *to try* is *essayer* or *essayar*. If you think of an essay as an *attempt*, you will appreciate the element of risk that a writer undertakes. What you are "attempting" or "risking" when you write an essay is to communicate ideas or insights that your readers do not already possess. You are attempting to bridge a gap between your understanding of some part of your world and your reader's different understanding. Our term *surprise* refers to an essay's success at bridging a gap. That is, an essay must bring the reader something new, something different or unexpected, something interesting, disturbing, or challenging.

Perhaps another analogy would help, this time from the area of physics called thermodynamics. The laws of thermodynamics state that heat will be transferred between two bodies of matter only if they are initially at different temperatures. The greater the degree of temperature difference, the greater the amount of energy transferred. Writers aiming for "surprise" in their essays might imagine themselves conveying energy (the writer's view of a topic) across a gap to a reader existing at a different temperature (a different view of the topic). What you want to avoid, to continue the analogy, is to be at the same temperature as your reader, that is, to say only what your readers already know, because then no different perceptions of the world will be transferred. As we will discuss in Part I of this text, surprise is not a simple feature of an essay that can be added or removed, but a complex product of the essay's content, form, and style. For now, however, it will suffice if you think of surprise as the element of newness or unexpectedness in your essay.

THE WRITING PROCESS AND THE GENERAL STRUCTURE OF THIS TEXT

This text has five parts. Part I introduces you to some basic skills and some important principles about writing. Parts II, III, and IV provide the formal writing assignments for the text, along with explanatory chapters and coordinated journal assignments for exploring ideas. Part V is a brief collection of essays by professional writers.

Part I—"Some Basic Principles and Skills"—will help you to stand back from the on-going process of writing an essay in order to appreciate, at a more abstract level, what is going on. The journal sequence which opens Part I and the microtheme chapter which closes it introduce you to some basic skills of writing. In between are some theoretical chapters which provide insights about principles. We believe that learning is most productive if the "how" of a process is tied occasionally to the "why." If you wanted to become an airline pilot, you would spend hundreds of hours learning the "how"--what levers to pull, what buttons to press, what gauges to watch, what actions to take at what moments. But as a pilot you would also be interested in some theoretical "why" questions: Why does a plane stall at a certain speed? Why does a plane fly in the first place? And so forth. Part I of this text discusses writing from this "why?" point of view.

The second main section of the text (Parts II, III, and IV) contains the formal essay assignments, together with a guided journal sequence for each section and one or more chapters explaining the thinking strategy that each kind of assignment demands. We classify formal essays into three broad categories that we have found useful for beginning academic writers: Part II deals with problem-solution essays, in which the body of your essay provides the answer to a question or the solution to a problem that you pose in the introduction. In these essays you imagine readers who want to learn information that your essay provides. Part III concerns issue-defense essays, in which the body of your essay defends your position on a controversial issue. In these essays you imagine readers who disagree with your position and thus must be persuaded rather than simply informed. Finally, Part IV treats story-based essays, in which you move beyond answers or positions to tell the "truth" you want to tell through story and image. In these essays you imagine readers who want to share a piece of someone's life without reducing it to a thesis statement. This kind of essay is something like a cross between a personal narrative and a short story.

It should be noted, of course, that these three types are not mutually exclusive. One might combine the three forms in any number of ways. You could, for example, use a story to present a problem or to defend a position. But we believe that these are useful distinctions for helping beginning college students get a handle on ways they can discover topics and organize essays for courses in any discipline.

The last section of the text—Part V—is a short collection of essays by professional writers dealing with issues of thinking, writing, and learning. These essays will be mentioned occasionally throughout the text both as illustrations of points and as examples of surprising ideas to stimulate thinking and controversy.

PART I

Some Basic Principles and Skills

Part I introduces you to some basic principles and skills that will help you gain experience as a writer. Much of Part I focuses on discovering ideas for your essays. The activity of discovering or inventing ideas is perhaps the least understood part of the writing process. In our view, the invention stage of writing does not begin when you receive a writing assignment. Rather, invention is a way of life. It involves a critical way of looking at the world, an awareness of gaps between your view of the world and someone else's, a sense of the problematic nature of ideas. Throughout this text we use the guided journal sequences to help you learn the skills of invention. The journal sequence which opens Part I—"Thinking about Thinking, Writing, and Learning"—introduces you to journal writing and to some basic techniques for stimulating ideas. You should work your way through this first journal sequence while you are reading Part I of the text.

The heart of invention, to our way of thinking, is the propensity to "problematize experience." Ideas grow when the mind wrestles with a problem. This way of looking at the world is the subject of Chapter 2—"Problematizing Experience: A Discussion of Reasoning for Writers." This chapter argues that problems begin with the thinker's awareness of contraries, or oppositions, the gap between two or more clashing ways of interpreting experience. If the journal sequences in our text help you learn "how" to find problems, Chapter 2 helps you understand "why" problem-finding is important.

It is one thing to explore ideas in a journal; it is another thing to shape those ideas for readers in a formal essay. As we explain in Chapter 3—"Form and Surprise: How to Turn Information into Meaning"—the act of organizing an essay is simultaneously the act of creating meanings. Experienced writers go through numerous drafts because the meanings they are creating evolve and change as they compose, thereby requiring new forms. Chapter 3 discusses these connections in detail.

While Chapter 3 is a theoretical discussion of how writers create form and surprise by turning information into meaning, Chapters 4 and 5 give you some practical suggestions for creating your own form and surprise. Chapter 4 explains three principles of form that will be useful to you as your ideas evolve, while Chapter 5, in turn, offers three principles of surprise. The two chapters together should equip you with enough "why" information to make sense out of the process you will go through in writing your formal essays.

Part I ends with a chapter on microthemes, which we see as something like practicing scales in music or figure-eights in ice-skating. These are skill-building exercises that help you learn, in discrete, manageable steps, some important techniques for organizing essays. As you will see, journal writing and microtheme writing involve quite different skills, skills which you must learn to integrate when composing formal essays.

Guided Journal: Sequence 1

Thinking about Thinking, Writing, and Learning

AN INTRODUCTION TO JOURNAL WRITING

The heart of the writing program set forth in this textbook is the Guided Journal, where you will learn how to use writing to discover ideas. And in discovering ideas to write about, you will also be learning creative thinking habits applicable to all disciplines.

For this first journal sequence, we suggest you write in your journals for one hour every day, preferably in three 20-minute segments. Before you gasp too hard ("an hour a day!"), think of learning to write as a lot like learning to play the piano or to figure skate. If you wanted to be good, you would expect to practice these skills at least an hour a day, especially if you were paying for lessons. There is something magical about an hour a day. We know of a running coach who teaches first-time joggers to run marathons within 18 months. His technique is to get beginners to run one hour non-stop every day—no matter how slowly, no matter if it takes someone a whole hour just to run around one block. Although on that first day beginners claim to die in agony, they soon notice that an hour of running comes more easily and that as they gradually increase their distances they are building up endurance to run for two and three hours at a time.

Of course, the analogy between writing and running can't be pushed too far. To the extent that writing involves generating ideas, then the analogy is helpful because writers, like runners, must develop discipline and endurance; they must learn to think intensely and productively for longer and longer periods of time. To the extent, however, that writing means sharing your ideas with others, then the analogy breaks down. Not even a professional writer can write non-stop for an hour and produce anything that is ready for someone else to read. Writing an essay for strangers takes lots of revising, and that is a kind of practice that this journal by itself won't provide.

Think of your journal, then, as a place to enhance your endurance for generating ideas. You may or may not share your journal writing with your instructor or peers. But if you do, you will not be judged as if you were writing an essay. In a journal, a good insight or an unusual question is far more important than a coherent paragraph or a well-composed conclusion. Journal writing is for yourself, not for others.

In this first journal sequence you will be exploring alternately two different topics—one we assign for you and one you choose on your own. The topic we assign concerns your ideas about thinking and learning. We want you to begin asking what it means to get a college education, to be an active thinker and learner in an academic setting. The topic you choose for yourself can be anything you are really interested in.

You should discover several benefits from doing this initial journal sequence. First, you should see yourself increasingly as an independent thinker who enjoys generating ideas for their own sake. Most of the ideas you discover in your journal will never find their way into your formal, graded essays for the course. Having an excess of ideas, however, is one of the hallmarks of a good writer. We want you always to see that each formal essay for this course will contain only a narrow portion of your ideas. Second, you will begin to practice habits of mind, such as searching for paradoxes, contradictions, and complications, that will be important for becoming a thinking writer in any academic subject area. Third, some of the ideas you discover in this sequence will be used directly in this course, either in the microthemes that your instructor may assign or in your formal essays.

Here is a brief list of the skills you will begin developing in this sequence: freewriting; looping; composing quick personal narratives; using "who, what, where, when, why, and how" to generate details; listening to views different form your own; looking for contradictions and complexities; and playing the believing and doubting game.

In Chapter 6 we have provided several microtheme assignments based on ideas you will generate in the journal; these will give you a different kind of writing practice. Whereas the journal frees you to write disorganized "searches" for yourself, the microthemes give you practice at writing single paragraphs shaped for readers. The journal encourages creativity and idea-generation; the microthemes encourage organization and logical development. In the journal you are trying to discover what you know; in the microthemes you are trying to convey what you have discovered to strangers.

Writing the Journal

Keep your journal entries in a separate notebook of whatever size and shape most inspires you to write (unless your instructor prefers a specific format). This sequence has 21 writing tasks. We recommend that you spend 20 minutes on each task, doing three tasks each day. Your teacher will inform you how many days a week to write. (Some teachers ask students to finish all 21 tasks in seven straight calendar days at the beginning of the term; others assign journal writing only on specified days during the week.) Whatever your assigned schedule, begin developing the habit of serious concentration during each of your 20-minute sessions. Just as you can waste time while practicing the piano, you can waste time writing in your journal. Journal writing, as we see it, is for serious students who plan to get their money's worth out of college.

Task 1

Freewrite for 10 minutes on the general topic "education." Rest for a minute or two. Then continue freewriting on "education" for another 10 minutes.

Explanation

Suppose you were given the following essay assignment:

Write an essay somehow connected to the general topic "education." The only restriction is that the essay *must* reflect your own personal ideas about some aspect of education and *must* contain within it at least one story about something that actually happened to you.

Chances are that upon receiving this assignment you would have little idea about what to write. What do you do then? One comfort is to know that a skilled writer would be just as uncertain as a beginner when such an assignment is first given. However, skilled writers have developed systematic thinking habits for tackling such problems. A skilled writer might, for example, generate a page or so of ideas about the topic before trying to focus on a likely theme.

One of the best "research-tested" means of developing ideas is a technique called "freewriting." When you freewrite, you put your pen on the paper and write non-stop for a set time period making sure your hand never stops moving. You don't worry about spelling, punctuation, grammar, or organization. Your pen, in fact, simply records the whirl of ideas that churn up in your brain. One student describes freewriting as taking a swim in the sea of his thoughts and recording what floats by. If you can't think of anything to say, write your last word over and over again, or write something soothing such as "relax" or "palm trees."

For this first session in your journal we want you to freewrite on the general topic "education," but to break your 20-minutes of freewriting into two 10-minute segments. Write "education" at the top of a blank page in your journal. Then set an alarm for 10 minutes and write nonstop, letting your ideas go wherever the trigger word "education" takes them. You will probably discover that after one or two minutes you run out of ideas; the purpose of freewriting is to break through this "idea-exhaustion" barrier, just as a runner must break through a pain barrier. When you run out of ideas, don't let your pen stop moving; discipline yourself to search for new ideas and keep going. Remember, you can write *anything*. Almost invariably an idea about education will pop into your consciousness and you can start pursuing it.

After 10 minutes, relax for a minute or two and then freewrite for 10 more minutes starting where you left off or beginning something fresh on the general topic "education." See if you can fill more lines with writing during your second 10 minutes than you did during you first 10 minutes. Keep that pen moving. Wait at least a half-hour before going on to Task 2.

Here is an example of a student's freewrite on this task:

The first thing that comes to my mind when I think of Education is a rock. My parents have always stood firm on a good education. They feel that you should receive your high school diploma and a college degree is what they strive for. Neither one of my parents got to have the opportunity of getting a college diploma. My mom got married right out of high school at the early age of 17. My dad was born into a large family in North Carolina that wasn't very rich. They were hard working people though. They did all get a high school diploma which his parents did enforce, but they never had enough money to send them to college. That is the reason why my parents feel that they have the money to send us to college. I myself feel it should be up to the kids. I like college, but my parents didn't force me to go they just left it up to me. They just suggested it and I think about it. Relax Relax Relax my dad thought it wasn't right to force kids to go to college. I do know kids that their parents feel that the only way is a college education. The kids just rebel and do go, but all they do at college is party all the time. I have noticed that this is what all new freshmen do around here. It is the first time away from home and they sure take advantage of it. Stay out late and party every night. I believe it is alright to party sometimes, but it has its limits.

Task 2

Reread your previous freewrite, searching for one idea that you liked best. Then freewrite for another 20 minutes on "education," but begin by developing in more detail this "most interesting idea" from your first freewrite.

Explanation

For this 20 minutes you will continue freewriting, but this time you should focus your efforts a bit more by searching for a dominant idea that began to emerge from your previous freewrite. This technique is called "looping" since you loop back to the most intriguing or interesting strand of your earlier freewrite. Begin with whatever you liked best in your first freewrite and see if the topic of "education" can lead you on to more ideas. Freewrite for 20-minutes (you can break this down into two 10-minute segments, if you like), again forcing yourself to break through the "idea-exhaustion" barrier. Set yourself a goal of increasing by 10 percent the number of words you can generate in 20 minutes of freewriting. Then wait for at least a half-hour.

Task 3

Freewrite for 20 minutes on "education," but this time focus on telling a story that actually happened to you.

This time, focus specifically on a story that actually happened to you that is in some way connected to "education." Don't worry for now exactly what that connection is or what your story might actually mean in a finished essay. Just tell your story in simple chronological order, but try to make it interesting by including specific details. Use the journalist's questions of who? what? where? when? why? how? to help you generate details and keep going. Name people's names, and tell exactly where and when events happened. Imagine that you are telling the story at a party.

If you would like to see an example of a personal story related to education, look at John Ramage's story about Dr. P. in Chapter 2 (pp. 49–51). Of course, Ramage shaped and polished his story through intensive revision. You don't have to do that for this journal entry.

Task 4

Freewrite for 20 minutes on "my own personal topics I might like to explore in this journal."

Explanation

Besides asking you to write on "education" for Journal Sequence One, we also want you to explore ideas related to a topic you choose for yourself. Because you will need to return to this topic throughout this journal sequence, you should consider your choice carefully. The topic you choose must be something about which you have direct personal experience—your immediate family, your memories of your grandparents, growing up in your hometown or neighborhood, sports and hobbies, music, problems you've had, absolutely anything so long as you can draw on personal experience for your exploration of the topic.

Let's begin by helping you find a topic. Using the freewriting technique, brainstorm on paper as many different topics as you can think of, searching for a single topic you would like to stick with. Let an idea float into your mind—let's say, "favorite relatives"—and then freewrite as rapidly as you can about why this would be a good topic. As soon as another possible topic hits you—say, "the drug scene at Washington High School" or "summer vacations" or "working at the Burgerbasket"—then drop "favorite relatives" and explore the next topic. Try to get through seven or eight possible topics in 20 minutes. Then let the problem "cook" in your subconscious for awhile. Before you start Task 5, take the plunge and commit yourself to a topic.

Task 5

Freewrite for 20 minutes on the topic you have chosen.

Explanation

Reread what you wrote in Task 4, and then choose a topic that you think you can stick with for quite a while. At the beginning of your freewrite for this task, write down your topic and put a box around it. We will be using as an example a topic chosen by John, an older student in one of our classes— "Early Memories of Growing Up in Cascade."

Now, for this task, spend 20 minutes freewriting about the topic you have chosen. Begin by collecting all the memories you can about this topic. Let your mind wander through your topic, recording your memories as you go. What follows is a ten-minute freewrite written by John.

Growing up in Cascade. Let's see. Memories begin to come flooding in. I see myself about 8 years old playing out in the deepest, freshest snow you can imagine. I am with Terrie and we fall in the snow backwards, swing our arms up and down and our legs back and forth making angels in the snow. We would get up and compare angels (the snow image had wings) and laugh and laugh and then make more angels all over the yard. Snow in the winter. Cascade had so much snow. Right outside our house was the main sledding hill where dozens of kids would gather every free moment to pull their sleds up the hill—those old flexible fliers, I can still see the worn paint and the scars in my old flexible flier—and then slide down yelling and screaming. We could go for hours at a time and then come in while one of the mom's fixed us hot chocolate. This was small town America and we all seemed to have moms at home and a close community. More snow. I can remember the great storm when the TV antenna was knocked off our roof and when the snow was so high you could climb on the roof directly from the snow bank and then slide off the roof into the snow. I remember going so deep in the snow once that I couldn't get out and I started to cry and my dad had to come pull me out. My rubber overshoe stuck in the snow bank and my dad pulled my feet right out of the boot. We had to go back later and dig the boot out. Relax, sledding, relax, relax, let's see. Once on one of the big sledding hills outside of town several older kids got the hood off an old car and used it for a toboggan. I remember the first time I got enough nerve to ride in it. It had sharp edges and was probably dangerous but I got in the middle and held on to my friends' arms as we started down the hill. You couldn't steer the hood; it just spun and swirled like a ride in a carnival. That same hill later on in the summer was the place where Eddie Butler found an old car door handle and told me it was a caveman's tooth and that cavemen were still alive back in these woods. I ran home scared to death and Mom wasn't there. I went next door to the telephone office and waited by the big central floor heater until my dad came back.

Tasks 6 and 7

Create two different "idea-maps" on the topic "traits I like best in teachers."

Explanation

For these entries, we will return to the original topic of education, particularly your ideas about thinking and learning. For these entries, assume that you have been given another essay assignment:

Write an essay that answers the question "What traits do you like best in teachers?" The only restriction is that your essay must illustrate these traits with examples of behavior from specific teachers that you have actually had. You may use negative examples. (A negative example is an "opposite case"; that is, you might illustrate your appreciation of a sense of humor in teachers by an example of a teacher who didn't have one.)

For this task, instead of freewriting, you will practice another technique for generating ideas called "idea-mapping." In idea-mapping, you draw a circle in the center of your paper. Inside the circle you write a trigger word or statement. Then you jot down ideas by branching off the circle, each branch becoming more and more specific the farther you get from the circle. Figure A shows an example of an idea map on another topic related to education—"problems with the grading system." As you practice idea-mapping, you will soon see how the map stimulates you to think of ideas. You add ideas to your map either by beginning a new branch off the circle or by adding smaller and smaller branches to existing branches. Smaller branches are sometimes related logically to larger branches, but sometimes you might have purely associational or whimsical relationships between smaller and larger branches. As with free-writing, the idea-map is *your* tool for helping you generate ideas. Use it in the way that works best for you.

When you do idea-maps, the shape and direction of your thinking is often determined by the organizational pattern you choose for the first spokes off the hub. For today's assignment, try two different patterns. On separate blank pages in your journal, draw the hubs and initial spokes shown in the examples in Figure B. Then try to make your pages almost black, filling all available space with ideas branching off ideas. In order to "stretch" your ideas sufficiently, force yourself to add at least three levels of subbranches to each main branch. Count your two idea maps (similar ideas can appear on both maps) as Tasks 6 and 7.

Task 8

Read the articles as explained below. There is no writing for this task.

Explanation

Starting soon we are going to ask you to summarize several lectures in courses you are now taking. First, read the following brief article by Richard Steiner, Professor of Chemistry at the University of Utah (the article first appeared in *the Journal of Chemical Education*). Then choose a course or courses in which to summarize lectures. If you are not taking any courses in which the teacher gives lectures, you may try summarizing the results of a class discussion as if you were a secretary taking minutes for a meeting. But choose a lecture if possible.

Later on in this course you may also be asked to summarize articles as well as lectures. Because either kind of summary requires you to be an open-minded "listener," listening either to words in the air or words on a page, please read at this time Carl Rogers' article "Communication: Its Blocking and Its Facilitation" on pages 393–398. You will need to read this article both for an appreciation of the value of listening and for our

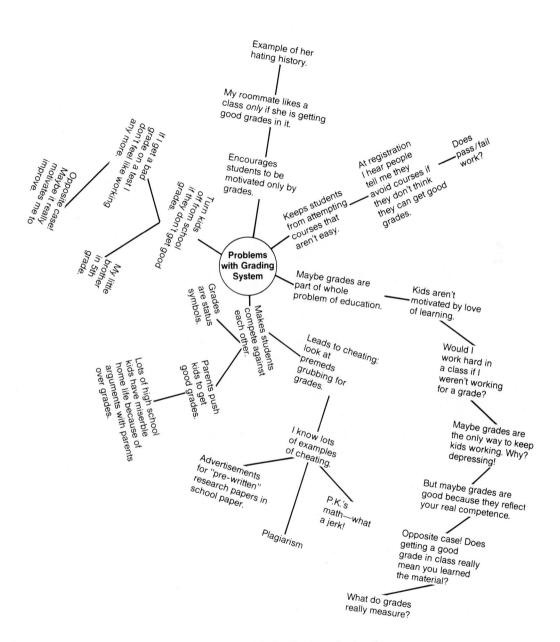

FIGURE A   An Idea Map on "Problems with the Grading System"

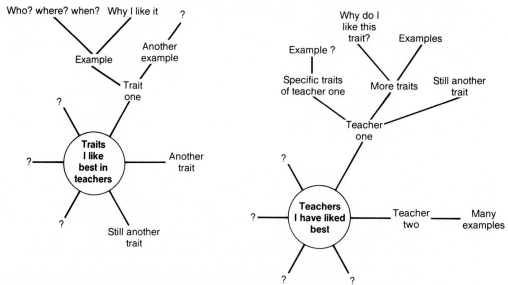

FIGURE B   Starter Diagrams for Idea Maps on "Traits I Like Best in Teachers"

up-coming discussions of the "believing and doubting game." Because you may appreciate having a bit of extra time, for this journal assignment you need only write a short sentence indicating that you have read the Steiner and Rogers articles.

Chemistry and the Written Word*

Recently, chemical educators have voiced concern over the apparent inability of students to understand and apply the principles of chemistry. At the same time educators in all fields have expressed concern that the writing ability of students is not what it should be. In short, these two statements indicate that many students cannot think and cannot write. Having said this, an obvious question is whether or not these inabilities are linked. In 1967 Peter Woodford wrote: "It is surely no accident that greater lucidity and accuracy in thinking should result from the study of clarity and precison in writing. For writing necessarily uses words and almost all thinking is done with words." Piagetian learning theory, upon which many curriculum changes are presently based, supports Woodford's observation. The restructuring of material to form a cohesive written statement is related to the "experience" phase of Piaget's theory. Therefore, it appears that by increasing the amount of written work

* From Richard Steiner, "Chemistry and the Written Word," in *Journal of Chemical Education* 59 (1982): 1044. Reprinted by permission.

required of students, and critiquing that work for content and style, we could achieve an increased understanding of course material and improved writing ability. A corollary to this hypothesis is that an early evaluation of a student's ability to write coherently should expose those students who will require extra attention. The question now becomes: How can increased writing be accomplished in our chemistry classes without severely usurping faculty time spent on other academic pursuits?

I decided that an effective way to utilize writing assignments as a way to promote understanding was to require written summaries of my organic chemistry lectures. Students were instructed to discuss briefly (one page) in writing the key points and relationships in each lecture. This was done outside of class and turned in at the beginning of the next class. The writing program was incorporated for the last third of the course. About 70 students participated and it took about two hours each time to read the papers. Written comments on sentence structure, readability, and chemistry were made wherever appropriate. Although the papers were not graded, a numerical value was given in order to correlate writing ability to test scores. Values of 1 to 5 were assigned with 5 being a clearly written, chemically correct paper; a 3 indicated minor errors in chemistry or writing; and a 1 indicated major errors in writing and understanding. After six such assignments an exam was given.

A look at the written work of the people receiving the ten worst exam grades indicates that only two did better than average on the written assignments; two did average work; three did minimal work on the assignments; and three did not do them at all. On the other hand, a look at the written work of the 12 people scoring over 90% on the exam showed that five turned in superior written assignments and five were about average. Only one student did minimal written work and one student (the curve-setter on the two exams prior to the writing experiment) did not do the assignments. These results, although admittedly not studied in a rigorous statistical manner, indicate a positive correlation between good writing and test scores. Further support for this relationship comes from the fact that, of the people doing consistently good written work, only three were below average on the exam, and of those doing consistently poor written work, only two were above average on the exam.

A question arises as to whether those students "naturally endowed" with good writing skills normally perform better or whether the assignments actually helped students focus their attention on the important points and helped those already skilled at writing to develop an ability to organize material. Though I do not doubt the former is true to some extent, I believe there is evidence that the latter is also true. The class average was 15 points higher than previous averages on exams and, of the 13 people who improved their score by more than 20 points, only three did below average written assignments.

The above data indicate that the writing assignments directly contributed to student understanding. However, another factor may have contributed to the improved test scores. As a result of reading these assignments I got an idea of what the students thought was important. If I felt they overlooked something I could re-emphasize it. As a result, there was a much better sense on the part of the student as to what would be tested. I believe that this communication between the instructor and the students is an important result of this writing experiment. In fact, one of my motivations for assigning the written work was the feeling that my students and I were not really agreeing on the most important (i.e., "testable") material in each lecture. I thought that by summarizing each lecture they would be forced to see major concepts instead of a series of individual examples. Overall, I think the writing method produced the desired result.

Task 9

Out of all your memories of education, choose a particularly vivid scene. It could be a fight on the school ground, a moment when you were especially excited about learning, an incident in class. Then describe that scene to readers, trying to convey specific details so that readers can close their eyes and see the scene as vividly in their imaginations as you see it in your memory.

Explanation

Before doing this freewrite, you might wish to read pages 116–122 in Chapter 5, about the importance of specific details in writing. This journal entry will let you practice generating the kinds of details discussed in those pages. In Task 3, you told a personal story about education. If you used lots of details to tell that story, then you already realized that readers depend on details to help them imagine for themselves the personal experience you are describing. If you didn't use very many details, now is the time to practice using more.

To help you think of details, use the journalist's questions of who? what? where? when? why? and how? that you used in Task 3. But there is another good technique also: this is to imagine your scene from the perspective of your five senses—sight, hearing, smell, taste, and feeling—and to think of details that each of your senses would notice.

For this task you will still be freewriting, in that you will write as rapidly as you can for 20 minutes without letting your pen stop. But this time don't let your mind wander off to new topics. Stay focused on the problem of describing a scene vividly for readers. This strategy is called "focused freewriting."

Task 10

Describe a scene related to your own personal topic, on the model of the scene you wrote for Task 9.

Task 11

Summarize a lecture from a course you are now taking. (If you aren't taking any lecture courses, you can substitute "minutes" from a class discussion.)

Explanation

In Task 8 we prepared you for this exercise. In your journal, write a summary of a recent lecture from a course you are now taking, based on your class notes. Follow the instructions Professor Steiner uses for his organic chemistry classes—that is, your summary should be one page in length, setting forth the main ideas in the lecture and explaining the arguments the professor used to support each point. Try to make your summary useful as a study guide to a student enrolled in the course who missed the lecture. This exercise should help you rethink the lecture material and see why writing can be a way of learning. The act of writing the lecture in your own words should help you understand the material more clearly.

Task 12

Crossbreed the word "education" with several randomly chosen words as described below.

Explanation

This task is a creativity exercise, which you will enjoy if you just let yourself go wherever your mind wanders. Here are two columns of words. The first column lists "concrete" words (words naming material objects you can see and touch) and the other column lists "abstract" words (words naming concepts or ideas). Before beginning this writing task, add three additional words of your own choosing to each column.

Concrete		Abstract	
parents		justice	
dog		sex	
milkshake		freedom	
your word	_____	your word	_____
your word	_____	your word	_____
your word	_____	your word	_____

Now you are going to try an idea-generating technique called "crossbreeding." To do a crossbreeding freewrite, you take the assigned trigger word "education" and crossbreed it with one of the words from your list by freewriting for as long as possible searching for any connections you can think of between the two words. Let your mind go free—be fanciful, frivolous, fun. For example, you can freewrite on "education and milk-shakes" or "education and justice" or education and any of your own words. Sometimes your freewrite will be triggered by associations in your own life between the two terms (maybe in grade school your mother rewarded your performance in a school play by buying you a milkshake); at other times you will discover playful likenesses between the terms (you might say, "Good ideas are like milkshakes: cool, rich, and refreshing, made up of various ingredients that need to come together in the right proportions."

Here is an example of a twenty-minute freewrite one person did on the crossbreeding topic "education and onions."

Let's see, this is dumb dumb dumb relax relax come on ideas education and onions let's see onions make me cry. What is there about education that makes me cry? I can think of all sorts of things that make me cry—education in school has sometimes made me cry but also things that make me cry are also educating. Relax relax relax keep going what things that made me cry are educating? When I think of crying I think of the time my parents were both in the hospital. They are very old and my mom had asthma and my dad had some unknown disease. The nurses put both of them in the same hospital room and called it the honeymoon suite. The thing I remember is when my mom got better she walked over to my dad's bed once and kissed him. It taught me something about the meaning of marriage. I probably learned more about marriage from that one episode than from all the marriage and family courses they have in this dumb college. What other things about education and onions can I think of? Actually onions are also used for spices. They make hamburgers taste better but they also smell up your breath. Could education in some way spice up your life but also smell up your breath? That is kind of a funny idea. I think learning new things in a way spices up your life but maybe the folks back home who do not go to college think that education has just smelled up your breath. Here comes that stuck-up college brat. He has so much education on his breath that I can't get in the same room with him. I think the guy I work with in the summer thinks of college kids this way. He dropped out of high school and really feels uncomfortable around me because I am going to college. I think on the one hand he feels inferior to me but he also feels in some ways a lot smarter and more worldly wise. That is an interesting idea, though, the way onions can represent something good and bad at the same time. What other things about onions are there? I just looked at my stupid watch and I have 4 more awful minutes to go. Sometimes this freewriting seems like a totally absurd game. I don't see how any of these ideas are good for anything. Education and onions is such a [expletive deleted]. Relax, you dumb [expletive deleted]. Palm trees, just swim here a while, palm trees, palm trees, let's see. You peel skin off of onions going deeper and deeper into the onion, each new skin looking fresh and moister. Does that lead anywhere? Is education at all like peeling the skin off an onion? My literature teacher says that you can find ideas in poems beneath the surface. Is that what you do when you think? Do you take an idea and then peel away the surface of the idea and look at it fresh. Then do you peel another idea away? This would be a good way of looking at education if when you peel an onion you actually got somewhere. Too bad onions don't have pearls in the middle like oysters so that when you peel away enough layers you got a wonderful reward—a pearl of an idea in the center. But I think when you peel onions you only end up with an infinite number of similar peels with nothing special in the middle. You just have a process and the process makes you cry. Is this what thinking is all about?

Do two ten-minute freewrites. In the first one crossbreed the topic "education" with a concrete word from your list. In the second one cross-breed "education" with an abstract word.

Task 13

Crossbreed your own personal topic (chosen at the end of Task 4) with two of the words from your list in Task 12. Do a ten-minute crossbreed using a concrete word and then another one using an abstract word.

Explanation

Many students report that this exercise gives them some surprising ideas about their own personal topics. Here is John's cross-breeding of "Early Memories of Growing Up in Cascade" with "justice."

Justice. Justice. What can a kid remember about justice? How about the time I hit Frankie over the head with a rock. I can't remember what we had been fighting about. I can see us in the alley between our houses. I was standing in front of our old wooden, barn-like garage yelling at Frankie who was walking slowly toward the woodpile in back of their kitchen. I was furious at him for something and picked up a rock, a big one, about the size of a pool ball and threw it at him. It hit the back of his head and he ran screaming into the house. I ran home and shortly his mother called mine. Funny, I can't remember how I was punished. All I can remember is seeing Frankie a day later with a huge golf-ball sized lump on his head. I was terrified the second I saw the rock hit him because I realized I could have seriously injured him. I felt awful—my own anguish punished me enough. I can remember the knot on his head but I can't remember if I got in trouble or not. Funny.

All the time I *am* writing the last part of this I think of Crazy Pete. I was scared of him. He was kind of the town idiot and I can picture him coming over to see my dad and dad sneaking out the back telling mom to tell Crazy Pete that he was out. Crazy Pete would usually just go away. As a child I didn't know why Crazy Pete was around. Why didn't they lock him up or put him in an institution or what? Why do I remember Crazy Pete so well from my childhood? I don't think my own kids will have the experience of living in a town with Crazy Pete's who are apparently harmless but scare little kids. Is it just to lock up Crazy Pete's? How does our society handle its Crazy Pete's?

Task 14

Do the following entry in two parts. Freewrite for 5 minutes on the initial question "Would you sign up for Dr. Sparkle's class or Dr. Lunt's?" as explained below. Then read the assigned article and freewrite for 15 minutes on the same question.

Explanation

Suppose you are going to register for an introductory course in economics taught in large lecture sections. One of the instructors for this course, Dr. Sparkle, is widely regarded among students and teachers as the best lecturer on campus. She has won two Distinguished Teacher awards and regularly receives student evaluations of 4.9 on a 5-point scale. The other instructor, one Dogwood J. Lunt, younger brother of Elwood Lunt, Sr., is something of an embarrassment to the Economics Department: he hasn't scored above 2 on student evaluations in the last ten years, and the incomprehensibility of his lectures is exceeded only by their dullness. As you stand in the registration line, hoping against hope that Dr. Sparkle's section won't close before your number is called, you discuss your fears with this strange-looking, bearded philosophy major standing in front of you. He tells you cryptically, "Don't take Econ 1 from Dr. Sparkle; take it from old Dogwood Lunt. You'll learn more."

Would you take this philosophy major's advice? Why or why not? Freewrite for 5 minutes exploring the paradoxical possibility that you might learn more economics from a bad teacher than from a good one.

Now read the short article "Poor Learning from Good Teachers" by Fritz Machlup, pages 399–405. (Please do not read this article until you have finished the 5-minute freewrite above!)

After reading the article, freewrite again, this time for 15 minutes, about your reactions to the philosophy major's advice. Now would you sign up for Sparkle's course or for Lunt's? Why or why not? Try to explore how this article might affect your study habits or the way you might in the future evaluate the effectiveness of your teachers. We hope this article "interfered" with your initial response to the philosophy major's advice. (By "interfered" we mean "slowed you down," "altered or deepened your thinking," "created complications where there were none before.")

Task 15

Play "the believing and doubting game" with either of the two following assertions:

"Competitive school sports help build a person's character."
or
"Grades are an effective means for motivating students to do their best work."

When you "believe," generate all the arguments and examples you can think of in favor of the assertion. When you "doubt," generate all the arguments and examples you can think of against the assertion.

Explanation

We now want to introduce you to a thinking technique that one writing teacher, Peter Elbow, has called the "believing and doubting game." Elbow suggests that whenever you encounter a new idea you should develop the systematic habit of first believing the idea and then doubting it.[1]

You can see the similarities between Elbow's believing and doubting game and the distinction Carl Rogers makes (in the article you read for Task 8) between listening and judging. When you play the believing game with a new idea you "listen" carefully to it and open yourself up to the possibility of its being true. Often, as Rogers states, practicing believing a new idea is frightening because new ideas can threaten one's world view.

The doubting game is the opposite of the believing game; it involves what Carl Rogers calls the critical or judging faculty, as opposed to the listening faculty. When you doubt a new idea, you try your best to falsify it, to find counter examples that disprove it, to find flaws in its logic. It is easy to play the doubting game with ideas you don't like. But Elbow insists that we also practice doubting ideas that are dear to us.

If we carry the believing and doubting game to an extreme, we are in danger of never making decisions, of endlessly weighing the pros and cons of every issue. If we don't play the believing and doubting game at all, we are in danger of never growing intellectually, of forever doubting ideas we don't like and forever believing ideas we already possess. Part of our maturity as educated persons is learning when to give up the believing and doubting game in order to make a stand, or, conversely, when to give up a stand in order to play the believing and doubting game. For many people, a college education is a shattering experience precisely because risking belief in new ideas threatens old ones. In fact, when education begins to "take hold," you will feel your world view being constantly challenged.

[1] Peter Elbow, *Writing Without Teachers* (London: Oxford University Press, 1975), pp. 147–191.

For each of the following believing and doubting exercises, draw a line down the middle of your journal page; write "believe" above the left hand column and "doubt" above the right hand column. Then choose an assertion. In the "believe" column, freewrite as rapidly as you can in search of all ideas, personal examples, and other evidence you can find to help you believe the assertion. In the "doubt" column look for all the countering ideas, counter examples, and other evidence that tend to falsify the assertion and therefore help you doubt it.

For your task for this session, choose either the assertion on competitive school sports or on grades as motivating forces, and play the believing and doubting game with it.

Task 16

Play the believing and doubting game with one of these assertions:

> *"Making daily entries in this journal is helping me become a better writer."*

or

> *"If I catch someone cheating on an exam or plagiarizing a paper, I should report that person to the instructor."*

Explanation

Once again, generate as many arguments for and against the assertion as you can. Think of personal experiences related to the assertions.

Task 17

Summarize another lecture. This time, draw a line down the middle of the page. On the right hand side, write your regular summary of what was said in the lecture. On the left hand side, make your own personal commentary on the lecture by jotting down questions that the material provokes, noting disagreements you might have with the lecturer, connecting points made in the lecture to your personal experience, or analyzing the importance of the lecture material.

Explanation

In this task the left hand column will contain commentary that you would normally not put into a summary on the grounds that you were adding your own ideas to someone else's words rather than just listening. The purpose of the left hand column is to start a dialogue with your instructor. The right hand column summarizes your instructor's ideas. The left hand column presents your own thinking about what the instructor said—your questions, your agreements and disagreements, your analysis. The purpose of this assignment is to make you aware of some of the things you do when you receive information since no one ever just soaks up information like a sponge. Part of us "listens" to the information coming in. Another part of us questions it, analyzes it, judges it.

Task 18

Write about your own personal topic (the one you chose at the end of Task 4) from the perspective of a different person.

Explanation

A good way to practice "walking in someone else's shoes," is to imagine seeing a topic through the perspective of another person. Return now to your own personal topic, the one you chose at the end of Task 4, and think of several people whose ideas about your topic might be different from your own. Then choose one of those people and freewrite for 20 minutes about your topic *from the viewpoint of the other person.* For example, in writing about Cascade the older student John considered it from the perspective of the little girl in his class who, because she dressed funny and was always dirty, was always being teased and mocked by the other kids.

Task 19

Write five or six assertions concerning your chosen topic about which you can play the believing and doubting game.

Explanation

Another way to deepen your perspective on your topic is to play the believing and doubting game with it. The key is to begin with good assertions that lead to controversy. To help you think of assertions, you might ask yourself this question: "When people disagree about my topic, what do they disagree about?" Here are eight assertions that John wrote for his topic "Early memories of Growing Up in Cascade." Each of these could lead to productive exploration through the believing and doubting game.

1. My mother was happy living in Cascade.
2. People are generally happier living in small towns than in cities.
3. Our parents should have stopped us kids from sledding in that old car hood.

4. A child growing up in the 80's faces problems much more complex than those faced by a child growing up in the 40's and 50's.
5. To be happy, families need to have Moms who stay at home.
6. Our society should lock up its Crazy Pete's. (Note: Cascade's Crazy Pete wasn't dangerous; he was just weird.)
7. My present values and way of life have been deeply shaped by my early childhood in Cascade.
8. My father was respected by everyone in the community.

Task 20

Choose one or two of the assertions you created in Task 19 and play the believing and doubting game with them. As before, make two columns and practice first arguing for your assertion and then arguing against it.

Explanation

See if your switching between opposing roles deepens some of the ideas you have about your topic.

Task 21

Reread your journal and make a brief listing of the parts of it you like the best.

Explanation

We want you now to reread your journal to get an overview of the kinds of ideas you have generated. We hope that you have enjoyed writing in your journal so far. Many people keep journals throughout their lives as a way of recording and exploring their ideas and of reflecting on their experiences. Whether you would consider such a discipline for yourself, we hope you have seen how journal writing can cause you to recall forgotten ideas and to reflect on them in creative ways. We hope too that you have seen how writing can be a mode of learning, a way of discovering and shaping ideas about a topic. Often the journal is just a catalyst. The remaining journal sequences in this text will help you continue to generate ideas and to see experience "problematically." For now, as you reread your journal and make a list of your favorite parts, be aware of what you have already accomplished.

CHAPTER 2

Problematizing Experience: A Discussion of Reasoning for Writers

Dialectical Quotes

I. a. If you want to talk to people, if you want to convey information, if you want to learn something from them, indeed if you want to learn something from the world itself—to perceive something, or know it or remember it—*there is no alternative to respecting the requirement of consistency.* (our emphasis)
   —*Michael Scriven, philosopher*

   b. A foolish consistency is the hobgoblin of small minds.
   —*Ralph Waldo Emerson, philosopher and poet*

II. a. X cannot equal not-X
   —*The* PRINCIPLE OF NONCONTRADICTION *upon which logic rests*

   b. My love [X] is [equals] a red, red rose [not-X].
   —*A* METAPHOR, *upon which poetry rests*

III. a. "...this disposition of abstractions, to generalizing and classifications is the great glory of the human mind."
   —*Joshua Reynolds, painter*

   b. To Generalize is to be an Idiot.
   —*William Blake, poet and painter*

IV. a. All Generalizations are the products of Idiots. [MAJOR PREMISE]
The above Major Premise is a Generalization. [MINOR PREMISE]
The above Major Premise is the product of an Idiot. [CONCLUSION]
—*A SYLLOGISM, used by logicians to test the validity of statements.*

b. All Cretans are liars.
I am a Cretan.
Therefore I am a liar.
Therefore I am not a Cretan.
—*A LOGICAL PUZZLE used to demonstrate the limits of logic*

THE USES OF CONTRARIES: AN INTRODUCTION TO ACTIVE REASONING

What is a reasonable person to make of all these apparently contradictory quotations? Choose one from each group and defend it to the death? If a person were compulsively "logical," she might feel compelled to do that very thing. On the other hand, if a person were compulsively anti-logical, he might say something like, "Well, it all depends on your point of view, you know. Diversity is the spice of life, I always say. Live and let live. I personally can agree with every one of those statements." Neither of these approaches is truly reasonable insofar as neither one can consistently rescue us from intellectual dilemmas.

Indeed, learning how to deal with these sorts of contraries is one of the most crucial tasks of education. Many of the problems we regularly face, in and out of school, appear to us in the form of contradictions, inconsistencies, or incompatibilities like the contradictory and self-contradictory statements which precede this chapter. We must contend with sometimes contradictory feelings, like a desire to be well liked versus a desire to be less dependent on others' opinions of us; contradictory goals, like an aspiration to be a successful businessperson versus an aspiration to live a non-pressured life with time for our families; contradictory ideologies, like the desire to provide generous social services versus the desire to reduce taxes; contradictory points of view, like the view that abortion is wrong versus the view that children should be born into families who want them. Most of the time when we find ourselves using our reasoning powers, it is because we've been provoked by such problems; we find ourselves faced with two or more alternative truths or paths which we must choose between or somehow reconcile.

How well we deal with these dilemmas is a good test of our reasonableness. Often in life we can't escape the dilemma, and, like twentieth-century physicists who have learned to live with the contradiction that light acts like both a wave and a particle, we must muddle along trying to embrace simultaneously two opposing views. But the mark of reasonable persons is the way they try to resolve contradictions. They will examine both sides of the contradiction, trying to see the strengths and weaknesses of alternative positions. Sometimes the dilemma will be resolved if one of the sides seems significantly weaker than the other. More frequently a person will have to choose one position and yet acknowledge its tentativeness.

At other times, however, reasonable people may make an even more complicated sort of choice. They may be able to "synthesize" the two contradictory sides in such a way that a new, third thing is produced. Thus, in having to choose between A and B, the thinker discovers a new position—C. The value of such a synthesis is that it allows us to modify and thereby possibly improve each of the contradictory elements.

In synthesizing ideas, then, you are playing a role like that of a labor negotiator who tries to convert the contradictory positions of labor and management into a compromise agreement. Sometimes, this compromise will simply be a "middle way" sort of compromise in which a company yields on one issue (higher wages) while the union yields on another (fewer fringe benefits). But at other times the synthesis will be more radical. Faced, for example, with a company's offer of $18/hour and a union's demand for $22/hour, a negotiator might suggest that wages be based on productivity or on a percentage of the company's gross income rather than on hours worked. This "radical" solution is the truest sort of synthesis insofar as it creates a truly new "third thing" out of the contradictory parts.

The process of synthesizing theses and antitheses is called dialectic thinking. Let's illustrate this process by attempting to synthesize the contradictory statements about generalizations from our opening dialectical quotes—the ones which see generalizing as, alternatively, a product of idiots or a glory of the human mind.

Let's begin by clarifying the problem itself. A "generalization" is an abstract statement that makes an assertion about a whole class of ideas or things. "Students growing up in Japan study harder than students growing up in America" is a generalization. In contrast, a "particular" is a statement about individual persons, places, or things—statements that are potentially verifiable and thus can potentially be called "facts." "My brother Joe studies six hours per day while our Japanese exchange student Tatsu spends his time playing video games" is a particular. This particular about hard-studying Joe (the American) and non-studying Tatsu (the Japanese) is a specific case that doesn't fit the generalization that Japanese students study harder than American students. Obviously, then, the generalization can't hold true for *all* American and Japanese students. If the generalization is true, it is true only in a statistical sense; yet the generalization seems to lump all American and all Japanese students into identical classes. In fact, the generalization about comparative study habits of American and Japanese students tells us nothing about individuals. Arthur may or may not study harder than Kazumi; Kiyoko may or may not study harder than Susan.

Blake's concern as a poet and painter is for the individual, for the infinite variety that makes one thing different from every other similar thing in the universe. Thus, to generalize is to lie, to falsify. The countering point of view, however, is that the ability to generalize is one of the glories of the human mind. This view points out that neither science nor philosophy could exist if people did not notice similarities among things as well as differences. Mere particulars have no meaning. To set up lists of particulars —A studies harder than B, C studies harder than D, and so on—remains pointless until someone notices a pattern that can be stated in a generalization. Although the generalization that Japanese students study harder than American students tells us nothing about individuals, it can tell us a great deal about the differences between two cultures. If we could not generalize, we would live in a kaleidoscopic world of intensely perceived, but meaningless experience.

This, then, is the problem that leads to the contradictory views of generalizations. In order to try to synthesize the contradictory positions, we're going to paraphrase a statement made by the German philosopher Immanuel Kant: "Generalizations without particulars are empty; particulars without generalizations are blind." In other words, generalizations *by themselves* are meaningless, just as are lists of particulars *by themselves*. We can't know what to make of a list of particulars until some generalization is introduced to account for why all these things have been put in a list. And we can't begin to assess the truth or adequacy of a generalization until we see how it relates to particular facts or cases. To put it still another way, we can't possess meaningful knowledge about study habits of Japanese and American students until we have *both* a generalization and also numerous particulars supporting and contradicting the generalization. Meaning is communicated in the relationship between the generalization and accompanying particulars.

Probably none of the people we've quoted in our opening section of dialectical quotes would disagree too strenuously with our tentative synthesis of their opposing positions. None of them intended that their statements stand on their own outside the context of the contrary and complementary thoughts which surrounded them. William Blake, the poet who associated generalizing with idiocy, was himself a great one for generalizing in proverbs like the one that we quoted. One of Blake's other proverbs, which might prove to be particularly useful in this discussion, goes like this: "Without Contraries there can be no Progression." In other words, unless you are willing to consider the possible untruthfulness of a generalization or to envision a state of affairs contrary to the one the generalization asserts, you are unreasonably accepting a half-truth. Reasonable people are, thus, always most interested in particular bits of evidence which don't appear to be consistent with generalizations they believe to be true. But their goal is not simply to prove that the given generalization is wrong or that all generalizations are ineffectual; their goal is to create new generalizations which better fit the particulars.

In disciplines like economics or philosophy or English, one can readily see this concern for contraries because economists and philosophers and literary critics all spend a good deal of time attacking each others' theories. But even in the sciences, where proofs appear to be less debatable, there is an ongoing concern for contraries. Scientists, for example, test their hypotheses by trying to figure out ways to disprove them. If a scientific hypothesis is incapable of being proven false, in fact, it is not considered a good hypothesis.

All reasonable people, in sum, are as much interested in how they might be wrong as they are in proving they are right. They are, in the words of poet Gerard Manley Hopkins, more fascinated by "All things counter, original, spare, [and] strange" than by things which are agreeable and familiar. They view contradictions as challenges which they will wrestle into syntheses.

For Class Discussion

As a class or in small groups, try reasoning your way toward a possible resolution of one of the following contraries. As you discuss the dilemma, try to observe the thinking processes going on. Are you and your classmates weighing the advantages and disadvantages of one side over the other? Are you trying to think of a compromising middle ground? Are you trying to create a synthesis that allows you some of the best features of both sides of the dilemma?

1. As an American Indian, I love my native culture and want to preserve it for my children. This culture can be maintained only if Indian peoples remain on reservations. But if we remain on reservations, we can never enter the mainstream of American life.
2. As a teacher I want to grade students on the basis of effort and improvement in order to encourage them to do better. But if I grade on effort or improvement, I will no longer be able to uphold standards.
3. Good leaders can make decisions quickly. But people who make decisions quickly don't understand the complexity of the problem.
4. As a black person I feel obligated to support black political candidates. But if I vote on the basis of race I am not acting as a unique individual.

THE CASE FOR LINKING DIALECTIC THINKING TO WRITING

And what, you might be asking yourself, does all this talk of contraries have to do with writing? In our opinion, a great deal. For one thing, it is difficult to write anything significant if what you write can not possibly be disagreed with or seen from an alternative point of view. Good writers try to ask "risky" questions that invite opposing answers. They try to show why their answers are good ones, not the only ones. And they do not merely declare their answers, but, like good scientists, test them in such a way that alternative answers are confronted, not ignored.

The force that drives thinkers—whether scientists in their laboratories or writers in their study—is a sense of a problem. Latin American educator Paulo Freire, who has devoted his life to helping third world peoples become critical thinkers about the political and social problems of their existence, claims that people become *awakened* into critical thought when they learn to problematize experience by seeing alternatives to the way things are.[1] When told that A is true, reasonable people respond by asking "Why not B also?" thus initiating dialectic thinking. Applied to the political history of the United States, Freire's message might look like this.

> **Person A:**   We can't rebel against King George. We are British citizens. (the way things are)
>
> **Person B:**   Why can't we redefine ourselves as Americans? (alternative case)

We think that Freire's notion of problematizing experience identifies the driving force behind most reasoning acts. Until we pose for ourselves a problem, we exist in an automatic world, thinking conventional thoughts and acting out conventional behaviors. As soon as we realize, however, that we can, if we choose, think *different* thoughts, act in non-traditional ways, then our reasoning powers are awakened. Of course, acting non-traditionally, by itself, doesn't prove that we are acting reasonably; the act of reasoning is the act of questioning and testing, of trying to decide whether it is better to act traditionally or non-traditionally. Our point is that the process of questioning and testing begins when the thinker poses a problem, which in turn begins as an uncomfortable sense of contrariety.

The posing of problems is essential, we think, for all persons who aspire to be better writers. If you ask writing teachers what most disturbs them about student writing, few will put poor grammar or bad spelling at the top of their lists. What they will complain about instead is lack of engaging content—the sense that freshman English essays tend to sound alike. In our view, these students are churning out "the way things are" essays because they don't see themselves as problem-solvers confronting authentic problems.

Let's illustrate with two examples of typical writing assignments in

---

[1] Paulo Freire, *Education for Critical Consciousness*, trans. Myra Bergman Ramos (New York: Seabury Press, 1973), p. 97.

college—one on a highly controversial topic where possibilities for contraries seem obvious and one on a bland topic where finding contraries might at first seem unlikely.

Suppose you are assigned to write a persuasive paper on the controversial topic "abortion" and want to argue that abortion is wrong. A "way things are" writer will not see a problem here—abortion is wrong, period—and is apt to trot out all the prefabricated arguments against abortion that anyone familiar with the issue has heard dozens of times before. Such writing, we argue, is unreasonable. It is possible, however, to make a reasonable argument against abortion, once the writer accepts the problematic nature of the issue. Here are some examples of contraries that a reasonable writer might be willing to pose:

- I think abortion is wrong, but I also think that abused and neglected children constitute a powerful wrong.
- I believe that abortion is wrong, but I think that bringing a severely abnormal infant into the world might also be wrong.
- One of my friends says, "Abortion is wrong *for me*, but I am willing to let others choose whether it is right or wrong for themselves." But if abortion is wrong for anyone, it must be wrong in some universal sense. I wouldn't say that stealing is wrong for me but may be right for someone else. Therefore what reasons make me believe that abortion is truly wrong?

By posing these contraries, the writer is seeing his or her issue problematically and reasonably and has a better chance of producing a surprising, memorable, useful essay than a "way things are" writer. The reasonable essay will, indeed, still oppose abortion, but it will do so by examining opposing points of view, weighing their strengths and weaknesses, and asserting the writer's position with a conscious sense of complexity. Such an essay is far more apt to be persuasive than an essay that rehashes prefabricated arguments.

But the topic of abortion is naturally controversial. What about a really bland topic like that traditional beginning-of-the-term assignment, "Why did you come to college?" This question, too, can be problematized. There are, of course, plenty of "way things are" responses: "I came to college to get a good job," or "I came to college to gain more knowledge so I can become a better citizen." But a problematizing thinker will find complexity in the topic.

- Suppose I came to college to get a good job. What constitutes a "good job" in our culture? On the one hand a good job means high salary. On the other hand, a good job means doing something valuable for society or doing something really interesting. Our society provides few jobs which combine high salary with valuable service and high interest. So what is it for me? Money, service, or interest?

- If I'm after money, why not invest my college money in the bond market and become a long distance truck driver?
- Although I say I came to college to get a good job, maybe going to college is the "way things are" in our culture. Maybe going to college is just a prestige thing that prevents many people from being happy with jobs that our grandparents might have loved, like becoming a mechanic or carpenter —working with your hands and having free time.

This is just a start on the contraries that a thinker could pose. Our point is that beginning writers must learn to pose problems of this sort if they are to develop the full range of their writing skills. The journal sequences in this text, as well as Chapter 7—"The Art of Asking Questions"—will help you learn to do so.

For Class Discussion

1. Choose one of the following topics and make a list of five or six contraries patterned after the kind of thinking shown in the previous examples on "abortion" or "why I came to college."

education	buying clothes	environment
justice	working in groups	cities
babysitting	feminism	relations with parents

2. Prior to class, read Caroline Bird's essay "The Dumbest Investment You'll Ever Make" in Part V, pages 385–392. In class, discuss the strengths and weaknesses of her argument. Then, working in small groups or as a whole, create a list of "real reasons" why you and other members of your class have chosen to go to college.

HOW WE GOT HERE: PERSONAL EXPERIENCE AS THE SEED OF REASONABLE THINKING

One assumption underlying dialectical thinking is that truth isn't fixed, it's organic. Truth, in Blake's phrase, "progresses," gets continually fuller and more articulated, like a plant. And, also like a plant, when we want to know where an idea is headed, it's often helpful to look back to its sources—its roots and seeds. Along the way, it might be helpful to examine some of the counter-truths which have shaped and modified it as it grew. What we're going to do now is to examine a personal source for some of the ideas in this textbook. It might help you to understand your own ideas better if you see them at least partially in the context of rejected alternatives. What follows is a tale from the undergraduate experiences of coauthor John Ramage. The purpose of the tale is at least twofold: (1) to illustrate what happens when there is a breakdown in the sort of dialectical thinking we've been discussing; and (2) to trace an idea back to its roots by way of showing how sharing your sources can help your readers understand your thoughts more fully.

I should have seen trouble coming that first day in Dr. P's logic class. There were plenty of signs. Even before the bell rang, as I sat listening to the nervous small talk of my new classmates, I was struck by the fact that they all seemed to be math majors. Curious, I thought to myself, why would so many math majors be taking a philosophy course?

And then there was the syllabus. It was as thick as the Old Testament. And like the Old Testament, it was full of "shalt's" and "shalt not's" and punishments and wrath. And finally, there was Dr. P. himself, a tall, angular man, all joints and knobs and sharp edges with an enormous Adam's apple that bobbed madly up and down when he talked, like a marker buoy in a typhoon. His attire—a manure brown jacket, burgundy and gray plaid pants, a silky vest with what appeared to be "scenes from an aquarium" printed on it, and a polka dot bow tie—served mainly to set off his ungainliness. He could have been arrested for visual assault.

In the beginning, the course went well for me. We studied the twelve (or was it seventeen?) "informal fallacies" of logic. I was thunderstruck, fascinated by how many ways there were to louse up an idea from the beginning of a sentence to the end. I loved the Latin names for each of the fallacies, and they rolled off my tongue like legal judgments. "*Post hoc, ergo propter hoc*, nit wit. Just because one thing follows another thing it does not mean that the first thing caused the second. Take him away, sheriff!"

Each day, Dr. P. would hand out paragraphs and sentences, each containing several logical errors apiece. He would then ask us to "put on your logic glasses and find the flaws in the arguments." And as he said this, he would point to his own inch-thick lenses and the eyes which swam behind them like two pale blue fish.

I always whizzed through these exercises, finishing well before the allotted time was up. As soon as I was done, I would turn my paper over to hide my answers from the prying eyes of the neighboring math majors who struggled to get halfway through the exercise. They had, I airily assumed, gotten in over their heads with this course.

But then we began the section called "symbolic logic." No more tidy sentences packed with informal fallacies. Now we dealt with disembodied symbols—pages of A's and not B's and therefore C's. I am afraid I don't remember that much of what we *did* do in symbolic logic. You cannot remember what you cannot understand, and I understood very little. My confusion was based on my inability to appreciate *why* we were performing all these mental operations with these pointless symbols. Faced with strings of unions and intersections and other strange sounding operations to be performed upon As and Bs, I might as well have been asked to perform brain surgery on a grampus.

Suddenly, I understood why there were so many math majors in the course. It was their turn to breeze through the exercises, elaborately turn their papers over, and hide their answers from my desperately rolling eyes. When I pleaded with one of them to tell me what it all meant, he looked at me quizzically and replied, "Just what it says. Don't try to understand why. Just do it and it's easy." But how could I do that? I was a philosophy major. I wanted to know *why* things were, not merely what. These math majors, I righteously concluded, were a pretty pedestrian lot. A bunch of number-and-letter-crunchers.

And if the math majors struck me as narrow, Dr. P. came to seem downright sinister. Whereas he had previously seemed benignly eccentric, an oddly constructed man in a hodge-podge of clothes, I began now to see him as a sort of alien being, trying to whisk me off into a fantasy world of made up letters and strange formulas which were little more than magical incantations. The farther away we got from the world of words and things where I had my moorings, the more otherworldly and evil he appeared. Those crazy clothes I had snickered at in the beginning, I now recognized were a uniform, a warning—beware earthlings, you too can be turned into an A or a B.

In the end, I skulked out of the course with a barely passing grade and a fund of elaborate self-justifications for not doing well. Looking back, however, I now think those justifications unreasonable. Faced with a sort of intellectual rite of passage, a test of intellectual maturity, I flunked, whatever my grade said. And my failure was as much of the will as of the intellect.

I had failed more than anything to understand that all learning requires periods of uncertainty and doubt and a faith that certainty lies somewhere ahead. The math major's advice to me was basically sound. He was simply telling me to keep the faith, to suspend the "Why?" question until I mastered the process, to let the "Why?" take care of itself later. And poor Dr. P., I now see, was a scapegoat for my feelings of alienation. I projected my own feelings of estrangement onto him and turned him into a grotesque ogre.

But at the same time, I don't want to let Dr. P. completely off the hook. Specifically I fault him for failing to take my own alternative point of view as a student into account. At no time did he consider that there might be a gap between his own assumption that symbolic logic was an innately significant and rewarding discipline and my own concern that logic was not directly or even indirectly relevant to problems I felt compelled to address—should I join a fraternity? break up with my girl friend? register for the draft? Although I couldn't have said it this way at the time, I now see that Dr. P. was an unreasonable man, despite the irony of his being a brilliant logician. He was unreasonable precisely because, with regard to his own teaching speciality and his relationships with students, he seemed unwilling to problematize experience. Because he assumed that logic was valuable, period, he felt no need to communicate to his students the place and purpose of logic in the overall scheme of things. He did not explore at all the development of logic, its sources in history, or the counter-truths, rejected alternatives, and inadequate precedents from which it evolved. He simply presented logic to us as a given and unalterable system. By implication, logic seemed to him synonymous with rational or reasonable thinking. Logic was his thesis and there was no antithesis.

But as some of Dr. P.'s own actions appeared to indicate, there is an important difference between spotting illogic in other people's statements and generating truly reasonable responses to problematic questions. One day, for example, Dr. P. used logic to "prove" to a classmate who was a religious fundamentalist that arguments for the existence of God were illogical and thus wrong. I couldn't help but feel that he was unreasonably overstepping his authority as a teacher to attack an important personal belief of a student and overextending the authority of logic to a realm in which logic's persuasive power was minimal. On another occasion he proudly recounted to us that he informed his daughters that there was no such thing as Santa Claus as soon as they were old enough to believe in such a preposterous creature so inconsistent with the facts of human nature and the laws of gravity. To be sure, his logic was impeccable, but the whole larger issue of whether or not children should be allowed to believe in palpable fantasies went unaddressed.

We'll return in Part III to the question of just where logic fits into the larger scheme of things and also explore some complementary systems of thought. For now, I want to suggest how my encounter with Dr. P. has influenced my life as a teacher and how it in turn has helped shape the text you are now reading. By failing to explore the alternatives to logic, Dr. P. set up an absolute world where authority reigned, a world very different from the world of clashing views that writers must encounter. In Dr. P.'s self-contained intellectual universe, every problem was *solvable* once you learned how to perform the right operations on the right symbols. But you can't, through symbolic logic, prove that abortion is right or wrong, or even discover why you came to college. Dr. P.'s class taught me that, for writers, "reason" is different from logic. As you can now appreciate, this chapter is our attempt to ground reasonable behavior on the ability to problematize experience rather than on the ability to manipulate the syllogisms of logic.

Even more importantly, Dr. P.'s course led me to see that it is crucial when introducing people to new knowledge and alternative points of view to reassure them that their feelings of anxiety and uncertainty are natural and even healthy. I learned that any teacher or text that guides people through new territory needs to tell people why they are making that journey by explaining certain choices and indicating certain "roads not taken." I want to show my students that although I might take approach A in conducting such and such a class, other teachers might take approaches B or C. I want to do this to remind students that every road is a choice.

PUTTING REASON TO WORK: PLAYING WITH THREE PROBLEMS OF WRITING

This story of Dr. P. should help you understand why our approach to teaching writing is grounded in a particular assumption about reasoning as a dialectical process of opposing views and why almost all the formal writing assignments later in this text require you to confront contraries. In the rest of this chapter we want to apply this process to three universal problems of writing, each of which originates in a sense of contraries. Our purpose in doing so is twofold. First, we believe that the writing problems of many people can be traced back to these three general problems. And second, we want to continue to model for you the dialectical process whereby the identification of a problem urges the thinker/writer to explore possible solutions. In effect, we will be killing two birds with one stone: (1) showing how the problematizing of experience (in this case problematizing the experience of writing) can help us generate arguments, and (2) allowing us to continue our theoretical discussion of issues in writing.

Problem 1: The Writer's Mind at War with Itself

Perhaps the first problem faced by any writer is that writing imposes contrary demands on the mind. On the one hand, you must generate surprising ideas and insights by creatively exploring your experiences and your subject matter. On the other hand, you must be quite severe on many of the ideas you generate, critical of the ways the parts of your essay fit into a whole, and willing to slice out a passage, no matter how much you like the sound of it, if it does not support your main idea. In short, you must be both a Yea-sayer who says "Yes" to experience and alternative points of view and a Nay-sayer who can say "No," like a good logician, to things which are inconsistent or do not fit.

Most of us feel comfortable doing one or the other of these sorts of tasks and, in turn, tend to downplay the importance of the one we do not do well. People who enjoy the chaos of creativity like to regard themselves as imaginative risk-takers and often see the organization of ideas and the necessity of providing relevant evidence as bothersome and dull duties imposed arbitrarily by unimaginative teachers. Typically, these persons thrive under the freedom of journal writing but feel their spirits wither under the restrictions of shaped writing such as the microtheme assignments in Chapter 6. Many other people, meanwhile, pride themselves on "common sense" and a pragmatic "no-nonsense" approach to writing. When given a problem, they like to answer it quickly, often by summarizing what the experts think, and view everything else as "padding." Typically, these people regard journal writing as a waste of time but enjoy the pleasing form of short shaped essays. Thus we have the "journal" people, who may have trouble focusing, limiting, and shaping their ideas, and the "microtheme" people, who appreciate form in writing but don't see much need to discover their own good ideas, which they regard as little more than "subjective opinion."

What do we do, then, when faced with the contradictory demands of being creative risk-takers full of good ideas and also being well-organized, concise writers whose essays have no extraneous words or parts?

One of the first things reasonable people do when faced with a contradiction such as this one is to break the problem into component parts and solve them one at a time. The best way to resolve this dilemma, we believe, is to separate the parts temporally. Indeed, most of the problems writers have in trying to satisfy the contradictory demands of writing arise because they try both to create and criticize *at the same time*. No matter what their bent, be it toward expansive connective thinking or narrow critical thinking, troubled writers often try to write one "perfect draft" which simultaneously incorporates both demands. Thus writers should strive for expansive, creative, yet messy and disorganized rough drafts, shutting down the critical mode that tries to say "nay" to ideas that don't fit or sentences that don't make sense. Then later they should turn on the nay-saying mode, shaping and focusing their ideas and improving their sentences. Unfortunately, trying to do it all at once, by shifting back and forth between the creative and critical modes of thought, is for most people like slamming a speeding car into reverse—clunk goes the transmission.

Given that it is so hard to write a perfect draft, you might well wonder why so many inexperienced writers try to do it. Much of the psychological reason is that people simply can't bear the uncertainty of living with an admittedly imperfect draft long enough to solve one problem before tackling the next. When they write a part they know is bad, they want to try to fix that part immediately instead of letting it be for a while and pushing on to write the rest of the draft. It's so hard being the Beast before we can be the Beauty (or, to use the embryo metaphor from the last chapter, being the caterpillar before we can be the butterfly).

The ability to do this, to live with a fair amount of imperfection while working toward a less imperfect solution, is sometimes referred to as "satisficing." It is, it strikes us, a very helpful thing to be able to do and characterizes many reasonable people. It is especially helpful in writing, primarily because most of the problems associated with writing are, as we have seen, self-created. Anything we can do to avoid working at cross-purposes with ourselves will simplify our task significantly.

To sum up our solution to this first dilemma: the problem of having to be both a creative yea-sayer to a diversity of ideas and a criticizing nay-sayer to everything that doesn't fit is resolvable if writers work first in one mode and then gradually shift to the other, keeping in mind all the while that only the final draft really matters.

Problem 2: Stereotyping, or, The Absence of Contraries

So far in this text we have argued that inexperienced writers must learn to "problematize experience" in order to create surprising essays instead of "the way things are" essays. However, we haven't yet examined possible explanations for why inexperienced writers might have difficulty problematizing experience.

We will suggest in this section that one cause may be a common habit of perception called stereotyping, which we will define as a failure to perceive contraries in certain fields of experience. Stereotypes are powerful blocks to creativity, so powerful that reasonable people must consciously train themselves to beware of them. The insidious power of stereotypes can be appreciated only if we recognize how hard it is to tell when they have invaded our thinking.

A good way to begin a study of stereotypes is to consider for a moment what it is like to be a victim of one. Let's take a subtle example—the way many students of your generation have been stereotyped as bad writers. As many of you probably realize, there has been a great deal of talk in recent years about a "writing crisis," as if loss of verbal skills were a national epidemic like swine flu. Listening to people talk about you as part of the "illiterate" generation who grew up on TV and video games and who would rather listen to rock music than read, you might feel a bit distorted, as though you were watching yourself in a funhouse mirror. It's you all right, but a pinched, distorted version of yourself.

So if you were faced with the task of responding to critics of student writers, how might you begin? Your first response, and it's a good one, is probably to point out exceptions to the rule that today's college students are not good writers. If you had several examples of decent student writers, the weight of these examples would limit the applicability of any general statement about the low level of writing skill among today's students. You would then be in a position to put forth some more carefully reasoned generalizations about the state of student writing.

Note here that you are not in a position to simply contradict the stereotypical view that college students today are generally bad writers. You are simply in a position to say that if there has been a decline in writing skills among college students, it hasn't been universal. Evidence from personal experience can never "prove" the universality of anything. But it certainly can prove the non-universality of anything. Stereotypical thinkers tend, however, to believe that their experiences are universal; they thus create hard-and-fast class distinctions on the basis of flimsy evidence.

In our view, the underlying cause of stereotypical thinking is a habit of mind known as dualism. A dualistic thinker is one who sticks every particular and unique phenomenon into one of two classes—right or wrong, us or them, lazy people or hardworking people, good writers or poor writers. The relationship between the two classes is typically antagonistic or adversarial, and keeping them separate "to avoid confusion" takes up much of the dualist's time and energy. This means, in turn, that it is difficult, if not impossible, for the dualist ever to synthesize contradictions and to progress toward fuller and more complex notions of truth.

This dualistic habit of mind is particularly detrimental to writers in that it prevents us from acknowledging or adhering to what philosophers call the Principle of Charity. This principle requires us to cast all counter-arguments and alternative proposals in the best possible light before we attempt to refute or modify them. It demands that we carefully read and listen to all points of view different from our own without distortion or interruption. It even asks us to supply missing steps or evidence in an opposing argument so that it can be as strong as possible. The Principle of Charity is, in sum, a sort of Golden Rule of reason which instructs us to treat all other points of view in the same way we would like our point of view treated by others. Whereas the dualist's first impulse is to say, "Because it's different it must be wrong," the reasonable person's first impulse is to say, "Because it's different it presents an opportunity to learn."

In short, a good response to a stereotype ("today's student writers are awful . . .") is to begin the dialectic process of opposing views. But we don't simply deny the stereotype and stop ("today's student writers are *not* awful . . ."). Rather, we acknowledge a partial truth in the stereotype and then seek to qualify it. ("Yes, there probably has been a decline in the quality of student writing, but . . ."). The reasonable response to a stereotype, then, is to play the believing and doubting game with it, a reasoning process we describe in Journal Sequence 1 (pp. 37–38). When we believe and doubt, we seek to find particulars that support the stereotype and others that oppose it, leading to a more accurate generalization and a richer sense of truth.

But what about people whose personal experiences seem only to reinforce their stereotypes, whose experiences, it would seem, *never* disconfirm their beliefs? (Those are the hard-core bigots and sexists of the world.) It is more likely, actually, that their perceptions, not their experiences, are overly narrow. It should be noted that some people never learn from experiences related to their pet stereotypes because their stereotyped vision shapes the perceptions they receive. They *have* experiences without *reflecting* on those experiences, without "seeing" what they really saw. Older is not necessarily wiser. But it should also be noted that all of us are prone to see things selectively and to derive different messages from our experiences. If we don't have a concept or a picture of an experience in our heads beforehand, it may well pass us by unnoticed. As one psychologist has put it, rather than saying "seeing is believing" we ought to say that "we only see what we believe."

When a belief is particularly strong, it can become impervious to experience. A hard-core sexist will simply not see competent, emotionally stable women working outside the home, nor will an instructor who believes that today's college students are awful writers "see" an imaginative intelligence at work in an essay if the essay also contains spelling errors and comma splices. Such extremely stubborn beliefs are referred to as prejudices (from "prior to judgment"), and no amount of persuasion or experience can touch them. While we may not be able to avoid selective perceptions, we can at least be aware of our tendency to see things incompletely and to seek alternative points of view.

One helpful way of "catching yourself" imposing your beliefs on a perception is to look at an optical illusion. An optical illusion is a perception which gives the appearance of being one thing but which we can eventually recognize as being another. Look at this famous one, for example, entitled "My Wife, My Mother-in-law" (Figure 2-1).

FIGURE 2-1 A Famous Illusion: "My Wife and My Mother-in-Law" (Source: *American Journal of Psychology*, 1930, 42: pp. 444–445).

Whom did you first "see" here, the young wife or the elderly mother-in-law? If you are like us, you probably first saw the attractive young wife with her plumed hat and her lovely profile. You may in fact have had a good deal of difficulty seeing the elderly woman. We had to force ourselves to stare at the young woman's "necklace" very hard and say "mouth" before we could begin to see the second image here. Only then did the delicate chin become a not so delicate beak. After we were able to see both images once, it became easier to see the second image; but still, we tend to see one before the other.

In part, the reason we see one image more easily than the other may have something to do with cultural conditioning. In the above illusion, for instance, people from Turkey will tend to see the old woman first, while Americans will tend to see the young woman. Is it a coincidence, do you suppose, that age is more respected in Turkey or that Americans esteem youthful beauty? (Plumed hats were associated with female beauty in turn-of-the-century America when artist Charles Gibson popularized the "Gibson Girls" who invariably wore such hats.) Older people in America often complain that younger people patronize them, do not seek their advice, and even fail to "see" them as real people. In fact, the very title of this illusion suggests Americans' prejudice against older people, especially older women.

Perhaps we are making too much of this little trick. But we can hypothesize these *possible* connections between perception and cultural stereotyping on even this slender experience. If we were ever to write an essay comparing stereotypical attitudes toward age and sex in American and Turkish cultures, we certainly could not stop with this experience. But we very well might start here.

Many great ideas and theories grew out of similarly slight experiences, followed by a good deal of speculation and investigation. Arthur Koestler, who studied scientific innovators over many centuries, characterized them as people who combined a skeptical questioning spirit with "an open-mindedness that verges on naive credulity toward new concepts." This habit of mind is the exact opposite of stereotyping. According to Koestler, in his book *The Sleep Walkers*, "creative people possess that crucial capacity of perceiving a familiar object, situation, problem, or collection of data in a sudden new light or new context: of seeing a branch not as a part of a tree, but as a potential weapon or tool; of associating the fall of an apple not with its ripeness, but with the motion of the moon. The discoverer perceives the image of a camel in a drifting cloud."[2] Koestler argues, then, that we are succumbing to stereotyped perception whenever we see an object or event as simply "the way things are." Creative people are always seeing new possibilities in the ordinary.

Let's close this section by relating the problem of stereotyping back to

---

[2] Arthur Koestler, *The Sleepwalkers* (New York: Grosset and Dunlap, 1959), p. 519.

student writing. Is it possible that students write "way things are" essays not simply because they are writing to the teacher rather than to a broader audience but also because they have stereotyped their teachers? Some students seem to hold the stereotypical view of English teachers, popularized in some media, that sees us largely as a tribe of disagreeable little twits whose objective in life is to correct people's grammar.

This stereotype might encourage some students to believe that English teachers want a certain kind of vapid writing—faceless, superficially correct and well-organized but dull, full of vague generalities that are neither supported nor opposed with specific details. They use jargon and a lot of imprecise but impressive sounding language to say as little as possible. They write what they think teachers are looking for; they seldom consider writing about things that matter to them in their own conversational voices because they assume that "teachers aren't interested in what we *really* think." "They don't care what we say, just how we say it." One writing teacher, Ken Macrorie, has labeled this sort of writing "Engfish," though no self-respecting fish would write this way unless he were stuffed.

So believe us when we say that writing teachers are people too, interested in other people. They want you to make generalizations, but they want you to test them against the wealth of particulars arising out of your personal experience—the whole range of memories stored in your brain, the sum total of what you have done, thought, dreamed, read, observed, heard, and felt. This is the source of contrariety in your mental life, your defense against stereotyping.

For Class Discussion

1. Practice thinking dialectically about a stereotype by going through the following exercise. Choose a fairly common stereotype of an ethnic group (WASPs, Italians, Jews, Blacks), a profession (truck drivers, college professors, secretaries), or a social role (feminists, cheerleaders, jocks, housewives, gays). Then go through this procedure:

   a. Describe the stereotype.

   b. Out of your collective personal experience choose several examples of people that on the surface at least seem to fit the stereotype.

      (1) Why do these people fit?

      (2) In what way do these people not fit the stereotype—how are they deeper, more complex than the stereotype? (The "yes, but ... " strategy)

   c. Choose people who do not fit the stereotype.

      (1) How are these people different from the stereotype?

      (2) What features do these people, in fact, share with the stereotype? (The "no, but ... " strategy)

2. The following critique of student writers was written by one Dr. Elwood Lunt, notorious grammarian and classroom terror. How are his views shaped by stereotypical thinking? How should he rewrite his essay if he wants to exhibit more reasonable thinking? How do you respond to Lunt's ideas here? How do you imagine the authors of this text might respond to them?

The Writing Crisis: Problem and Solution

A Modest Proposal
by Dr. Elwood P. Lunt, Sr.
Prescriptive Grammarian
Right or Wrong State University
Blindspot, Montana

College students of today write abysmally. They cannot even spell correctly, and their handwriting is atrocious. Their verbal scores on standardized tests have dropped dramatically over the past fifteen years. From the mid '60s to the mid '70s alone, SAT verbal scores dropped by 32 points! Today's students don't have the foggiest notion about how to use periods, semi-colons, and commas —and no wonder, they don't have even a rudimentary understanding of grammar. In my prescriptive grammar class more than 40 percent flunk, and I never go beyond diagramming sentences! In fact, the final examination I use for my college course is the same one I took in the 8th grade from Mr. Grundy. (I'll bet I studied harder in the 8th grade than today's party-going students study in college.) Not only can today's students not do grammar, they also can't write interesting essays. Our composition director complains that more than half of all final exam essays are boring, cliché-ridden drivel. And now look at the fads developing in some of our supposedly "up-to-date" writing classes. One teacher claims to teach "thinking" as well as writing, (imagine, teaching someone "to think"—you've either got it or you don't!) And another teacher raves about "the interactive method" where he has students working together in groups, supposedly "helping" each other with their papers. This is the dumbest fad ever to hit academia. Talk about your blind leading the blind! The helpless helping the helpless! Dull, unimaginative minds giving insipid ideas to other dull, unimaginative minds! Aargh! This "teacher" compounds his own ignorance with nonsense by asking these students to write about personal experience. What personal experiences have they had that could possibly interest an intelligent mind? No one should write about personal experience until they are old enough to run for president. What can educators who care about the future of this country possibly do? How can we solve this writing crisis?

I propose we abolish all faddishness in writing courses and get back to the basics. Specifically, I mean that no student should be allowed to write an essay until he has mastered traditional grammar. I have tried for years to make my grammar class a prerequisite for freshman writing, but so far the liberal student-coddlers in my department have outvoted me. Second, no teacher should be allowed to ask students to write about personal experience. Instead, students should begin to write by imitating the great masters, first by copying out model sentences and then by imitating the sentences with ideas of their own. In order to cut down on cheating, students should receive *no* help with rough drafts and should have their finished essays graded rigorously for spelling and grammar. I doubt we can expect students to improve their thinking or actually to give us good ideas unless we reform the whole educational system. But surely we can expect them to get their sentence structure right. Let's at least do that!

Problem 3: The Mind of the Reader at War with Itself

So far in this chapter, we have been discussing problems of writing primarily from the viewpoint of individual writers and their relationship to their subject matter. We have examined both emotional and intellectual blocks to good writing and thinking, such as the fear of uncertainty and the problem of stereotyping. But in all this, we have left out one important variable. The audience. In some cases, audience is much less a problem than in other cases. When you write a letter to a close friend, for example, you can depend upon a "charitable" reading of your writing. Consequently, you can focus on what you want to say and be as funny, glib, and elliptical as you care to be. But in other cases, when your audience is hostile or demanding, or, worse yet, unknown, the problem of audience is uncomfortably real.

In writing this book, for instance, we knew only that we were writing for "today's college students." Unfortunately, we are less sure about who "you" are than is our friend Elwood P. Lunt. In our classrooms, we encounter all sorts of people, including increasing numbers of women, older students, and minorities. But as individuals you can't be lumped into any one category. Some of you have just left home for the first time, while others have just sent your youngest child off to college. Some of you like Bach; others prefer Huey Lewis and the News. Some of you like pondering over fairly complex reading material, like this chapter; others would prefer to find their complexity in a computer circuit or a chemistry lab. Some of you are reluctantly taking this course because it is required; others are cheerfully taking this course because you like to write.

We can make few useful generalizations about all the individual members of our audience that would simplify the task of writing this book. So here, in addressing the problem of audience, we'll restrict our discussion to the universal needs of all readers. We do so because you must *always* consider the universal needs of readers and can sometimes consider *only* those needs. Later on in the book, we will discuss specific strategies for thinking about the needs of individual audiences.

Thanks to the study of reading by psychologists and writing scholars, we can draw a few conclusions about the universal needs of readers. Whether you are writing to biologists, philosophers, English teachers, women or men, there are a few things that all people require from your writing to make it understandable and meaningful. Unfortunately (there's always a catch), the two main generalizations that we can make about the needs of readers are incompatible. They constitute a contrariety, a problem.

The first thing every reader needs when he reads is a sense of direction (form). Just a couple of sentences ago, for example, we told you that the two major generalizations we can make about the needs of readers constitute a contradiction. So right away, you know that this "first thing" is a generalization about the needs of readers and it will be followed by a second, contradictory generalization about the needs of readers. You begin anticipating what our second generalization will be as soon as you know that the first generalization is "readers need a sense of direction." Some of you may wish we had told you in general terms what both generalizations were right at the beginning so you could "predict" more accurately what was to come. Some of you even wish we would shut up and get on with this explanation because the longer you have to hold on to your prediction, the more it fades from your mind. But you will just have to wait.

Some people who study the process of reading call this habit of making predictions "making and matching." You make a prediction or picture of what you think will be said and then match that prediction to what you actually get. If your predictions are all haywire, if you think the writer is going to say "nose hockey is fun" and instead she says "Otto burst in the swimming pool," then we generally say we cannot make sense of what is written.

One simple way of testing how readable a piece of prose is involves leaving out every fifth word and seeing how well readers do at putting the right word or a close synonym back in. This is called a Cloze test. Obviously,

some things are _____ to be more easily _____ than others depend-

ing on _____ the readers are and _____ the subject is. If _____

have never taken a _____ in botany before and _____ first chapter of

the _____ is designed to introduce _____ to lots of new _____

terms, your level of _____ will probably not be _____ high, no

matter how _____ the author tries to _____ you for what is

_____ . But given that situation, some botany texts will do a better job

than others of helping you predict what is coming and will be more readable, and more comprehensible, as a result. So, while the imperative to make your writing as readable and predictable as possible is universal, there is no single standard you can use to measure how successful an author has been.

We know then that it is important to give our readers signals about what is coming in the next sentence or paragraph and to fulfill the expectations we create. The fuzzier our predictions, the longer we leave them hanging in the readers' minds, the more faith we are requiring of the readers. According to writing theorist E. D. Hirsch, the best writing is that which "leaves the reader in uncertainty for the shortest possible time." Thus, for example, if we are going to contrast two things, our readers should know that is what we intend to do. We should probably tell them at the outset just what sort of contrast we see between the two things we are comparing. And when we shift from talking about the first thing and start talking about the second thing, we need to say we are shifting. Like this.

The second contradictory generalization we can make about readers' needs is that they also require a certain amount of uncertainty (surprise). If a reader can precisely predict *everything* you are going to say, why should they bother to read your whole essay?

Indeed, perfectly predictable writing fails to tell us anything we did not already know. Clichés are like that. Essays that tell us that death is unpleasant are like that. Essays that first tell us everything they are going to say and then say it are like that. Teachers who lecture word-for-word out of a book you have already read are like that. Just as you want to avoid confusing your reader with a collection of unpredictable statements, you want also to avoid boring your reader with a collection of safely certain statements. A reader who asks "So what?" is just as lost to you as the one who asks "Say whuuh?"

All effective writing, then, by its very nature contains some element of uncertainty in it. It was with this knowledge in mind then, that novelist Andre Gide advised his readers, "do not understand me too quickly ..." And this knowledge also lies behind writing specialist Peter Elbow's statement that "the writing that I value, that demands something of me as a reader, that turns its back on whatever comes quickly to mind, requires repeated and ongoing effort."

So what are we to make of this contradiction? What sort of synthesis can we make of the thesis ("give your reader a sense of direction or form") and the antithesis ("surprise your reader")?

In our earlier contrary dealing with the necessity for writers to be both critical and creative thinkers, we suggested that you divide your problem temporally by writing a rough draft and then by switching gradually from your creative to your critical self, bringing order and form to the surprise of your developing ideas. In our new dilemma, though, readers cannot really separate their need for direction and their need for surprise temporally. A reader cannot read once for form and then once for surprise. (Though we do something like this when we scan an article to get a sense of its content and shape prior to reading it carefully and, as we shall see, when we read a certain variety of unpredictable texts.) But the contradiction between the need for uncertainty and the need for predictability can be resolved if we approach a synthesis from a somewhat different direction.

To achieve a synthesis, we would like to propose here an analogy between reading and learning. Specifically we are going to compare psychologist Jean Piaget's solution to the problem of how people learn to our own problem of how people read. The terms of our analogy go something like this: a writer is to a reader as a teacher is to a learner.

According to Piaget's description of learning, we can conclude that learners have the same sort of problem that confronts readers. All learning involves a certain amount of novelty or surprise. When we say we "learned something new" today, we are really being redundant since we would never say that we "learned something old today." If a child already knows how to tie her shoes, then shoe-tying is not for her a learning situation unless, say, she learns a new sort of knot. If, on the other hand, we go in the other direction and hand a three-year-old a 9th grader's algebra problem, we will probably get a three-year-old's version of "say whuuh?"

Too much novelty, thus, is as deadly as too little for learners as well as readers. From his observations of how his children learned, Piaget concluded that the best learning situation was one of "moderate novelty." The puzzles his children were eventually able to solve but which stretched them in the process were those which were similar to but not identical with problems they had solved earlier. One further phenomenon encouraging to all writers is that Piaget's children *enjoyed* "moderately novel" puzzles and problems. According to Piaget, human beings appear to have a need for uncertainty in controlled doses, and writers who can exploit this need will not only educate but entertain their readers.

So when you confront the problem of balancing your reader's need for direction and form against his need for novelty or uncertainty, we suggest that you think of him as a learner. Think of yourself as a teacher. Make "moderate novelty" your goal. As a writer, be like a good teacher who wants to tell students things they did not already know, to make them think. Every good teacher imparts new knowledge to her students, drawing on her special expertise and/or personal experience to provide multiple fresh perspectives on her topic. But remember, too, every good teacher gives her students a lot of help at the "local" level by carefully introducing new topics and making sure the transitions and connections between her ideas are clear and explicit; she introduces new ideas by comparing them with old ones and summarizes connections between new and old material. She constantly takes her students places they have not been before, but she also takes them back to where they have been and provides them with sufficient direction to follow her into unexplored territory.

We noted earlier that there are certain situations in which a relatively high degree of unpredictability was unavoidable. At this point, we would like to suggest that with certain types of writing, unpredictability is not only unavoidable, but desirable. If we put predictability and surprise on a continuum rather than thinking of them as warring needs, we would place some types of writing farther to the predictability end of the continuum and other types farther to the surprise end no matter what the audience.

Your readers, flexible and reasonable people that they are, are accustomed to reading these different sorts of writing and even have different ways of reading them that are appropriate to the demands you make of them. These two different ways of reading can be called "piecemeal" and "global." Writing that appears to be straightforward and reasonably predictable we read piecemeal, a "chunk" at a time. Each chunk that is read piecemeal should be clearly connected to the chunks that precede and follow it. Typically, each chunk is perceived as a component part of a larger whole, which the writer describes briefly in the introduction to the essay. Depending on the assignments your instructor chooses from this text, probably two-thirds of the essays you write for this course will permit piecemeal reading.

Scientific writing is perhaps the clearest example of a sort of writing that requires piecemeal reading and a corresponding sort of writing. This sort of writing attempts to eliminate all surprises in organization and style, limiting surprise to content alone—the new ideas and information that the writer intends to pass on to fellow scientists. Typically, scientific writing begins with a relatively long and precise title that clearly classifies, labels, and predicts the content. Next, most scientific writers provide an "abstract," which briefly summarizes what is in the piece. Subsequently, the article follows a strict format in which the problem is introduced and described, the procedure employed in solving the problem is explained, the findings are presented, and then the significance of the findings is discussed. In writing this sort of piece, scientists seek as much clarity as possible—hence the highly predictable form and the narrowing of surprise.

On the other hand, when we read writing that is by its nature full of surprises—surprises in form and style as well as content—we read "globally." When we do this, we do not require the writer to make perfect sense at every stage. Rather, we relax, keep the faith, and let the whole piece unfold. Then, when we have finished reading the whole piece, we go back and make sense of the parts as pieces of a whole that has gradually taken shape for us. The piece is then a "globe," like a globe of the world, and until we can see the whole thing we cannot say how close or far away places are from one another, or whether something is north or south of something else. The beginning makes full sense only when we reach the end; the parts make sense only when we see the whole.

Story-based essays of the kind described in Part IV of this text are examples of this kind of writing as is the "opposing scenes" assignment in Chapter 8. Other examples occur regularly in fictional writing and to an extreme degree in poetry, which we expect to be full of surprises (poet Ezra Pound said that the whole point of poetry was "to make it new"). The wonder of poems is how they make sense only when contemplated as a whole, and often only after they have been read globally a dozen or more times.

CONCLUSION

You have now reasoned your way through several of the major problems faced by all writers, and in the process you should have become aware of several principles that guide reasonable people's thinking in any problem situation. You have learned: (1) the need to pose contraries by actively seeking and charitably attending to counter-evidence and alternative view points; (2) the necessity of breaking problems down into their constituent parts; (3) the value of "satisficing" or living with imperfection long enough to *approach* perfection; (4) the danger of allowing certain assumptions or beliefs to harden into inflexible categories (stereotypes) which blind you to individual members of a class, to contrary viewpoints, and to experience itself; and (5) the usefulness of analogies in providing unlikely solutions to complex problems. In general, you might note from the above points that reasonable people are characterized by their desire to be both consistent and flexible. That is, reasonable people make generalizations that they try not to contradict or ignore as they deal with specific cases; but they are also willing to alter generalizations when the evidence of particular cases mounts up against them. According to philosopher Immanuel Kant, this ability to move nimbly back and forth between the generals and the particulars is the essence of reasonable thought. "Stupidity," according to Kant, "is nothing more or less than the inability to apply generalizations to particular situations."

The specific writing problems we have attempted to solve or assist you in solving include (1) how to resolve the contradiction between the two major intellectual demands that writing places on you—to be a midwife who helps bring ideas and words to birth, and to be a surgeon who excises defects and incongruities from those newborn ideas; (2) how to counteract stereotypes, which tend to lock you into dualistic thinking and prevent your attentiveness to counter-examples and opposing points of view; and (3) how to resolve the contradiction between the needs of readers to be able both to predict what is coming and to be surprised by what is coming. All of these specific problems are illustrations of the fundamental reasoning principle described in the chapter: the posing of problematic contraries followed by a dialectic search for resolution.

For Class Discussion

1. Examine the following chart of maxims for writers derived from E.D. Hirsch's study of writing handbooks. Discuss each maxim insofar as it aids the reader of prose in predicting what is coming or being surprised by what is coming:

   - Choose and restrict your subject.
   - Use definite, specific, concrete language.
   - Avoid clichés, jargon, and circumlocution.
   - Write in unified and complete paragraphs.
   - Vary sentence types.
   - Make clear the connections between sentences.
   - Don't say too many things at once.
   - Use appropriate words.
   - Keep related words together.

2. Prior to class read Peter Elbow's article "Embracing Contraries in the Teaching Process," pages 406–419. In class, discuss Elbow's solution to his dilemma. What are the two poles of his problem? Would you call his solution a compromise or a synthesis? Do you think his solution is satisfactory?

3. As a class, make a list of contraries that you sometimes feel in your role as students. Do teachers sometimes place conflicting expectations on you? Do you feel contraries when you study? Listen to a lecture? Participate in small group work? You can explore ideas from this list for some of the tasks in Journal Sequence 1, if you choose. These ideas can also become seeds for essays in Chapters 8 or 12.

CHAPTER 3

Form and Surprise: Turning Information into Meaning

PRELIMINARY EXERCISE: CONVERTING DATA INTO A PARAGRAPH

Read the following essay assignment developed by Professor Andrea Lunsford, a composition researcher from the University of British Columbia. Before proceeding, take 5 minutes or so to plan out how you would organize an essay using the information below, or, even better, take a half hour to write the essay yourself.

1. New York City lost 600,000 jobs between 1969 and 1976.
2. In 1975, twenty buildings in prime Manhattan areas were empty.
3. Between 1970 and 1975 ten major corporations moved their headquarters from New York City to the Sunbelt.
4. In 1976, New York City was on the brink of bankruptcy.
5. Between February, 1977, and February, 1978, New York City gained 9,000 jobs.
6. Since January, 1978, one million square feet of Manhattan floor space has been newly rented.[1]

[1] Andrea A. Lunsford, "Cognitive Development and the Basic Writer." *College English* 41 (1979): 38–46.

67

7. AT&T has just built a $110 million headquarters in New York.
8. IBM has just built an $80 million building at 55th Street and Madison Avenue in New York.
9. Co-op prices and rents have increased since 1977.
10. Even $1 million luxury penthouses are sold out.
11. There is currently an apartment shortage in Manhattan.
12. The President recently signed a bill authorizing $1.65 billion in federal loan guarantees for New York.

After reading and thinking about this information, how would you describe the current economic trend in New York City? Using your answer to that question as an opening sentence, write a paragraph in which you explain and offer support for your conclusion by using the information provided above.

Once you have planned your own response to this assignment, read the two students' essays below. Then consider the questions that follow.

Essay 1

After a slump in the early seventies, New York City's economic situation is now on the upswing. In the first part of the decade the metropolis's economic outlook was bleak. New York City lost 600,000 jobs between 1969 and 1976. Between 1970 and 1975, ten major corporations moved their headquarters from New York City to the Sunbelt. In 1975, twenty buildings in prime Manhattan areas were empty. By 1976, New York City was on the brink of bankruptcy, but then things began to look up. Between February, 1977, and February, 1978, New York City gained 9,000 jobs. Additionally, AT&T has just built a $110 million headquarters there and IBM has constructed an $80 million building in the city. Since January, 1978, one million square feet of Manhattan floor space has been newly rented leading to an increase in co-op prices and rents. With even $100 million luxury penthouses sold out, there is currently an apartment shortage in Manhattan. To spur the recovery further, the President recently signed a bill authorizing $1.65 billion in federal loan guarantees for New York City. Bouncing back from a brush with bankruptcy in the middle seventies, New York City, with jobs, businesses, people and money returning, is emerging economically healthy.

Essay 2

Recently a bill authorizing $1.65 billion in federal loans from the President was guaranteed for New York City. Between 1969 and 1976 New York City lost 600,000 jobs. New York City was on the brink of bankruptcy. Because in the years 1970 to 1975 ten major corporations moved their headquarters from there to the Sunbelt. Also in 1975 twenty buildings in prime Manhattan were empty.

But between February, 1977 and February, 1978, New York gained 9000 jobs. One million square feet of Manhattan floor space has been rented since January, 1978. AT&T and IBM have spent over $150 million on buildings in New York.

There is a shortage of apartments in Manhattan. Why? Because rents and co-op prices have risen since 1977. And even luxury penthouses that are worth one million dollars are sold out.

Why does all this happen? The price of living goes up twice or more each year.

Which of the two student essays above do you think is better? Why?

TURNING INFORMATION INTO MEANING: A SHORT ILLUSTRATION

A fundamental concept in the study of writing is the difference between information and meaning. You will see this difference for yourself if you work your way conscientiously through the following exercises—what we like to call "the shortest writing assignment ever invented." Please have some scratch paper handy; you will get the most benefit from this chapter if you do each exercise yourself before you proceed with your reading.

Exercise 1

Here is a short list of information. Write an initial sentence that will convert this list of information into an essay.

- Dingy, gray paint is peeling from the walls.
- Several light fixtures are burned out.
- The windows are dirty.
- It is raining out.

An essay differs from a list of information in that an essay makes a point. What point might a writer have in mind if she wanted to mention peeling paint, burned out light fixtures, dirty windows, and rain? Although lots of variations are possible, you might write an opening sentence something like this:

Sitting in this room depresses me.

This sentence turns a list of information into a little essay:

Sitting in this room depresses me. Dingy, gray paint is peeling from the walls. Several light fixtures are burned out. The windows are dirty. It is raining out.

Now try your hand at a contrasting exercise:

Exercise 2

Here is a short list of information about Room 107 in Grimm Hall. Add five more pieces of information that could also be plausibly true about the room.

- Dingy, gray paint is peeling from the walls.
- Several light fixtures are burned out.
- The windows are dirty.

Since the three pieces of information given seem to indicate that the room is poorly maintained, many people try to stick logically to this idea as they make up their lists of new information. They might include "facts" such as these:

- The blackboards are coated with chalk dust.
- The floors have big splotches of mud on them.
- Paper litters the floor.

However, the assignment itself doesn't specify information about "poor maintenance"; it asks for any kind of information. So the following data about the room would also fit the assigned task:

- The room is rectangular and contains fifty movable desks.
- The clock on the wall above the door is white and black.
- The fluorescent lights in the ceiling fixtures are made by General Electric.
- Seven of the desks are constructed for left handers.

Obviously, once people start listing raw information, they can keep going forever. A vision drifts before us: After three days of feverish notetaking, Larry the Listmaker is still listing facts about 107 Grimm Hall. Larry vows not to stop until the volume of paper produced by his lists equals the volume of the room.

Unlike Larry, reasonable people don't like meaningless lists of information; hence our natural tendency is to complete Exercise 2 with data about "poor maintenance" rather than with random data about light bulbs and left-handed desks. Our minds intuitively see "meaning" in the given list of data—"Grimm Hall is poorly maintained." But this statement is not an individual piece of datum about the room. Rather, the statement "Grimm Hall is poorly maintained" is a generalization that expresses the meaning found in some of the data about the room—the burned out light bulbs, the peeling paint, and the filthy windows—but not in the other equally true data about the number of desks or the brand of the light bulbs.

Exercises 1 and 2 should now make clear, then, that a sentence like "Sitting in this room depresses me" (or "Grimm Hall is poorly maintained") is fundamentally different from a sentence like "There are fifty moveable desks in the room." The first sentence is a generalization while the second sentence is a particular. Obviously, reasonable people seek some kind of coordination between generalizations and particulars, some sort of weaving back and forth between them. In Chapter 2 we discussed this balance theoretically, introducing our discussion with Kant's observation that "generalizations without particulars are empty; particulars without generalizations are blind." The exercises about Grimm Hall illustrate this balance at the nuts-and-bolts level. Let's now examine this balance in more detail.

In Exercise 1 you created a mini-essay because your discourse began with a generalization ("Sitting in this room depresses me") followed by supporting details about the room that are all related to the writer's feeling of depression. This little essay can be displayed graphically in a tree diagram.

Diagram 1

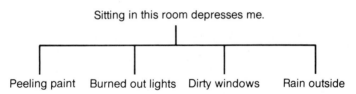

Here the main point—that the room is depressing—is supported by "depressing" details. However, in a long list of random information about the room, there could be no single generalization that would show a logical relationship among all the details.

Diagram 2

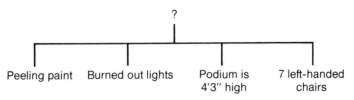

This second diagram shows what we mean by "information without meaning." This tree could be extended to the right indefinitely if we included every conceivable fact that Larry the Listmaker discovered about the room, but all those facts would add up to nothing because they would support no central point. On the other hand, a meaningful essay is severely limited with respect to the kinds of data that can be included in it. Diagram 1 (p. 71) necessarily *omits* most of the information about the room since all those facts about the number of chairs, the height of the podium, and the brand of light fixtures are irrelevant to the writer's point that the room is depressing, or to another possible point that the room is poorly maintained. We should see then that a meaningful essay is *always* limited and partial; a writer creates it by consciously omitting details as well as by including them. It is precisely because good essays are limited that they are risky, attackable, and hence surprising.

We can restate our point, then, by saying that a list of information becomes meaningful only when each piece of information is related logically to some overriding generalization. One of the most common complaints that college professors make about student writing is that it often contains information without meaning. Research papers are prime culprits. Students paste together all the information they learned about topic X, but they don't select and arrange the information in order to support a challengeable thesis about topic X. One professor at our university calls this kind of writing "data dumping."

If you return now to the two student essays about the economic situation in New York City in the opening exercise of this chapter, you can see that Essay 1 is meaningful while Essay 2 is closer to a data dump. Essay 1 begins with an accurate generalization about all the data: "After a slump in the early seventies, New York City's economic situation is now on the upswing." (This sentence asserts the meaning of the essay.) The data are then arranged to support this meaning. The first half of the essay includes all the "downswing" data, followed by a transition that prepares readers for the "upswing" data in the second half. ("By 1976, New York was on the brink of bankruptcy, *but then things began to look up.*")

Essay 2, on the other hand, fails to identify any pattern for the data it presents. Rather than beginning with a generalization (as the assignment specifies), the writer begins by citing the information about federal loan guarantees. Theoretically, this could be an artful opening for the paragraph if the writer viewed the federal loan guarantee as a crucial moment in a series of events. But he doesn't. Instead the writer proceeds simply to list all the "bad" data, then all the "good" data, and then some data which the writer clearly doesn't know what to make of, and finally to write a conclusion asserting a point that has nothing to do with any of the data presented. Most of us would find it easier to make sense of the original list than of this muddled version.

Why does the second writer have so much trouble with this assignment? We offer two possible explanations. First, the writer may not understand that essays must convey meaning rather than mere information. Thus, the writer might not appreciate the importance of making his point explicit, in this case by beginning with an overall generalization about the New York economy. Our second possible explanation, however, acknowledges that this assignment is really more complex than many persons would at first recognize. Manipulating verbal information so as to keep a meaningful balance between generalizations and particulars is as challenging to the intellect as solving complex mathematical problems. A lot of research data suggest that many capable college students (some studies suggest well over half of them) have difficulty transforming a short list of data, such as the New York City data, into a meaningful mini-essay, not because they aren't intelligent but because they haven't had the right kind of practice and because the skills of arranging verbal material into a hierarchical pattern are fairly late to develop. If this explanation is correct, then the second writer needs not only to understand what "meaning" means in an essay but also to get systematic practice in producing short pieces of organized writing. The microtheme assignments in this book are especially designed to help students master these kinds of organizing skills.

TURNING INFORMATION INTO MEANING: LARGER PATTERNS

Of course, the series of sentences about peeling paint and burned out lights make a mighty slim essay. However, such a tiny piece of discourse can be seen as a little building block of meaning that can be fitted into a longer essay. Try the following exercise:

Exercise 3

Try to construct generalizations and particulars for a longer essay that would include the mini-essay about Room 107 in Grimm Hall. Make your ideas fit this tree diagram. Work on the diagram a few minutes before proceding.

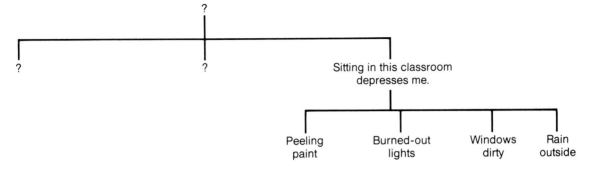

Here are two student solutions to this puzzle. Note that in the second solution, the student had to exclude the detail about the rain. (We'll see why shortly.)

Solution 1

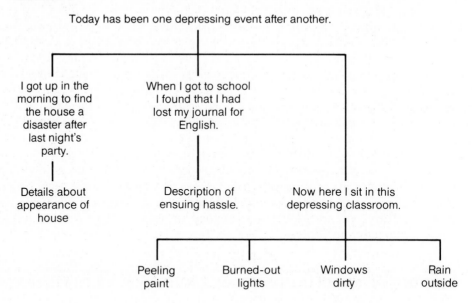

Solution 2

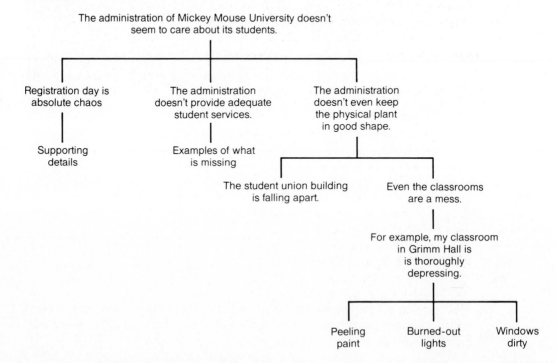

In these solutions you can see that the "depressing room" sequence becomes a building block for larger essays. In Solution 1, the depressing room becomes one of three examples of the writer's depressing day—the messy house, the lost journal, and the depressing room. In Solution 2 the depressing room is reduced to a quite minor building block nesting three levels down the hierarchy. The details about the peeling paint and so forth support the small generalization that the room is depressing. The generalization that the room is depressing, along with the generalization about the crumbling student union building, become pieces of information supporting the larger generalization that the administration doesn't maintain its physical plant. In turn, the information about the poorly maintained physical plant, along with information that registration day is chaotic and student services are inadequate, become supporting information for the essay's major generalization (its thesis statement) that the administration of Mickey Mouse University doesn't seem to care about the happiness of its students.

This is what we mean when we say that an essay is organized hierarchically: smaller parts fit into larger parts, all of which contribute to a unified whole. It is because the smallest blocks are working parts of the whole essay that the detail about rain is appropriate for Solution 1 but not for Solution 2. Because the whole of Solution 1 concerns the writer's depressing day, the gloomy rain supports the writer's point since it is one more detail contributing to the writer's depression. But Solution 2 is about MMU administrators' lack of concern for students, as evidenced partly by their failure to maintain the classrooms. But while the administration of MMU may be responsible for the dirty windows, it is hardly responsible for the rain. Thus, whether or not a detail belongs in an essay depends on whether the detail is relevant to the generalizations which give the essay meaning.

We should also mention at this time a point we will develop more fully later. So far we haven't considered the problem of contradictory evidence—what to do with all those pieces of data that don't fit our thesis, that complicate our attempts to make meaning. What if Micky Mouse University chose to neglect its physical plant in order to pour money into scholarships and teachers' salaries? What if MMU was a vibrant, intellectually stimulating place while neighboring Cinderella College, with its perfectly computerized registration system and its manicured lawns, was Dullsville academically? Would it then be fair to say that the administration of MMU doesn't care about its students? In the face of complex, often contradictory data, thesis statements are much riskier to make than our earlier examples may have suggested. On the other hand, it is complex, contradictory data that allow essays to be surprising. Much more on this in later sections of the text.

CHANGING THE LENGTH OF YOUR ESSAYS: THE PRINCIPLE BEHIND EXPANSION AND CONTRACTION

We have said that meaningful writing involves a weaving back and forth between generalizations and particulars. The few sentences about the state of repairs in Grimm Hall, which we have been using as an example, hardly seem long enough to be a model for college-level writing. Yet college-level essays don't have to be long. At our university we know professors who regularly require very short essays (around 200 words). Perhaps the most common length for college essays is 3–5 pages, although long research papers (10–30 pages) are still frequently assigned to upper division students. And, of course, graduate students are writing book length dissertations. How can you learn to adjust your writing to fit the various length requirements you might be assigned in college?

We think this is an instructive question because the advice many writing handbooks give is misleading. Moreover, the correct answer, we think, reveals an important principle about the construction of essays. Many handbooks explain that the length of an essay is a function of the breadth of its topic. You could write a long research paper on, say, the Puritans' conception of marriage, but if you were limited to only one page you would need to limit your topic further to something like a description of a typical Puritan wedding ceremony. In other words, the shorter your essay, the narrower your topic must be.

But it is possible, theoretically, to write on any topic—broad or narrow —at almost any length, depending on the extent of the details you choose to include. You could indeed write a research paper on the Puritans' conception of marriage, but you could also write a book on that topic or, if you wanted to, a two-page essay, or a paragraph, or a single sentence. In these latter cases the shorter versions would be summaries of the longer ones. Your single-sentence essay would be the thesis statement for the research paper or book; your single-paragraph essay would be an abstract or précis. Conversely, a one-page description of a typical Puritan wedding ceremony could be expanded indefinitely by including more details (if you used the technique of flashbacks you could turn the description of a ceremony into a novel). We will therefore prefer to talk about two modes of writing—the summarizing mode and the detailed mode—and to argue that each mode has its appropriate purposes.

To put the matter in other terms, if a professor designs a very short writing assignment (say, 100–200 words), he or she can think of it either as a piece of a longer essay or as a summary of a longer essay. In the first instance (the detailed mode), your discourse will be like one of the body paragraphs inside a long essay. In the second case (the summarizing mode), your essay will be like an overview of the whole argument of a longer essay without the details. To illustrate, let's suppose you had to write several mini-essays, one in the detailed mode and two in the summarizing mode (a very short one and a slightly longer one). Here are example assignments followed by appropriate responses:

Assignment 1 (detailed mode)

Examine the tree diagram for Solution 2 (p. 74) and write a detailed paragraph about the poorly maintained classrooms in Grimm Hall (the far righthand branch). Invent whatever details you need to support your point.

Possible Solution

Not only is the student union building falling apart, but even the classrooms are disgracefully maintained. A typically depressing example is Room 107 in Grimm Hall, where I have my English class. In at least a dozen places around the room, the dingy gray paint is peeling off the walls. In one particularly ugly spot students have colored the plaster beneath the peeled paint with children's crayons. Additionally, several fluorescent lights are burned out. Our teacher claims he has called Maintenance several times to complain, but as yet they haven't been replaced. Perhaps the clearest indication of poor maintenance is the filthiness of the windows in Grimm Hall. In Room 107 the windows have huge mud splotches near the top, which have streaked down like veins in a leaf. It is now June and the windows have looked like this since spring term started in March.

Assignment 2 (summarizing mode)

Examine the tree diagram for Solution 2 (p. 74) and then write the following: (1) a 50-word summary of its argument, and (2) a 125–175 word summary of its argument.

Possible Solution: 50-word version

The administration at Mickey Mouse University doesn't seem to care about the happiness of its students. Registration day is chaotic, student services are seriously inadequate, and the physical plant, including the student union building and the classrooms, are poorly maintained.

Possible Solution: 125–175 word Version

The administration of Mickey Mouse University doesn't seem to care about the happiness of its students. For example, registration day is chaotic. Unlike

Cinderella College, where, according to a friend, registration takes only 30 minutes, registration here at MMU keeps students more than 6 hours standing in long confusing lines. Another example of the administration's disregard for students is the inadequacy of student services. The health facility is over-crowded, the bookstore is understaffed, there is no day-care facility or women's resource center, nor is there a writing center or university-sponsored tutoring service. Finally, the administration isn't even maintaining the physical plant. The roof in the student union building has leaked for more than a year and the linoleum floors are so worn they look slummy. And even the classrooms are disgracefully maintained. My English classroom, for example, has paint peeling from the walls, numerous burned-out light bulbs, and windows streaked with mud since March.

These examples should make clear that there is no absolute distinction between the two modes, which blend into each other on a scale going from generalizations supported by extensive particulars to generalizations with almost no supporting particulars. In the longer summary version, for example, more than 50 percent of the essay is still devoted to details and examples, but the details are not as elaborate or as extensive as they are in the detailed mode.

It follows, then, that pieces of writing can be expanded or contracted almost at will. You can contract a large essay either by summarizing it or by taking one of its parts and reshaping that part into a new, smaller whole. Conversely, you can expand a piece of writing either by making it a part of a larger whole, or by expanding it from within by adding further development to the existing generalizations. This principle of expansion and contraction makes it possible for us to give you very short writing assignments and yet be confident that you are gaining skills for writing longer essays.

TURNING INFORMATION INTO MEANING: FORM AND SURPRISE

So far we have used the simple example of the classroom with peeling paint, burned-out lights, and dirty windows to illustrate how an essay is not a listing of information but a weaving back and forth between generalizations and particulars. We have used the details about Room 107 in Grimm Hall to support two quite different meanings: "Sitting in this room depresses me" and "The administration at MMU doesn't maintain the university's physical plant."

Let us now move from these greatly simplified examples to show you the same principles at work in a complex, college-level thinking task. The example we will use was provided by an instructor at Wayne State University in Detroit in a Humanities course for engineers entitled "The

Impact of Technology on Society"[2] It illustrates how human minds turn information into meaning. As we shall see, the creation of meaning simultaneously creates a form and surprise.

Students in this course were studying a disaster in which Michigan residents were accidentally poisoned when they ate beef from cattle fed FIREMASTER (a flame retardant with poisonous PBB) instead of NUTRIMASTER (a supplemental cattle feed). The mix-up occurred because of the similar names of the two products and the similar 50 pound brown bags for packaging. Even though cattle ranchers and government officials knew that the cattle had eaten FIREMASTER, the cattle were not destroyed because of conflicting test results about the effects and dangers of PBB, officials' uncertainty about how much was dangerous, the enormous economic costs of destroying the cattle, the dilemma of who was responsible for compensating victims, apparent political cover ups, and so forth. Students struggled for 20 minutes or so trying to get straight the complex raw data—who did what, when, and why?—and then were asked, as a group, to summarize the causes of the accident.

The mind at this point is given a task—to turn raw data into meaning. But what is the meaning? What caused this accident? Who is responsible for it? Eventually someone suggested a possible generalization: "The government was most responsible for the foul up." Then the arguments began, with other students showing why it wasn't the government who was most responsible but maybe the cattle ranchers. No, it was the Michigan Chemical Company, whose packaging mistakes led to the trouble. Then someone else suggested a new generalization (and hence a new meaning): "There were many causes of the PBB tragedy." But this sentence led to no clear classification scheme (2 causes? 8 causes? 12 causes? How could they be grouped?)

Finally someone said, let's list the information so we can see it all. After several minutes of brainstorming, the class listed the following pieces of raw data:

Possible Causes

- Michigan Chemical Company (bag mix-up; poor labeling)
- general unfamiliarity with PBB chemical
- government response slow
- Farm Bureau initially claimed feed OK
- FDA concerned with quarantine of farms, not solution to overall problem
- FDA safety levels set too low
- legislative arguments over who should pay victims

[2] Julie Klein, "The Post-Mortem Plan: Teaching Writing Across the Disciplines," *Exercise Exchange* 28 (1983): 33–41.

- conflicting test results (differences in Michigan tests vs. out-of-state tests)
- bureaucratic delays

The data made visible led to renewed discussion, and the class finally suggested still another generalization:

"There were many levels of complicity in the PBB tragedy: business, government, political management, and scientific procedures."

Our point is that each of these different generalizations asserts a different meaning, that is, interprets the data in a different way. Similarly, each different meaning commits the writer to a different shape for an essay, a different way of selecting and arranging the data. The data *are given*—the class could see the various pieces of data displayed on the board—but the meaning *is made* by human minds. (It is precisely the generalizations that are *not* displayed on the board as data.) The act of writing has forced the class to make meaning, and the making of meaning, in turn, forces them to impose shape on the data. Without meaning, the data lie there pointlessly, just so many unrelated facts to be memorized. This is why writing is a mode of learning. Writing forces you constantly into the creative act of making meanings.

The complexity of this process can be further illustrated if we imagine members of that Humanities class going on to write a formal essay on the causes of the PBB disaster. Their final generalization arrived at in class demands something like the following form, which could serve as a diagram for a preliminary draft.

There are many levels of complicity in the PBB tragedy:
business, government, political management, and scientific procedures

This initial shape is apt to evolve considerably as a writer tries to wrestle the data into an essay. For example, the writer will have to make many more meanings as he or she moves from part to part. What generalization, for example, can be used to summarize the complicity of business in the first branch of the tree diagram? ("Business was careless and irresponsible"? "Despite good intentions, business found itself caught in a web of unpredictable accidents"? "Although all business people shared in responsibility for the disaster, the chemical company was more to blame than the ranchers"? "Although all business people shared in responsibility for the disaster, ranchers appear most to blame"?) Each slightly different way that the mind interprets the data alters the way the data must be selected, worded, and arranged.

And as the writer struggles to create a meaning for that section of the essay dealing with business, she is forced to reconsider the thesis statement for the entire essay itself (that is, the final generalization decided upon in class, the one at the head of the previous tree diagram.) Does that generalization really give the reader a clear enough vision of purpose and meaning? Is it a good thesis statement?

Certainly this sentence would give the reader a general sense of what to expect from the essay. And for an essay exam it would probably suffice as a statement of meaning. But for a different audience and in a different context, a writer would probably have to make substantive revisions. It is unclear just exactly what is meant by "levels of complicity," and the shape predicted by the thesis doesn't seem focused. (For example, are the four branches arranged in order of complicity going from most guilty to least guilty? From least guilty to most guilty?) We could sharpen the point in any number of ways. One way would be to change the shape of the essay. We could, for instance, start by giving the background of the tragedy and introducing the major characters in the drama, and then, in the best tradition of the whodunit detective story, we could ask who should bear primary responsibility. We could discuss each of the possible agents in turn, arriving by the end of the essay at the most guilty party. Either that, or we could begin with the thesis itself, but sharpen it by identifying the party we wish to blame most and placing the other parties in a subordinate context through the use of an "although clause": "Although many parties share the blame for this tragedy, X and Y seem particularly culpable."

What this example illustrates, finally, is that meaning gives rise simultaneously to form and surprise. First, meaning demands form because the data must be selected and arranged to support the controlling generalization. Various details about the PBB disaster will be included or omitted according to the meaning chosen and, if included, will be placed in different contexts with different emphases depending on the precise wording of the thesis.

And just as meaning creates form, so meaning also creates surprise because the meaning is new (the writer made it; it didn't lie there in the data). Whether ranchers or the chemical company were more responsible for the PBB disaster is not a piece of data but a thinker's interpretation of data—a meaning that the thinker creates. If a reader had not previously considered the writer's meaning, or if the reader had not been committed to a different meaning, then the surprise created by the writer's thesis would be especially fresh.

Note too that because the writer made the meaning, the writer can be wrong. The act of composing an essay is thus the act of supporting and defending a meaning, of taking a stance with a risky assertion, which in turn initiates the process of dialectic—the clashing of opposing views. A rancher, angry at one writer's suggestion that ranchers shared in complicity for the PBB disaster, writes a counter-essay freeing ranchers from blame by placing greater blame on the FDA. An FDA official, alarmed at the rancher's view, writes still a different argument. And so the dialectic continues. And so writers take risks, surprising readers with their interpretations of data and supporting their interpretations with formed arguments.

But it should be clear that this process of making meanings—of creating generalizations that account for complex data—and then of arranging the discourse into an effective shape with clear sentences and pleasing style is a slow and evolving one. The students studying the PBB tragedy spent several hours discussing the event before they arrived at a tentative thesis, a thesis that must itself evolve considerably if the ideas are to be shaped into an essay. Each draft, in fact, will be a way of learning further just what meanings must be made. As we explained in Chapter 1, experienced writers go through the writing process to "discover what they know." The next two chapters will present six principles that may help you clarify your goals as you work your own way through the writing process.

For Class Discussion

1. To begin this exercise, each member of the class should freewrite for 5 minutes on the following question: "What was the most unfair examination a teacher ever gave me?" Next, working in groups of 5–7 students, read your freewriting aloud to the other members of your group. Then, as a group write a single-sentence generalization that could serve as a thesis statement for an essay that answers this question: What kinds of exams do students think are unfair? [In this exercise each of your freewrites constitutes a piece of information. The generalization composed by your group asserts a meaning.]

2. Look at the portrait by Picasso (Figure 8–3, p. 220). Working in small groups, try to decide why Picasso may have chosen to paint a portrait in this unusual way rather than in a traditional way. Then, as a group, write a generalization that could serve as a thesis statement for a short essay that presents your group's conclusions. [In this exercise, the Picasso portrait itself is the raw information; your analysis of why Picasso painted this way asserts a meaning.]

CHAPTER 4

Three Principles of Form for Writers

PRELIMINARY EXERCISE: TWO ESSAYS FOR COMPARISON

This chapter and the one following give you six practical suggestions for improving the quality of your essays. To illustrate our suggestions, we will be referring throughout to the following two student essays, both written in response to the topic—"the impact of television on society." Essay 1— "TV"—illustrates what we mean by "Engfish" essays, the term we used in Chapter 2 to refer to surpriseless, "canned" essays, technically "correct," but dull and pointless. Essay 2—"Boob Tube: Entertainer Turned Controller"—is presented in two versions, an early draft and final draft. We have chosen this essay because its final version is controversial. In numerous writing-across-the-curriculum workshops that we have conducted for faculty, "Boob Tube" invariably produces heated discussion.

Many English teachers would give "Boob Tube" an A. On the whole, however, instructors from other disciplines, especially the physical and social sciences, have a lower opinion of "Boob Tube" than do English faculty. Why such controversy? The answer to this question should become clear to you as you proceed through the principles of form and surprise in Chapters 4 and 5. As you take part in this conversation about "Boob Tube," you will be growing in your understanding of how teachers from different disciplines judge writing. For now, read the two essays carefully, including the early draft version of "Boob Tube."

Essay 1

TV

It seems that everyone today watches a lot of television. Kids watch cartoons, many people like to watch afternoon soap operas and at night there's the news and the prime time shows. Also many times during the week sports fans like to watch their favorite sports shows be it football, basketball, baseball, or some of the lesser watched sports like golf and bowling. What is the impact of all this TV watching? In my opinion TV has its good aspects and its bad aspects. *Thesis*

As for the good aspects, there is entertainment. I personally like to watch the soaps and look forward everyday to learn about the new things that will happen in the lives of those particular characters that I enjoy watching. My family likes to watch sports and also many of the prime time shows although some are pretty silly. Besides entertainment, there's all the educational things you can learn on TV such as the news, Sesame Street, and all the educational specials, like wildlife shows and Cosmos. The present generation is a lot more informed than other generations because of all the things you can learn on television.

As for the bad aspects, there is too much sex and violence on TV. Some of the things that go on in some of the prime time shows make me blush. One show had a scene of a rape in it and a lot of police shows show drugs and murders. I don't think they make enough good decent shows anymore. Another maybe bad thing about television is that you can watch it too much and not do other good things like read or go for a walk. A lot of times I think we'd be better off if we just turned the TV off for awhile.

In conclusion, I have shown that TV has good aspects and bad aspects. Whether it is good or bad for a given person depends on the personality and values of that particular person and how that person reacts to it. You can't say it is all good or all bad. It's up to the individual whether or not TV is good for that individual.

Essay 2 (early draft with paragraphs numbered)

Boob Tube: Entertainer Turned Controller

1. Is television starting to control our lives completely? It has long been apparent that communication between family members is becoming worse. It is now meddling with our children's diets and state of mind.

2.   In the average home, the most important part of the family's daily existence is the huge-screen, remote-control, full-color of their television set. The father of the family comes home from a hard day at work, sits down in his favorite chair and reaches for—not his wife, not his slippers, not even his newspaper—but his remote control. It's become a matter of convenience to watch television instead of reading the daily newspaper.

3.   The rest of the family filter in and out of the room, the only thing that is said is "There's a good show on the other channel", or "We always have to watch news!" There is no small talk, or important talk about the day's events. When dinner time rolls around in between the news and prime time viewing, the family rushes through dinner, hardly saying a word. Everyone watches the clock timing their gulps to the tick of the clock, knowing they'll be able to eat dessert in front of the television.

4.   A communication barrier is apparent in the above situation. It isn't caused by the father or mother, but by television. If they actually all sat down, shut the television off and talked, would they know what to say?

5.   The communication problem is simply one of the things we are allowing television do to our lives. Our children acquire an unrealistic view of the world. Their favorite shows, usually dealing with some sort of violence, show their heroes shot and healed in one episode. Television depicts a fairy tale world surrounding someone all of us would like to be—a hero. Do our children know how unrealistic their favorite shows really are?

6.   Children are always being told to "go watch TV" while the parents are entertaining or going about everyday chores. These parents aren't actually aware of what some television shows do to their children, in a very innocent way. In the news very recently a small boy shot his older brother in a fit of rage, just like he saw on television the night before. Lawyers tried to prove the boy was influenced by television to the point of madness, they were unsuccessful. This one incident alone stands as an example of the way television influences our children's lives to the point of controlling them.

7.   Some Saturday morning, sit down with your kids and watch the commercials on "children's prime time". You'll see mostly cereal and candy commercials, all with catchy little jingles, most of which your children probably know by heart.

8.   Most of these cereals have been proven to have in excess of 50% sugar. This sugar can have a serious effect on your child. If a child consumes too much of this appealing, sugar-coated cereal, he can develop diabetes, tooth decay, hyperactivity, and, most surprising of all, a dependency on sugar. This addiction can cause withdrawal pains when sugar is taken out of their diet. These pains can be as unpleasant as the withdrawal pains an alcoholic experiences after having alcohol taken out of his diet.

9.   All of these things, the communication-gap, children's violence, and consumption of foods with high sugar content, are caused in some way by our huge-screen, remote-control, full-color television set. Look around you, you decide if television is controlling our lives or merely entertaining us.

Essay 2 (final draft with paragraphs numbered)

Boob Tube: Entertainer Turned Controller

1. There it is, the center of attention in the living room and the center of the family's daily existence: a full-color, remote-controlled television set. The father of the family comes home from a hard day at work, sits down in his favorite chair, and reaches for—not his wife, not his slippers, not even his newspaper—but his remote control. It has become a matter of convenience to watch television instead of reading the daily newspaper. Is it possible that the boob tube, instead of providing entertainment and education, might be taking over our lives? I think it is possible indeed. TV is ruining communication between family members, and it may be messing with children's minds and even ruining their diets.

2. Take a look at the way TV destroys family communication. After Dad comes home and flops himself down in front of the tube, the rest of the family filters in and out of the room. The only thing that is said is, "There's a good show on the other channel," or "We always have to watch news!" There is no small talk, or important talk about the day's events. Dinner time rolls around. In between the news and prime time viewing the family rushes through dinner, hardly saying a word. Parents and kids watch the clock, timing their gulps to the tick of the clock, knowing they'll be able to eat dessert in front of the television. This TV-caused communication barrier is frightening. If the family actually all sat down, shut the television off, and talked, would they know what to say?

3. The communication problem is simply one of the things we are allowing television to do to our lives. We are also letting TV mess with our children's minds. For one thing, TV gives children an unrealistic sense of the world. Their favorite shows, usually dealing with some sort of violence, show their heroes shot and healed in one episode. Because wounds heal so fast, children don't really appreciate the consequences of violence, especially when all the violence seems so fun and entertaining to watch. Also, children come to except that life's *accept* problems can be solved neatly and quickly in a half hour since they are used to seeing problems solved easily on TV. Another way TV messes with children's minds is the way it induces them to imitate their TV heroes. In the news very recently a small boy shot his older brother in a fit of rage, just like he saw on television the night before. Although lawyers were unsuccessful in trying to prove the boy was influenced by TV to the point of madness, this episode suggests the potential danger in TV watching, especially for children. Television thus depicts a fairy tale world where pain heals quickly and where violence is glamorized. What a distortion of reality!

4. If psychological damage isn't enough, TV is also ruining our children's physical health by promoting poor diets. Some Saturday, sit down with your kids and watch commercials on "children's prime time." You'll see mostly cereal and candy commercials, all with catchy little jingles, most of which your children probably know by heart. Most of these cereals have been proven to have in

excess of 50 percent sugar. This sugar can have a serious effect on your child. If a child consumes too much of this cereal, he can develop diabetes, tooth decay, hyperactivity, and most surprisingly of all, a dependence on sugar. This addiction can cause withdrawal pains when sugar is taken out of their diet. These pains can be as unpleasant as the withdrawal pains an alcoholic experiences after having alcohol taken out of his diet.

5.   All of these things—the communication-gap, the messed-up minds, and the consumption of foods with high sugar content—are caused in some way by our huge-screen, full-color, remote-controlled television sets. Look around you and decide whether television is controlling our lives or merely entertaining us.

THE TENSION BETWEEN FORM AND SURPRISE: A REVIEW

As we discussed in previous chapters, form and surprise aren't separate ingredients that you simply mix like sugar and water to form an essay. Rather, they are opposing principles that must be synthesized in ways that defy simple explanation. Form and surprise are like two sides of an arch. By opposing each other they create balance and stability. Moreover, if one is taken away, the other simply collapses. You cannot really have surprise without form. To be surprised it is necessary to have expectations, and form provides us with expectations. In a purely formless world one may be bewildered or confused, but not really surprised. On the other hand, a well-formed essay that doesn't surprise a reader is pointless and boring. Readers read to gain different perspectives on their world, not to hear what they already know.

The paradoxical relationship of form to surprise can be illustrated by the way that professional writers often violate "rules" described in writing handbooks. For example, many writing handbooks explain that a well-formed paragraph should begin with a topic sentence. In this text, so far, we have certainly seemed to support this rule. In Chapter 3, during our discussion of the difference between information and meaning, we said that a writer should begin with a generalization that asserts a meaning and then should support that meaning with details. So far, our model paragraphs, particularly Essay 1 on the New York City assignment (p. 68) and all of our mini-essays about Room 107 in Grimm Hall, have been textbook examples of the "begin with a topic sentence" rule. And yet the majority of paragraphs written by professional writers don't follow this rule. A dozen years ago a composition researcher named Richard Braddock analyzed paragraphs selected randomly from essays in such literary magazines as *Harper's*, *Atlantic Monthly*, and *The New Yorker*. He found that fewer than 40 percent of them followed the textbook rule of beginning with a topic sentence.[1] Does this mean that the handbook rule is incorrect?

Probably not. As with other contradictions we have examined, we can reasonably seek a synthesis of the opposing principles rather than simply eliminate one of them. (Thus, "There are exceptions to every rule" is a quite different statement from "There are no rules.") Professional writers frequently break the topic sentence rule because they seek a balance between form and surprise at a more complex level than the rule acknowledges. The real principle of writing is not "begin each paragraph with a topic sentence" (this advice is simply one strategy for realizing the principle), but "convey meanings to a reader with a sense of ease, clarity, and pleasure appropriate for your message, purpose, and intended audience."

For some purposes, a writer is much more apt to follow the topic sentence rule than for other purposes. In Chapter 2 we talked about the difference between a piecemeal and a global way of reading, each dependent on the way an essay is structured. In piecemeal reading, individual paragraphs and groups of paragraphs make almost complete sense as soon as they are encountered. Each piece of the essay is clearly predicted in advance, and the relationships between part and part and part and whole are made explicit as the essay proceeds. Piecemeal reading is analogous, say, to a tour of a building in which you have a detailed floor plan in front of you at all times.

A reader shifts to global reading, however, when the sense of a floor plan is absent. Global reading is analogous, say, to a river voyage where you are carried along by the flow of the writer's prose to an uncertain destination, a destination which is suggested, perhaps, but not laid out in detail. The rule about beginning paragraphs with topic sentences creates prose which can be read piecemeal. Such prose is highly appropriate when clarity, precision, and ease of reading are important goals. And even in piecemeal reading, topic sentences can often be omitted from paragraphs if the meaning is clearly implied. But if your goals include giving your reader a sense of mystery about where your essay is heading, then you may well choose to avoid the carefully mapped and signalled structure typical of essays to be read piecemeal. Your essay will still have form, but your reader's whole sense of it will be apparent only in retrospect, after the essay has been read and digested. Most of the formal assignments in this book focus on essays to be read piecemeal, but a few of them, such as the "opposing scenes" assignment in Chapter 8 and the story-based assignments from Chapter 13, will let you experiment with essays that demand global reading.

The three principles of form explained in the rest of this chapter apply mainly to prose that can be read piecemeal. As we have suggested, this is the

---

[1] Richard Braddock, "The Frequency and Placement of Topic Sentences in Expository Prose," *Research in the Teaching of English* 8 (1974): 287–302.

most common kind of writing and is especially appropriate for academic essays, technical and professional reports, grant proposals, or any other writing where clarity and ease of reading are at a premium. If you choose to break these principles, your prose will require a global method of reading, with all the advantages and potential dangers of this more complex technique.

PRINCIPLE 1: ACHIEVE FORM BY WORKING TOWARD A FINAL DRAFT THAT CAN BE TREE-DIAGRAMMED.

A tree diagram is a way to display visually the hierarchical structure of ideas in an essay. When you read, you necessarily read linearly across the page, going not from one main idea to the next main idea but from one idea to its supporting argumentation and details and then on to the next main idea. If Main Idea 1 occurs on page 2 of an essay, you might not get to Main Idea 2 until page 7. When you display your essay in a tree diagram, however, Main Ideas 1 and 2 will be next to each other at the top of your diagram. Page 91 shows the tree diagram that the writer of "Boob Tube: Entertainer Turned Controller" used while drafting the final version of her essay.

This diagram could also be displayed as a traditional outline:

Thesis: TV is ruining communication between family members, and it may be messing with children's minds and ruining their diets.

I. TV destroys family communication as illustrated by typical dinner scene.
II. TV messes with children's minds.
   A. TV creates an unrealistic sense of the world
      1. Wounds heal rapidly
      2. Problems solved in half hour
   B. TV perhaps causes children to imitate violence as illustrated in recent court case.
III. TV ruins children's diets.
   A. Commercials cause children to eat too much sugary food.
   B. Sugar is dangerous.

However, we prefer tree diagrams to traditional outlines because they seem to be far more powerful for most writers. Because they display a hierarchy spatially, they enable writers to visualize the logic of the structures they are creating. Writers who create illogical traditional outlines can understand and correct their problems when they switch to tree diagrams.

*Tree Diagram of "Boob Tube"**

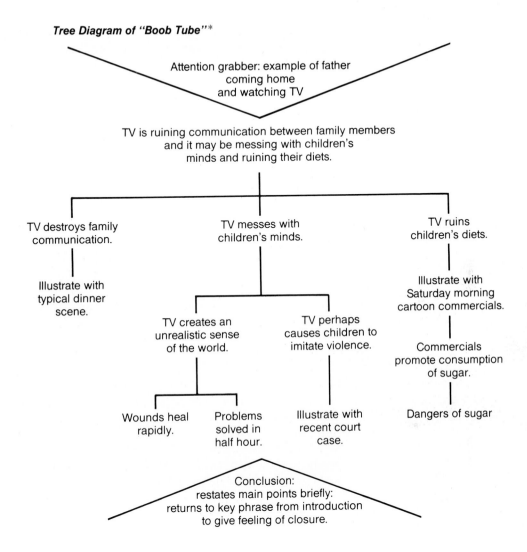

A second advantage of tree diagrams is that they avoid the intimidating baggage accompanying traditional outlines, such as confusion about the use of arabic and roman numerals or the placement of spaces and periods. A particularly inhibiting rule of traditional outlining is the injunction never to

* *Note:* In this diagram the thesis statement for the essay comes at the top of the tree diagram. All the introductory material that precedes the thesis statement (the introduction) is represented in a V above the tree. Similarly, the conclusion is represented as an inverted V below the tree diagram. Thus the tree itself outlines only the body of the essay but not the introduction and conclusion.

have an *A* without a *B* or a *1* without a *2*. This rule is based on the principle of division, whereby you can't divide a whole into just one part (that is, if you divide something, you must have at least two pieces). But a tree diagram can show levels of generalization and specificity as well as division into parts. So if you wanted one branch of your tree diagram to show that a generalization is being supported with just one example, your tree diagram would look like this:

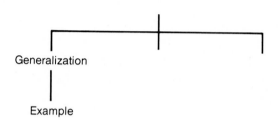

If you tried to display this same structure in a traditional outline, you would have

A. Generalization
   1. Example

and some stuffy English teacher might tell you you were being illogical. "Hogwash," you can now reply. "The logic of my tree diagram is superior to your 'division into parts' logic, Mr. Jones." This stunning retort ought to get that teacher off your back!

Although some writers are able to make fairly complex diagrams of their intended essays before writing a rough draft, most writers can only sketch out a rough plan that changes considerably as they begin drafting. And some writers can't make tree diagrams at all until they have written several drafts to help them discover what they want to say. The tree diagram for "Boob Tube: Entertainer Turned Controller" was made, with some help from the instructor, between the early draft shown on pages 85–86 and the final version of the essay.

This tree diagram, the writer reported, helped her "see" her essay as a hierarchical structure that could be read in piecemeal fashion, each part related clearly to other parts and to the whole. To appreciate how the diagram guided the writer toward a coherent form, try comparing and contrasting the early draft version and the final version of the essay. This comparison should help you appreciate how the tree diagram helped the writer. Once the writer completed the tree diagram and appreciated the importance of showing meanings to readers at the beginning of each paragraph, she was able to write a new draft with the satisfying sense of finally "seeing what I mean."

Using Complete Sentences in Tree Diagrams

The tree diagram used as the map for "Boob Tube: Entertainer Turned Controller" has complete sentences at the top levels of the tree, a practice we strongly recommend. You can see why if you compare the previous tree diagram with this "phrase only" version:

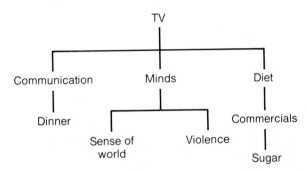

The problem with a "phrase only" version is that phrases by themselves convey information but not meaning. Only sentences convey meaning because sentences, by definition, have both subjects that name topics and predicates that make assertions about topics. A brief discussion here about the nature of sentences will make this point clearer.

In all languages of the world the concept of "sentence" remains remarkably similar no matter how differently the grammars of different languages create different sentence structures. A sentence names something (the subject) and then makes an assertion about the thing named (the predicate).

Name something	Make an assertion about it
Peanut butter	has more protein, gram for gram, than carrots.
Justice	is hard to come by in some parts of the United States if you are poor or black.
Television	may cause children to act violently.

As this list should help you see, meanings are created by predicates. Because a "phrase only" tree diagram lacks predicates, it has only limited value in helping a writer convert information into meaning. If the meanings in an essay are already clearly formulated by the writer, then a "phrase only" tree can be useful as a shorthand way to jog one's memory. But if the writer is using a tree diagram to help discover and create meanings, then a complete-sentence tree diagram is a far more powerful tool. What you actually accomplish in making a complete-sentence tree diagram is to construct drafts of actual key sentences in your essay: the thesis statement (at the top of the tree) and the major topic sentences for paragraphs (at the head of each main branch). A complete-sentence tree diagram will effectively convey to another person not just the shape of your essay but the meaning of your essay also. (Imagine that you hadn't read "Boob Tube: Entertainer Turned Controller"; don't you agree that its argument is clearer in the "complete sentence" tree diagram than in the "phrase only" diagram?)

For Class Discussion

As a class or in small groups, list and discuss the changes the author of "Boob Tube" made in the final version of her essay as a result of creating a tree diagram.

PRINCIPLE 2: ACHIEVE FORM BY DEVELOPING AN UNDERSTANDING OF UNITY AND COHESION

Together the terms "unity" and "cohesion" name essential characteristics of form in an essay. "Unity" refers to the relationship between each part of an essay and the larger whole. "Cohesion" refers to the relationship between each part of an essay and the parts immediately preceding and following.

When a sequence of parts has neither unity nor cohesion, you get nothing but a jumble, like this:

Ellen likes nose hockey, but I don't care if it is March. Not when AT&T is being divided up into little companies. Typewriters especially are getting outmoded. I have a four-cylinder Toyota, and my dog's name is Misty.

The above sentences are related neither to each other nor to a larger whole.

A more subtle problem of form occurs if sentences show cohesion by being related to each other but not unity by being related to a larger whole.

I am writing this essay with a pen I bought at our bookstore. Our bookstore is in the bottom of the Student Union Building, which was recently remodeled by a construction firm from Cooper City. I especially enjoy Cooper City in the summer because of its fine swimming pool. It was, in fact, at the Cooper City swimming pool that I met Martha, whom I have dated now for seven glorious months. Our dates have sometimes ended in fights, however. I also fight with my little brother who is on the 6th grade basketball team. Basketball is an exciting . . . .

If one isn't paying attention closely, the above passage seems to make sense because each sentence is linked to the one before it. But the individual sentences don't contribute to the development of a larger whole. The passage begins with pens and ends with basketball. We might encourage this kind of associational wandering in freewriting, where you are searching for creative ideas, but it is a disaster in shaped writing where you seek to convey unified ideas to a reader.

A converse problem of form would be a series of sentences that exhibit unity without cohesion. In the following example all the sentences would seem to support a unifying assertion, but the connections between sentences are confusing:

I am a bundle of neuroses. My pen is a fine-pointed ballpoint. Round barrels are better than polygon ones. When my pen started skipping I threw it across the room. I had other pens in my backpack, but I went to the bookstore and bought a new one. I write double-spaced on legal-sized yellow pads. My creative juices won't flow. I like silence, so I go to an unused classroom in the Psychology Department. I also work at the cafeteria. I spread my rough drafts over the table and get out my scissors and tape and piles of scratch paper.

Although confusing, all the sentences in this example seem to support a unified point about writing. The passage is worth revising. What the writer needs to do now is link sentences in such a way that their relationship to each other, as well as to the controlling idea of the paragraph, is clear. Here is a revision:

When I write rough drafts, I have all sorts of neurotic needs. First, I have to have exactly the right kind of pen. I require a fine-point, black ballpoint with a round barrel rather than a polygon barrel. The other day when my "perfect pen," which I had just purchased at the bookstore, began skipping, I threw it across the room in a fit of rage. Although I had other pens in my backpack, they wouldn't do for rough drafting, so I went back to the bookstore to make another purchase. Next, I have to write double-spaced on one side of legal-sized yellow pads. Unless I have exactly that kind of paper, my creative juices won't flow. Finally, I have to have exactly the right location. When writing a first draft I demand complete silence, so I hole up in an unused classroom over in the Psychology Department. When I revise drafts, however, I like noise, so I work with scissors, tape, piles of scratch paper, and all my drafts spread out over a cafeteria table. If I don't have exactly the right pen, the right paper, and the right place, it's curtains for my essay.

The Causes of Noncohesive Prose and Some Cures

One of the most important discoveries that composition researchers have made is that both beginning and highly experienced writers write noncohesive prose. Such prose tends to characterize almost any writer's rough drafts. The difference, however, is that experienced writers have learned how to revise their early drafts in order to create cohesion for readers. To understand how to revise for cohesion, one needs to understand why a lack of cohesion occurs naturally in early drafts of an essay.

Consider again the writing process as we have been describing it. When you start the earliest drafts of an essay, you generally don't have a clear picture of what you really want to say. Writing the first draft is often a way of discovering your ideas and making meanings. Early in the writing process, you are worrying mainly about getting your ideas clear *for yourself*. As ideas start becoming clear to you as writer, the prose is still not ready for readers because important connections between ideas and important nuances of meaning, although clear *in your mind*, have not yet been made clear on paper.

The best way to revise your prose is to role-play a stranger who doesn't have any access to ideas inside your mind. Read your draft slowly, asking yourself where a stranger would get lost. Revising in this way generally helps you create cohesion in your draft. Let's look at how the writer of the "neuroses" passage might have used this technique to create the revised version of the passage.

What Writer Said in Incohesive Version	What Writer Actually Meant
I am a bundle of neuroses.	When I write drafts, I have all sorts of neurotic needs.
My pen is a fine-point ballpoint.	One of my neurotic needs is for exactly the right kind of pen, which is a fine-point ball point.
I write double-spaced on legal-sized yellow pads.	This is another one of my neurotic needs.
My creative juices won't flow.	This is what happens to me if I don't have the right kind of paper.
I like silence so I go to an unused classroom in the Psychology Department.	Another neurotic need is that I have to be in the right location when I write. This piece of information shows I have to have silence to write a rough draft.
I also work in the cafeteria.	This piece of information shows further my neurosis about location.

The subsequent revision of this paragraph is cohesive because it better shows the connections between ideas. Although from the writer's perspective the cohesive version contains the same meaning as the noncohesive version, it better conveys that meaning to readers.

Beginning writers can learn to create unity and cohesion in their essays if they appreciate the strategies used by experienced writers. Here are three important ones:

Using Transitions and Other Logical Connectives

In the revision of the "neuroses" passage, the writer uses the words "first," "next," and "finally" to identify the transitions between the three main examples of neurotic needs. Other kinds of transitions or logical connectives used in this passage include "although," "when," "if," "so," and "however." These connectives indicate the logical relationship between successive parts of a discourse.

In prose that possesses neither unity nor cohesion, a sentence can be followed by an infinite range of other sentences. But in unified and cohesive discourse, the possible logical relationships between parts is surprisingly limited. Although different language experts will classify the system of connectives in somewhat different ways, the following list of transitions is widely accepted:

- *sequence:* first, second, third, next, finally, earlier, later, meanwhile, afterwards
- *restatement:* that is, in other words, to put it another way,—(dash), : (colon)
- *replacement:* rather, instead
- *example:* for example, for instance, a case in point
- *reason:* because, since, for
- *consequence:* therefore, hence, so, consequently, thus, then, as a result, accordingly
- *denied consequence:* still, nevertheless
- *concession:* although, even though, granted, of course
- *similarity:* in comparison, likewise, similarly
- *contrast:* however, in contrast, conversely, on the other hand, but
- *addition:* in addition, also, too, moreover, furthermore,
- *conclusion or summary:* in brief, in sum, in conclusion, finally, to sum up, to conclude

Repeating Pronouns and Key Meaning Words

In the "neuroses" passage, the writer's purpose is to show his neurotic needs when he writes drafts of essays. Note how often the writer repeats words associated with writing: "When I *write* rough *drafts*..."; "They wouldn't do for rough *drafting*...”; “Next I have to *write* double-spaced...”; “When *writing* a first *draft*...”; “When I *revise drafts*...”; all my *drafts* spread out.” Although the key word “neuroses” isn’t repeated, the concept of neurosis is highlighted throughout. Instead of “My pen is a fine-pointed ballpoint,” as in the original draft, the writer revises: “First, I have to have exactly the right kind of pen.” This compulsive “have to” is then repeated in each part. “Next, I *have to* write double-spaced.” “Finally, I *have to* have exactly the right location.” Note also that key words for each of the three parts of the paragraph are also repeated inside their respective parts: “pen” in the first part, “paper” in the second part, and references to “location” in the third part. The same effect of linking key words is achieved if you use pronouns instead of the original noun.

Adding Intermediate Generalizations

In the noncohesive version of the “neuroses” passage, the writer goes directly from the topic sentence “I am a bundle of neuroses” to a specific detail: “My pen is a fine-pointed ballpoint.” The link is clear in the writer’s mind (“having to have the right kind of pen is an example of my neurosis”), but this linkage isn’t spelled out for the reader. Perhaps the most important revision the writer makes for this paragraph is to add three intermediate generalizations, which we can call “subtopic sentences” and which would occur at the head of the main branches of a tree diagram of the passage.

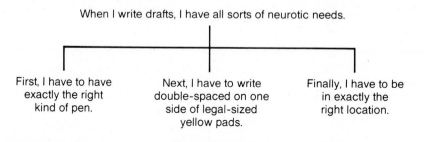

When I write drafts, I have all sorts of neurotic needs.

First, I have to have exactly the right kind of pen.

Next, I have to write double-spaced on one side of legal-sized yellow pads.

Finally, I have to be in exactly the right location.

Unity and Cohesion at the Level of the Whole Essay

So far we have discussed unity and cohesion at the level of the paragraph, but the same principles apply at the level of the essay where each paragraph should be related to the essay’s thesis (unity) as well as to its neighboring paragraphs (cohesion). In a short essay meant to be read piecemeal, the opening of each paragraph often makes three kinds of links.

1. A link from part to whole: that is, some reference back to the thesis statement.
2. A link from part to preceding part: that is, some reference back to the previous paragraph.

3. A link from part to following part: that is, a forecasting of the content of the upcoming paragraph.

The final version of "Boob Tube: Entertainer Turned Controller" clearly shows this kind of linking, as you can see by looking at the thesis statement of the essay and the opening sentences of each paragraph.

For Class Discussion

1. Add appropriate transitions to fit the following contexts:

   a. Working in groups is probably good practice for helping students develop job skills. _____, students often waste time in groups by turning them into socializing sessions.

   b. Working in groups is probably good practice for helping students develop job skills. _____, group work teaches the need for compromise.

   c. There are several things students don't like about the word-processing programs in our writing center. _____, our programs don't allow you to scroll rapidly to the middle of your essay. _____, if your text is ten pages long, it takes a number of key stroke commands to get page 8 to show on the screen. _____, many commands require you to push two keys at once, making you move your hands away from typing position. I frequently find myself typing a line or two of nonsense because I get my hands off position. _____, you can see only a little bit of your text at a time. _____, you can see only three or four lines on either side of the line you are currently revising. Despite these disadvantages, _____, many students still prefer word processing to the scissors and tape method of revising. _____, we recommand that the writing center continue its experimentation with word processing for students.

2. Examine Carl Rogers' "Communication: Its Blocking and Its Facilitation" (pp. 393–398). Identify all of the devices used by Rogers to attain cohesion. Discuss the effectiveness of these devices.

PRINCIPLE 3: ACHIEVE FORM BY LAYING OUT THE WHOLE BEFORE PRESENTING THE PARTS

This principle, which is central to writing discourse that can be read piecemeal, is perhaps the first principle you would begin to break if you were writing an essay you wanted to be read globally. By "laying out the whole before presenting the parts," we mean to give your readers a quick overview of your whole essay before proceeding to your argument itself. Another way of stating the same advice is this: "Give your readers the meaning before you give the information," or, perhaps more accurately, "Give your readers a general sense of your meaning before you provide them with the information that renders your particular meaning clear." So long as the reader is left to discover *how* and *why* your meaning is true, you've left room for surprise.

At the paragraph level, this means to begin your paragraph with an overview generalization showing the point or purpose of the paragraph (its meaning) and then to provide the supporting details. The psychological effect of this procedure on your readers can be illustrated by a comparison of the following two paragraphs. Which one is easiest for you to make sense of?

1.   First you turn the computer on by locating the switch on the back of the unit. Once the cursor begins to flash, type in the command WS and wait for the main menu to appear at the top of the screen. Note that in the middle column of the menu is the command D for "open a document file." For now just type in your first name. The computer will whiz and whirr a moment, flashing the message "new file" on the screen. When it quits whirring, you can begin typing in your text.

2.   Beginners are often intimidated by a word processing computer, but a "smart typewriter" is surprisingly easy to learn to use. Here is the simple procedure for getting started on the computers in Room 315. First you turn the computer on by locating the switch on the back of the unit. Once the cursor begins to flash, type in the command WS and wait for the main menu to appear at the top of the screen. Note that in the middle column of the menu is the command D for "open a document file." For now just type in your first name. The computer will whiz and whirr a moment, flashing the message "new file" on the screen. When it quits whirring, you can begin typing in your text.

[handwritten marginalia: 1st sentence = relates to the reader. Gives the reader a sense of security. "no need to worry." attitude. "Smart typewriter" "simple" "easy" (a person can relate to a typewriter before they can to a computer)]

If you are like most readers, version 2 helps you get your bearings because you know what you are reading and why you are reading it before you get to the specific details. If you were skimming this passage and didn't care a fig about how to operate the computers in Room 315, you could skip this paragraph after reading the opening sentences. With version 1, however, you would have to read the whole passage carefully, trying to figure out why you were reading it, and only then decide that you didn't want to read it in the first place.

Laying out the whole, in other words, helps a reader establish a cognitive map for the essay and thus to appreciate the function and meaning of individual parts as they unfold. The rhetorician Kenneth Burke has described form as "an arousing and fulfillment of desire." "A work has form," he continues, "in so far as one part of it leads a reader to anticipate another part, to be gratified by the sequence." An effective introduction sets up the reader's expectation for what is coming. When the body of the essay fulfills the reader's expectation, the whole essay produces a satisfying sense of structure.

Thesis Statements, Purpose Statements, and Blueprint Statements

In "laying out the whole before presenting the parts," writers generally have at their disposal three main techniques: a thesis statement, a purpose statement, or a blueprint statement. A thesis statement is a one-sentence summary of the argument of an essay. (In long essays, writers sometimes use several sentences to summarize the argument.) A purpose statement usually begins with phrases like "My purpose is to . . . " or "In the following paragraphs I intend to . . . " and provides a statement of the author's reasons for writing the essay—his purpose or intention. A blueprint statement describes the form of the upcoming essay, usually announcing the number of main parts and describing the function or purpose of each one. Purpose statements and blueprint statements are very common in academic writing, but occur less frequently in popular essays for the general public.

[handwritten margin note: Definitions Here in this ⇐ ¶. See also: next pg. in margin]

Writer's Versions of Thesis Statements, Purpose Statements, and Blueprint Statements

Each of these kinds of statements, when composed on separate sheets of scratch paper, can serve as guides for the writer during drafting; they do not necessarily have to occur in the finished essay itself. We will refer to the following illustrations of thesis statements, purpose statements, and blueprint statements as "writer's versions," meaning that these statements are intended as guides for the writer during drafting. After we present the examples, we will discuss in more detail the difference between writer's versions and reader's versions of these statements and give some suggestions on when to include them in the introductions of your essays and when to omit them.

A helpful way to illustrate writer's versions of these statements is to show how a writer could compose them for a paragraph as well as an essay. For example, the New York City paragraph that we discussed in Chapter 3 (p. 68, example 1) can be mapped in the following ways:

Thesis Statement

After a slump in the early seventies, New York City's economic situation is now on the upswing.

[handwritten note: Refer to Essay pg. 68]

Purpose Statement

The purpose of this paragraph is to report recent economic trends in New York City.

Blueprint Statement

The first part of my paragraph discusses the bleak economic conditions in New York during the early '70s. The second half of the paragraph discusses the recent upswing.

The same techniques can be used to map whole essays. The following sentences describe "Boob Tube: Entertainer Turned Controller." Note that we provide a short version and a long version of the thesis statement for the essay. The short version summarizes the main point of the essay; the long version summarizes the main point and, in addition, summarizes the major supporting points. We also include two versions of a blueprint statement, one with thesis elements and one without. A thesis element is any phrase that actually summarizes portions of the argument.

Thesis Statement (short version)

[handwritten: For Essay, refer to pg. 85]

Television is beginning to control our lives in several ways.

Thesis Statement (long version)

[handwritten left margin: Thesis = what you're writing about. Purpose = Why you are writing it. Blueprint = Structure = how you will present it.]

Television is beginning to control our lives by ruining communication between family members, by messing with children's minds, and even by harming children's diets.

Purpose Statement

This essay examines several ways that television is beginning to control people's lives.

Blueprint Statement (without thesis elements)

Part One describes the effect of TV on family communication; Part Two discusses the effect of TV on children's views of reality; Part Three examines the effect of commercials on children.

Blueprint Statement (with thesis elements)

Part One describes the way TV interferes with family communication; Part Two discusses the way TV messes with children's minds by suggesting that TV gives children an unrealistic sense of the world and may induce them to imitate violence; Part Three examines the way commercials urge children to eat too much sugar.

Finally, here are examples for Carl Rogers' article on listening (pp. 393–398).

Thesis Statement

We often block communication by our tendency to judge other people's ideas before we really listen to them; the solution is to learn to listen with understanding.

Purpose Statement

The purpose of this essay is to describe how listening with understanding can improve human communication.

Blueprint Statement

I begin by describing how our tendency to judge before we listen blocks human communications. I then offer my solution, which is to listen with understanding. I suggest both the powers and difficulties associated with such listening, and then suggest ways that such listening can be used more effectively in our lives and even in international politics.

Composing writer's versions of thesis statements, purpose statements, and blueprint statements for your essays is an excellent aid during the drafting stage of writing, even if you later choose not to include these statements in your actual essay. We thus suggest that you write "for yourself" a thesis statement, purpose statement and blueprint statement for every essay you write. These statements will serve as planning and shaping aids as you progress through various drafts, helping you "nutshell" your ideas at those moments when you can't see the forest for the trees. Writing these three kinds of statements for yourself will force you to look at your essay from three different perspectives: the thesis statement focuses on the content of your essay, what your essay actually says; the purpose statement focuses on the goal of your essay, its intended effect on a reader; the blueprint statement focuses on the shape of your essay, its part-by-part structure.

If you like, you can write these three statements on separate sheets of scratch paper, not in your drafts themselves, to emphasize that they are notes to yourself to help you discover the point and structure of what you are creating and not actual "readers' versions" that you will place in your essay. (We know a sociologist who calls these working statements his "butcher paper statements'' because he writes them on butcher paper and tapes them on the wall next to his writing desk.) If you are like most writers, these statements will probably change with successsive drafts as you struggle toward a final version of what you want to say.

The Differences Between a Thesis Statement and Purpose Statement

Although writers often compose sentences that combine both a purpose statement and a thesis statement, it is helpful to think of them somewhat differently. Generally, purpose statements are easier to write because they identify the essay's topic without summarizing its content. Thus the difference between the two is like the difference between a ''phrase only'' tree diagram and a ''complete sentence'' diagram. Note the difference between the following statements:

Purpose statement: My purpose is to explain why I like physics better than chemistry.

This statement implies the question ''Why do you like physics better than chemistry?'' but doesn't answer it. In other words, the purpose statement doesn't summarize the content of the essay.

Thesis statement: I like physics better than chemistry because ideas in physics are easier to visualize.

One sentence that answers the question

This is a thesis statement because it summarizes the argument. Because the thesis statement forces you to generate an argument, it is the most powerful of all the nutshelling statements you can write. If you think of an essay as the writer's attempt to answer a reader's question, then a thesis statement is a one-sentence summary answer to that question.

Reader's Versions of Thesis Statements, Purpose Statements, and Blueprint Statements

The examples we have used so far have all been ''writer's versions'' of mapping statements designed to help the writer get a clear nutshell vision of her essay from several perspectives. The question you must still face is whether to include these statements in your actual essay. How explicitly should you lay out the whole in the introductions of your essays? Your first option, of course, is not to lay out the whole at all but to depend on your reader's ability to sense the whole unfolding as your discourse progresses (global reading).

However, if you are writing an essay whose content and purpose make piecemeal reading appropriate, you still have many decisions. You can just sketch in the whole by presenting a short version of your thesis statement, or you can give your reader an elaborate map complete with long thesis statement, blueprint statement, and purpose statement. These are your choices, but we can give you a rule of thumb: too much mapping can insult your reader's intelligence unless your essay is long enough and complex enough to demand such mapping. Ideally, the joints of your essay should be carefully constructed and therefore largely unnoticeable. Once your mapping passages begin to call attention to themselves, they can begin to distract and annoy your reader. For most of the essay tasks in this text, a short version of your thesis statement will be sufficient, and, in fact, in our form-specified assignments we will guide you toward an effective placement and timing for your thesis. In longer essays, however, you will be on your own.

This rule of thumb against too much mapping, however, can be discounted considerably for the writing you will do in college because academic prose tends to have very explicit mapping in the introduction. The following examples, all taken from academic journals, show how frequently academic writers not only summarize their content at the beginning (thesis statement), but also state their purpose (purpose statement) and map out their essay's shape (blueprint statement).

This article addresses two issues concerning the relation between learning and creative problem solving in science [purpose statement]. First, the question of what good problem solvers pick up from reading a text that poor problem solvers seem to miss is addressed. Then, an experiment is described that explicitly attempted to emphasize the type of information that good problem solvers acquired to see if this instruction intervention could enhance problem-solving performance [blueprint statements].

The above introduction from Bromage and Mayer[2] uses both a purpose statement and a blueprint statement. There is no thesis statement because the actual content of the essay isn't summarized.

The following introduction, from an article by Ede and Lunsford,[3] includes all three mapping devices—a thesis statement, a purpose statement,

---

[2] Bruce K. Bromage and Richard E. Mayer, "Relationship Between What is Remembered and Creative Problem-Solving Performance in Science Learning," *Journal of Educational Psychology* 73 (1981): 451.

[3] Lisa Ede and Andrea Lunsford, "Audience Addressed/Audience Invoked: The Role of Audience in Composition Theory and Pedagogy," *College Composition and Communication* 35 (1984): 155.

and a blueprint statement. The passage quoted occurs after an opening summary of a debate among writing teachers about how to treat "audience."

> To many teachers, the choice seems limited to a single option—to be for or against an emphasis on audience in composition courses. In the following essay, we wish to expand our understanding of the role audience plays in composition theory and pedagogy [purpose statement] by demonstrating that the arguments advocated by each side of the current debate oversimplify the act of making meaning through written discourse [thesis statement]. . . . After discussing the strengths and weaknesses of the two central perspectives on audience in composition . . . we will propose an alternative formulation, one which we believe more accurately reflects the richness of "audience" as a concept [blueprint statement].

For Class Discussion

1. Look at the introductions to several of the articles in Part V of this text and discuss the extent to which they "lay out the whole before presenting the parts." Can you identify thesis statements, purpose statements, and blueprint statements?

2. Imagine that you are Fritz Machlup; as a class compose a "writer's version" of a thesis statement, purpose statement, and blueprint statement for his essay on pp. 399–405, "Good Learning from Poor Teachers."

3. The following passage occurred at the end of the introduction for a college research paper on theories of education. Try creating the top branches of a tree diagram for this essay.

> My purpose in the following paragraphs is to reveal the complexity of the arguments surrounding the open curriculum controversy. I will examine first the views of three educators influenced by Rousseau—A. S. Neill, John Holt, and Jerry Farber. Each of these people believes that the goal of education should be the joyful pursuit of self-discovery and that children should be free to explore their own natural interests. I will then turn to two opponents of the open curriculum—Max Rafferty and B. F. Skinner. Rafferty believes that the goal of education is the acquisition of intellectual skills rather than self-discovery. B. F. Skinner believes that the concept of freedom is an illusion and thus opposes the notion that students can "choose" their own curriculum.

WRITING INTRODUCTIONS AND CONCLUSIONS

Of all the formal aspects of the essay, two which frequently trouble our students are the introduction and the conclusion. Again and again, students come to us with questions about how to begin or end their work. Most writers seem to find it difficult, if not terrifying, to commit themselves to their topics in the beginning or declare themselves done at the end. To relieve some of that anxiety, we'll offer some brief advice here about this formal dimension of writing.

Introductions

For most beginning writers, introductions are easier to write than conclusions, especially if an essay is designed for piecemeal reading where the introduction "lays out the whole." The introduction arouses expectations, either by explicitly signalling what's coming (piecemeal reading) or by setting in motion a sequence whose precise outcome is unknown (global reading). A quick survey of academic and nonacademic writing reveals a broad range of specific forms that the introduction can take. Depending on the length, complexity, purpose, and audience of the essay, a good introduction may, besides providing mapping statements, describe a problem, provide its historical context, present a dramatic vignette, persuade us of the importance of the topic, and so forth. In every case, however, good introductions create a tension that can be fully resolved only by the whole essay which follows. Since the nature of the introduction depends so heavily on the nature of the body of the paper, writers many times find it helpful to wait until the rest of the essay is written before writing the introduction.

We have found that a few simple pieces of advice can help a student create a decent introduction:

1. Have a good lead. The lead is the opening few sentences of the essay, which should be aimed at getting the reader's attention and attracting interest in the subject. (You might note the improved lead in the final version of the student essay on animal research in Chapter 1, pp. 13–14.)
2. Have a subsequent section of the introduction that develops a sense of a problem or a question or an issue. This strategy helps set up the essential tension of an essay and also creates your reader's expectation about what follows.
3. For essays to be read piecemeal, have a thesis statement, a blueprint statement, or a purpose statement, or, if you want to delay presenting your thesis until later, end your introduction with a focusing question that the body of your essay will answer.

Conclusions

If we turn now from introductions to conclusions, we will find a different set of problems. In our view, the purpose of the conclusion, and hence the challenge to the writer, is twofold. First, a conclusion should change a reader's focus from the individual parts of the body of the essay back to the whole of the essay, rather like a zoom camera shifting from a close-up to a distance shot where you see the whole landscape at once. The second challenge, which is far more difficult, is to underscore or clarify the significance of what's been said. Your problem generally is to find the form of a conclusion that best meets your need to clarify and underscore the significance of your essay.

It would be impossible to catalogue all the kinds of conclusions common in academic and popular writing, and indeed such a list would probably leave you more bewildered than enlightened. Instead, we'll briefly discuss four of the most common sorts of conclusions and suggest occasions when each might be useful.

1. Perhaps the most common kind of conclusion, especially in technical and business writing and often in academic writing, is the summary. (Carl Rogers uses this method in his article on "Communication: Its Blocking and Its Facilitation.") The summary is an excellent method of helping the reader see the essay whole, but it can be weak in helping the reader appreciate the significance of what's been said. Skillful summary conclusions don't simply repeat earlier points, but classify them or otherwise clarify them in such a way that readers feel like they are getting another perspective on the material and not simply a rehash of it. In our view Carl Rogers' summary conclusion is weak; once readers recognize that he is simply relisting his main points, many readers just quit reading. For a summary conclusion to be effective, the body of the essay should be complex enough or long enough to warrant a review. In a short, straightforward piece of writing, a summary conclusion can be insulting to the reader, besides being dull.

2. The next option is what we sometimes call in our classes the "web" conclusion, based on the metaphor of a spider web. If you touch a spider web at any point, your touch can be felt at other points on the web. By analogy, any topic is connected to a web of other topics. If your essay focuses on one part of the web, you can show in your conclusion how your topic touches another part of the web. You thus show the significance of your issue by relating it to other issues. You see your essay whole, but in the context of a still larger whole, just as one intersection on a spider web is part of a much larger structure.

Thus in a web conclusion writers show the relevance of their subject in a larger context. For example, in the student essay on the ethics of using animals in medical research, the writer's conclusion relates that specific issue to the larger issue of whether humans and animals are "brothers" or whether humans are more important than animals. A paper on gun control, meanwhile, might end by placing the controversy within the larger context of an individual's rights versus a government's authority; or an essay arguing for a pass/fail grading system might end by discussing whether people in our society are motivated primarily by rewards and punishments or by love of what they are doing. Thus, a web conclusion can show a surprising dimension of your topic's significance instead of merely summarizing what was said. Many of the student examples in Chapter 12 on issue-defense essays have "web" conclusions.

3. Another option—known as the "proposal conclusion"—is found frequently in persuasive writing or in writing that tries to solve a practical problem. Having critically discussed an issue or problem in the body of the paper, the proposal conclusion calls for action. It states the response the writer wants the reader to make, showing briefly the advantages of this action over alternative actions or otherwise describing its beneficial consequences. A slight variation is the "call for future study" conclusion, which shows what kind of additional research is needed before the problem that has been examined can be completely solved. Such conclusions are very common in scientific writing.

4. Finally, perhaps the trickiest of the four conclusions is the "scenic or anecdotal" conclusion, which uses a scene or anecdotal story to illustrate the significance of your theme without stating it explicitly. The purpose of the scene is not to explain the significance of your essay, as a web conclusion might, but to help the reader experience that significance. Thus, a paper arguing against the current trend to remove developmentally disabled people from institutions and place them back into society might end with the scene of a former mental patient, now an itinerant bag lady, collecting bottles in a park. Such scenes can show your reader the emotional significance of a topic you've treated intellectually in the body of the paper.

Of course these four categories of conclusions are neither exhaustive nor mutually exclusive. It is possible to imagine a conclusion that mixes all these types—several sentences summarizing your essay, a short passage showing the relationship of your topic to some broader issues, a brief call to action, and a final concluding scene.

One final tip. Professional writers often achieve a feeling of closure or completeness in their essays by having their conclusions "return full circle" to something in the introduction. In the jargon of free-lance writers, this is the "hook and return" strategy. Thus the lead of your essay might be a vivid illustration of a problem—perhaps a scene or anecdote. Your conclusion would then return to the same scene or story, but with some variation (the next day, five years later, different point of view) to illustrate the significance of your essay. This sense of return can give your essay a strong feeling of unity.

Having now examined three principles of form in an essay, let's turn next to three principles of surprise.

CHAPTER 5

Three Principles of Surprise for Writers

In Chapter 4 we discussed strategies for achieving form in an essay, but we talked little of surprise, except to say paradoxically that form and surprise are opposing principles like the two sides of an arch. While "form" can be defined fairly satisfactorily as the principle of shape or organization in an essay, "surprise" is a broader, more complex and elusive term, harder to describe and explain, than is "form." Thus, before we turn to three principles that will aid you in creating surprise in your essays, we should attempt to define "surprise" more fully.

WHAT DO WE MEAN BY SURPRISE?

To understand surprise, we should first ask why readers read essays at all. As an initial hypothesis, we might say that persons read essays for the utilitarian purpose of gaining information. Thus an essay has surprise if it brings you new ideas or helps you understand something in a new way. So far, in fact, we have been defining surprise as this element of newness in an essay's content.

But there is a further dimension to surprise also, something more allied to pleasure than to a purely utilitarian desire to learn something new. Like listening to music or playing basketball or watching a cat purr, reading is a source of pleasure and a means of play. We can never account for our desire to read solely on the basis of gaining information. Many people report the same kind of aesthetic pleasure from reading a well-made essay as they do from listening to a symphony or observing a beautiful painting or a beautiful bridge. In other words, an essay—even a short essay of the kind you will write for this course—can be a work of art. When composition teachers run out into the hall to share a particularly good freshman essay, they are usually reacting not only to the ideas the essay conveyed but also to the aesthetic pleasure it gave.

Yet we don't think it is possible to specify, for certain, the exact source of this pleasure. An encyclopedia article on dinosaurs can give considerable pleasure to someone who wants to know about ancient reptiles since learning information itself can be pleasurable. In a larger sense, the sudden flashing of new comprehension that an essay can give can even be joyful, so much so that the ancient Greek philosopher Socrates described learning as an intensely pleasurable, erotic experience—the satisfaction of desire. Today we often symbolize the pleasure of learning in the myth of Archimedes, who ran naked through the streets shouting "Eureka, I have found it!" after he discovered how to measure the volume of the king's crown while he was taking a bath. Our point is that language can convey to us a new understanding or vision of something that affects us emotionally as well as intellectually. In one sense, the pleasure we receive is a response to the essay's content. But in other senses that we shall be exploring in this chapter, our pleasure is also a response to the essay's craft, its beauty.

We will re-define "surprise," then, as that element of an essay that brings pleasure to readers, both in our comprehending the writer's meaning—new information, new insight, new understanding, new "seeing" of another person's human experience—and in our appreciating the writer's art-istry—his or her skill at creating and shaping language. Surprise is an inter-twining of content and form and style. It is our response to what the author says and how he says it, a response which is unique to that particular piece of writing.

But when we refer to the content or ideas of an essay, we must hasten to qualify our term "pleasure" to mean also "negative pleasure" or "that which disturbs or troubles." Thus an essay can be surprising (and hence pleasur-able by our definition) if it threatens our view of the world or in some other way disturbs or troubles us, as well as if it gives us warmth and satisfaction. With this sense of surprise in mind, let's turn now to three principles for achieving it.

PRINCIPLE 1: ACHIEVE SURPRISE BY TRYING TO CHANGE SOME ASPECT OF YOUR READER'S VIEW OF THE WORLD

Have you ever attended a basketball game where the cheering of the crowd seemed to ignite the home team and turned the game around, as if crowd and team formed a kind of symbiotic relationship? Whatever psychology is at work here, almost every performer has experienced it, and it always involves some sense of a relationship between performer and audience, as if, in some mysterious way, the audience draws the performance out of the performer just as the performer draws from the audience a sense of rapt attention and pleasure. Actors report that it is difficult to perform onstage unless they establish rapport with their audience during the opening scenes. Teachers too are moved by the rapport they establish with students, so that if you want your teachers to be better at teaching you need to draw the performance out of them by being responsive students.

What many beginning writers don't understand is that writing too is a performance that requires a symbiotic relationship with an audience. (Some writing, of course, like some piano playing is private, for the self, like your journal writing, but this is an exception.) But the problem, of course, is that for writers the audience is absent so that the writer has to invent the relationship, as it were, has to picture the expressions on the reader's face, has to create the audience as an act of imagination.

One of the best strategies for reaching out to an audience is to imagine your essay as a response to a question that interests your readers—either an information-question such as "Did dinosaurs care for their young?" or an issue-question such as "Should local school boards require the teaching of creationism as an alternative to evolution?" Because a question expresses a reader's curiosity and need, the question-answer structure can create a link between writer and reader.

In answering a reader's questions, an essay can surprise a reader by potentially changing his or her view of the world. There are at least three different ways that this change can occur.[1] First, an essay can enlarge a reader's vision of the world. This kind of essay is primarily informational; it answers questions by giving readers new ideas or new data, adding to the reader's store of knowledge. Second, an essay can affect the certainty or clarity with which a reader views a certain portion of the world, either by making a vague idea clearer or a supposedly clear idea more tentative and uncertain. For example, a reader puzzling over the question "Can abortion be morally justified?" may believe instinctively that abortion is wrong but

[1] Our summary of these three ways is indebted to Richard Young, Alton Becker, and Kenneth Pike, *Rhetoric: Discovery and Change* (New York: Harcourt Brace, 1971).

have no intellectual sense of how to create an argument to support such a belief. An article presenting moral arguments against abortion could help the reader clarify ideas that were previously only dimly felt. In such a case the reader's original opposition to abortion would be strengthened. On the other hand, an essay *justifying* abortion on moral grounds and showing weaknesses in anti-abortion arguments could unsettle the reader by causing him to doubt his original position, thus complicating his view of the world. Finally, an essay can actually change or restructure a reader's view of some portion of the world. Such essays are often threatening to our identity, disturbing us into becoming in some sense different or "changed" people. For example, an essay which explains the existential view that we define ourselves by our choices and must accept full responsibility for our identities could cause some people to reexamine and question some of their most fundamental assumptions about life.

Surprise, then, can be measured partially by the kinds of change experienced by a reader upon completing the essay. It should be noted that surprise does not reside simply in a surprising thesis or claim but in the persuasiveness of the claim as the essay unfolds. Unless the claim is made plausible, no change will seem likely and hence the essay will have no surprise. For example, the "shocking" headlines featured on many tabloid newspapers turn out to be pretty surpriseless stories once we read them because the arguments in the story itself don't support the claim of the headline.

If we imagine our essays as in some sense intended to change our readers' view of the world by answering our readers' questions, then we have discovered a powerful technique for bringing surprise to our essays. The author of "Boob Tube: Entertainer Turned Controller" (pp. 87–88) is successful in seeing her essay as a risky answer to the issue-question "What effect is TV having on our lives?" Her assertion that TV is beginning to control our lives could potentially change a reader's view of television. As we will see later, the writer is not particularly successful in making this claim persuasive, but she does an excellent job of taking a surprising stance, of having a risky thesis. And if the thesis wasn't risky, if the reader already agreed with it, there would be no opportunity for change.

The writer of "TV" (p. 85), however, violates this principle of surprise. The thesis "TV has good aspects and bad aspects" is neither new information nor a risky position on a controversial issue. This essay could not possibly change a reader's view of the world because every idea in it is already shared by readers. The essay simply rehashes the obvious. The writer needs to abandon the present draft entirely and begin a search for a problem or puzzling question that will challenge readers. How about an opening like this?:

Although TV, as everyone agrees, has good aspects and bad aspects, perhaps some of the "good aspects" that people take for granted are not so good at all. Consider, for example, the common assumption that the Evening News is "good" because it keeps people informed about current events. Hogwash. The Evening News only makes people *think* they are informed. Actually, as I shall show in this essay, the Evening News is dangerous to our society for a number of reasons.

If this introduction arouses your curiosity about why the Evening News is dangerous, then you have been hooked and are ready to be surprised.

But to convert from the Engfishy thesis "TV has good aspects and bad aspects" to the surprising thesis that the Evening News is dangerous, the writer herself must come to have a new relationship with her subject matter. She must learn, as we explained in Chapter 2, to "problematize experience," to discover surprising questions where others see only "the way things are." Encouraging you to see in new ways, and *to want* to see in new ways, is one of the main aims of this text, both in the journal sequences and in our design of the longer essay assignments.

Changing a Reader's World View: Asking Power Questions

One way of imagining yourself changing your reader's world view is to place yourself in the powerful role of a writer who can bring new or unexpected insights to a reader. Beginning college writers can truly do this if they search for their own "power questions." A "power question" should have three characteristics:

1. You must be the only person in your writing class who can answer the question.
2. The question must interest other persons in the class (or you must think of some technique for getting them interested).
3. It must demand an essay response rather than a "short answer" response (no trivia questions such as "What was my Aunt Bertha's middle name?).

Here are some examples of "power questions" from students in our own classes:

- "What is the best way to bleed the last nickel of insurance payments from a stingy auto insurance adjustor?"—Marv Drake. (Every car owner in the class wanted to learn Marv's strategy.)
- "How can a short person become an effective striker in volleyball?"—Sheila LaBere. (Something in this question also gets people interested whether they know anything about volleyball or not—perhaps it is our human admiration for the little guy.)

- "How do you get a cow to adopt an orphan calf?"—Andy Orham (The ranchers in our class perked up at this question, exchanging their own orphan-calf solutions. The rest of us too soon got interested in the controversy.)
- "What can a baby sitter do to keep little kids from crying when their parents leave the house?"—Kelly Gornall. (Anyone interested in child psychology wants to hear the answer to this one.)
- "How can you get your average Pete and Polly Polyester interested in art?"—Nancy Stone. (Nancy's solution was to paint a water color for them using a razor blade instead of a brush.)

You will get a chance to practice asking and answering your own "power questions" as part of Journal Sequence 2 and to turn one of your power questions into a formal essay in the first "problem-solution" assignment in Chapter 8.

For Class Discussion

Come to class with several of your own "power questions" written out on a sheet of paper. Then share your questions with your classmates. Which questions most interest the class? Would you like to read essays by your classmates answering their power questions? Why or why not?

PRINCIPLE 2: ACHIEVE SURPRISE BY MOVING UP AND DOWN THE SCALE OF ABSTRACTION

We have said that in a good essay a writer weaves back and forth between generalizations and particulars. A failure to shift back and forth from the abstract to the concrete and vice versa can be both confusing and dull. To write on one level of generality is akin psychologically to talking in a monotone: deadening. Certainly we've all been bored by people rattling on, giving us endless details about matters of no significance to us. What a pleasant surprise if such a speaker were suddenly to pop up out of his stupor of details and show us in a flash what it all meant and why it was important to us to know. By showing us particulars without telling us what they all mean, the speaker induces confusion rather than surprise.

This sort of failure, the failure to ascend to a higher level of generality, has already been developed in our discussions of the difference between information and meaning in Chapter 3. In this section, we're going to focus primarily on the failure to go in the other direction: from the general to the particular. The failure to surprise a reader more often comes from the failure to develop a generalization through greater particularity than from a failure to move in the other direction.

Levels of Generalizations and Details

But before we can talk about this movement from one level of generality to the next, we need to explain further just what we mean by the terms "generals" and "particulars," "abstractions" and "details". Many writing textbooks stress particulars by citing rules that go something like this: "Use definite, specific, concrete language," or "Support generalizations with colorful details." In many writing situations, this is excellent advice. John Ramage followed it, for example, in his story of Dr. P. when he described his professor as a "tall, gawky man with inch thick glasses and an enormous Adam's apple" wearing a "manure brown jacket, burgundy and gray plaid pants, a silky vest with what appeared to be 'scenes from an aquarium' printed on it, and a polka dot blue tie." These details help you experience Ramage's world. They don't just tell you that Dr. P. dressed weirdly; they *show* you.

So in many instances the terms "particular" or "detail" mean words that convey sensory experience itself, words that show how something looked or sounded or felt or tasted or smelled. But the rule "use definite, specific, concrete language" can be misleading because this rule, like most rules, exists within a system of contraries. The word *detail*, like the word *large*, is a relative term, not an absolute one. (A marble is large compared to a white corpuscle but is small compared to a basketball.) Thus it is awfully difficult to pin down exactly what we mean by the terms *generals* and *particulars*. Words are not labeled "abstraction" or "detail" in the dictionary precisely because their level of generality depends on how they're used in a particular context. Thus, for example, what might be major generalization in a comparative anatomy lab ("the mouse's bone structure exhibited numerous similarities to the cat's") might turn out to be an incidental detail in a philosophy paper on evolutionary theory.

Indeed, students can sometimes get into trouble as they shift from one context to another trying to find the appropriate mix of generals and particulars. For example, if you are writing a philosophy paper comparing Plato's view of reality to another philsopher's, you might want to discuss Plato's allegory of the cave, in which Plato compares life in the material world to a shadow-like existence away from the sun. In such an essay an extended description of the dampness and texture of a cave's walls would be inappropriate since these details are irrelevant to the philosophical point. So the most particular sentences in this philosophy essay might be more abstract than the most general statements in a personal experience essay about, say, a time when you and your brother got lost in a cave. Our point is not that one kind of writing uses abstractions while the other uses details. Our point is that both essays move up and down the scale of abstraction from one level of generality to another, but that they begin at different levels on the scale.

Using Details Effectively

Following our own advice to shift from one level of abstraction to another, let's now take a look at some concrete examples of how people create surprise through these kinds of shifts. In order to illustrate different kinds of abstractions and details, we asked a graduate student at our university to write several essays for us. At the time, this student was earning a masters degree in wildlife management and had just published with colleagues a scientific article on an improved technique they had discovered for live-capturing bighorn sheep. We asked this student to summarize his scientific article into a two-paragraph, problem-solution shape (this is the first assignment in Chapter 8) and then to expand it again into a longer essay written for a popular audience, such as readers of *Field and Stream*, rather than for fellow scientists. These three versions of the same topic are printed in Part V—"Readings"—on pages 420–427. The rest of this section refers to these essays.

The Use of Details in the Two-paragraph Version

In the two-paragraph version of the essay, the writer summarizes the scientific report using the two-paragraph, problem-solution shape that we describe in Chapter 8. This shape develops a dimension of surprise by posing a problem for the reader in the first paragraph and then solving it in the second. Having felt the nature of the problem, we are surprised by the writer's answer.

But because of its limited range of movement up and down the scale of generality, the short version lacks dimensions of surprise possible in either of the longer versions. From the perspective of a scientist, the short version lacks the surprise of persuasiveness because without particulars scientists can't know whether the writer's conclusion is justified. (If another scientist said, "We tried net-guns too, but they didn't work," scientists would need the details of both cases in order to decide whom to believe.) And from the perspective of a reader looking for a good story, the short version lacks the surprise of drama. You know the results of the writer's work, but you don't experience it in process. It is like returning from a day's shopping to learn the final score of a football game you are interested in. You are "surprised" to learn the results, but this surprise is nothing like the tension and suspense of watching the game itself.

Use of Details in the Scientific and Popular Versions

In comparing the detailed versions of the essay—the scientific and popular audience versions—we get a clearer sense of how writers use different sorts of abstractions and particulars in different contexts for different purposes. In the scientific essay, the writer's purpose is to inform other scientists that the net-gun method works better than the darting method. The writer imagines skeptical readers who are always ready to cross-examine him. What kind of drug did you inject? How accurately did you place the darts? Did you use the same helicopter and pilot in employing each method? What stress was placed on the sheep in both cases? By imagining such questions, the writer moves from generalizations to details suitable for this scientific audience—precise identifications (the particular company manufacturing the equipment mentioned), exact measurements (dosages of drugs, the range within which all hits were made, the exact down times of the sheep), and objective observations (number of sheep involved, levels of stress exhibited by sheep as measured by observation and blood parameter tests—with specific mention of a "countering example," an earlier experimental report citing deaths of two sheep during a net-gunning capture).

It is clear then that the writer's choice of details is shaped by his purpose. His first obligation is to communicate what happened with sufficient precision that other scientists can replicate his experience, either to test it further or simply to use what the author had taught them. Hence, such details as where the drug was purchased and its concentration are extremely important. By the same token, a philosophical discussion of, say, the ethics of animal experimentation and capture are beyond the scope of his essay, as are details about what the author was actually feeling during the drama of the chase.

When we turn to the third version of this student's essay, the abstractions and details reflect a different audience and purpose. The author is now writing to a popular audience who will ask him different sorts of questions. "What's it like to shoot at bighorn sheep from a helicopter? Were you scared? How dangerous is it? Did you really jump out of helicopter on the edge of a cliff?" and so forth. The popular audience wants the writer to recreate the experience so that they can re-live it with him. The writer's task now is to choose details that enable the reader to experience vicariously the excitement and danger. So the writer turns to sensory details that create an imaginative world for the reader.

The helicopter hovered a few feet above the ground while Dick and I leaped out into a cloud of swirling snow, landing hard on the rocks and frozen ground. We raced to the edge and started to inch our way down an icy rock chimney to get to the ram.

With these kinds of details, we experience a dimension of surprise different from that of the scientific essay. In the scientific essay, the sheep-capture problem is a puzzle which the author helps his readers solve. The tension is intellectual—the tension between the writer's claim and the surprise of the details that finally make the claim persuasive. The tension in the third essay, however, is emotional and psychological, the sort that comes from wanting to know what will happen next. The writer is no longer describing an experiment but a process of particular personal experiences leading to an unknown outcome. All the details in the third story serve to reinforce this tension by allowing us to see the dangerous surroundings and weather, to sense the urgency of finding a solution (time and money are running out), and to identify with the actors in this drama (even the sheep) who stand to gain or lose. So, for all their obvious differences, the two essays do manage to move up and down the scale of generality in a way which is appropriate for their context and potentially satisfying to the type of reader they are addressing.

Let's now return for a moment to the student essay "Boob Tube: Entertainer Turned Controller," which we told you at the start of Chapter 4 was so controversial. You can best appreciate that controversy in light of our discussion of generalizations and details. Many English teachers will give "Boob Tube" an A, and cite, as one of their reasons, the student's considerable success in the use of details. These readers enjoy this writer's description of the family gulping dinner to be ready for the prime time shows, and it is easy to picture the father reaching for the remote control of his huge, full-color TV set while his wife goes unhugged. These details create in our imaginations a world dominated by TV. Thus, for these readers, part of this student's growth as a writer can be measured in her appreciation for the power of detail.

But other readers ask if these details are appropriate for the essay's apparent purpose. Teachers outside of English, especially scientists, tend to think the essay is a failure. What they object to is the way the writer invents data. To support the point that TV destroys family communication, the writer makes up a hypothetical example of a family that chugs down their dinners and then uses this example to "prove" the assertion. Whereas scientifically inclined readers are expecting the surprise of "hard data" to make the claim persuasive—research evidence, say, derived from a survey of the dinner conversation habits of randomly selected "heavy TV" families compared with the dinner conversation habits of an equal number of "light TV" families—they are given instead colorful sensory details more appropriate for personal experience essays. For these readers the writer's failure to provide particulars suitable to the essay's thesis discredits the essay entirely.

It is evident then that the writer hasn't yet solved problems of audience and purpose, as we discussed in Chapter 1, and must face again the task of revising the essay, at least if she wants to reach a scientific audience. Obviously these problems of audience and purpose bear on the problem of content. Since many readers object to her use of a hypothetical family, perhaps her best recourse is to describe the TV habits of a family she has actually observed and then to create some kind of argument suggesting that this family is typical of other families. This kind of radical revisioning of an essay, as difficult as it is to undergo, is typical of the writing process of mature writers.

The debate over "Boob Tube" suggests how complex the teaching and learning of writing can be. While you are making progress according to the criteria of some teachers ("Use specific, concrete details"), you get zapped by other teachers who seem to blindside you before you know their rules ("These details must be appropriate for a scientific audience"). As you take a variety of courses in college, you will begin learning the process of argumentation in different disciplines and the kinds of details used to support claims. No matter what discipline, when you write an essay trust in the writing process itself by letting peers read your rough drafts and give you advice about purpose, audience, and the kinds of details therefore appropriate for your evolving essay.

For Class Discussion

1. Reread John Ramage's story of Dr. P. (pp. 49–51) and discuss his use of various kinds of details throughout the story. Ramage's story functions as a unit that is itself a detail, supporting other points within the whole chapter. What is the function of Ramage's story within the whole of Chapter 2?

2. One way to train yourself to use sensory details is to practice writing descriptions using a sensory chart. In small groups, observe together any scene—your university cafeteria, the library, a basketball crowd, a chemistry lab—and pool your observations by listing details about the scene on a "sense chart" with a column for each of the five senses. (The chart guides you to write down what you see, hear, smell, taste, and feel.)

Sight/Eyes:

_____

Sound/Ears:

_____

Taste/Tongue:

_____

Odor/Nose:

_____

Touch/Fingers:

_____

To help you fill out this chart with rich details, imagine what the scene is like from each of the five senses in turn. What would this scene be like if you could only smell or taste? What if you were deaf and blind and could only touch? In Chapter 6 you will have the opportunity to write a paragraph describing this scene, or another one of your choice, incorporating details from all five senses. In such a paragraph, your purpose is to make the scene live in the imagination of an absent reader.

3. To help you learn to use numerical details common in business, technical, or scientific writing, try this task. Working in small groups, create a short questionnaire on some issue related to your writing class—for example, a questionnaire on student attitudes toward journal writing. Display your results in a table or graph. Then either individually or as a group, write a short report to your institution's Director of Writing describing students' responses to your questionnaire in statistical terms. (This assignment is another option in Chapter 6.)

PRINCIPLE 3: ACHIEVE SURPRISE THROUGH EFFECTIVE STYLE

Style refers to the manner in which you put words together to form sentences and paragraphs. Elements of style include your choice of words and your craftsmanship in arranging words into effective sentences. In some cases, one's prose style can be as distinctive as one's style of dress or style of dancing. Hemingway, for example, is well known for his spare, lean style with lots of short sentences. Faulkner, however, often writes a dense, tangled, heavily descriptive style with sentences that occasionally go on for more than a page. The King James Bible is richly poetic and appeals to those who think that a religious text should sound elevated, formal, and slightly archaic, like a solemn ritual. The contemporary Bible *Good News for Modern Man*, on the other hand, tries to sound like everyday speech—the Bible turned into the language of a popular novel. Beginning writers, too, have distinctive styles, and by the middle of a term composition teachers can often tell which students wrote which essays simply by the style of their sentences.

Although it is useful to talk about individual prose styles, it is more profitable to talk about ways that skilled writers change their styles for different audiences and purposes. In reading Chapter 2, you probably noted a dramatic shift in style as John Ramage began his story of Dr. P., and even inside that story the style of the first half differs considerably from that of the second half. Similarly, we saw in the previous section of this chapter how the writer of the bighorn sheep essay changed his style for different audiences and purposes. Thus, rather than making universal judgments about one kind of style being better than another, we prefer to stress the value for beginning writers of learning to adopt different styles for different purposes.

The Impact of Style on Surprise

In the simplest sense of the word, style is *how* you say what you have to say. Style is the sum of all the choices you make when you select the words which express just the meaning you have in mind. People who do not think consciously about style, who make word and sentence choices automatically without an awareness of *choosing*, tend to sound monotonous. They are like the pilotless drone planes used by the military for target practice. They drone anonymously on, the automatic pilot holding them at a constant air speed, flying them at a fixed altitude and in a fixed direction. The only people who bother to follow their flight are the people paid to shoot them down.

Contrast the monotonous flight of the drone plane to the antics of a stunt plane flown by an experienced pilot. People enjoy watching the stunt plane, pay money to do so, because the pilot is forever doing the unexpected, exploring all possible choices of speed, direction, and altitude, and testing the limits of the plane's freedom of choice. And each stunt pilot has a recognizable style, a unique way of combining all those choices into a coherent routine.

Of course, not all good writing styles will be as flamboyant as a stunt pilot's routine. But all good writing styles will result from conscious choices of how to say things and from a commitment to exploring the available resources of language to expand one's choices. Sometimes, a particular style will resemble the colorless flight of a drone plane but will still strike us as effective. When the writer's style is straightforward and easy to follow, we almost don't notice a "style" at all, until we try to imitate such writers and discover that they have made a concious commitment to do the excruciatingly difficult task of stating complex ideas simply, without over-simplifying those ideas.

One of the key differences between novice writers and experienced writers is the proportion of time each spends on the "how" of writing. Beginning writers tend to worry mostly about whether or not they've violated any rules. They think of the "how" of writing as a set of prescrip-tions or laws that must not be broken and yet are really never understood. They often yearn for someone to tell them exactly what they are supposed to do for "style" so that they can eliminate all possibility of error. For beginning writers, this freedom of choice in how to say something is often a dismaying experience.

Experienced writers, on the other hand, are more likely to discover what they have to say while wrestling with the complexities of how they're going to say it. Thus it is that a great writer like James Joyce could spend seven years writing *Ulysses*. Joyce already had models for his plot and his characters and his themes; he was a fluent and brilliant writer—but still he required all those years struggling mostly with the "how" of his novel. The better the writer, the more likely it is that he or she will spend considerably more time revising rough drafts for style than does a beginning writer. Experienced writers "listen" to the sound of their sentences, often reading them aloud for their rhythm and balance. They combine sentences, recast them, try them in several different versions on scratch paper, looking for the right combinations of sound and sense. They worry about their sentences the way a violin-maker worries about the fitting of joints and the sanding of finishes. The pleasure we get from the work of expert craftspeople—whether writer or violin-maker—is thus always a surprising pleasure, an unusual sense of being in the presence of quality.

A Brief Analysis of Style

To accept the responsibility for creating your own style of writing is to accept one of the most interesting challenges posed by the craft of writing. If you think back to the two essays on TV cited earlier in the chapter, you can see that two writers can be distinguished as much by how they speak as by what they say. "Boob Tube" is more surprising than "TV" because the writer took more responsibility for her choices about how to discuss the effects of television. For one thing, she adopted a conscious point of view toward her subject. She chose to treat it humorously. By inviting her readers to laugh at her "typical" family of "videots" she invited them to see the reductive effects of TV viewing. Besides experimenting with point of view, the author also gives careful attention to her choice of words, particularly verbs. In telling us, for example, that family members "filter in and out" of the room, she tells us not just *what* they do (come into the room and leave the room) but *how* they do it (quietly, aimlessly). Her choice of verbs, in short, supports the impression that she wants us to form about her exemplary family.

The less successful essay—"TV"—doesn't adopt any real point of view toward the subject. It's not funny, but, on the other hand, it's not serious either insofar as the writer communicates no sense of engagement with the subject matter. Some things about television are said to be good, others bad, but it's not clear why they are good or bad and there is no developed sense of how, on balance, the writer finally feels about the subject. Without a controlling point of view, the author has no real reason to choose one word over another; consequently, the language is bland and anonymous. It is the sort of essay we might write on automatic pilot.

Differences in style, such as the ones noted above, are often easy to sense, but excruciatingly difficult to describe. Indeed, there's a whole branch of study called stylistics which has developed a very specialized vocabulary for articulating these differences. Such studies can be dauntingly difficult for the novice. This difficulty follows from the fact that linguists have shown us in recent years that even an ordinary paragraph involves an enormous number of choices on the part of the writer. That is, two writers can say essentially the same thing, following the same code for linguistic correctness, in a multitude of different ways. It would take us another entire book to begin to define and demonstrate all these different stylistic options.

Luckily, we don't have to do this. We don't have to because most writers, even professionals, rely on a handful of stylistic options (actually, categories of options) to guide the thousands of particular choices they make in the course of writing a paper. By way of making you more aware of your own stylistic options, we offer the following four sorts of choices that good writers would make in suiting their prose to their particular needs. While certain sorts of writing (for example, scientific or technical writing) severely limit one's stylistic options, a good writer can always find a way of stating something more gracefully and pleasingly, with less strain on the reader, than an indifferent writer. Here then are four choices to keep in mind as you turn from writing prose to crafting it: (1) you can choose from among different ways of shaping each sentence (simple/complex, long/short); (2) you can choose from among the wealth of available words the precise words for the job (abstract/concrete, colloquial/formal, metaphoric/literal); (3) you can choose your relationship with your reader (intimate/distant; informative/ entertaining); or (4) you can choose from among different attitudes toward your subject matter (humorous/serious, ironical/straight-forward). Of course, these choices are interrelated. Your relationship with your reader might well limit your word choices; your attitude toward the subject might well influence your decisions about sentence shape. But nearly always, there's some room for choice and some possibility for "surprising" your reader in a pleasant way.

Probably the best way of understanding style is to see it in action. To that end, let's study two very different styles and see the concrete results of authors exercising their options in different ways to suit their particular needs.

In the first example, Tom Wolfe is discussing how his visit to a hot rod show inspired him to write a different kind of essay about hot rodders:

I don't mean for this to sound like "I had a vision" or anything, but there was a specific starting point for practically all of these stories. I wrote them in a fifteen-month period, and the whole thing started with the afternoon I went to a Hot Rod & Custom Car show at the Coliseum in New York. Strange afternoon! I was sent up there to cover the Hot Rod & Custom Car show by the *New York Herald Tribune*, and I brought back exactly the kind of story any of the somnambulistic totem newspapers in America would have come up with. A totem newspaper is the kind people don't really buy to read but just to have, physically, because they know it supports their own outlook on life. They're just like the buffalo tongues the Omaha Indians used to carry around or the dog ears the Mahili clan carried around in Bengal. There are two kinds of totem newspapers in the country. One is the symbol of the frightened chair-arm-doilie Vicks Vapo-Rub *Weltanschauung* that lies there in the solar plexus of all good gray burghers. All those nice stories on the first page of the second section about eighty-seven-year-old ladies on Gramercy Park who have one-hundred-and-two-year-old turtles or about the colorful street vendors of Havana. Mommy! This fellow Castro is in there, and revolutions may come and go, but the picturesque poor will endure, padding around in the streets selling their chestnuts and salt pretzels the world over, even in Havana, Cuba, assuring a paradise, after all, full of respect and obeisance, for all us Vicks Vapo-Rub chair-arm-doilie burghers. After all. Or another totem group buys the kind of paper they can put under their arms and have the totem for the tough-but-wholesome outlook, the Mom's Pie view of life. Everybody can go off to the bar and drink a few "brews" and retail some cynical remarks about Zora Folley and how the fight game is these days and round it off, though, with how George Chuvalo has "a lot of heart," which he got, one understands, by eating mom's pie. Anyway, I went to the Hot Rod & Custom Car show and wrote a story that would have suited any of the totem newspapers. All the totem newspapers would regard one of these shows as a sideshow, a panopticon, for creeps and kooks; not even wealthy, eccentric creeps and kooks, which would be all right, but lower class creeps and nutballs with dermatitic skin and ratty hair. The totem story usually makes what is known as "gentle fun" of this, which is a way of saying, don't worry, these people are nothing.[2]

In the second example, Bertrain Morris is summarizing a view of the world called "mechanistic materialism," a view that he will eventually oppose:

Being atomistic and reductive, mechanistic materialism is also characterized as a self-contained system, in which everything in the universe happens as a consequence of motions predetermined by mechanical necessity. This necessity is expressed in causal laws. Bodies move, not haphazardly, but predictably, in accordance with a pattern. The causal forces in the world are motions of bodies which predetermine the motions of other bodies, just as one billiard ball striking another causes it to move with a certain motion in a certain direction. Motion is conserved, if not in the obvious movements of bodies, then in the form of heat or some other form of energy. But heat, too, is a form of motion, at least according to the kinetic theory, which applied to gases proved to be a dramatic confirmation of the mechanistic hypothesis. Thus, in the kinetic theory of gases, the higher the temperature of a gas, the more forceful the bombardment of the molecules against the sides of its container, and consequently the greater the pressure that the gas exerts. If, moreover, light, electricity, and magnetism can be similarly interpreted as forms of energy convertible into motion, the mechanistic theory becomes virtually complete.[3]

Without knowing anything about style you would still be able to hear considerable difference in these two passages. You might well conclude without knowing the two authors that they are very different people. But in fact that may not be so. In person, the authors might be quite different from what their prose would lead us to believe. In choosing a style, an author is not so much choosing a way of expressing a personality as subordinating personality to the needs of writing. If Wolfe were to write a textbook explaining the Second Law of Thermodynamics to students, his style would undoubtedly still be different from Morris's, but it would also be different from the one used in the above piece. In fact, in other writings, Wolfe's style is considerably less flamboyant. You might see, for example, his treatment of some of the technical matters in his book *The Right Stuff*.

[2] Reprinted with permission from Tom Wolfe, *The Kandy-Kolored Tangerine-Flake Stream-line Baby* (New York: Farrar Straus and Giroux, 1965).

[3] Harry Girvetz et al., *Science, Folklore, and Philosophy* (New York: Harper & Row, 1966).

Assuming then that the authors' styles result more from conscious choice than from an unconscious overflow of personality, let's review their particular decisions about the four options.

With regard to sentence types, both writers exhibit a fair amount of variety. Both move from simple sentences ("This necessity is expressed in causal laws." "There are two kinds of totem newspapers in the country.") to much longer and more complex ones. On the whole, Wolfe would appear to favor longer sentences, though not necessarily more complex ones. His phrases tend to pile up in parallel fashion to create one strong cumulative effect (". . . a sideshow, a panopticon, for creeps and kooks; not even wealthy, eccentric creeps and kooks, but lower class creeps and nutballs with dermatitic skin and ratty hair.") Morris, meanwhile, uses complex sentence structures more to qualify ("Motion is conserved, if not in the obvious movements of bodies . . . .") and to clarify logical relationships. In addition, Wolfe uses sentence fragments ("After all." Mommy!") for dramatic effect, while Morris's sentences are written in full conformity with the standard code for sentence construction.

In the matter of word choice, Wolfe uses words which are sometimes simpler and more concrete than Morris's ("ratty hair," "chestnuts and salt pretzels") and sometimes more obscure ("dermatitic"). Morris's language is both more abstract and more formal on the whole. He uses concepts like "motion" and "kinetic theory," but in a very fixed and precise way. When he introduces a technical term like "mechanical necessity" he proceeds to define that term. Wolfe's vocabulary is slangier, grittier ("nutball"), closer to oral speech than Morris's. And just as Wolfe will break grammatical rules occasionally, he'll also invent words. Some of these words he will define later ("Totem newspaper") while others he leaves for the reader to figure out ("Frightened chair-arm-doilie Vicks Vapo-Rub *Weltanschauung*" [that italicized jaw-breaker at the end of this phrase is German for "world view"]). Another thing to note about this last example from Wolfe is that it tends towards the figurative. Wolfe is equating a world view with two items that the proponents of that world view might use (chair-arm-doilies and Vicks Vapo-Rub). Wolfe generally favors figurative language, in particular, outrageous metaphors such as the above example. Finally, Wolfe's language tends to be much more highly emotionally charged than Morris's. From his words we can tell not just what Wolfe thinks, but how he feels about his subject. Morris's tone, meanwhile, is studiously neutral.

In their relationship to their audience, Wolfe would appear to be much more intimate than Morris is. He writes to us in the first person "I" voice in a loose, conversational way. Moreover, he seems to assume that his audience is predisposed toward his unfavorable view of "totem newspapers" and middle class Americans. (His railing against them suggests a conspiratorial, "we're in this together" attitude rather than the sweetly reasonable "how can

I convince you" attitude.) His assumption that we know what he's talking about when he invents new terms or makes far-ranging comparisons again suggests a sort of in-group relationship with his readers. And finally, Wolfe will thrust a dramatic scene upon us by way of illustrating a point, a scene which is vividly immediate ("the picturesque poor in Havana"). By contrast, Morris, writing in the third person, will stand aside and let physical laws explain particular phenomena. Morris's relationship to his readers is more like that of a teacher's relationship to his students than anything else. He draws our attention to things on the board, formulas and diagrams, which he unobtrusively takes us through by pointing with a piece of chalk. Wolfe, meanwhile, is more like a sidewalk orator who's buttonholed us on our way to the bus stop to enlist us in some cause.

The differences which are so apparent in the first three categories of stylistic options are equally apparent in the authors' attitudes toward their subject matter. Wolfe uses humor, exaggeration, and irony (saying one thing while meaning another) to make us laugh at and dismiss the attitudes, institutions, and people he finds unacceptable. His distortions of the material appear to be as much to make us laugh as to persuade or inform us. His distortions are, moreover, so obvious that few people would mistake them for lies or inaccuracies. Morris's attitude toward his subject is obviously much more accepting. Having "listened" sympathetically to what mechanistic theory is all about, he's now summarizing that position in a way that would be unobjectionable to even the staunchest proponent of the mechanistic view, even though he will ultimately point up weaknesses in the view. He is attempting to present that information straightforwardly with a minimum of distortion. It is, in sum, a respectful attitude toward the topic, as respectful as Wolfe's is irreverent.

Now, in terms of the relationship between style and surprise, it would appear that Wolfe, by breaking grammatical rules, inventing new words, experimenting with his sentences, and treating his subject humorously and ironically is the more "surprising" writer. Certainly he's the more adventurous stylist. But surprise is, remember, also a function of what you say as well as how you say it. Here, Wolfe's essay probably contains considerably less novel material than does Morris's. While you may not know who George Chuvalo is (a heavyweight boxer from the 1950s and 1960s renowned for his ability to absorb punishment), you can probably figure out most of what Wolfe is saying about him from the context. Wolfe is, finally, a journalist whose subject matter is the sort of everyday stuff with which all of us are to some degree familiar. (The whole point of "New Journalism," the sort of writing Wolfe is said to be doing, is to offer a fresh perspective on events which the news treats more straightforwardly.) But Morris, in defining for us just what "mechanical necessity" entails, is probably taking most of us into fresh territory. He's taking us beyond our workaday sense of what that means and deepening our understanding of the operation of physical laws. His is not a new perspective on the matter, but it's a very clear one whch most of us will appreciate.

For Class Discussion

1. Analyze the stylistic differences between the two versions of the bighorn sheep essay in the previous section in terms of sentence construction, word choice, attitude toward reader, and relationship to content.

2. Here are two passages of prose which have been "deconstructed" into a series of kernel sentences. A few words have been changed and all connecting words and figurative language have been left out. Prior to class, recombine them into effective paragraphs written in your own style. Then in class compare your version first with those of your classmates and then finally with the original model. Be sure you understand that the original version is not the *correct* answer; it is only one option among thousands. Your instructor has access to the originals of these passages.

Take a light vessel. *and*
~~The vessel should have a~~ narrow mouth.
Apply ~~the vessel~~ *it* to your lips. *and*
Suck the air out of the vessel. *and*
Discharge ~~the air.~~ *it*
The vessel will hang from your lips.
The vacuum will draw your lips into the vessel.
The lips will fill up the exhausted space.
There is a vaccum in the vessel.
The vaccum is continuous.
Take a cup.
The cup is egg-shaped.
The cup is the sort doctors use.
The cup is made of glass.
The cup has a narrow mouth.
Doctors suck the air out.
Doctors place a finger over the vessel's mouth.
Doctors invert the cup.
Doctors place the cup into liquid.
Doctors withdraw their fingers.
Liquid is drawn into the cup.
The liquid is drawn into the exhausted space.
The motion of the liquid is upward.
Upward motion is against the nature of liquid.

—*Hero, Greek scientist* A.D. *60*

A budget is literally a document.

The document contains words and figures.

The document proposes expenditures.

The expenditures are for certain items and purposes.

The words describe items of expenditure.

The items of expenditure include salaries, equipment and travel.

The words describe purposes.

The purposes include preventing war, improving mental health and providing low income housing.

The figures are attached to each item or purpose.

We presume that budget-makers have an intent.

The intent is to make a connection.

The connection is between what's written in the budget and future events.

We can conceive of the budget as a prediction.

We can conceive of the budget as intended behavior.

The purposes will be achieved only if funds are granted.

The purposes will be achieved only if funds are spent in accordance to instruction.

The purposes will be achieved only if the actions involved lead to the desired purposes.

The budget is a link.

The budget links financial resources to human behavior.

The budget accomplishes policy objectives.

How correct are the predictions postulated in a budget?

The success of budget predictions can only be determined by observation.

—from The Politics of the Budget Process by Aaron Wildavsky

CHAPTER 6

Practicing Form: Microthemes about Thinking and Learning

THE DIFFERENCE BETWEEN JOURNAL WRITING AND MICROTHEME WRITING

By the time you start writing these microthemes, you will probably have gotten a good feel for journal writing. As you will soon discover, writing microthemes is a quite different sort of task because microthemes are written "for others" while journals are written "for self." We use the term "microthemes" for very short writing assignments that focus on the development of a few specific skills. Many instructors in other disciplines like microtheme assignments because they are relatively easy to grade and can be designed to enhance your learning of the subject matter while giving you additional practice in writing. Moreover, when instructors give the same microtheme assignment to all students, they can provide feedback by discussing model microthemes in class. Students frequently find that they learn more about writing from comparing their microthemes to the models than they do from traditional teacher comments.

Think of these microtheme assignments as skill-building exercises, something like scales in music or figure-eights in ice-skating. The subject for the tasks in the first four microthemes will be the process of teaching and learning—a topic you have already been exploring in your journals. Because these microthemes are designed to increase your awareness of "form" in writing, you will often be asked to follow a prescribed structure. Our purpose is to help you internalize a basic skill needed for creating form in writing—the skill of relating general statements to specific details and of making transitions as you move up and down the various levels of abstraction. An efficient way to learn these skills is to begin with fixed-form paragraphs.

The specific techniques you will be learning in the microthemes are these:

- The ability to introduce a microtheme with a topic sentence, which is the most general sentence in the essay.
- The ability to divide development for the topic sentence into parts, when necessary, and to introduce each part with a smaller generalization that we will call a subtopic sentence.
- The ability to support generalizations with specific details or other argumentation.
- The ability to use a variety of sources for details.
- The ability to write transitions that link each subpart of the microtheme back to the topic sentence.
- The ability to use transitional words and expressions to create cohesion between sentences.

From just this much explanation, you can tell that these kinds of structured writing tasks will involve very different thinking and writing skills from the freewriting you have been doing in your journal. As we have suggested, microthemes are intended as writing for readers. Therefore, the ideas in your microthemes must be shaped to meet readers' needs —readers whom we can call "strangers" because they will know you only through the paragraphs that you write.

Microtheme 1: A Paragraph with Parallel Subparts

As a group, write the second paragraph for a two-paragraph essay on the topic "How Teachers Could Improve Their Teaching." The introductory paragraph is provided, as is the topic sentence for the paragraph your group will write. Your paragraph will be built with parallel subparts. Here is the introductory paragraph plus a framework for the paragraph you will write:

We students hear about an education crisis all the time. Teachers tell us that we watch too much television, that we don't study enough, that many of us haven't learned the basic skills, and that we are interested only in grades rather than education. Some of these charges may perhaps be true. But if there really is an education crisis, then maybe teachers should accept part of the blame too. Perhaps we would be better students if our instructors were better teachers.

Although all of us have had plenty of good teachers, we have also had plenty of bad ones—teachers who bored us, insulted us, ignored us, short-changed us. After much discussion about the best and worst teachers we have had, our group would like to answer the following question: What can teachers do to help us become better learners?

Our group believes that teachers could help us become better learners if they followed three simple principles of good teaching. First, teachers should ... [here you will identify your first principle and develop it with details]. Second, teachers should ... [your second principle along with supporting details]. And finally teachers should ... [your last principle and supporting details].

This first assignment is a group paper. Imagine that you are writing to teachers at the college or secondary level and that your purpose is to offer useful suggestions to teachers on how they can improve their teaching so that you can improve your learning. Each principle of good teaching in your microtheme should be supported by specific details based on personal experiences of members of your group. These details should show how each of the teacher behaviors you recommend leads to better student learning. Thus, the opening sentence of your microtheme stresses a connection between good teaching and good learning. Each part of your microtheme must follow up on the promise to develop that connection. Your paragraph should be approximately 300–400 words in length.

The shape of the paragraph you will write is shown in the following tree diagram.

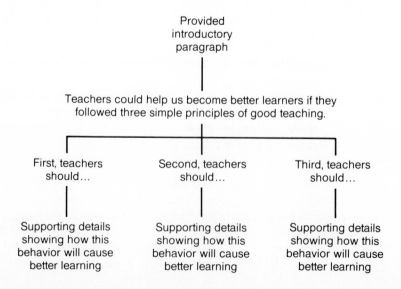

Discussion

This assignment introduces you to a very common strategy for organizing sections of writing. A writer begins with a generalization that is then developed in equal parts. Each part begins with a narrower generalization that is developed with its own details. Writing teachers call these parts "parallel" or "coordinate" because each part makes an equal contribution to the development of the whole. Frequently the parts could be arranged in a different order. To make sure the reader doesn't get lost, writers use two "mapping" techniques:

First, writers use transition words to introduce each of the parallel parts. The most common of these transitional words or expressions are these:

first . . . ; second . . . ; third . . .	likewise
moreover	equally important
either . . . or . . .	furthermore
in addition	another
first . . . ; next . . . ; finally . . .	and also

Second, writers sometimes, but not always, make each subtopic sentence begin with the same grammatical structure for a parallel "echo-like" effect. Both of these techniques are evident in the subtopic sentences provided in this exercise:

First, teachers should. . . . Second, teachers should. . . . And, finally, teachers should. . . .

This organizational pattern occurs frequently in writing. In order to get the feel for using this technique in your own prose, watch for it in textbooks and articles. Here are some examples of the ways writers use this technique:

• When they want to divide a concept into various categories:

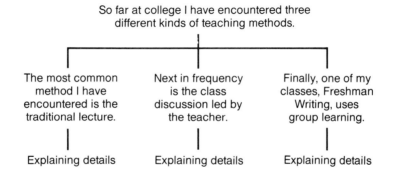

So far at college I have encountered three different kinds of teaching methods.

The most common method I have encountered is the traditional lecture.	Next in frequency is the class discussion led by the teacher.	Finally, one of my classes, Freshman Writing, uses group learning.
Explaining details	Explaining details	Explaining details

• When they want to supply a list of reasons for an opinion.

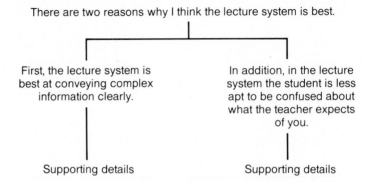

• When writers want to develop a point by giving several examples:

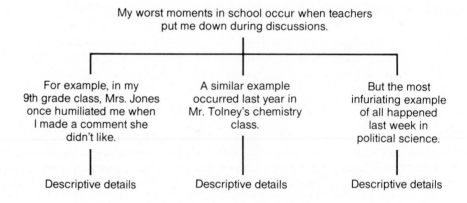

In all these examples, the main generalization is developed through a series of equal subparts. In each case, what will make the writing surprising is the aptness of the subtopic sentences and the liveliness of the details. Specific details such as descriptions or quoted snatches of conversation are especially effective elements of surprise because they are almost always novel to the reader. Your readers may already be familiar with your general point, but the specific details and evidence you cite will almost surely be new to them and cause them to think about your topic in a new way.

Writing Your Microtheme As a Group
This writing task is a group project in which all members of your group collaborate to decide on your three pieces of advice and then to write the paragraph.

Probably the best way to begin is with group brainstorming. Spend ten minutes or so brainstorming things teachers could do to help you become better learners. Get as many ideas as possible down on paper without criticizing or judging any of them. Since you will have already explored ideas about good and poor teaching in your journals, your group should be able to think of many possible "principles of good teaching."

After your brainstorming sessions, your group should negotiate consensus on three main pieces of advice you wish to give teachers. Each piece of advice must be summarized as a complete sentence beginning with the words "teachers should." You should then discuss what details or arguments you could use to support each piece of advice. Illustrate your points with actual personal experiences from members of your group. Remember that the topic sentence you are required to use commits you to relate good teaching to good learning. You must show how each "principle of good teaching" will increase your *learning* in a course, not simply increase your enjoyment of the course.

When you are ready to start writing, divide your group into two subgroups—the DRAFTERS and the REVISERS. Each member of the DRAFTERS group should write a rough draft of the paragraph independently and pass it along to the REVISERS. When the REVISERS get copies of each of the rough drafts, they should collaborate to write a single second draft that incorporates the best features of the individual rough drafts. They are free, however, to add material or change material in order to improve the essay. Finally, all members of your group should work together to edit the paragraph.

Here is how this procedure might work. The three drafters (Mary, Angelo, and Kim) write independent drafts and give them to the revisers (Sam and Jefferson). Working together, Sam and Jefferson produce a single second draft. At this stage the whole group edits the final draft. Angelo volunteers to type it and, as a reward, the other members buy him a pizza.

Moving Beyond the Microtheme

Although this assignment asks you to use the parallel parts pattern to organize a single paragraph, it should be easy to see how the pattern can be used in longer structures. Each part could become a paragraph by itself or even a whole group of paragraphs. The writer would simply introduce the group of paragraphs with a general statement indicating that a parallel sequence is beginning and then write clear transitions at the beginning of each subpart. You can see this technique in Carl Rogers' article (pp. 393–398). For example, paragraph 10 ends with the sentence "I will try to list the difficulties which keep it [good listening] from being utilized." The next three paragraphs present these difficulties.

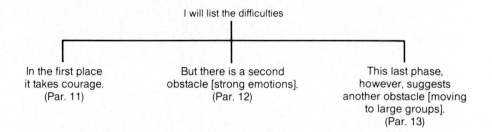

You will find similar examples of the parallel parts method used for short or extended passages of writing in just about everything you read.

A Student Example

The following microtheme was recently written by a group of students in freshmen writing. The names of teachers have been changed to protect the innocent (guilty?).

Our group believes that teachers could help us become better learners if they followed three simple principles of good teaching. First, we think teachers should show less favoritism toward individual students. Anita remembers a history teacher, Mr. Jones, who gave his undivided attention to three students within the class, and centered all lectures, homework, and tests around these individuals. Anita recalls that "He would find out the class schedule of his three favorites and then schedule his tests and homework assignment around their other classes. It got to the point that no one even cared if they learned anything because they were so mad at the teacher." Second, we think teachers should include humor in their lectures. This helps keep a relaxing atmosphere in class and can even help students remember main points. Pete recalls his government teacher who could blend humorous anecdotes into his lectures to highlight main points. The "element of surprise" helped Pete remember important points because he could associate the subject matter with a joke. Finally, we feel teachers should assign a wide variety of homework, ranging from fact-memorization to research papers. Jeff feels that some of his teachers lacked effectiveness because they continually assigned fill-in-the-blank homework which only required skimming through the chapter. He felt that this detail did not allow students to think on their own. "Just filling in the blanks does not give you the chance to be creative and is easily forgotten." Our group does, however, feel that fill-in-the-blank homework can be effective in moderation, but that longer, more detailed assignments should also be given. Vicki stated that she likes to do research papers because she can learn different things about the subject. For example, she remembers a time in her speech and communication course during her senior year when she had to write an essay on the "Moonies." She knew very little about them when she began, but during the course of her research learned many interesting facts, including how they arrange their marriages, how they organize their communal living, and how and why they sell their products to the public.

To appreciate how tree diagramming can help you structure your writing, you might wish to note how the organization of this essay can be displayed:

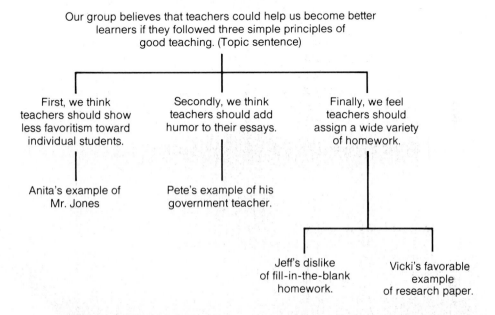

Microtheme 2: Another Parallel Subparts Paragraph

Write a 250–300 word paragraph that beings with one of the following opening sentences:

1. *"Working in groups has affected my understanding of the writing process in several ways."*
2. *"Journal writing has helped me learn several new techniques for generating ideas."*
3. *"Writing summaries of lectures has affected my thinking and learning habits in several ways."*
4. *"So far, journal writing has not been effective for me for several reasons."*

Develop your microtheme using the "parallel subparts" method used in Microtheme 1—include at least two subparts but no more then four. Imagine your audience as a group of college instructors from various disciplines interested in how students perceive the effects of working in groups, writing journals, or writing summaries of lectures.

Discussion

This microtheme assignment requires the same organizational strategy as in Microtheme 1, but here you are asked to work individually rather than write your microtheme as a group. Your main thinking problem for this microtheme is trying to determine just what it is you have learned about the writing process from working in groups, about generating ideas from writing journal entries, or about your thinking and learning habits from summarizing lectures. You will then need to classify that information into several parallel subparts. Your instructor may give you time for small group discussion of these problems.

Microtheme 3: Writing a Summary

Write a 100–word summary of Peter Elbow's article "Embracing Contraries in the Teaching Process" (pages 406–419) or another article chosen by your instructor. You can go over or under the 100–word limit by no more than 15 words. As an option, teachers may specify longer summaries such as 150, 200, or 250 words. The longer the summary, the more details you can include.

Discussion

A summary is an extremely condensed version of an article—so condensed that all the specific examples and details of the essay are eliminated leaving only the major points. With practice a person can write summaries of varying lengths, from very short summaries (one or two sentences) to quite long summaries (four or five pages, say, if you are summarizing a book). A one-sentence summary of an article we generally call the article's "thesis statement—the whole article reduced to a single sentence. Longer summaries (sometimes called abstracts) regularly occur at the beginning of articles appearing in scientific journals, and sometimes authors will conclude an article with a summary of their main points.

We introduced the concept of summarizing in Chapter 3, where we discussed the differences between the summarizing and the detailed modes of writing. When you summarize an article, you omit the article's supporting details leaving only the skeleton of main ideas. If you imagine this skeleton displayed as a tree diagram, you can understand why it is possible to write summaries of different lengths. A very short summary captures only the ideas at the very top of the tree diagram. The longer the summary, the farther down the tree diagram the summary writer can go.

We believe that summary writing is an excellent skill-building exercise for a variety of reasons. [Note that we are here using the "parallel subparts" organizational technique you practiced in Microthemes 1 and 2. Watch for our transitions "first," "second," "third," and "finally."]

First, summary writing is an exercise in "listening." As you will remember in the Carl Rogers article assigned for Journal Sequence 1, Rogers warns us not to evaluate someone else's ideas until we have walked in that other person's shoes, understanding that person's ideas so thoroughly that we "could summarize them for him." In composing summaries, a writer temporarily abandons his own world view in order to adopt another person's world view.

Second, besides being an exercise in "listening," summary writing gives you practice in careful reading. As you will see, writing a summary requires you to understand the main ideas of an essay, which must be distinguished from minor points and from supporting examples and details. In order to determine the main ideas, you need to understand the organizational structure of the article, which in turn makes you sensitive to the kinds of structural "signals" writers use (like the "first," "second," "third," and "finally" we are using here) to help their readers perceive structure. By seeing how other writers structure their prose, you can pick up lots of hints on how to structure your own.

Third, summary writing helps you learn to write concise, efficient prose. Because this assignment limits you to 100 words, you will need to eliminate all deadwood and combine sentences into efficient grammatical structures that can capture complex ideas. In short, summary writing forces you to make every word count.

And finally, summary writing is an essential skill for writing research papers, which almost always include summaries of other people's ideas from articles, books, or interviews. In a later assignment in this text you will have the opportunity to write a short research paper by summarizing several articles. And in this present assignment we will show you how to write a summary as a paragraph you could insert in a research paper.

How to Write a Summary

These following steps should help you to prepare your first summary. As you practice writing summaries, you will find yourself doing many of these steps automatically, making the process much quicker and easier than it will seem the first time.

1. Read the article you will be summarizing at least twice, "listening" to the whole argument. By the second time through you should be responding to the article, jotting notes and questions in the margins,

underlining what you think are the main points, but withholding judgment and criticism. (Any disagreements you have with an article should *not* go in a summary, which is simply "listening.")

2. Locate the main divisions of the article and break it down into its principal main parts. (Most articles have no more than three or four main parts.) In many articles the author will predict the principal parts through a blueprint statement or purpose statement somewhere in the introduction. In Carl Rogers' article, which we will now use for an example, the blueprint statement occurs in paragraph 2:

> It is, then, from a background of experience with communication in counseling and psychotherapy that I want to present here two ideas. I wish to state what I believe is one of the major factors in blocking or impeding communication, and then I wish to present what in our experience has proven to be a very important way of improving or facilitating communication.

This statement tells us that the essay is divided into two main parts—the first part identifying a problem that blocks communication, the second part setting forth a solution. In Rogers' article the first part occupies paragraphs 3–5 while the second part occupies paragraphs 6–15. We know where Part 1 ends and Part 2 begins because Rogers provides a very obvious transition to highlight this major joint:

> But is there any way of solving this problem, of avoiding this barrier? . . . .

When you write your summary, try to keep the same proportions as in the original. Because Part 2 in Rogers' article is about three times longer than Part 1, a writer should keep the same proportions in the summary—three times as many words for Part 2 as for Part 1.

3. Once you know the main divisions of the article, reread it carefully, and in the margins try writing a brief one-sentence summary of each paragraph seeing how each paragraph relates to a hierarchy that you are trying to construct. Then make a tree diagram. By following carefully the author's transitions, you should be able to determine whether a given paragraph advances a new point or somehow develops a previous point. Theoretically, you should be able to make a tree diagram that includes information from each paragraph, but often you will need to diagram only the main branches of the argument. Our tree diagram for the Rogers article is shown in Figure 6-1.

4. You are now ready to write a draft of your summary by turning your tree diagram into prose. Since summaries include only the main ideas of an article while omitting the specific details, most summaries will

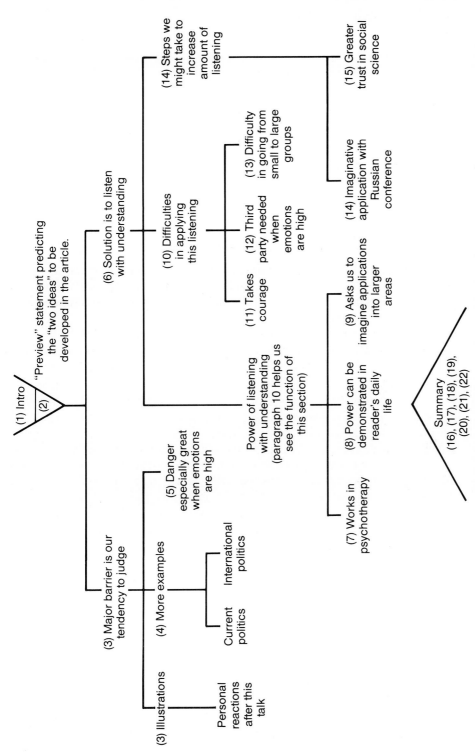

FIGURE 6-1 Tree Diagram of Carl Rogers' Article—"Communication: Its Blocking and Its Facilitation" (Numbers in parentheses refer to paragraph within the article.)

143

be successful if you capture the ideas contained in the top three or four levels of the tree diagram.

5. Revise your draft carefully to bring it into the 85–115 word space limit. Try to create graceful sentences without padding or deadwood. Write your summary either as an author's abstract or as a paragraph you could insert in a research paper. The difference between an abstract version and a research paper version are explained below. (Some instructors may ask you to write both versions of the summary.)

Differences Between "Author's Abstract" Summaries and "Research Paragraph" Summaries

Summaries as Author's Abstracts

In an abstract version of a summary, you write from the viewpoint of the author of the article. Such a summary is called an "author's abstract" because you write it as if you are the original author simply summarizing your own ideas. Thus you don't include phrases like "In this article, Carl Rogers says . . . ," nor do you refer directly to the author. Rather, you pretend you are the author. Here is our 100-word "author's abstract" for the Carl Rogers essay:

A major barrier blocking interpersonal communication is our tendency to judge other persons' statements, especially where feelings are intensely involved. The solution, found potent in psychotherapy, is to "listen" to the other person, understanding an issue from that person's point of view so well that you can summarize it to his satisfaction. Such listening takes courage since you risk becoming changed by the experience. When emotions are high a neutral third party can facilitate communication by listening to both sides and thus moving the disputants toward mutual problem-solving. This method, which works for small groups, has important implications for large group problem-solving, even for international politics.

Summaries as Passages for a Research Paper

In this version you write from you own point of view, and thus you must add phrases called "attributive tags" such as "Rogers says," "according to Rogers," or "as Rogers points out." An "attributive tag" attributes ideas to the source you mention; it indicates that you are summarizing the ideas of someone else rather than giving your own ideas. In a research paper version of a summary, you would also use quotation marks for any phrase that you copy directly from the source. We often ask students when writing research paper versions of summaries to make up a context for their summary, imagining that it is a paragraph coming somewhere inside a longer research paper. Here is our "research paper version" of the Carl Rogers summary:

In contrast to Dr. Mudfuddle's views, Carl Rogers has used his experience as a psychotherapist to devise a humanistic technique for improving interpersonal communication. In his essay, "Communication: Its Blocking and Its Facilitation," Rogers claims that a major barrier to communication is "our natural tendency to judge, to evaluate, to approve or disapprove, the statement of the other person or the other group." The solution, Rogers believes, is to "listen" to the other person, understanding an issue from that person's point of view so well that you can summarize it to his satisfaction. Rogers warns that such listening takes courage since the listener risks becoming changed by the experience. Because "listening" becomes increasingly difficult when emotions are strongest, Rogers recommends that a neutral third party facilitate the communication, moving the disputants gradually toward mutual problem-solving. Because this method has been proven effective in small groups, Rogers believes that it can be used successfully for large group problem-solving, even for resolving international issues.

Microtheme 4: A Contrast Paragraph

Write a 250–350 word paragraph that contrasts journal writing to microtheme writing (or an alternative comparison/contrast topic chosen by your instructor). Use examples and details from your own experiences.

Discussion

A paragraph comparing or contrasting two items forces you to move back and forth nimbly between generalizations and particulars. You *compare* two items when you are pointing out similarities; you *contrast* the items when you point out differences. For this exercise we ask you to contrast two items, but the techniques of organization are the same whether you are dealing with similarities or differences.

To write a comparison/contrast paragraph you begin with the two items to be compared (or contrasted) and then, often after considerable thought, you decide upon points of comparison (or contrast). If you were constrasting, for example, downhill skiing and cross-country skiing (Items A and B), you might choose for your points of contrast kinds of equipment used, kinds of skills needed, and kinds of pleasure derived (Points 1, 2, and 3). If your paragraph were to show both comparisons and contrasts, you would probably begin your paragraph with a brief summary of the similarities between downhill skiing and cross-country skiing and then devote most of your paragraph to the underlying differences.

In organizing the main body of a comparison or contrast paragraph, you have two choices: the "side by side" pattern, in which you discuss all of Item

A and then all of Item B, or the "back and forth" pattern in which you discuss all of Point 1, comparing or contrasting A and B on that point, and then proceed in a similar fashion to Point 2, 3, and so on. The following tree diagrams show how each pattern is shaped.

Side by Side Pattern

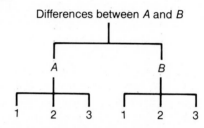

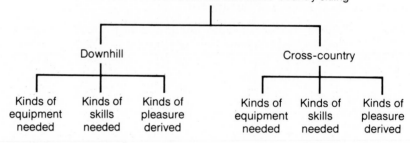

Back and Forth Pattern

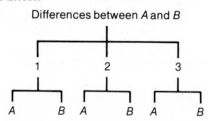

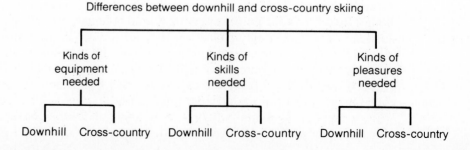

There are no cut-and-dried rules on when to use the side-by-side pattern or the back-and-forth pattern. However, since the back-and-forth pattern requires you to be a bit more nimble in your use of transitions and subtopic sentences, it generally provides you more intense practice at developing skills. We therefore ask you to use that method for organizing this microtheme unless your instructor says otherwise.

We have illustrated the two methods by writing our own microthemes on the "lecture method versus the group learning method of teaching."

Back and Forth Pattern

The lecture method and the group learning method differ in a number of ways. A first difference is the role of the teacher. In the lecture method, the teacher must spend considerable time preparing each lecture, often revising lectures each year. And during class time the teacher dominates by doing most of the talking. In contrast, the teacher of a group learning classroom appears to have no role at all. She either leaves the room or else wanders about from group to group. Actually, however, the teacher's role is significant because she must design good group tasks, coordinate them, monitor group work, and later be on her toes during class discussion. A second difference between the two methods is the role of the student. In a lecture classroom students generally listen and take notes. In group learning, on the other hand, students actively generate their own ideas, each member contributing insights for the success of the group. A final difference between lecture and group learning is the relative advantages of each. The lecture is probably best at passing on "content" to students. A good lecturer can also model for students the process of problem-solving. But group learning is probably best for helping students become active questioners and problem-solvers and learn some of the group skills needed in most businesses and professions.

Side by Side Pattern

The lecture method and the group learning method differ in a number of ways. The lecture system obviously places visible demands on the teacher, who must spend considerable time preparing lectures, often revising them each year. And during class time the teacher dominates by doing most of the talking, while the students generally listen and take notes. Such a system has several advantages. The lecture is particularly effective at passing on "content". A good lecturer can also model for students the process of problem-solving. In contrast, the group learning system differs considerably. The role of the teacher in a group learning classroom appears invisible. She either leaves the room or else wanders about from group to group. Actually, however, the teacher's role is significant because she must design good group tasks, coordinate them, monitor group work, and later be on her toes during class discussion. The students' role, too, is different. In group settings students actively generate their own ideas, each member contributing insights for the success of the group Finally group learning has different advantages. It is probably best for helping students become active questioners and problem-solvers and for learning some of the group skills needed in most businesses and professions.

Signalling Form in Your Microtheme

To help your reader follow your line of thought throughout your contrast paragraph, you will need to use two kinds of transitions. To move from one main point of contrast to the next, you will use the parallel subparts method that you used in Microthemes 1 and 2. This strategy includes making your subtopic sentences parallel for an echo-like effect and using such transitions as "first ...," "second ...," and "third." For moving between items, however, you will need to use a different kind of transition such as the following:

- *To point out differences:* however, conversely, nevertheless, in contrast, on the other hand, whereas, although, but, yet
- *To point out similarities:* similarly, likewise, equally, in like manner, in the same way, just as, in similar fashion

For Class Discussion

1. As a class or working in small groups, create tree diagrams for both the "side by side" and the "back and forth" versions of the sample microthemes contrasting the lecture method and the group learning method.

2. On page 149 is a partially completed tree diagram for a comparison microtheme. (In this case, the microtheme points out similarities instead of differences, but the organizational problems are similar.)

   As a group project, write a draft for the first one-third of this microtheme following this tree diagram. What would be a good opening sentence? How would you introduce the first point of similarity? How would you go from the first point of similarity to the details about building a house? How would you switch from the details about building a house to the details about writing an essay? How would you move from the details about writing an essay to the second main point of similarity on "developing a design"?

   After you have written a draft for the first third of this microtheme, try to plan out the whole essay. This is a good illustration of how an "unfilled" tree diagram can help you generate ideas.

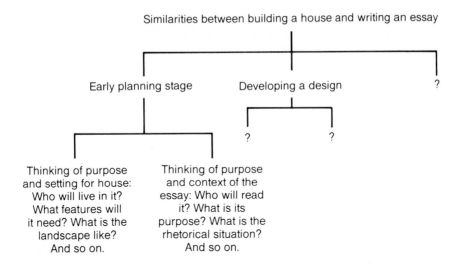

Microtheme 5: Using Different Sources of Detail

In this task you have three different options, each of which asks you to write a microtheme using different sources of details. Option 1 focuses on using sensory details to write a descriptive paragraph. Option 2 focuses on the use of statistical details. Finally, Option 3 lets you use your understanding of someone else's ideas as a source of details.

Option 1: A Descriptive Microtheme

Reread Chapter 5, pages 116–121, on the need to move up and down the levels of abstraction. Class Discussion Exercise 2 on page 121 asks you to observe a scene and fill out a sense chart recording the details of your observation. For this microtheme, describe that scene so that an absent reader can picture it vividly in his or her mind.

Option 2: A Statistical Microtheme

In that same chapter, Exercise 3 (page 122) asks you to conduct a small survey in your class either through interviews or a questionnaire. For this task write a brief report to the Director of Writing at your university setting forth the results of your survey.

Option 3: A Microtheme Based on Your Grasp of Ideas

Suppose you are Fritz Machlup. Write the conclusion for the following letter based on information in the Machlup article you read for Journal Sequence 1 (pp. 399–405):

Editor of *Academe*

Dear Editor:

Some readers of your journal have apparently misunderstood parts of my article "Poor Learning from Good Teachers" which recently appeared in *Academe*. I have received nasty notes in the mail and several angry phone calls, all from professors and administrators who accuse me of promoting bad teaching. "Hey, Fritz, you dunderbrain!" they say. "What do you want teachers to do? Tear up their lecture notes and go into class mumbling, fumbling, and stumbling like incompetent dodos?!" If it weren't for nice letters from Professors Dogwood Lunt and his brother Ellwood Lunt, I would think I had been universally misunderstood.

Let me clear up this misunderstanding by stating my ideas in a somewhat different way. [Complete this letter using no more than 300 additional words without using any of the original wording in Machlup's article—that is, do not copy passages from the original.]

Discussion

These final microtheme tasks will help you see how the details needed for supporting generalizations in an essay can come from different sources. Option 1 uses sensory details for support. Option 2 uses statistical details. Finally, Option 3 uses as details your paraphrase of someone else's ideas. In the essays you will write for your formal assignments in Chapter 8, 12, and 13, you will have occasion to use all three kinds of sources. These microthemes give you a chance to practice each kind in isolation.

PART II

Problem–Solution Essays

Part II includes two chapters and a journal sequence. We suggest you begin doing the journal sequence while you are reading Chapter 7 and that you try to do at least a week of journal writing before you begin writing your formal assignments from Chapter 8.

Chapter 7—"The Art of Asking Question"—will help you increase your skills as a question-asker and problem-finder. Question-asking helps writers generate ideas on a topic by stimulating thinking and the search for data. Question-asking can also help a writer discover a focus and purpose for an essay since almost any essay can be understood as an answer to a question. A writer's task is to discover a question that both writer and reader can perceive as a problem.

Journal Sequence 2 focuses on both asking questions and exploring answers to them. Once again the journal provides a risk-free environment for practicing skills. You will practice a variety of techniques for inventing questions. You will also practice two complementary skills for exploring answers to questions: (1) shaped writing if you have an answer in mind for the question, and (2) exploratory writing, such as freewriting or idea-mapping, if you don't know an answer.

Chapter 8—"Problem-Solution Essays"—provides a sequence of formal essay assignments aimed at developing your skill at formulating problems and then exploring solutions to them in shaped essays ready for strangers.

CHAPTER 7

The Art of Asking Questions

It seems to me, then, that the way
to help people become better writers
is not to tell them that they must
first learn the rules of grammar,
that they must develop a four-part
outline, that they must consult the
experts and collect all the useful
information. These things may have
their place. But none of them is as
crucial as having a good,
interesting question.

—*Rodney Kilcup, Historian*[1]

A GENERAL INTRODUCTION TO QUESTION-ASKING

There are lots of anecdotes about creative people. Almost all the ones we know support Thomas Edison's contention that genius is 10 percent inspiration and 90 percent perspiration. Although we can quibble about the

---

[1] Rodney Kilcup, "A Modest Proposal for Reluctant Writers," *Newsletter of the Pacific Northwest Writing Consortium*, Vol 2, No. 3 (Sept 1982), p. 5.

proportions, there is no doubt that creative people have an uncanny knack of seeing old things in new ways (inspiration) and also a dogged stick-to-it-iveness that keeps them plugging away at a problem long after other people have given up (perspiration).

Part of that "inspired" 10 percent is the ability to ask good questions, to see problems where other people see business-as-usual. But we have also found that through perspiration, persons can train themselves to ask better questions and to explore the questions they raise systematically. We believe, in fact, that the difference between "inspired" students who write surprising essays and uninspired students who write Engfishy ones can often be attributed to that 90 percent perspiration factor. Good writers spend more time and use their time more productively.

One way to spend your time as a writer productively is to learn to find what historian Rodney Kilcup has called a "good, interesting question." Let us preview, for a moment, the main points we will be making in this chapter, points which you will put into practice as you write the formal essays for this course.

1. A writer should try to see her essay as the answer to a good question.
2. This question should be perceived as a "problem" by both the writer and the reader.
3. A one-sentence summary answer to the question serves as the thesis statement for the essay.
4. The thesis statement should contain some sense of tension, some feeling that the thesis is risky and surprising.
5. A writer usually doesn't begin the writing process with either the problem or solution clearly formulated. (Through journal writing and the composing of early drafts of an essay, the writer comes to discover what he wants to say. Thus writing is a way of discovering your own ideas, of making your meanings.)

Question-asking, then, not only helps you discover something to say about a topic, but also a purpose for saying it. A list of questions about a topic can urge you to generate data and ideas. It can guide your research or spark your own creative thinking. We can refer to this phase of question-asking as *divergent thinking* because you will be exploring a wide range of possible ideas about a topic, bouncing around different points of view, different ways of playing with your topic, different ways of formulating questions. Eventually you will settle upon a question that particularly interests you, a question you would like your essay to answer. This stage of question-asking involves *convergent thinking* because it will lead to an eventual focus and thesis for your essay. By learning to pose a question in such a way that the reader's curiosity is aroused—so that the question becomes a problem—a writer begins to sense both a shape and purpose for the essay.

DEVELOPING THE HABIT OF QUESTION-ASKING

In this section we will suggest some initial strategies for question-asking and hope that you get the question-asking habit. If you do Journal Sequence 2 at the same time you are reading this chapter, you will get plenty of practice both at asking questions and at exploring answers to them.

Using Question-Asking to Narrow a Topic

Often when you are given a writing assignment in college you will be given just a topic area: "Write a paper on some aspect of the Middle Ages" or "Write a 15-page research paper on something to do with computers." Your eventual goal will be to pose an interesting question about your assigned topic and then to write an essay that responds to it. By choosing one question out of dozens of possible questions you will narrow and focus your topic. A good strategy for beginning your thinking is to freewrite on trigger questions such as these: "What questions about X interest me?" or "What aspects of X puzzle me?"

Thus a writer might begin freewriting on "What questions about computers interest me?" or "What do I find puzzling about the Middle Ages?" Here is a sample 10-minute freewrite on the question: "What questions about computers interest me?"

Let's see. What questions about computers interest me? I am really interested in how computers work. I know that they work on the binary system and that they use circuits that are either off or on. But the whole process is so incredibly mysterious. I remember when we first got a small pocket calculator and I would punch in a number and then hold it up to my ear to see if I could hear it working. It was absolutely quiet. How could anyone ever think to invent one of those? What is the history of computers? Did one person invent the computer the way Alexander Bell invented the telephone? I wonder how home computer companies compete with each other. A friend of mine got an Apple McIntosh the first week they were on the market and we were over doing McPainting and all sorts of things you couldn't do on regular computers. Did Apple computer know that people wanted to Mcpaint or was it a big gamble? Keep writing, keep writing, keep writing. What about computers in the—hold it, I just thought of another Apple question. I remember seeing the first 1984 TV commercial with the gorgeous athletic woman throwing the hammer through the television screen. What a great commercial. Nobody knew it was about computers. I wonder how successful that commercial was and the whole story behind how it was made. That would be a fun research project. I wonder how I could get the info? Back to computers in the schools. My little brother's grade school just got a bunch of computers and they don't really know what to do with them. They just play games. I wonder if any school districts really use computers in an innovative way. Time's up.

This freewrite raised a number of questions that could serve as topics for research essays: how computers work, the history of computers, competition and innovation among computer companies, the history behind one famous computer commercial, and the uses of computers in elementary schools.

Stimulating Question-Asking with Idea Maps

Another strategy for narrowing a topic is to create an idea map that uses questions, wherever possible, as the start of new branches. Some writers like to begin an idea-map with five or six general questions used as triggers for each branch, as shown in Figure 7-1.

Beginning with these "starter branches," you can pursue your ideas on each branch, asking questions whenever they come to mind. Each new question can become the head of a new branch (see Figure 7-2).

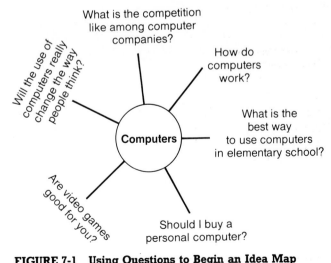

FIGURE 7-1   Using Questions to Begin an Idea Map

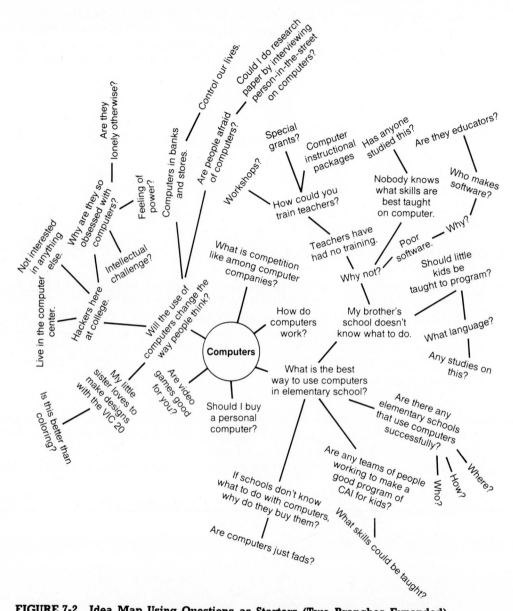

FIGURE 7-2   Idea Map Using Questions as Starters (Two Branches Expanded)

Playing the Question Game

Another good way to get in the habit of question-asking is to play a simple game (for those of you with children, this is a fun game to play with grade school kids as a way to help them increase their own thinking skills.) In this game you begin by generating a list of random nouns such as *snow, peanuts, garbage, the moon, bacteria, houses*, etc. You then ask questions about each of these topics, trying to fit questions into each of the following three categories:

1. *Questions you can presently answer.* Give bonus points if a person can ask a power question for this category. You have asked a power question if you are the only person in your class who can answer it, if the answer requires a brief essay as opposed to a mere fact or short answer, and if you can make the question interesting to others.
2. *Questions you can't answer at this time but that you think you could answer after some research or thinking.* Questions in this category often lead to good focusing ideas for college essays.
3. *Questions you don't think anyone has yet answered.* These questions serve to remind us that collective human knowledge hasn't reached its limits, that there is still plenty of research to be done.

What is surprising about this game is that Category 1 questions often dissolve into Category 2 or 3 questions once we try to answer them. Questions we thought we understood turn out to be confusing and puzzling once we try to explain our answers.

Here are some sample questions from students in our classes for the words *moon, peanuts,* and *bacteria.*

1. Questions I think I can answer

- How do we know the moon causes tides?
- How do you make homemade peanut butter?
- Are bacteria ever good for us?

2. Questions I can't answer now but could through research

- What new information about the moon did we learn from the space landings?
- How do astronomers measure distance to the moon?
- How do bacteria cause disease?
- What major problems do peanut farmers face in the United States?

3. Questions I don't think anybody can answer

- How does gravity really work?
- How was the moon formed?
- Can we discover a way to grow peanuts without light?
- How could one totally control the process of mutation in bacteria?

One of the exciting things about college is discovering that the more you learn about a given topic the easier it is to ask Category 3 questions. A freshman student might not know many Category 3 questions about bacteria, but a bacteriologist could rattle off dozens of unknown things about bacteria in a couple of minutes.

For Class Discussion

1. Working in small groups, create an extensive idea-map on a topic of your choice (or one chosen by your instructor) by writing an interesting question to head each branch.

2. As a class or small group, brainstorm a series of questions about one or more of the following topics. Try to generate at least 20 questions in 10 minutes. Have one person record the questions while the rest of you blurt them out as soon as you think of them. Or, as a variation, play the question-asking game by placing your questions in the three categories described above (those you can answer, those you could answer through research or thinking, and those nobody can answer).

garbage	Ancient Rome	bridge-building	cats
Presidential elections	luge-racing	birth	death
pizza	secretaries	automobiles	energy

THE DIFFERENCE BETWEEN A QUESTION AND A PROBLEM

Throughout this text we will use the terms "problem" and "question" almost interchangeably. These is some difference between the meanings of the terms, however, since "question" is generally a broader, more inclusive term than "problem." In other words, all problems are questions, but all questions aren't problems, just as all cats are animals but all animals aren't cats. It will therefore be helpful to look more carefully at what we mean by "problem."

In general usage, "problem" is a narrow term meaning something like an uncomfortable situation that we would like to overcome, as in "I have a problem with my boyfriend," or "a problem with the fine-tuning adjustment on my TV." In this text, however, we stipulate a much broader definition of "problem." In our usage, a problem is any question that has no immediately obvious answer but that stimulates your curiosity. For us, a "problem" is a good question, an interesting question, a question which arouses a desire to know and whose answer brings surprise. Often the difference between a question and a problem is an affective or emotional difference rather than a conceptual difference. Whereas a mere question can produce an indifferent "so what?," a problem arouses the excitement of wanting to find out, of wanting to learn. Let us illustrate with an example from an introductory physics course.

One of the most popular teachers on our campus is a physics professor who, early in his course, likes to startle his class by dropping a heavy book on the floor. After the crash, he asks quietly, "What made the book fall?" From all over the room comes the obvious answer, "Gravity." "No," he answers. "No, no! Gravity is a just a name for something we don't understand. Nobody in the world knows what makes the book fall. The word 'gravity' just lulls us into thinking we understand something when we don't." As a physics teacher, his goal is to turn the apparently silly question, "What makes the book fall?," into a problem—the same profoundly puzzling problem that drives research physicists forward in their current search for the mystery particle, the graviton. He wants to dispel students' comfortable sense that physical phenomena in our everyday world can be easily explained. His course explodes with questions. Why does a flute sound different from a clarinet? What direction does a compass point in Australia? Why are astronauts weightless in a satellite? All these questions become problems the instant you feel your curiosity welling up, the instant you sense that obvious answers aren't really satisfactory. Psychologists sometimes define a problem as your awareness of a gap between where you are and where you want to be. If you believe a book falls because of gravity, you have no problem because you feel no gap, no sense of your mind needing to explore new territory (you are already where you want to be). If you don't know why a book falls and don't care, you also have no problem: this time because you don't want to be anywhere else. Even though you may feel a gap, you have no desire to bridge it. As a writer, your job is to pose problems for readers, make them want to cross the bridge you build for them, and then take them on a surprising journey into new places.

We suggest, then, that problems form the core of surprising essays. One of the chief premises of this book is that a thinker can best think his way toward a solution to a problem by writing about it. In a sense, good essays originate in problematic questions that writers have posed for themselves, questions they seek to answer through succeeding drafts of an essay. The finished essay then provides the reader the answer the writer has discovered. What was a hard journey for the writer ideally becomes a pleasing, surprising journey for the reader, who benefits in a few minutes from what took the writer a long time to discover and learn to explain.

The difference then between a problem and a question is not a matter of wording or content, but of curiosity and engagement. Good writers are problem-finders, people who can pose questions in such a way that readers feel difficulties, uncertainties, or knowledge gaps that they would not otherwise have felt. Any question-answer structure can give form to an essay, but a problem-solution structure will give it surprise. From now on, then, think of a problem as any question that has no immediately obvious answer and that awakens the reader's curiosity and desire to learn or discover.

For Class Discussion

Prior to class, look back over the questions you've asked so far and write down three good questions that you perceive as problems. Share your questions with your classmates and be prepared to discuss why you find them problematical.

USING QUESTION-ASKING STRATEGIES TO IMPROVE YOUR STUDY HABITS

Now that you've been introduced to question-asking in general and appreciate the difference between a question and a problem, we would like you to try some specific question-asking techniques that could greatly improve your study habits. One of the best ways to practice question-asking for your courses is to try to understand teachers' thinking processes when they invent questions for an exam. What kinds of questions appeal to teachers and why? In this section we are going to help you second guess teachers by having you invent exam questions for courses you are currently taking and then practice answering them in your work in Journal Sequence 2. The studying strategies we will suggest here are very similar to those recommended by Fritz Machlup in his article "Poor Learning from Good Teachers," which you read for Journal Sequence 1.

In general, when teachers make up exam questions, they try to be aware of the level of difficulty of the question and match that difficulty level to the goals of the course. To appreciate how teachers' minds work, you should understand the difference between knowledge/comprehension questions and analysis questions.

Knowledge/Comprehension Questions

The lowest levels of difficulty are questions that test knowledge and comprehension. Questions in this category do not ask students to go beyond what is covered in the text or in class. At the lowest level would be questions that test only memory and recall, that is, your ability to remember information. At a higher level are questions that focus on meanings, that is, on your ability to understand and explain relationships among data. For example, a science professor usually will not want you just to memorize a formula, but to know how the formula is derived and why it works. Similarly, a history teacher does not want you just to memorize dates, facts, and names of historical figures. History teachers are interested in connections among ideas. They try to identify the major characteristics of a historical period, analyze the causes of historical change, and explore various historical interrelationships, such as the relationship between people's beliefs about their position in the universe and the kinds of governments they value or the kinds of art they produce. When testing at the knowledge and comprehension level, however, teachers don't expect you to figure out these connections and relationships for yourself, just to understand the connections and relationships as they were explained in class or in the text.

If we were giving you an essay exam on this textbook, here are some knowledge and comprehension questions that we might ask:

- What is meant by "form" and "surprise"?
- What reasons do Bean and Ramage give for preferring tree diagrams over traditional outlines?
- What is the difference between a question and a problem?

One of the best ways to study for a course is to practice asking yourself knowledge/comprehension questions about the material. Several psychological studies, in fact, have demonstrated that students can increase their comprehension of material if they train themselves to see information in texts or in lectures as answers to questions. A psychology professor at our university teaches his students to use the right-hand margins of textbooks (or class notes) solely for asking the questions that the corresponding pages of the text or notes are answering. Thus, if your textbook or class notes are explaining the process of photosynthesis, you might write in the right hand margin, "How does photosynthesis work in a plant?" If your text or notes are discussing John Calhoun's views on the meaning of federalism, you would write in the margin, "What were John Calhoun's views on the meaning of federalism?" Psychologists have demonstrated that the mind processes and stores information more efficiently if the information is understood as the answer to a question. Apparently the question-answer structure mirrors in some mysterious way the neural structures in the brain. Thus the simple act of writing out the questions that a textbook or lecture answers channels the information to the brain in a way that makes it easier to process and store. Evidence suggests that the technique is most effective if you ask the questions yourself, rather than having textbook authors put questions in the margins for you. [Thus in the margin next to this paragraph you would write, "Why is it valuable to ask knowledge/comprehension questions in the margins of your texts?" This paragraph answers that question.]

Once you have written knowledge/comprehension questions in the margins of your texts or notebooks, you can review the material later simply by covering up the text and mentally answering each of the questions you have in the margin. For particularly complex questions you can practice answering the questions in writing, as in an essay exam, which forces you to consider the material deeply and to appreciate the relationships among its parts.

For Class Discussion

In groups, make a list of 5–10 good knowledge/comprehension questions about this textbook or about another subject shared by all members of the group. Make the questions suitable for an essay exam for the course. Remember that a knowledge/comprehension question doesn't ask you to go beyond what the textbook or instructor says, just to understand the material as it is presented.

Analysis Questions

So far we have dealt with knowledge/comprehension questions. A more difficult category of questions is called analysis. What distinguishes "analysis" questions from "knowledge/comprehension" questions is that in answering analysis questions you must do your own original thinking as opposed to simply understanding someone else's thinking. When teachers construct questions in this category, they always introduce something new, something that was not covered directly in the text or in class. Similarly, when college students write critical essays or research essays outside of class, they are expected to pose for themselves analysis questions that go beyond what was covered by the instructor.

Here are some examples. Suppose your history teacher tells you that there are five main causes of the French Revolution. If you copy down the five causes and study them for an exam, you are operating at the level of knowledge and comprehension. If, however, you say, "Why are there just five causes of the French Revolution rather than four causes or six causes?," you are operating at the level of analysis. You are "thinking for yourself" by following the reasonable habit of imagining an alternative case and thereby posing a problem. Instead of simply memorizing the five causes for the French Revolution, you now begin thinking like an historian. You see that "five causes" is not a fact, but some historian's interpretation of facts, an interpretation that may or may not be convincing. (Remember in Chapter 3 the humanities class trying to classify the causes of the PBB disaster?) If you wanted not only to think like an historian but also to *act* like an historian—say for a research project when you were a senior—you would need to go back to the primary sources that historians use (government documents, eyewitness accounts of events, contemporary treatises on politics and philosophy, data on the economic condition and political attitudes of various social classes, and so forth). During the process of examining these individual parts of a large problem, you might discover weaknesses in the "five causes" interpretation. Perhaps that historian overlooked or overemphasized certain primary sources, held biases or prejudices that distorted the interpretation of data, or simply oversimplified the data to fit a neat scheme. If you propose an alternative hypothesis, say *six* causes of the French Revolution, or even if you simply reorder the original five causes, you are forming a new interpretation of history by putting data together into a new whole. This is the kind of thinking we hope you will learn to do while in college.

Let's try one more example. You have recently read an article by the psychologist Carl Rogers, but you might not know that Rogers is a controversial figure among psychologists. Particularly, his views have been opposed by "behavioral psychologists" associated with a famous Harvard professor named B. F. Skinner. If during lectures an instructor compared the ideas of Rogers and Skinner, showing the underlying differences in their views about human nature, and then asked you to recall those differences on an essay examination, you would be operating at the knowledge/comprehension level. If, however, an instructor handed you several articles by each of the two men and told you to compare their ideas about human nature yourself (asking you in effect to do the thinking that the teacher had to do in order to prepare the lecture), then you would be operating at the level of analysis.

What baffles many freshmen students about college is the importance college professors place on analytical thinking. Beginning students tend to study at the knowledge and comprehension level, while professors prefer questions that demand analysis. One of the best ways to develop these analytical skills is to practice asking yourself analysis questions and then to explore answers in your journal.

Here are some analysis questions we might ask about our text. Notice that all of these questions assume your knowledge and comprehension of the material, yet require you to do something new, to go beyond what was done or said in the text.

1. "Haste makes waste." "He who hesitates is lost." Attempt to reconcile these two contradictory quotations using some of the reasoning techniques modeled for you in Chapter 2.
2. What kinds of students would most benefit from doing the guided journal exercises as set forth in *Form and Surprise*, and what kinds would least benefit?

A special subcategory of analysis questions is called evaluation. In general, evaluation questions ask you to make independent judgments about the value, worth, effectiveness, strength, or validity of ideas. In responding to evaluation questions, you must make judgments and support them with arguments—tasks that involve complex reasoning skills. (We will spend more time discussing the kinds of reasoning evaluation questions demand when we get to issue-defense essays in Chapters 9 and 10.)

For now, you should concentrate on learning to ask evaluation questions as one particularly important kind of analysis question. In general, evaluation questions take two forms: (1) Is X good or bad?; and (2) Should we do X? Here are some evaluation questions based on our text:

1. "Carl Rogers is a naive romantic if he thinks 'listening' will solve real interpersonal crises. People aren't that simple." Do you agree? (Underlying frame of this question: "Is Carl Rogers' argument good or bad?")
2. Should writing teachers give group essay assignments such as Microtheme 1 (p. 133)? (Underlying frame: Should we do X?)

As a studying technique we hope you will get in the habit of asking your own analysis questions about ideas in all your classes, thereby helping you do some original thinking about your courses. As you are studying in your other courses, you might try some of the following techniques for asking analysis questions.

- *Play the believing and doubting game with ideas and concepts in the course and with ideas voiced in class discussion.* (Underlying frame: "Believe and doubt X.") Someone says that John Calhoun was motivated primarily by racism. Believe and doubt that statement. Your psychology teacher says that all human behavior, just as all animal behavior, can be explained in terms of stimulus-response conditioning. Believe and doubt that statement.
- *Relate what you are learning in class to your own personal experience.* (Underlying frame: "Does X make sense in terms of my life?") What would people in my family think of John Calhoun's views on states' rights? Is my view of evil more like Ahab's, Ishmael's, or Starbuck's? Does Erik Erikson's description of how a person achieves a mature identity fit my own experiences?
- *Imagine alternative cases, perhaps triggered by "What would happen if . . .?" or "What would have happened if . . .?"* (Underlying frame: "If X, then what? If not X, then what?") Would the Civil War have occurred if

John Calhoun had never existed? What would happen to plant life if a volcano caused the earth to be covered with black clouds for a year?

- *Ask comparison/contrast questions linking the topic you are currently studying to other material in the course, to ideas in other courses, or to ideas and events in your own personal life.* (Underlying frame: "How is X like Y?" "How is X unlike Y?") What are the similarities and differences between Calhoun's view of government and that of other Southern politicians? Between Calhoun and Henry Clay? How do Erikson's views of child development compare with Piaget's? Is photosynthesis the same in all plants? How does photosynthesis in a redwood tree compare with photosynthesis in algae?

- *Try to imagine how the author of the textbook you are reading came to know the knowledge being conveyed.* Push this process back to the original discoverers of the knowledge and try to imagine the processes they went through. Try to ask some of the same questions they might have asked. This technique not only helps you imagine how other people ask analysis questions, but will also help you discover new ones of your own. (Underlying frame: "What can I learn about X by asking how person Y learned about X?") How do historians know what John Calhoun's political philosophy was? Are there letters, speeches, newspaper accounts in existence? Does our library have them? Was Calhoun consistent in all his speeches? If I read all the original materials would I agree with this textbook's summary of his views?

- *Ask evaluation questions about the material you are studying.* (Underlying frame: "Is X good or bad?" "Should we do X?") A particularly good technique is to evaluate an idea first from your perspective and then from someone else's perspective. Were Calhoun's ideas good or bad? How would Henry Clay evaluate Calhoun's ideas? How would a southern plantation owner in 1833 evaluate Henry Clay's compromise arrangement concerning South Carolina's nullification of the 1832 tariff? What are the strengths and weaknesses of Piaget's theory about children's cognitive growth?

- *Use some of the additional question-asking procedures we will discuss later in this chapter (under the heading "Heuristics").*

For Class Discussion

As a class or in small groups ask a series of analysis questions about the general topic "writing." Invent at least one question for each of the strategies we have suggested: a believing/doubting question, a personal connection question, an alternative cases question, a comparison/contrast question, a return-to-the-origins-of-the-idea question, and an evaluation question.

TURNING QUESTIONS INTO THESIS STATEMENTS: GOOD QUESTIONS, SURPRISING ANSWERS

So far we have concentrated on the asking of questions. However, the heart of an essay is not your question but your answer. Often your question itself will be an ordinary, garden-variety kind of question: "Is *Citizen Kane* an important movie?" "What are the strengths and weaknesses of Carl Rogers' essay 'Communication: Its Blocking and Its Facilitation'?" "What do the sexual stereotypes in Beetle Bailey cartoons tell us about American society?" Whether any of these questions will lead to a good essay depends on your answer. Thus, our chapter on question-asking would be incomplete if we didn't include some discussion also of question-answering. Our rule of thumb: have a surprising answer.

To suggest what we mean by "surprising answer," let's shift, for a moment, to a slightly different context in order to create an analogy. A classic test of creativity is a person's responses to the question "How many uses can you think of for a brick?" Psychologists measure a person's creativity by scoring both the number of responses and the quality of each response. (A "high quality" response is an unusual use of a brick that seems plausible: "Smash brick with hammer and use the dust as an abrasive for cleaning a cooking pot on a camping trip" would be a high quality response; "Use brick as ketchup for hamburgers" would be a low quality response.)

A colleague of ours used to give this test to her writing students during the last fifteen minutes of the opening day of each term. She told them to jot down all the uses of a brick they could think of, after which time they could leave for the day. She discovered two interesting facts: first, the amount of time they spent on the puzzle was a fairly accurate predictor of the grades they eventually earned in the course. And second, nearly everybody, both the creative and non-creative types, wrote the same uses for a brick at the top of their lists: build a wall, build a fireplace, make a brick sidewalk, etc. Thus, the difference between the creative and the less creative people showed up, not at the beginning of their lists, but at the end. The less creative types wrote down the obvious uses for bricks and then left the room, while the more creative types went on to think of surprising uses.

The point to emphasize here is that creative thinkers don't leap immediately to creative responses; rather, they work their way first through the non-creative, ordinary responses that everyone thinks of. And for good reason. It would be a strange mind indeed that could imagine unusual uses of X without also imagining usual uses of X. After all, building a wall or a fireplace is an *excellent* use of bricks—perhaps the best use of bricks. These just aren't surprising uses.

Our "uses of bricks" example provides a helpful analogy for discussing surprise in an essay. In most cases, a surprising essay responds to a question by taking the reader through "knowns" (the ordinary expected answers that writer and reader already share as common ground—the equivalent of using bricks to build houses) toward "unknowns" (the unusual, unexpected answers with which the writer surprises the reader—the equivalent of grinding up bricks for abrasives.) In Chapter 2 we referred to this process as a movement back and forth between the familiar and the unfamiliar, the old and the new. Thus an analysis of Carl Rogers' essay on communication might begin with the obvious comments that almost any writer would make: the article is thought-provoking; listening to others is indeed a valuable habit; we all have had the experience of judging someone without listening carefully enough; it would be nice if everyone listened in a Rogerian fashion. But a surprising analysis would go beyond this to say something more. The nature of the surprise can't be predicted (or it wouldn't be surprising), but we know it must be both something the reader hadn't thought of *and* something that is plausible. One of the our students, for example, argued that Rogers' theory of "listening" is naive because it doesn't take into account human sinfulness—humans will often choose to do evil no matter how much they listen. If you hadn't considered that idea before and if you find the argument plausible, then the thesis surprises you.

The "uses of bricks" example also gives us another perspective on journal writing. Since creative people generally begin with obvious ideas before moving on to new insights, journal writing can often be seen not as a place where you create surprising ideas but where you siphon off all your unsurprising, ordinary ideas. In fact, one teacher in our department calls journal writing "sludge" writing. She says you can't have a new idea until you free your mind of the sludge of common, uninspired ideas. For her, the journal is where you dump your garbage so you can put all your good ideas in your formal essays.

So far we have argued that an essay's thesis should be surprising, yet should allow the writer to discuss the familiar and unsurprising as a way of establishing common ground with the reader. We turn now to a discussion of what constitutes "surprise" in a thesis statement. No overall description is possible, but one or more of the following features are usually attributes of a surprising thesis:

- Gives the reader new information or clarifies a confusing concept.
- Takes an argumentative stance, acknowledging opposing views.
- Works through two or more differing answers to the same question, attempting to resolve the differences or to underscore a dilemma.
- Shows that a commonly accepted answer to a question isn't satisfactory.
- Shows that a commonly rejected answer to a question may be satisfactory.

- Gives a new solution for a problem.
- Identifies a new problem (even if no solution is provided).
- Identifies an unexpected effect or implication of something.
- Identifies an unexpected cause of something.
- Shows that two or more commonly accepted notions about something are contradictory.
- Shows underlying differences between two concepts normally thought to be similar.
- Shows underlying similarities between two concepts normally thought to be different.
- Opposes a commonly accepted viewpoint.
- Supports an unpopular viewpoint.
- Finds paradoxes or contradictions in some area of experience that others regard as nonproblematic.

All these potential features of a surprising thesis have one element in common: Underlying all of them is a sense of *tension*, that is, a clashing of opposing possibilities. "Whereas most people believe X, I believe Y." In a surprising thesis, the writer assumes in some sense an opposing stance whereby he or she attempts to make some sort of change in the reader's world view. One of the best ways to help you create surprise in your thesis statements is to begin them with an "although" or "whereas" clause in which a viewpoint counter to your own can be summarized. (Often, the "although" clause will be omitted from your actual essay, but the act of imagining the "although," of visualizing the world view you are attempting to change, will help you achieve focus and surprise in your thesis.) Here are some examples:

Question

"Are Indian reservations still valuable in today's culture?"

Thesis Without Tension

"Indian reservations have good points and bad points."

Thesis With Tension

"Although my friend Sam Running Rabbit believes that Indian reservations are necessary for Native American people to preserve their heritage, I believe that the continuation of reservations actually harms most Native Americans."

Question

"What effect has the telephone had on our culture?"

Thesis Without Tension

"The invention of the telephone has brought many advantages to our culture."

Thesis With Tension

"Although the telephone has brought many advantages to our culture, it may have also contributed unexpectedly to the increase of violence in our society." [See Ellen Goodman's essay on pages 221–224.]

Even essays intended only to give information will possess tension if the writer conceives the new information being conveyed as competing with old or mistaken information in the reader's mind. For example, the thesis statement required for Microtheme 2—"Journal writing has taught me several different techniques for generating ideas"—can be given tension if the writer conceives it this way:

"Although my reader probably believes I learned nothing from writing in the journal, actually I learned several new techniques for generating ideas."

An essay on this topic would probably omit the "although" clause, but if the writer imagines an "although" clause, he will be more apt to put in the convincing specific details needed to change the reader's mind.

We suggest, then, that as you formulate thesis statements for your essays for this course, you try to see your thesis in competition with possible opposing theses, which you summarize in an "although" clause. The clash between the opposing views will help create the tension which underlies any surprising thesis.

For Class Discussion

1. Prior to class re-read your entries on education from Journal Sequence 1. Do you now see your entries as "surprising writing" or as "sludge writing"? Be prepared to discuss your evaluation of your journal entries with your classmates. Try to share at least one surprising idea that emerged from your journal.

2. Working in small groups, develop 3–5 thesis statements about education that contain tension. Try to begin each one with an "although" clause that summarizes opposing views.

USING HEURISTICS TO ASK ANALYSIS QUESTIONS

When you first started freewriting you needed to learn how to break the "idea-exhaustion barrier." A similar barrier may occur when you try to generate questions about a topic. Frustrated students often ask if there are any tricks to the trade, any mental techniques that can stimulate creative question-asking. The answer is yes. Such mental techniques are called "heuristics" after the Greek word *heuresis* meaning discovery or invention (related to our word *"Eureka*! I have found it!").

If you have any doubt that heuristics can work, just consider for the moment how a simple heuristic might increase your score on the creativity test we discussed in the last section: "How many uses can you think of for a brick?" Psychologists have shown that as long as your mind pictures a brick, you will tend to think of only those conventional uses of bricks you have stored in your momory. Yet creative people think wildly, shifting perspectives, making unusual links between concepts. To help yourself "think wildly," consider this simple trick—the "many attributes" heuristic.

The "Many Attributes" Heuristic: An Introduction to Using Heuristics

STEP ONE: List the attributes of X (that is, the features, characteristics, or qualities of X). Here is what you might jot down for "brick":

hard object	holds heat
rectangular surface	won't conduct electricity
dense object (won't float)	crumbles into a gritty powder when struck with
dull rust color	a hammer
a rectangular solid	waterproof
won't rot	has a smooth flat surface

STEP TWO: Don't think X; think attribute. In other words, don't ask yourself "What are the uses of a brick?" Instead, ask "What are the uses of a hard object? What are the uses of an object that won't float? What are the uses of a rectangular solid?" This technique will increase most people's ability to think of uses for an object. Instead of a single question containing the word "X," which your mind may perceive in a stereotyped way, this heuristic gives you numerous questions without the word X. In effect, it gives you more playing room for your mind.

The Psychology of Using Heuristics

Before moving on to heuristics designed especially for writers, let's pause briefly to analyze some thought processes involved in using the "many attributes" heuristic, since these processes are common to your use of all heuristics.

- *Breaking the problem down into appropriate sub-problems.* It is often easier to solve a large problem if we break it down into a series of smaller, easier-to-solve problems. There are no rules, of course, for telling you what sub-problems are appropriate for what purposes, but, in general, almost any problem can be broken down into smaller parts. Thus, in the "many attributes" heuristic it is easier for your mind to handle a series of narrow questions like "What are the uses of a hard object?" than it is to handle the all-at-once question "What are the uses of a brick?"
- *Delaying closure.* Note that before getting to the end goal of thinking of uses of a brick, we had to make a list of the attributes of a brick—an additional step that added considerable extra time without any promise of successful results. This intermediate step was a form of interference, keeping us from working directly on the problem we wanted to solve. Unskilled problem solvers jump quickly to a possible solution, accept it, and quit. More creative problem solvers aren't satisfied with first answers, but keep gnawing away at the problem.
- *Courage.* Delaying closure requires courage. In Chapter 2 we identified lack of courage as one cause of the "perfect draft" syndrome. We want our problems solved quickly, our drafts beautiful the first time. Creative people, however, endure imperfection, chaos, ugliness, the frustration of being stuck, because they have faith that this is a temporary condition that they can work beyond. Moreover, they believe that if they bypassed or hurried through the stage of imperfection and confusion, their final work would be less creative. If you think of heuristics as something to do when the mind gets stuck, you will be prepared to use them courageously on the problems you must solve. When others give up, you will have a technique for keeping going.

For Class Discussion

Try applying the "many attributes" heuristic as a group activity. You are applying for a position as a member of an engineering design team for a top secret corporate project and, as part of a battery of tests, you are assigned to a group given the creativity task: "How many uses of X can your group think of?'' Substitute a word of your choice for X (a tin can, sand, coffee grounds, popcorn, a thermometer, an egg, an old slipper, a used composition textbook).

In the rest of this section, you will be introduced to a variety of heuristics designed to help writers pose questions and thus discover ideas for essays. First, however, a word of caution and comfort. Heuristics don't work for everyone, nor can any one person feel comfortable using more than a couple heuristic procedures as an ingrained thinking habit. Moreover, a heuristic which works well for one kind of topic or rhetorical problem may not work at all on another topic.

Don't approach the following heuristics, therefore, the way you might approach a new section of chemistry or math, as content you've got to learn or risk failing a test. You can be a good thinker and writer without learning any of these procedures. Moreover, if approached in the wrong spirit, heuristics may even be harmful if trying to learn them damages your sense of play and makes you think you have new rules to memorize. Heuristics work only if they help you learn to ask better questions.

The "Set Questions" Heuristic

One of the most time-honored heuristic is a set of common questions into which you can plug almost any topic. There are many such sets available, ranging from an elaborate system created by Aristotle in classical times to simplified versions designed by today's composition teachers. Of course, not all modern versions are simple: rhetorician Richard Larson once published an article listing more than a hundred set questions that can get writers thinking about their topics.

Our experience seems to indicate that this heuristic works best for beginning writers if the number of questions is kept small. Here are ten good questions that can generally get you started thinking about any topic:

1. How can X be defined or described? (Your goal here is to focus on the unique, distinguishing features of X, the features that make X different from Y.)
2. What can X be compared to or contrasted to? (Your goal here is to explore X by finding other subjects that seem like X but really aren't. Highlight X by showing how it is similar to or different from Y. This question can also stimulate you to think metaphorically.)
3. What cause and effect chains is X part of? (Your goal here is to think of all the causes of which X is an effect and all the effects of which X is a cause.)

4. What is the function or purpose of X? (Here you explore X from the perspective of its "ends" or "goals"—the role it plays in the human or natural order.)
5. If some part of X changed, what else would change? (This is another way of looking at X in terms of cause and effect changes, but it urges you to pose hypothetical cases.)
6. How has X changed over various time periods? (After describing the changes in X, you should go on to ask what have been the causes and effects of these changes. You should also ask how X will change in the future.)
7. What is controversial or paradoxical about X? (This is generally among the most productive of all questions. Your goal is to find the points of opposition within the topic, the contraries that lead to dialectic thinking.)
8. What is my own view of X? (When answering this question explore why you have this view. What forces or reasons have led you to take the position you do?)
9. Who opposes my view of X? (Here ask also what forces or reasons have led your opponents to take their view.)
10. What is the value of X? (Is X good or bad? What is the signficance or importance of X? In answering these questions, explore the criteria that lead you to your decision.)

The best way to use the "set questions" heuristic is to run through the list of questions rapidly, seeing which ones pose interesting problems that you might try to solve in an essay. When one of our classes tried this heuristic on the topic "good teachers," the very first question began generating interesting arguments which several students went on to explore in formal problem-solution essays: "How can we define the concept 'good teacher'?" Almost all the other set questions also posed interesting puzzles for analysis. "What can a good teacher be compared to?" (a good parent? a good leader? a good friend? a good resource, like a library? a good role model for thinking? a good actor?) "What is the function of a good teacher?" (to impart knowledge? to initiate change in students? to impart love of learning? to facilitate mastery of material?) "If some part of a good teacher changed, what else would change? (If a good teacher suddenly started to follow some of Fritz Machlup's advice, would he or she still be perceived as a good teacher?)

For Class Discussion

Use the set questions heuristic to explore in class one of the following topics: love, justice, industrial pollution, pornography, punk rock, a good student, poverty. After the class has posed a number of questions, each student should choose at least one that he or she might like to "answer" in a formal essay. Discuss why you think your answer to your chosen question might be surprising.

The "Journalist's Questions" Heuristic

The mental "trick" involved in the "many attributes" heuristic is breaking the main problem down into a sequence of sub-problems that are easier for the mind to handle. An excellent parallel heuristic for writers is the journalist's "six questions"—"who?," "what?," "where?," "when?," "why?," and "how?," Each of these questions constitutes a different perspective on a single event. Suppose you were investigating for a sociology class an incident at a little league baseball game in which a group of parents attacked an umpire over a controversial call. (This actually happened in a town near ours several years ago.) Your goal is to try to provide a sociological explanation for this event. You could begin by breaking this large task into subtasks. "Who" were the parents and umpire involved? (You must find out as much as possible about their personalities and backgrounds.) "What" happened? (You must trace the sequence of events preceding and following the confrontation as well as describe the confrontation itself.) "When" and "where" did it happen? (Here you are interested not only in specific dates and places but also in the nature of the town itself and in surrounding events going on at the same time as the confrontation.) "Why" did the event occur? (Here you would not only ask each participant why the event occurred but also question other observers and bring in your own insights from sociology.) "How" did the event occur? (You would now focus on the means used. Was it a fist fight or a shoving match? Did people throw things? Was there a crowd mentality involved or was the incident isolated to a few individuals?)

As you know from Journal Sequence 1, the journalist's questions also help you find specific details when you are describing a scene or giving the background of an important event. Thus the heuristic can be used to ask broad, theoretical questions about a topic or used "up close" to help generate specific details within a paragraph.

For Class Discussion

"Take Back the Night," a women's group on your campus, is writing a booklet on rape to be distributed to all students, both male and female. You are part of the team charged with writing the booklet. At an early meeting of the group you all decide to divide up research tasks. Your group would like to find out all it can about attitudes toward rape on your campus, including women's fears about rape, about past incidences of sexual assault on campus, and about possible actions people at your university can take to make the campus a safer and healthier place. Use the journalist's heuristic to help your group set up an initial list of research questions. Then discuss an appropriate way a group might divide up the research task.

The "Pentad" Heuristic

One reason the journalist's six questions heuristic may be so powerful is that it includes all the "wh-" interrogative words in our language; perhaps these words have evolved because they provide the major perspectives we need to explore any event.

Drawing on this idea as developed by a twentieth century rhetorician and philosopher named Kenneth Burke, writing teachers have transformed the journalist's "six-question" heuristic into a more elaborate and powerful heuristic sometimes called the *pentad*. (The name comes from *penta* meaning "five"—like *pentagon*. As you will see, the pentad reduces the journalist's six questions to five by combining *when* and *where* into one word, *scene*.)

The pentad works best for exploring the causes of any event involving human beings, but with some imagination it can also be used to study events in which the main actors are animals or physical objects. The pentad teaches you to see a complex web of causes behind any event, even those that on the surface seem easy to explain. If you think you came to college in order to become an accountant or an attorney, the pentad will cause you to look at your decision from a variety of perspectives. Did you really "choose" to come to college, or did your family or peers really "choose" for you? If you think you did the "choosing," did your culture and environment shape you in such a way that your "choice" was inevitable? How did your goals in life influence both your decision to come to college and your decision to become an accountant rather than an artist or an engineer? How did your culture shape those goals? (Would you have had the same goals had you been born into a different family? a different country? a different social class? a different age?) How did twentieth century economics, politics, and technology shape your culture? These are the sorts of questions the pentad will help you pose.

We have found that students can best appreciate the pentad if they visualize it as a 5-pointed star within a pentagon (see Figure 7-3). To appreciate how the pentad works, you will need to understand what is meant by each of the terms at the points of the star. In the pentad, ACT refers to any event, process, or action that you wish to explore. ACT could refer to any human event, such as the writing of this textbook or an assassin's attempt to murder the president. ACT could also refer to an event without human actors, such as the creation of a black hole or the spawning runs of salmon. ACTOR/AGENT is the person or persons who perform the act; the

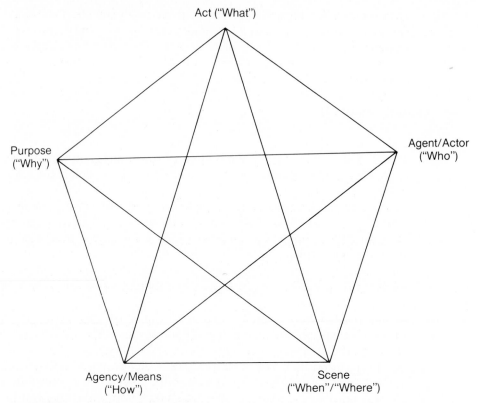

FIGURE 7-3   The Pentad Heuristic

actor/agent can also be an animal or a natural force, such as the Colorado River if your "act" is the formation of the Grand Canyon. In analyzing ACTOR/AGENT focus on the characteristics that make that actor or agent unique. For humans, focus especially on personality traits. SCENE should be interpreted broadly to include not just specific times and places but the broader cultural and environmental contexts in which the event occurs. AGENCY refers to the manner or method by which the action was done or sometimes to the instruments or techniques used in doing the action. For example, if the ACT is the formation of the Grand Canyon, AGENCY is the slow action of water eating against rock. If the ACT is the assassination attempt on the president, AGENCY is the kind of gun used, the assassin's strategy for getting within shooting range, and so forth. Finally PURPOSE refers to the motivation, aims, and goals of the actor/agent, if the actor is a human being. If the actor/agent is an animal or a natural force, then PURPOSE is a troublesome term since modern science concerns itself with causes, but not purposes. From a scientific perspective, pressurized gas and molten lava had no "purpose" in blowing the top off Mount St. Helens. Certain religions, however, claim that every event in the universe has a purpose from a divine perspective.

The power of the pentad heuristic is that each of the perspectives can be cross-bred with each of the other perspectives, giving you a systematic procedure for shifting your point of view. (Note how in Figure 7-3 each point is connected to every other point.) The perspectives look like this:

1. *Act to Actor/Agent:* What is the relationship between the act and the personality of the actor? (Explores psychological causes of the act.) If the agent is nonhuman, focus on the unique characteristics of the agent. How do these account for the act?
2. *Act to Scene:* What is the relationship between the act and the scene or environment including the social and cultural context of the act? (Explores sociological or behavioral causes of the act or explains act from sociological perspective.)
3. *Act to Purpose:* What is the relationship between the act and the actor's purpose? (Assumes actor has "free will" and explores act from the perspective of the actor's goals or purpose.)
4. *Act to Agency:* What is the relationship between the act and the means or instruments available? (Explores to what extent the act occurred because certain means or instruments were available.)
5. *Actor/Agent to Scene:* To what extent is the actor's personality shaped or influenced by the environment?
6. *Actor/Agent to Purpose:* What is the relationship between the actor's personality and the goals the actor chooses? What do the actor's goals reveal about the actor's character and values?
7. *Actor/Agent to Agency:* How are the available or chosen means a reflection of the actor's character of personality?
8. *Scene to Agency:* How are the available means related to the surrounding environment and cultural context of the act?
9. *Scene to Purpose:* To what extent are the actor's goals shaped by the surrounding social or physical environment?
10. *Agency to Purpose:* What is the relationship between the actor's purpose and the means available or chosen?

The best way to see how these perspectives work is through an example. Here is how an undergraduate student used the pentad to help him think of questions for a research paper on mountain pine beetles:

Actor/Agent: The mountain pine beetle. *Act:* Infestation of the Gallatin Canyon and resultant destruction of trees. *Agency:* Beetle bores into a lodgepole pine, lays eggs. The larvae stage eats the inner bark, moving horizontally around the tree trunk. Thus the tree is girdled and dies. *Scene:* Infestation throughout the Rocky Mountains, but for the purposes of this exploration, the Gallatin Canyon area south of Bozeman, Montana. The pine beetle is presently active in the area. *Purpose:* The trees are a source of food for the beetle's larvae. From a holistic ecological view the beetle is replacing fire (prohibited by man) as the end point in the natural forest succession cycle.

Act/Actor: Why does the beetle infest only mature lodgepole pine trees? To what extent is the cycle of infestation related to the beetle's hormonal makeup? Why do the larvae eat horizontally?

Actor/Agency: Does the beetle "choose" lodgepole pine because it's easier to bore into? Since it is the larvae and not the adult beetle that actually kills the tree, which should be the target of any proposed solution? If the beetle were inhibited from flying could the disease be controlled?

Act/Scene: Why was the Gallatin Canyon infested? When the first signs of the disease appeared, what was done about it? Did the date of the Gallatin Canyon infestation correlate to dates the disease appeared elsewhere?

Act/Purpose: Could another food source be substituted for the trees? If fire is allowed to run its natural course would the disease be controlled? The results of infestation seem to be detrimental to man (economically). Are they?

Act/Agency: How does the infestation spread? How does girdling kill the tree? How does the method of attack determine which trees are hit?

Actor/Scene: How did the beetle get to the Gallatin Canyon? Were conditions in the Gallatin advantageous to the beetle? Are these conditions changing?

Actor/Purpose: If the beetle was eradicated and fire was still prohibited, what would be the next growth limiting factor for lodgepole pines? How has the cycle between the beetle and the pine run in the past?

Agency/Scene: Does the season of the year have any correlation to the beetle attacks? Are the beetles limited by temperature? How long do the larvae remain in the trees?

Agency/Purpose: Compared to fire, is the beetle more or less efficient in recycling the nutrients of the trees? Could the larvae be changed genetically so that they eat vertically, thus letting the tree live?

Scene/Purpose: Were the trees ripe at this time for infestation (did they need to be drastically thinned)? Are Gallatin Canyon pines more susceptible to infestation than the same species elsewhere? How does the climate that lodgepole pines inhabit affect the beetle's life cycle?

As you can see, the pentad helped this student think of many questions, some of them unusual questions that could lead to a creative research paper. When you try using the pentad for yourself, you should keep in mind three things: First, don't worry whether the questions you think of actually fit neatly into a specified category. Whether a question is ACT-SCENE or ACT-AGENT isn't crucial. As long as the pentad stimulates you to keep asking questions, it is working. Second, some perspectives don't work very well with some topics. Often, for example, it is difficult to know what to say for AGENCY. Third, be reminded that a writer would never respond to all those questions in a single formal essay. Sometimes one perspective alone could produce the focusing question for a long research project. A heuristic such as this works best at the early discovery stages of writing when you want your mind to play with dozens of possibilities before you begin narrowing down your topic.

For Class Discussion

1. Prior to class, use the pentad to ask questions about any event, process, or action that interests you. This event could either be something from your personal life (your falling in love with X, your mother's decision to quit her job, your decision to major in computer science, whatever) or some aspect of one of your courses. Then in class share your perception of how effectively the heuristic worked.

2. In small groups, study the Picasso painting on page 220 and the accompanying writing assignment (an option for one of the essay assignments in Chapter 8), and use the pentad to explore the question "Why did Picasso paint in this strange way?" Ask questions about this painting from all the cross-breeding perspectives of the pentad.

3. In small groups, use the pentad to explore any other puzzling social phenomena, the causes of which are complex and intertwined: child abuse, the popularity of rock groups with bisexual identities, the new interest in weight lifting and body building among women, the condominium craze, the growing rise of anorexia and other eating disorders, the growing interest in soccer, the differences between the study habits of dedicated students and lackadaisical students, and so forth.

The "Particle/Wave/Field" Heuristic

This heuristic, developed by the linguists and rhetoricians Richard Young, Kenneth Pike, and Alton Becker, helps you switch your perspective systematically on a topic.[2] It works superbly on some topics but is very difficult to apply to others. Only practice will help you get the feel for the heuristic.

The method asks you to regard your topic first as a static, unchanging entity (particle), noting its distinguishing features or characteristics and

---

[2] Richard Young, Alton Becker, and Kenneth Pike, *Rhetoric: Discovery and Change* (New York: Harcourt Brace, 1971), pp. 121–130.

trying to determine how it differs from other similar things. Then you view your topic as a dynamic changing process (wave), noting how it acts, how it changes through different dimensions of time, how it grows or develops or decays, and so forth. Finally, you view your topic as part of a network or system or ecological environment (field), trying to see the interrelationships of its parts and its relationship to other things. (See Figure 7-4.)

Although it takes practice to use the particle/wave/field heuristic on complex topics, beginning writers find that it can quickly help them generate ideas on topics relating to their personal lives. For example, suppose you are

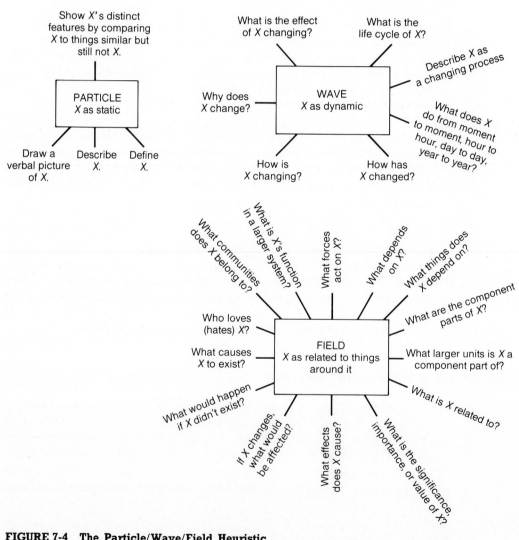

FIGURE 7-4   The Particle/Wave/Field Heuristic

going to write a story-based essay (Chapter 13) about your favorite aunt and are jotting down ideas on an idea-map. Viewing her through the particle perspective, you would jot down features that make her unique, that is, all the particular features that make her your special aunt and no one else. You might list her physical characteristics, her personality traits, her odd habits, her way of talking, etc. Then you would shift to the wave perspective and think of your aunt in action and changing through time. What is her daily routine like? What does she like to do? How does she change from hour to hour throughout the day? How has she changed in the last year? What was she like as a little girl? What will she be like when she is very old? Finally, view your aunt from the field perspective, relating her to both her physical and social environment. What kinds of settings do you picture your aunt in? What does her house look like? Where does she most like to be? Who are her friends? What social groups does she belong to? How do other people regard her? How are her personality and values reflected in the physical and social network of which she is a part?

The point of the particle/wave/field method is not to generate a pigeon-holed list of items that fit neatly into each category. Rather, the method works best when you use it loosely and playfully. Like other heuristics, the method reminds you to vary your perspective, to shake loose memories that you can later use for details in your paper and to discover connections and angles of vision that you might not otherwise have had.

For Class Discussion

1. Observe the chart explaining the "particle/wave/field" heuristic (Figure 7-4). To what extent are the questions on that chart duplications of questions in the "set questions" heuristic? To what extent do questions generated with the "particle/wave/field" heuristic overlap the questions you can generate using the pentad?

2. Prior to class, use the "particle/wave/field heuristic" to explore ideas about one of your favorite places. Pick a favorite place (a room in your house, a hideaway under some old stairs, a cabin in the woods, a favorite pool hall) and generate ideas about it using the particle, wave, and field perspectives. Then share your feelings about this heuristic with the class.

3. Suppose you are taking classes in art history or in earth science and are asked to write a research paper relating to gothic architecture or to earthquakes. Working in small groups use the "particle/wave/field" heuristic to ask possible research questions about one of these topics.

The "Range of Variation" Heuristic

This heuristic helps you avoid oversimplification when you attempt to describe or define something. With this heuristic you ask yourself "How much can X change and still remain X?" Or "How many variations of X are there?" For example, if you were explaining the concept "dog" to someone who had never seen dogs, you would have to mention their incredible variety—from tiny toy poodles to Great Danes, from purebreds to mutts. Yet all these dogs have a quality "dogginess" that distinguishes them both from cats and from hamsters. The "range of variation" heuristic forces you to think of variety as you describe or define.

For advanced writers, we have found that this heuristic is a challenging thinking exercise. For example, if we asked a political science major to define the term "Democrat" for, say, a Japanese exchange student, this heuristic would encourage that student to consider all the varieties of "Democrat," from Jessie Jackson to Geraldine Ferrarro to Ted Kennedy to Uncle Hank the truck driver. Before attempting an overall definition, the student would first explain to the Japanese visitor the wide range of variety within the category. This is a complex thinking task, as you can tell, but one that can increase the sharpness of one's thinking considerably.

The "range of variation" heuristic can also help you generate ideas for descriptive or narrative essays in which you want to portray a fairly complete picture of X. If you wanted someone to understand your friend Pete, how many different photographs would it take to capture his many moods and facets? How many different Petes are there on different days? It might help you to rename this heuristic something like "the many faces of X" or "the many moods of X."

For Class Discussion

1. You are now a photographer assigned to produce a publicity brochure for your college or university. You have space for ten photographs. In small groups, decide what photographs you should take to suggest the "essence" of your college to prospective students. [As an alternative, suppose you could now have ten photographs from your childhood, photographs that would capture the fullness of your early childhood memories. What would those photographs be? Can you describe some of the scenes in words for your classmates?]

2. How many variations are there of each of the following X's?

lovers	Christians/Jews	football fans
rock music	good teachers	effective advertisements
sexist behavior	sports cars	risk

ASKING EMPIRICAL RESEARCH QUESTIONS FOR SCIENCE

The heuristics in the previous section are all aimed at helping you ask open-ended analysis questions for generating ideas for essays. The kinds of analysis questions asked by scientists, however, especially the questions that lead to laboratory research and to the publication of experimental findings, are somewhat different from the kinds of questions you have practiced so far. This section deals specifically with question-asking in science, from speculative, open-ended questions to precise research questions.

Albert Einstein once claimed that he began to formulate his theory of relativity by asking himself, "What would it be like to ride on a beam of light?" This is one of those wonderful puzzle questions that human beings often pose for themselves, questions that stretch the very limits of analytical thinking. Many years later, long after Einstein had published his theories, a group of scientists verified Einstein's hypothesis that energy and matter were related by demonstrating, during a solar eclipse, that the sun's gravity bent light rays coming from a star directly behind the sun (see Figure 7-5). These two events—Einstein's speculative musings and the later design of a precise scientific experiment—suggest two kinds of thinking that scientists engage in, and each demands its own type of question-asking.

The first kind of thinking is unchanneled and speculative. It usually begins with the scientist's perception of a problem—some kind of puzzling phenomena, a contradiction or inadequacy in a theory, a fact that doesn't match a current explanation. Scientists frequently express their curiosity in open-ended, speculative questions, like Einstein's beam of light question or like the analysis questions you have been asking in your journal (see, for example, the student's "pentad" questions on the mountain pine beetle). Such questions spark creative thinking and often lead the scientist to what we might call a hunch, or, more formally, a hypothesis. At this stage an experienced scientist's thinking and question-asking technique shifts remarkably, from open-ended speculative questions ("indeterminate questions," as we will call them shortly) to very precise "determinate-empirical questions" that guide actual laboratory or field research.

It is at this stage—the movement from open-ended speculation to the formulation of precise research questions—that many students have trouble. Recently a psychology professor named Robert Morasky completed an extensive study of the way scientists ask research questions and developed procedures for helping students improve their question-asking skills.[3]

---

[3] Robert L. Morasky, "Model of Empirical Research Questions (MERQ)," unpublished paper, 1985.

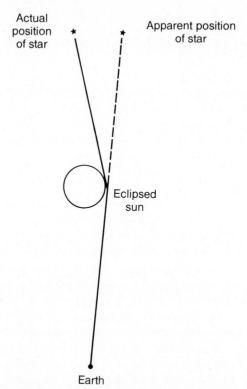

FIGURE 7-5   Demonstrating the Interrelation of Matter and Energy

Having watched dozens of students botch laboratory experiments because they weren't sure what question their experiment was supposed to answer, Morasky is convinced that students should be trained to ask good research questions. This section will introduce you to some of the techniques developed by Professor Morasky.

Specifically, beginning students have trouble asking determinate-empirical questions and thus attempt to guide their research with broader and vaguer indeterminate questions. What, then, is a determinate-empirical question as opposed to an indeterminate question?

First, by calling a question "determinate" we mean that it has a simple, definite, correct, factual answer. The answer may not yet be known (hence the need for research), but such an answer is assumed to exist. The most focused kind of determinate question asks simply for a "yes," "no," or "don't know" response. An indeterminate question, on the other hand, is open-ended and cannot adequately be answered with a yes/no response or with brief factual data, demanding instead an essay answer or a sequence of "maybe" answers. For example, Einstein's question—"What would it be like to ride on a beam of light?"—is indeterminate because it doesn't call for a yes/no answer and because nothing short of a complex essay would begin to be an adequate response. On the other hand, the research question posed by the scientists who tested Einstein's theory—"Will the sun's gravity bend a beam of light?"—is a determinate question because a single "yes" or "no" response will answer it. Suppose those scientists hadn't formulated a determinate question and asked instead an indeterminate question, such as "How will the sun's gravity affect a beam of light coming from a distant star?" Because this last question permits as answers a number of "maybe" alternatives (maybe intensify it? maybe change its color? maybe bend it? maybe slow it down? maybe speed it up?), the scientists would have been less certain what they were looking for and hence less certain of designing a precise experiment on the first try. (Of course they could try another experiment the next time a solar eclipse came along on a nice cloudless day!)

The act of stating research questions in a yes/no format forces scientists to clarify exactly what knowledge they need to gain from a piece of research and hence to design an experiment that yields exactly that knowledge. [You can get the hang of formulating yes/no questions if you practice playing the old party game of "Twenty Questions" where your goal is to guess what someone is thinking of in twenty questions or fewer. The rules permit only yes/no determinate questions. Thus, "What color is this object?" would not be a permitted question since it doesn't have a yes/no answer. However, you could ask "Is this object red?" If you think of Mother Nature as giving out only yes/no responses to scientists' questions, you will learn to design better experiments.]

It should be noted, however, that not all yes/no questions are determinate. A major exception is the yes/no "should" question, such as "Should abortion be legal?" or "Should the United States spend more money on space research?" These questions ask for value judgments about which reasonable people will differ, not for factual data about which reasonable people must agree. Because these questions can't be settled by an appeal to facts, "should" questions are indeterminate. Chapters 9 and 10 on issue-defense essays deal extensively with "should" questions.

The second feature of a determinate-empirical question is that its answer must be empirical, that is, based on observations of events in the material, physical universe. Thus the question "Does God exist?" (or "Do ghosts exist?") is non-empirical because both God and ghosts, by definition, are non-material beings. For the physical sciences, empiricism presents fewer problems than for the social sciences because the events being observed are material ones. But the social sciences examine human phenomena that are often difficult to think of in physical terms. For example, the brain is a physical (material) organ upon which brain surgeons can operate; the "mind," however, is a mental concept (we have no mind surgeons) that can't be touched or weighed, and scientists and philosophers often disagree about whether or not the brain and the mind are synonymous. Similarly, such terms as "personality," "intelligence," "aggression," "sexual stereotyping," "job satisfaction" are all concepts that social scientists investigate, yet none of them is an empirical concept. Social scientists attempt to solve this problem through the technique of operational definition, which translates a nonempirical concept into an empirical one that can be observed and measured. "Personality" might be defined operationally as a score on a personality inventory test, just as "intelligence" might be operationally defined as a score on an IQ test. Or, to measure the extent of latent sexism within a certain social group, a scientist might define such sexism operationally as "the frequency of sexist jokes that persons in this social group tell at work." It should be noted, however, that scholars often disagree about the adequacy of these operational definitions.

Once students understand the concept of a determinate-empirical question, they can increase their skill at asking them. Professor Morasky has designed a simple heuristic for generating determinate-empirical questions based on his observation that nearly all such questions fall into one of five categories.

Category 1: Existence Questions ("Does X exist?")

Scientists doing research in this category are looking for the existence of a substance or event. One branch of physics today is dominated by the search for the hypothetical particle, the "gravitron" ("Does the gravitron exist?"). If you wanted to do research on the effect of the women's liberation movement since the 1960's, you might ask as one of your research questions: "Do traditional sexual stereotypes of little girls and little boys exist on children's birthday cards currently displayed at local stores?" Here are some additional existence questions, developed by Professor Morasky, that use the more complex language and vocabulary of professional scientists: "Do fragments of fungi exist in Precambrian sediments?" "Can human-modified bones of extinct fauna (50,000 years) be found in North America?"

Category 2: Quantitative Questions (How large/small/fast/much/many/bright is X?)

This is one of the few exceptions to the rule that determinate-empirical questions must be cast in a yes/no format; note, however, that a single piece of factual datum will adequately answer the question. In this category scientists are seeking quantitative data answering measurement questions.

"How hot is the surface of Venus?" "How much, if any, will the sun's gravity bend a beam of light from a distant star?" "What percentage of children's birthday cards currently displayed at local stores contain sexual stereotyping?" "How rapidly does the blood absorb lead under normal conditions?"

Category 3: Comparison Questions ("Is X greater/less/different than Y?" or "Does X demonstrate more/less of A than Y?")

Comparison studies are very common in science, perhaps because comparison/contrast itself is the means by which the human mind builds up complex ideas. Examples of comparison questions might be: "If I drop a heavy object and a light object off the Tower of Pisa, will the heavy object fall faster than the light object?" "Is the percentage of sexually stereotyped children's birthday cards currently displayed at local stores less than the percentage of such birthday cards displayed at local stores in 1970?" "Is radiation from Io greater in volcanic areas than it is in nonvolcanic areas?"

Category 4: Correlation Questions ("Does X vary with Y?" or "Is X positively [negatively] related to Y?")

Correlation questions are complex versions of comparison questions. They attempt to identify relationships among variables. For example, Galileo started out hypothesizing that the speed (X) at which an object fell varied with its weight (Y). That is to say, the heavier the object, the greater its speed of fall. When he conducted his famous experiment by dropping two weights from the Tower of Pisa (historians now tell us this event may never have occurred, but we like the story anyway), he discovered that weight and falling speed were not correlated at all. The answer to his research question—"Does the speed of a falling object vary with its weight?"—was a stunning "no," leading Galileo to formulate new theories about physical motion. Once scientists discover correlations between variables, they usually shift to quantitative questions and attempt to measure the degree of correlation. This is a relatively complex mathematical procedure, but perhaps some math wizards in your class already know how to measure correlations statistically. Some examples of correlation questions are these: "Does the frequency with which adults seek out non-sexually stereotyped children's birthday cards vary with their socio-economic status?" "Does the height attained by mature bean plants vary with the amount of sunlight they receive?" "Do students' evaluations of teachers vary with the grades they expect to receive from teachers?"

Category 5: Experimental Questions ("If Z occurs, then will X occur?" or "If . . . [an experimental group] receives [independent variable], then will the experimental group have higher/lower/greater/less [dependent variable value] than a control group?")

Experimental questions involve controlled laboratory experiments in which the experimenter systematically controls one variable (called the independent variable) and then measures that variable's influence on another variable (called the dependent variable). The experimenter must ensure that all other variables in the system are held constant. Experimental questions always have an if-then structure. A simple example would be this: "If the amount of voltage fed to an electric light bulb increases, then will the brightness of the light bulb increase?" Or, "If students receive systematic training in scientific question-asking, then will their ability to design research projects increase, as measured by pre- and post-examples of written descriptions of proposed research experiments?" In systems where change is irreversible, scientists must rely on control groups to conduct experimental research. (You can't, for example, go through college twice, trying it once without training in question-asking and then trying it again with this training.) The scientist establishes two groups—an experimental group and a control group—and then keeps all variables constant except for the independent variable, which she administers to the experimental group but not to the control group. If the variable being investigated (the dependent variable) changes within the experimental group but not within the control group, then the scientist can infer that the independent variable caused the observed changes in the dependent variable. Examples of experimental/control group questions include these: "If an experimental group of bean plants is exposed to rapidly blinking light, then will they grow as tall as a control group of bean plants exposed to constant light?" "If laboratory rats are injected with cigarette tars, then will they develop cancers at a greater rate than rats not injected?"

For Class Discussion

1. Working in small groups or as a class, imagine some zoology/botany "do-it-yourself" research each of you could conduct in your own dorm room or apartment (observing potted plants, mold on week-old coffee in misplaced coffee cups, fleas on your dog, cockroaches under your sink, whatever.) Invent some determinate-empirical questions you might ask to guide your at-home research. As a group, ask one or two questions in each of the categories beginning with existence questions ("Do fleas exist on my dog?"—a very legitimate research question!) and moving through quantitative questions, comparison questions, correlation questions, and experimental questions.

2. You and a group of friends decide you want to do some sociological research on the kinds of solutions people give to the following problem:

A boy is brought into a hospital with severe head wounds as a result of a car accident. The boy is rushed into the surgery room and prepared for surgery by a team of doctors and nurses. Several minutes later the hospital's chief brain surgeon rushes into the room freshly scrubbed. The surgeon takes one look at the boy and exclaims, "I can't operate on this child. He's my son!" Since the surgeon was not the boy's father, how might you explain this puzzle?

The answer is, of course, that the surgeon was the boy's mother, an answer that doesn't occur to a lot of people because of the power of sexual stereotyping. It occurs to your group that you could use people's solutions to this puzzle as an operative definition of sexual stereotyping by creating a "scale of stereotyped thinking" ranging from "extremely stereotyped" (a person never thinks of "mother") to "moderately stereotyped" (a person thinks of "mother" after playing with other hypotheses) to "not stereotyped" (a person says "mother" immediately).

Ask several determinate-empirical questions that would enable you to conduct sociological research using this story.

Guided Journal: Sequence 2

Asking Questions, Exploring Answers

INTRODUCTION

Journal Sequence 2 bridges the gap between Chapter 7—"The Art of Asking Questions"—and Chapter 8, which sets forth problem-solution essay assignments. The purpose of this journal sequence is twofold: First, its aim is to increase your skill as a question-asker by letting you explore on your own a broad range of ideas. Second, it should help you discover and explore ideas that you can use directly for various assignments in Chapter 8.

It would be a good idea for you at this time to preview Chapter 8 by looking briefly at each of the assignments. If your instructor has selected the formal assignments that you will be doing in Chapter 8, pay special attention to them. Briefly, all the assignments in Chapter 8 require you to begin by posing a problem that can be summarized as a one-sentence question. The assignments differ in the ways the body of the essay develops your answer to the question. Here in a nutshell are the kinds of essay assignments Chapter 8 sets forth:

1. A two-paragraph problem-solution essay. Your task here is to use your introduction to interest your reader in one of your "power questions" and then to present your answer in the second paragraph. This journal sequence will help you discover appropriate power questions.

2. A longer problem-solution essay in which the body of the paper shows several different possible solutions to the problem you pose in the introduction. As you do this journal sequence, be alert for questions that seem to have more than one possible answer.

3. A longer essay that begins by posing a question that seems to have a common, expected answer. After presenting that answer, however, your essay switches direction and provides a surprising answer. Look for questions that you think you can answer in an unexpected way.

4. An essay that explores a contradiction. Here you ask a question that has two opposing answers that seem to cancel each other out. One of your goals in this journal sequence is to find questions with this particular kind of complexity—questions that leave you in a quandary because opposing solutions seem equally attractive. Some teachers might ask you to do one of these essays as a short research paper.

5. An analytical essay based on an assigned topic. We call these "findings-discussion" essays, terms which we have borrowed from scientific writing. For this essay you will have to pose a puzzling question which your essay then attempts to answer, first by summarizing the data that relate to the question (findings) and then by analyzing the significance of the data (discussion).

As you do Journal Sequence 2, keep in mind the freedom the assignments in Chapter 8 provide since the choice of subject matter for most of them is entirely open to you. This journal sequence will help you get some control over that freedom.

Journal Sequence 2 focuses both on asking questions and on exploring answers to them. The journal sequence has four parts. Part 1 will help you discover those strategies for exploring questions that work best for you. In Part 2 you will use your journal as a thinking and studying tool for one of your courses outside of this writing class. Part 3 focuses on achieving "surprise" and "tension" in your exploration of a question—exercises to help you push beyond the obvious. Finally, Part 4 is an unstructured, open-ended opportunity for you to use heuristics to ask questions about topics of your choice.

This journal sequence will be less structured than Journal Sequence 1, allowing your instructor more flexibility to assign writing tasks according to his or her own purposes. We recommend that you spend 15 minutes of writing time per task. Your instructor will inform you how many tasks to complete each week. Throughout this sequence, exercises can be added or eliminated without harm in order to meet the needs and schedules of different kinds of composition courses.

PART 1: GETTING THE QUESTION-ASKING HABIT

Task 1, 2 and 3

Practice asking questions using the techniques described in Chapter 7, pages 154–158. You can use your own topics or select topics from the class discussion exercises in Chapter 7. Ask at least 20 questions. Include some you can answer as well as some you can't answer.

Explanation

These three tasks let you start this journal sequence by getting in the habit of asking questions. Try the techniques described in Chapter 7, especially freewriting on the trigger question "What aspects of X puzzle me?;" making idea-maps with questions to head branches; and playing the question-game. You can switch from one topic to another ("dogs," "life in the dorm," "issues related to my political science class") or you can ask all your questions about just one topic.

Task 4

Choose either the Beetle Bailey cartoons on page 250, the Picasso Portrait on page 220, or the two pictures of childhood on pages 252–253. Observe your topic for 5 minutes and then freewrite for 10 minutes on one of the following trigger questions: "What puzzles me about X?" or "What questions about X interest me?" If you run out of questions, try freewriting some possible answers to questions you have asked.

Explanation

Whereas the exercises you have done in Tasks 1, 2, and 3 ask you to generate ideas "from scratch" on topics of your choice, this task gets you thinking about the kinds of topics teachers often assign in college. At first the Beetle Bailey cartoons might not seem puzzling at all. But once you begin looking at them, lots of questions about our culture might begin to emerge. (For example, "Why are wives in our culture often stereotyped as unattractive shrews?") Questions about the Picasso portrait or the two images of childhood will probably come readily to mind. Depending on the assignments your instructor chooses, you may have an opportunity, later in this course, to write formal essays on one of these topics.

Task 5

Ask several "power questions" based on your own personal experiences. After each power question, write a one-sentence summary answer.

Explanation

Power questions were first discussed in Chapter 5 (pp. 115–116) and then again in Chapter 7 (p. 157). A power question has three characteristics: (1) you are the only person in your class who can answer it; (2) the answer requires a short essay; (3) the question interests your classmates. A power question, with its answer, will form the basis of your first formal essay in Chapter 8—the two-paragraph problem-solution essay.

In searching for power questions, you might try going back over your entries under "education" in Journal Sequence 1 and also your own personal topic in Journal Sequence 1. You can also try to find power questions within the topics you have chosen for this journal sequence. But feel free to draw power questions from any area of your own personal experience. Here is a power question based on John's exploration of his early childhood experience in Journal Sequence 1:

> **Power question:** How can a group of kids too poor to buy a toboggan have a 'community' sled ride?"
>
> **Answer:** If you can't afford a toboggan and yet want the fun of a community sled ride with your friends, get an old car hood from a junk yard.

Task 6

From the questions you have asked so far in this journal sequence, choose any question that you think you can answer but that you think your intended audience can't answer. Then, in a 15 minute session, write a shaped essay answer to your question aimed at your intended audience. Begin with a one-sentence summary answer to the whole question. Your answer should take at least a full paragraph.

Explanation

Asking questions, of course, is only one side of the creative process; the other side is exploring answers to the questions you pose. Clearly there are two categories of questions—those you can answer and those you can't—and they are going to require different strategies when you write responses to them in this journal.

In responding to a question that you can answer, you should practice "shaped writing," that is, organized and developed writing of the kind you have to do on essay exams or in formal essays. The microtheme exercises in this text are models of "shaped writing." As we have suggested in the microtheme exercises, the best way to practice shaped writing is to begin with a one-sentence summary answer to the whole question ("Lay out the whole before presenting the parts") and then to use the rest of the essay to support that one-sentence answer. Locate now a question that you can answer (perhaps one of the power questions from the previous task) and spend 15 minutes writing out your answer in a clear and organized way. This could become part of a draft for one of the assignments in Chapter 8.

Task 7

Now choose a question that you can't answer and explore an answer through 15 minutes of free writing.

Explanation

In your last task you practiced doing "shaped writing" in response to a question you could answer. But there is another whole breed of questions—those you can't answer. In these cases, there is no use trying to be organized because you don't know yet what you want to say. Writing in such a situation has to be "writing for yourself" rather than "writing for strangers." In this task and the one following, we will explain some techniques for "writing for yourself." Your goal will be to find which strategies work best for you.

The technique you will use for this task is simply to freewrite on your question. Research suggests that freewriting can actually increase the flow of your ideas. Many students who practice freewriting long enough to master the technique report that freewriting initiates intense concentration. Often while freewriting in response to a puzzling question, you can generate ideas that might lead to a solution to your problem or at least to a plan of attack through research. Here is a an example of a 15-minute freewrite on the question—"How do bacteria cause disease?"

People would probably think I am dumb asking this question. Everyone knows that bacteria cause disease. People might think that this is a dumb question. But maybe most people know how bacteria do that but I don't. Anyway I think it is a pretty good question so there. Relax, relax. I know that all bacteria don't cause disease. Some bacteria live in our bodies all the time. In fact, I think our bodies need some bacteria but I'm not sure about that. Maybe that's some other animal I heard about that have bacteria in their stomach all the time to help digest food. Is that humans or lizards or sheep or what? Anyway I wonder if scientists really know how bacteria produce disease when you get down to the nitty gritty chemistry of it. Relax, relax, relax, relax. Let's see what might be some theories. Maybe bacteria produce a poison that poisons you. Or maybe they eat up food that we need or some special substance that the body needs. Maybe they just take up space in the body or maybe they attach themselves to a certain kind of cell and prevent it from functioning in some way. This is pretty complicated. I wonder why different kinds of bacteria produce different kinds of diseases. I remember my small pox vaccination—this huge pussy hole in my arm—how awful small pox must have been to have those pox all over your body. Why would that bacteria produce pox while diphtheria produced a horrible sore throat? Do these bacteria like to live off just certain cells? How do they know where they are in the body? Do different bacteria produce illnesses in different ways? If you could look at them under a microscope could you tell whether they would be harmless bacteria or mean ones? Do they have little road maps of the body telling some of them to head for the throat and others to head for the skin? Why does a sore throat bacteria go to the throat? Why couldn't it be a sore lung bacteria? Maybe I should go to the library and read up on bacteria. I wonder if the articles will be too technical for me?

This brief freewrite produces a number of questions that could serve as the focus of a research paper in a science course. Now you freewrite for 15 minutes exploring possible answers to any question that puzzles you.

Task 8

Return to one of the topics you explored in your earlier journal entries and create and idea-map with questions heading each of the branches. (See page 155 in Chapter 7 for an example.) Then branch off each of the questions, exploring possible responses using the idea-mapping techniques you first learned in Journal Sequence 1.

Explanation

An idea-map is another journal-writing technique that can stimulate focused concentration. Most writers report that their minds work differently during idea-mapping than during freewriting, so try to determine which technique is most useful for you. Your idea-map here will be similar to those you created for Journal Sequence 1 except that you will have questions at the head of each branch to trigger your exploration.

Task 9

In a 15-minute piece of shaped writing answer this question: "What are the strengths and weaknesses, for you, of free-writing and idea-mapping as techniques for exploring answers to puzzling questions? Can you think of another technique that might work better for you? "

Explanation

This is the end of Part 1 of this sequence. You have practiced three skills: (1) asking questions; (2) giving shaped responses to questions that you can answer; and (3) trying freewriting and idea-mapping as ways of exploring questions that you can't answer. For this entry you are to evaluate what works best for you as a way of exploring answers to puzzling questions. From now on you will be responding in your journal to all sorts of questions that puzzle you. You will be free to choose whatever thinking technique works best for you. For this entry, just give that question some conscious thought.

PART 2: WRITING AS A MODE OF LEARNING IN YOUR OTHER COURSES

In Part 2 you will apply some of the techniques you learned in Part 1 to help you study for your other courses. This section of your journal will enable you to use writing as a mode of learning across the curriculum. We hope that one reward for doing this section of your journal will be improved grades in your other classes as well as the discovery of some new learning and studying habits. Additionally, you might decide to use material from your other courses as possible topics for one of your assignments in Chapter 8.

Task 10

Ask at least 10 knowledge/comprehension questions about the subject matter in other courses you are now taking. These should be questions suitable for an essay exam, even though your instructor may give multiple choice or short answer exams. Ask a few questions that you know you can answer, but also ask some challenging ones about the hardest material in your course. After each question place a check or an X. A check means you are confident you can answer that question; an X means there are aspects of the material you don't really understand.

Explanation

Knowledge/comprehension questions are explained in Chapter 7 (pp. 160–162).

Task 11

For each of the checked questions in Task 10 (that is, questions you are confident you can answer), write a one-sentence summary answer that would serve as your "thesis statement" in an essay exam.

Explanation

A common cause of low grades in college essay exams is an answer that looks more like freewriting than like shaped writing. A good strategy for improving your essay answers is to delay writing until you have formulated a one-sentence summary answer to the entire question. This summary answer should be the opening sentence for your exam. Such a "thesis statement" opening gives you a roadmap for your ideas and satisfies your reader's need for predictability and form ("Lay out the whole before presenting the parts"). Also, if you run out of time in an exam and don't get to write, say, the last third of your answer, the instructor will know in summary form what you were going to say from the opening thesis statement. In this task, then, you are practicing writing the opening sentence for your exam answers—an opening which announces your entire answer in miniature.

Here are examples of one-sentence answers to some of the knowledge/comprehension questions we asked about this text in Chapter 7 (p. 161).

Question: What is meant by form and surprise?
 Answer: Form is the element of organization or shape in an essay while surprise is the pleasure a reader receives either from learning new ideas or from enjoying the craftsmanship of the writer.
Question: What is the difference between a question and a problem?
 Answer: A problem is a "good" question, that is, a question that arouses a reader's curiosity, requiring an answer beyond the expected and ordinary.

Task 12

Now take one of the "thesis statements" you composed for Task 11 and, in a 15-minute piece of shaped writing, go on to develop an answer as you would in an essay exam.

Explanation

In this task you will practice writing an actual essay test answer. We advise you to see yourself as teaching the exam material to a new learner. This will force you to develop your answer clearly and keep you from falling into the "you know what I meant" syndrome that often results in low test scores. If possible, discuss this answer as well as your answers for Task 11 with other students taking the same course.

Task 13

Choose a question you marked X in Task 10 and freewrite for 5–10 minutes on this trigger question: "What is it about this material that confuses me?" Then plan a way to get the material clarified, either by restudying your textbook, asking a classmate, or seeing the instructor.

Explanation

Our point here is to emphasize your responsibility for identifying course material you don't understand and for developing effective study techniques for learning that material. Often freewriting about what you don't understand will help you start to clear up the confusion.

Tasks 14 and 15

Ask at least 10 analysis questions about one or more courses you are now taking. Ask questions in each of the six categories described on pages 164–165 in Chapter 7 (believe/doubt; personal connection; what if ...; comparison/contrast; return to the roots of the original knowledge; and evaluation questions).

Explanation

Analysis questions are explained in Chapter 7 (pp. 162–165).

Tasks 16, 17, and 18

Choose several of the analysis questions you asked in Tasks 14 and 15 and explore answers to them, either through freewriting, idea-mapping, or any other technique that works for you.

Explanation

Remember that asking analysis questions is a powerful way to think of topics for out-of-class essays you have to write for courses across the curriculum; the body of your essay will be your answer to a question you pose in the introduction.

You should appreciate how frequently analysis questions invite you to do research—either in the library to find out information or in a laboratory to conduct your own experiments. Additionally, many kinds of analysis questions call mainly for your own critical thinking—research spun out of your own mind rather than through the gathering of data in the library or a laboratory. What you should see here is that reasonable people are drawn into research by their desire to answer questions. As long as you see yourself capable of generating your own good questions, and as long as you feel questions turning into problems, then these early sections of Journal Sequence 2 will have been successful.

Task 19

Take 15 minutes to respond to the following questions:

1. *How might Journal Sequence 2 so far affect your future study habits? Explain.*
2. *How has this journal sequence so far affected your sense of yourself as a student?*
3. *How could you make the ideas suggested here work best for you after this course is over?*

Explanation

These questions will help you and your instructor take stock. Some students go on to make "writing as a mode of learning" a part of their regular study habits through college. One technique is what rhetorician Ann Berthoff calls a "dialectic notebook." You take notes on the righthand pages of your notebooks, asking knowledge/comprehension questions in the margins. But you devote the entire lefthand pages of your notebooks for analysis questions and freewrites. Fill the lefthand pages with your own musings, doubtings, and questionings of the material. The dialectic notebook captures the two intellectual roles you should try to play as a college student: (1) an absorber and learner of the information and knowledge being passed on to you from previous generations; and (2) a creative thinker and independent problem-solver, the kind of person who will add to the store of knowledge passed on to the next generation.

PART 3: SEEKING SURPRISE

For the next tasks, read pages 166–169 in Chapter 7 on ways of seeking surprise in a thesis statement. The next journal tasks will all be aimed at helping you get the "feel" for surprise. Any of the following entries could form the basis for formal essays later in this text.

Task 20

Choose one of the following real or hypothetical events and brain-storm as many consequences as you can think of that might poss-ibly be caused by the event: a cure for cancer; worldwide dis-armament; the elimination of athletic scholarships; the recent epidemics of sexually transmitted diseases such as herpes or AIDS; a heavy tax on families having more than two children; replace-ment of federal income tax with a large federal sales tax; social-ized medicine in the United States; a four-day work week; an event of your choice.

Explanation

This assignment is designed to get you thinking about the notion of "surprise" or "tension" in an essay as discussed in Chapter 7 (pp. 167–168). A thesis has tension and hence surprise when it plays unexpected ideas or insights off against predictable ideas that the reader already has. Your goal in this task is to think of possible consequences of an event that go beyond what everyone would expect. Make this task a game in which you search for the unexpected. Of course, in an essay you would have to create an argument showing that your unexpected consequences are in-deed plausible.

Choose one event from the list and brainstorm every possible conse-quence you can imagine. Use freewriting, idea-mapping, or simply listmak-ing—whatever works best for you.

Task 21

Think of several responses you might make to one or both of the following trigger questions: "What are some popular views about X that I think are wrong?" "What are some unpopular views about X that I think might be correct?" Substitute for "X" any topic of your choice.

Explanation

Here you are searching for tension by taking a minority view on a question. This thinking strategy is most powerful if you take a position opposing people closest to your own worldview. For example, if you are opposed to abortion, rather than attack a pro-abortion position, turn the knife of your thinking upon those who are most like you—those who share your opposition to abortion. In other words, what position can you take that is unpopular *among those who already share your opposition to abortion?* To put it still another way, try to make your argument surprise your friends as well as your enemies.

Task 22

Using freewriting, an idea map, or a simple list, respond to this trigger question: "In what ways in your personal experience or observation have you encountered contradictions or paradoxes such as contradictory value systems, equally attractive ideas that can't be true simultaneously, or other instances of opposing notions that leave you in a dilemma?"

Explanation

Chapter 2—"Problematizing Experience"—began with a series of "dialectical quotes," which seem to be self-cancelling generalizations and thus constitute paradoxes or contradictions. A paradox or contradiction occurs when two notions both seem equally plausible, equally attractive, and yet cannot both be true simultaneously according to the laws of logic. Such dilemmas are often the source of surprising writing, either when a writer points out a paradox in some area of human experience that a reader hadn't previously noted, or when a writer resolves a paradox by eliminating one of its sides or reaches a synthesis that permits us to accept the truth of both sides. Chapter 2 shows our attempt to reason our way through several paradoxes associated with writing and thinking.

In this journal task you are to discover your own paradoxes and contradictions. Some of the ideas you discover here could become topics for the "contradiction-quandary" essays in Chapter 8 and also for the "issue-defense" essays in Chapter 12. Here is a short list of contradictions one student has made:

- What is really meant by a paradox? Let me try to put this in my own words. Maybe a case where values conflict, where you believe one thing but in believing that one thing you really have to disbelieve something else that you still want to believe?

- That helps, let's see. I believe that it is good for a kid to get an after school job to learn about responsibility and to help pay expenses; on the other hand, I think the high school years are your last opportunity to be a kid and working takes too much time away from studying.
- Here's a paradox that just popped into my head. Our culture values two contradictory things at once. It values women's liberation but it also values preserving one's ethnic heritage. How can you preserve your ethnic heritage if your heritage exploits women? Can a Japanese woman be liberated and simultaneously walk two paces behind her husband to preserve her cultural heritage? Can you just keep part of your cultural heritage and change all the rest? Aren't we caught here in a bind between our vision of an ideal future and our vision of an ideal past?
- The ideas are beginning to float in. How about femininity and feminism? The feminists of the late sixties rejected traditional feminine appearance of frilly dresses, stylish hair, many feminine mannerisms, etc. Now there seems to be a return to feminine clothing. Can a true feminist dress and act according to the standards of feminine beauty in our culture since those standards seem to have evolved in a sexist culture?
- Can a cheerleader be a feminist?
- Why are nursing homes so popular in our culture? On the one hand, we value love and should, with those values, ask our elderly parents to live with us the way extended families in the past have lived. On the other hand, we value independence and autonomy and can't be burdened down with the responsibility of having elderly parents in our homes. Where would I like to live when I am old and feeble?
- How could Ronald Reagan, who came to office pledging the need for federal government to accept fiscal responsibility like a good, conservative family that saves its money, chalk up the highest federal debt in history?

Task 23

Think of as many causes as possible for one of the following phenomena: the failure of many sexually active teenagers to use birth control; opposition of many Americans to gun control legislation; growth of the home computer industry; popularity of rock groups with bisexual identities; inflation; support of many Americans for gun control legislation; a recent increase of popularity for natural methods of childbirth; the frequent defacing of subway systems in large American cities; during a time of rapid expansion of women into the male work force, the failure of women to enter the skilled trades such as carpentry, bricklaying, or plumbing (see Table, p. 246); Pablo Picasso's decision to paint the strange kind of portrait shown on page 220; the dominance of Blacks in college and professional basketball;

since the 1960s the steady decline of SAT scores among high school seniors; the popularity of James Bond movies; the success of the Star Wars trilogy; growth in the pornography industry.

Explanation

In our explanation of analysis questions in Chapter 7 (pp. 162–165) we illustrated analytic thinking with a discussion of the causes of the French Revolution. If your professor tells you there are five causes of the French Revolution and you memorize them, you are operating at the knowledge/comprehension level. However, if you do research into the historical documents of the period and decide that there are six main causes of the French Revolution, you are doing analytical thinking. Task 23 asks you to do the same kind of analytical thinking. How many causes are there for the current popularity of bisexual rock groups:? Or for the number of teenage pregnancies in an age of easy access to birth control? A hundred years from now, cultural historians will be asking these same questions in order to understand America in the 1980s. Do your own thinking about these questions now.

Once again, your goal is to push beyond predictable explanations imagining some possible causes that will at first surprise your classmates but then come to seem plausible as you explain your reasoning. Your thinking for this task could lead to ideas for the problem-alternative solutions essay assignment, the contradiction-quandary assignments, the findings-discussion microtheme assignments, or many issue-defense assignments later on.

PART 4: HEURISTICS AND SCIENTIFIC QUESTION-ASKING

We will leave the design of this section of Journal Sequence 2, covering heuristics and scientific question-asking, to the discretion of your instructor. From our own experience, we have found that a study of heuristics must be tailored to the needs and psyches of individual students. Some students love heuristics, learning to use them with the same kind of agility that other people have for playing bridge or doing crossword puzzles. Other students dislike heuristics, feeling that the imposition of artificial constraints gets in the way of their thinking. We believe students must approach heuristics with an open mind and a sense of play, free to try them in ways that work best for themselves and free to abandon them if they don't work.

We have developed our own methods of introducing students to heuristics, but we will outline it here as a recommendation only.

The most powerful heuristic, we believe, is the pentad, and we like to have all our students appreciate how it works. The value of the pentad is the way it expands a person's sense of the complexity of casual relationships.

The time spent studying the pentad can often increase a student's appreciation for other courses in the curriculum. For example, sociologists are apt to study human behavior from the perspective of SCENE (your actions are shaped by your culture and society) and psychologists from the perspective of ACTOR/AGENT (your actions are shaped by the interior workings of your psyche). We recommend therefore that every student create a series of questions using the various perspectives of the pentad and then explore answers to some of those questions using freewriting, listmaking, or idea-mapping.

In addition to experimenting with the pentad, we ask students to read the explanations of the other heuristics in Chapter 7 and to try out two or three of them on topics of their own choice. We have found that most students have by now developed the habit of journal writing so that they can sustain an exploration of ideas without explicit instructions for each day. We usually ask students to keep writing in their journals a half-hour per day and to use a week to ten days to experiment with heuristics on topics of their choice. Science students often prefer to spend their time designing scientific experiments, using the question-asking techniques in the last section of Chapter 7 rather than the general heuristics in the preceding section.

CHAPTER 8

Assignments for
Problem–Solution Essays

EXPLANATION OF PROBLEM–SOLUTION ESSAYS

Throughout this text we have claimed that essays are answers to questions. It follows that before you can write a good economics essay or a good nursing essay, you need to know the kinds of questions that economists or nurses ask, or the kinds of problems they like to puzzle over. Because beginning students tend to think of college as a place to soak up information (the teacher lectures, you take notes), it may at first seem strange that one of your primary tasks as a student is to learn to ask questions. In fact, we think that question asking is such an essential skill that we have devoted the whole of Chapter 7 and Journal Sequence 2 to helping you improve your ability to ask questions or pose problems, and throughout the text we have treated writing as a problem-finding as well as a problem-solving process.

In this chapter we will show you how asking questions can lead to well-focused essays. We will show you that the last part of an essay is frequently the answer to a question, or the solution to a problem, proposed in the first part. (Usually, of course, the writer uses the introduction to pose the question or problem and presents the solution in the main body of the paper.) This chapter will explain how to use the question-answer or problem-solution strategy to write college essays. A good question can give your essay a sense of purpose. A one-sentence answer to that question can serve as your thesis statement. And your whole essay can then be seen as a systematic attempt to support that thesis statement.

Throughout the chapter, we'll show you several variations of this strategy. Each variation leads to a different form or shape of an essay. But we encourage you not to focus on the shape the essay takes so much as on the processes of thought demanded by the shapes. The thinking strategies themselves—stating a problem and then exploring a solution to it—are common to all disciplines. The shapes that occur when you use this strategy are highly flexible once you master the thinking strategy. The shapes we recommend are thus only temporary aids to help guide you through the thinking process.

The simplest version of the problem-solution essay occurs when you ask a question in the introduction of an essay and then answer it in the body. Here is an example of this strategy from the magazine *Science Digest*.

How Movies Deceive

When we watch a movie the screen is actually dark for about half the time. This is because motion pictures are a series of still photographs (frames) projected one after another onto the screen, each of which is followed by a brief period of darkness. Why, then, don't we notice the dark intervals? Why do we see the series of still images as continuous?

Motion pictures rely on two fortuitous visual phenomena to produce their illusion: persistence of vision and the phi phenomenon. Persistence of vision is the result of the retina's inability to detect rapid fluctuations in brightness. There's a physiological limit to how fast the eye can deliver impulses to the brain. If a light is flashed on and off at more than about 30 times per second, it will appear to be on continuously.

But since individual frames in a movie are projected at the rate of only 24 per second, shouldn't we be able to detect a flicker in the image? The answer is no. Modern projectors show each frame two or three times in quick succession, and although only 24 different frames are on the screen each second, they appear a total of 48 or 72 times. The phi phenomenon allows a rapid, orderly sequence of still frames to be perceived as motion. The brain has a tendency to "fill in" missing gaps, so when we see an object first in one position and then in another, as we do at the movies, our minds assume that the object is moving. To take full advantage of this visual blending, movies are actually shot slightly out of focus.*

We can learn a good deal from this little essay about the intricacies of the problem-solution strategy and the movement from the asking of questions to

* Reprinted by permission of *SCIENCE DIGEST* © 1981 by The Hearst Corporation.

the shaping of our answers for others' consideration. Note, for example, how the writer arouses our curiosity about the problem with a bold declaration that "When we watch a movie the screen is actually dark for about half the time." He immediately creates a sense of tension between a reader's beliefs about experience and what actually happens. He has turned an ordinary activity into a mysterious one and sparks a desire to solve that mystery. By "problematizing" an unproblematic activity, he has made his solution valuable to other people.

At least as important as his ability to arouse our interest is his ability to satisfy that interest with a clear explanation of technical matters. Notice how he offers a simple one-sentence answer to the question in the first paragraph and then elaborates on that answer. He has done a good job of "laying out the whole before presenting the parts," something scientists quite commonly do in their writing. But you should also notice that his one-sentence answer is more tantalizing than definitive. Few of us know what he means by persistence of vision and phi phenomenon and must read on if we are to have any sort of satisfactory answer. Because the author explains the two phenomena with sufficient detail for us to see exactly how they answer his question, we feel we have learned from his essay.

Now look at the essay in Figure 8-1 for another example of the problem-solution shape, this time from *Newsweek*.

In this essay Walter Williams spends the "problem" half of his essay trying to convince his readers that the concept of social security is a mistake. His thesis for this section is that "social security is at once a bad deal, a lie, and a national obstruction." Williams doesn't simply name a problem; rather he also tries to explain in some detail *why the problem is indeed a problem*. Whereas many other economists were attempting to improve the social security system, Williams wants to show that the whole concept of social security is a mistake. Thus, before his readers will be interested in reading his solution to the social security mess, they need to become aware of the problem itself as he sees it. Again, a hallmark of a creative thinker is the ability to identify problems where others see just ordinary events that cannot be changed. Note how effectively Williams uses specific details, especially statistics, to show his readers why he thinks social security is a rip-off.

The "solution" half of the essay begins with a summarizing restatement of the problem itself and then presents the thesis for this section: "The solution is to make social security private, since *every* estimate shows that a private retirement program, such as a mandatory IRA, would be superior." As with the first essay, Williams first defines and arouses interest in the problem, summarizes the solution to the problem, and then develops that solution fully, showing how it fits the problem.

From reading these two essays one might get the idea that writing problem-solution essays is a relatively easy task. It's not, of course, and before sending you on to look at specific strategies, we'll mention a few of

A Skeptic's Challenge

By WALTER E. WILLIAMS

Social security is at once a bad deal, a lie and a national obstruction. To many Americans, this statement falls just short of attacking God, country and motherhood, so let me explain.

A bad deal. A study by Peter J. Ferrara, commissioned by the Washington-based Cato Institute, reports that a worker who enters the work force in 1980, earns an average salary all his life and then retires at age 65 would receive social-security payments of $15,000 a year in constant 1980 dollars for him and his spouse. Had the worker instead put the same amount of money he paid as social-security taxes into a private fund yielding a real return of 6 percent, the couple could not only retire on an annual income of $28,000 but also, when they died, leave a $500,000 estate to their children. If they didn't want to leave a bequest, the couple could enjoy an annual income of $45,000 until death.

A lie. An officially contrived misconception about social security is that the employer pays half the payroll tax. The truth of the matter is that both the employer share and the employee share come out of the *employee's* paycheck. The employer treats "his" share just as he treats any other fringe benefit: the employee's cash pay is adjusted downward to reflect the noncash pay. There are more lies. You're told that social-security payments are contributions. A contribution is *voluntary*. Social-security *taxes* are not. You're told that these "contributions" go into a trust fund for future payments. No such thing. Your only guarantee of future payments is the willingness of workers to pay increasing taxes. The maximum tax now is $4,342 a year and will probably be $10,000 by 1990.

A national obstruction. If a person were able to invest the money now taken by social-security taxes in a private retirement plan, that money would be available to investors for the purchase of plant and equipment. But no such thing happens with social-security payments, totaling $180 billion last year, because as soon as you pay social-security taxes, they immediately go to a social-security recipient. Martin Feldstein, chairman of the President's Council of Economic Advisers, has estimated that social security reduces private savings by about 35 percent. Feldstein concludes that because of reduced savings—and hence investment—our GNP is lower than it would otherwise be.

Despite conventional wisdom and political demagoguery, the social-security mess is not so much a problem for older people as it is for younger people. They are the ones who will pay increasingly higher taxes and find, in the autumn of their lives, a

Ken Heinen

> Social security is a lie, a bad deal and an economic roadblock. A mandatory private pension system would provide more for the elderly and spur growth in our flagging GNP.

bankrupted, politically unacceptable system. Recent surveys demonstrate pessimism among our young. A 1982 Washington Post-ABC News poll found that 66 percent of those under 45 and 74 percent of those under 30 believe that social security won't be in existence when they retire. A 1981 New York Times-CBS News poll found that 75 percent between ages 25 and 34 doubted that they would receive the social-security benefits they have been promised. The same poll found that 73 percent of all Americans had lost confidence in social security.

Solutions. Nobody with the slightest bit of compassion suggests turning old people out into the streets. Our first order of business is to recognize that social security, while well intentioned, was a mistake—a mistake that won't be corrected by raising social-security taxes, raising retirement age, reducing benefits or dragging federal employees and congressmen into the morass. These steps just postpone the crisis for three or four years, the time between elections. The solution is to make social security private, since *every* estimate shows that a private retirement program, such as a mandatory IRA, would be superior.*

How do we get from here to there? First we acknowledge that among current workers, those above a certain age have already paid so much into social security that they would do better staying in the system than abandoning it. That age is approximately 40. Everyone who is younger than that would leave the social-security system and kiss goodbye the money already contributed. The sweetener is that at 65 they will be as well off and most likely better off than they would have been with social security. Those people over 40 who desire to stay in social security would continue making payments and would receive benefits when they retire. All who are already retired would get the benefits now prescribed. There would be a shortfall of revenues against expenditures—perhaps more than $100 billion—that would have to be funded out of general revenues. While it is a frightening figure, we can count on it to fall rapidly.

Privatizing social security will make the nation better off economically by putting billions of dollars into our capital-starved economy. It will avoid social problems as well. For if we continue with the present system, a day will come when young people, paying 30 percent of their wages in social-security taxes to support some old people, will begin to get other ideas about what to do with old people. That's an increasing concern of mine as the years go by.

Walter E. Williams is a professor of economics at George Mason University in Fairfax, Va.

---

* I would reluctantly make such a program compulsory only to address the criticism that people would not otherwise prepare for old age.

FIGURE 8-1   An Example of a Problem–Solution Essay
(Source: Walter Williams, "A Skeptic's Challenge," *Newsweek*, Jan. 24, 1983, p. 26. Copyright 1983, by Newsweek, Inc. All Rights Reserved. Reprinted by Permission. Photograph: Newsweek, Ken Heinen.

the pitfalls that writers can encounter in working with problem-solution essays. For example, sometimes a writer might take a problem like shyness about working in groups and solve the problem by urging people to be more outgoing. Instead of showing us how to solve the problem, they've told us how things will be once the problem is solved. They've told us what the end looks like without providing us with the means to get there. In a slightly more advanced version of this sort of essay, the writer might offer us a few tips on how to go about overcoming shyness, but the tips will be so general and unrealistic as to be useless (Join a club!"). In either case, the writer's difficulty can probably be traced back to his or her failure to move to a lower level of abstraction where problems are defined with greater particularities and solutions are described in fuller detail.

The key, then, to writing successful problem-solution essays is to discover problems that allow you to surprise your readers. The assignments in this chapter all follow the basic organizational structure we have described: The opening paragraph poses a problem that can be summarized in a single-sentence question. The body of the essay explores the problem in more detail—sometimes by presenting the solution, sometimes by presenting several alternative solutions, sometimes by summarizing a conventional solution and then presenting an unanticipated solution, sometimes by arguing that the problem seems unsolvable, and sometimes by presenting a solution systematically, first by summarizing the relevant data and then by analyzing its significance.

For Class Discussion

Read Carl Rogers' article "Communication: Its Blocking and Its Facilitation" (pp. 393–398). How does that article employ the problem-solution strategy as we have defined it? Working in small groups, can you summarize Rogers' problem in a single-sentence question? Can your group summarize his solution in a single sentence.

ASSIGNMENT 1: A TWO-PARAGRAPH PROBLEM–SOLUTION ESSAY

Your essay for this task will have two paragraphs as shown in Figure 8-2. Write this essay for your fellow classmates and judge its success by how interesting you can make your problem to them and by how clearly they can understand your solution. Follow the format shown on the diagram, making sure that your opening paragraph ends with a one-sentence question and that your second paragraph begins with a one-sentence answer to the question. Your essay should be between 400 and 600 words. Although most

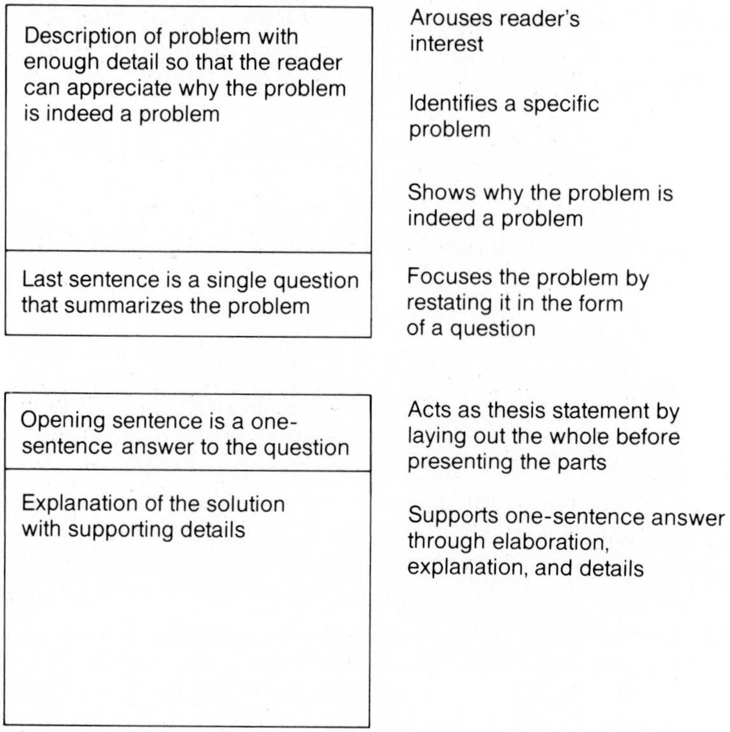

Description of problem with enough detail so that the reader can appreciate why the problem is indeed a problem	Arouses reader's interest Identifies a specific problem Shows why the problem is indeed a problem
Last sentence is a single question that summarizes the problem	Focuses the problem by restating it in the form of a question

Opening sentence is a one-sentence answer to the question	Acts as thesis statement by laying out the whole before presenting the parts
Explanation of the solution with supporting details	Supports one-sentence answer through elaboration, explanation, and details

Length = approximately 400–600 words.

FIGURE 8-2   Two-Paragraph Problem–Solution Shape

essays in real life wouldn't have such a rigid structure, marrying your thoughts to such a structure can make you more conscious of the structural guidelines all writers develop to allow readers access to their ideas.

The key to writing a good essay on this assignment will be the amount of surprise you can put into your essay: surprise at the level of ideas (Is your problem and/or solution unique, something your reader wouldn't expect?) and surprise at the level of specific details (Does your essay have sensory details, or other appropriate sorts of details and examples to show your reader your problem and solution?)

Option 1

Create a personal power question as explained in Chapter 5 (pp. 115–116) and again in Chapter 7 (p. 157); see also Task 5 in Journal Sequence 2. Remember that if you truly have a "power question" you should be the only person in your class who can answer it, and yet you should be able to get your classmates interested in it. The best power questions are taken from your own personal experience. Try to choose a subject area or skill that you are especially good at or that particularly interests you: for example, power questions about skiing, auto engines, getting around on subways, music, watching football, playing PacMan, catching fish without a hook, painting a room. Your goal is to teach your readers something about your topic, to find a question that you can answer, but they can't.

Here is a sample essay written by a student answering the power question: "How can you get the most money out of an insurance adjustor?" [Other examples of two-paragraph problem-solution essays occur on p. 59 (Elwood Lunt's solution to the writing crisis) and on p. 420 (the first bighorn sheep essay).]

Squeezing Blood from an Insurance Adjustor

You're in a car accident, and your vehicle is totaled. Soon you find yourself sitting at an old scratched oak desk facing an insurance adjustor. He might be the nicest guy in the world, but to you he will be a "villain." Invariably he will seem overweight, in his late fifties, and have a pudgy face with droopy eyes. This guy, your mind will tell you, must be the epitome of late middle-age losers who lost their pension or whatever at another job, so they rented an office, put up a desk, and called it an adjusting firm. This man, who now becomes your foe, will offer you two-thirds of what your wrecked car was worth. This creates a major problem if you want to get enough money to replace it. If you don't get enough, you'll end up borrowing money or settling for a junkier vehicle. So how do you go about extracting the last possible dime from an insurance adjustor?

In order to bleed the most money from the adjustor you must have some proof of the vehicle's worth and increase the marginal costs for the adjustor and insurance company. By proof of vehicle worth I don't mean blue-book price. If lots of work or after-market accessories have been put into your car, such as a new engine or tape decks, speakers, seat covers, and so forth, all you need is the receipts and that money can usually be added right on to book price. For example, I once had a 1963 Chevy pick-up that was rear-ended by a drunk doing about forty. As expected the adjustor offered a little over book price because he could see I'd put some work into the truck. This wasn't nearly enough so I started scrounging for receipts. You'd be surprised how much money can actually be tied up in a car. The adjustor had offered $900 and by the time I was finished we settled at $2000. The other thing that can help you get the amount you want is to increase the marginal costs for the adjustor and the insurance company. Marginal cost is an economic term that involves non-monetary as well as monetary costs. Non-monetary costs could be time, paperwork, wasted effort, loss of reputation, and so forth. In order to increase these costs for the adjustor you should be assertive. Set a goal amount that you want and stick to it. This will drag out the settlement, increasing the adjustor's time cost, possibly frustrate him a little, and at the same time increase the monetary cost for the insurance company. Every day that goes by the insurance company must pay more storage on your wrecked vehicle and possibly rent on a car if one is needed. An example of how well this can work occurred when my friend Bill had his Bronco wrecked. He had dragged the settlement out for a couple of weeks and was using a rental for getting to work. A business trip came up and if a settlement wasn't reached soon, the rental would have to be used. When the adjustor found this out, he offered to settle at Bill's amount immediately. So if you can get some proof of money spent on the vehicle and increase their cost for handling your account, you have a much better chance of getting top money from the insurance.

Option 2

To try the problem-solution shape at a more difficult level, ask an "analysis question" as defined in Chapter 7 (pp. 162–165). An analysis question requires you to do your own analytic thinking so that your "solution" is not so much a "right answer" as a plausible answer, a thoughtful answer. Generally "power questions" of the kind you might ask for Option 1 are pragmatic questions, questions about how to solve an everyday problem in the real world. The solutions to pragmatic questions are activities that you can carry out. The solution to an analysis question, on the other hand, usually involves explanations or theories rather than actual activities you can do. Thus, "What is the best way to teach children to play chess?" is a pragmatic question. An answer to that question involves an activity, something you could actually do. But the question "Why is chess a more difficult game for children to learn than Monopoly?" would be an analytic question. Its answer isn't an activity but an explanation. Both kinds of problems—pragmatic and analytic—are good material for writers, but they pose different problems. Here are some examples of analytic questions that might lead to good ideas for two-paragraph problem-solution essays.

- *What would happen to the earth's ecology if ice suddenly began to contract rather than expand when it freezes?*
- *Why does the poet e. e. cummings not use any capital letters in his poems?*
- *Why are rock groups with bisexual identities so popular?*

In each of these examples, the first paragraph would give the background for the question, convincing the reader that the question is problematic, perhaps by showing why the first answers that come come to mind aren't adequate. The second paragraph then answers the question. Sometimes a writer may wish to provide multiple answers in the same paragraph, using the parallel subparts method of organization as explained in Microthemes 1 and 2 ("Chess is more difficult for children than Monopoly for two reasons. First.... Second....).

Option 3

Choose a famous problem-solver from the history of science, engineering, sports, literature, the arts, medicine, the military, or some other field. Read about a specific problem that your person solved and then, pretending to be that person (identify who you are in your essay's title), describe your problem and solution in a two-paragraph essay. Here are some suggestions:

- *Archimedes and the problem of the counterfeit crown.*
- *Copernicus and the problem of the retrogression of the planets.*
- *Malcolm X and the problem of becoming educated while in jail.*
- *George Halas and the problem of the better backfield (Halas introduced the T-formation into modern professional football).*
- *Sheila Tobias and the problem of math anxiety.*

What Do I Do If My Solution Takes More Than One Paragraph?

When you are drafting your essay, you may discover that your solution will take more than one paragraph to explain. What should you do?

Different instructors will answer this question differently. Some will say to use as much space as you need to present your solution, even if the body of the essay therefore needs three or four paragraphs. Others will want you to work within our two-paragraph limit because it forces you to confront certain principles of conciseness and paragraph construction. Certainly our one-paragraph restriction for the solution section forces you to craft your answer carefully. When working under the restraint of limited space, you have essentially two options:

The first option is to think of your paragraph as a summary of a larger essay. As we discussed in Chapter 3, a characteristic of most well-organized writing is that it can be summarized by eliminating details. Thus, if the draft version of your solution is too long, you can shorten it by summarizing. We have illustrated how a long essay can be summarized into a two-paragraph shape in our examples of the "bighorn sheep" topic that we discussed in Chapter 5.) The long and short versions of the essay are on p. 420–427.)

There is always a danger, however, with summaries. Because you summarize by cutting out supporting details and illustrations, you often cut out the flesh and blood of your writing, leaving your reader with only a dry skeleton of your argument. In particular, what often gets left out are the specifics about how the problem was solved. Since readers find much of their pleasure and surprise in the details and examples, summary paragraphs are always in danger of being lifeless. Moreover, they can also be less than helpful insofar as the reader lacks sufficient information to replicate the solution.

The second option is to narrow the focus of your problem so that your solution is less complex or less broad. In other words, you simply chew less by biting off less. This option often forces you to rethink your essay completely. Sometimes you may have to choose a whole new problem that is easier to handle in a short essay. At other times you can simply ask a narrower, more focused question that will reduce the scope and size of the solution, allowing you to handle it in a single paragraph.

ASSIGNMENT 2: PROBLEM–ALTERNATIVE SOLUTIONS STRATEGY

Let's introduce this task with a brief discussion exercise:

Why do women live longer than men? Recent data indicate that the average life expectancy for a baby boy in American society is 70.7 years, while a baby girl can expect to live for 78.2 years. So far, scientists studying the causes of this difference have been unable to explain it satisfactorily.

How many hypotheses can you think of? As a class or in small groups, generate as many possible answers to this question as you can.

Problems with Alternative Solutions

A frequently encountered kind of problem-solution essay is one that informs readers about several possible solutions to a problem. Read the following essay—"Why Do Women Live Longer Than Men?"—which recently appeared in the popular science magazine *Science 85*. This essay by Sue Hoover Epstein, addressing the problem we just gave you, is a good example of the "alternative solutions" strategy written by a professional science writer. Try making a tree diagram or flow chart of the essay to get a sense of how the author has arranged the parts. Because this article is written in a journalistic style for non-technical audiences, its structure is informal, with many short paragraphs. Nevertheless, it is quite easy to map out the relationship of its parts.

Life expectancy is at an all-time high, trumpeted a brochure released by the Metropolitan Life Insurance Company last spring. But women have a clear statistical edge. According to the latest data collected by the National Center for Health Statistics, a baby boy born today can attain the ripe old age of 70.7, while a baby girl can reach 78.2. This eight-year disparity has yet to be explained by the medical community.

A female's ability to outlive a male was noted as early as the 17th century, but it wasn't until this century that the difference in life-span became a gaping chasm. In 1980 there were 131 women for every 100 men between the ages of 65 and 74, and by the year 2000, predictions run to 150 women for every 100 men in that age group. "The gap is widening all the time," notes Edward Schneider, associate director of the National Institute on Aging. "And we really don't know why."

While both men and women are living longer, women seem to have benefited most from the elimination of infectious diseases as the top killers. Because the gap in life expectancy is largest in industrialized societies, women may have some kind of natural resistance to the so-called diseases of civilization, like alcoholism and cardiovascular disorders.

But just how genetic and behavioral differences might affect life-spans has been the subject of few scientific inquiries. Several years ago, at the Second Conference on the Epidemiology of Aging, Erdman Palmore of Duke University estimated that "about half the greater longevity of women is due to genetic differences and about half is due to differences in life-style, such as less hazardous occupations and more careful driving, which produce lower accident rates, and less cigarette smoking, which produces less lung cancer and cardiovascular disease."

While most medical researchers agree that the phenomenon is the result of a combination of factors, not enough is known about them to explain the gap. An oft repeated refrain is that as more women enter the work force and take up smoking, the gap will close. Yet ever since World War II women have been working and smoking in greater numbers and are consistently increasing their edge. As the King of Siam would say, "It's a puzzlement."

Some think that women have reaped the benefits of the Industrial Revolution in the form of greatly improved medical techniques for childbearing. At the turn of the century, less than five percent of American babies were born in hospitals. By 1979, just about all U.S. births occurred in hospitals with a decline in maternal deaths. Men, on the other hand, continue to suffer the negative effects of financial responsibility and stress, which include a higher incidence of alcoholism and liver disease, of suicide and today's Public Enemy Number One: heart disease.

Another prevalent theory is that women have more contact with the medical care system. "Perhaps women are taught to take better care of themselves and to deal with health problems when they occur," suggests medical sociologist Marcia Ory. "However, national statistics indicate that while women report more illnesses than men, they have a lower incidence of life-threatening diseases."

In addition to taking advantage of expanded health services, it could be that a woman's life-style is healthier than a man's. On average, a woman doesn't drink or smoke as much as a man, she sleeps more and has a wider social network to relieve stress and combat loneliness. Others theorize that women have less exposure to physical and social stresses in the work environment, or different and healthier ways of coping with stress.

M. William Voss, director of the Department of Geriatrics and Gerontology at the University of Maryland, believes there's a strong psychological component to the higher mortality of males. "Many men," he notes. "seem to lose their reason for living when they retire. I've observed healthy farmers who've worked hard all their lives retire and move to town. They sit rocking on their front porches and a few years later have a heart attack and die."

A recent National Institute on Aging study indicates that widowed men fare worse after the death of a spouse than women do, suggesting that men's health may also be more severely affected by emotional blows. Recognition of these factors may help men better their life expectancies, but there's a growing body of evidence that suggests that women would still have an advantage in the battle for survival.

"Throughout the mammalian kingdom, there's no contest," asserts Estelle Ramey, professor of physiology and biophysics at Georgetown University School of Medicine. "Females appear to have the natural advantage from the moment of conception."

Ramey attributes this advantage to an inherent sex-linked resistance to life-threatening disease. Her research with Peter Ramwell indicates that a female's hormones work to give her a more efficient immune system. The different effects of the female hormone estrogen and the male testosterone point strongly to estrogen as a protective factor against heart disease. During their childbearing years, when estrogen levels are high, women have a significantly lower incidence of cardiovascular disease than men of the same age. And recent studies on the use of postmenopausal estrogen indicate that estrogen can aid in the prevention of heart disease.

But just how estrogen beefs up the immune system isn't fully understood. "We need much more research," says Ramey. "People are not notable for acting rationally about sex differences, and the denial of women's longitudinal advantages may have inhibited research in the past."

"There are many promising signs that more research is taking sex differences into account," says Ory. "We're beginning to understand that each individual's body chemistry works differently and that biology interacts with social factors."

But the total picture remains elusive. And the gap between life expectancies continues to widen.*

Composing Your Own Essay Using the Problem-Alternative Solutions Strategy

Choose a problem or question that you don't think has one definite answer, but rather several alternative answers, none of which is entirely satisfactory by itself. Begin your essay by introducing your problem, getting your readers' attention, and arousing interest in the problem. You can end your introduction either by summarizing your problem as a one-sentence question or by writing a thesis statement, purpose statement, or blueprint statement (see Chapter 4, pp. 101–106). Then in the body of your essay develop your alternative solutions, usually devoting one paragraph for each possible solution. For this essay you may also need to write a conclusion, usually one that goes beyond a simple summary to discuss the problem you have presented within a larger context of issues (see the discussion of conclusions in Chapter 4, pp. 108–110). However, sometimes your presentation of the last solution serves as a satisfactory conclusion.

Discussion

To help you think of ideas for your essay, go back over your journal searching for questions or problems that you think can be answered in alternative ways. For example, a question such as "What is the best way to train for a marathon?" will obviously have competing answers since runners and coaches all have their own personal theories and training strategies. If you have trouble thinking of your own problem or question for this assignment, you might consider one of the "suggested problems" presented at the end of this discussion.

Through freewriting or idea-mapping, begin searching for the details you will need in order to explain various answers to the question you choose. For example, paragraphs describing competing theories about how to train for a marathon will be fleshed out with specific details about what runners should do according to each theory. Your final goal is to write an essay that begins with your presentation of the problem or question, and then explains three or four possible solutions.

The following essay illustrates problem-alternative solutions strategy.

* Reprinted by permission of *Science 85* Magazine, © the American Association for the Advancement of Science.

Getting Matthew to Eat

One winter I had the privilege of babysitting a young boy named Matthew. Matthew's mother, a friend of my family, was going on a business trip for a week. She told me Matthew had not been eating well lately and I would have to do my best to get him to eat. After his mother had left and I was preparing lunch, Matthew informed me, very strongly, that he did not intend to eat. When I inquired why, I soon realized that at the ripe age of three, Matthew believed he had reached the prime of his life. He did not wish to get any older. Since eating made a person grow, Matthew was convinced that if he did not eat he would continue to be three forever. At this point, I realized I clearly had a problem. How could I convince a determined three-year-old that he must eat?

During the course of my week with Matthew, I tried four ways to solve the dilemma. My first inclination was to let him starve. I believed that when he got hungry enough he would eventually eat. That evening Matthew went to bed without any lunch or dinner; I was convinced that he would be ready to eat anything by morning. The next day, Matthew didn't say a word; he just got dressed and went downstairs to watch TV and play with his GI Joe. By noon, I was genuinely worried and feeling very guilty that I had let this poor child go for over twenty-four hours without even trying to feed him a meal. I now realized that Matthew was determined enough to starve himself and I should make it my duty to change his mind.

Remembering something I'd read in a psychology book gave me my second idea. It said that there are three things that motivate people: love, fear, and sex. Obviously, sex was out, and love would be difficult because I was not Matthew's mother. The only choice was to persuade the child with fear. Since Christmas was only two weeks away, I told Matthew that Santa Claus would not come if he was a bad boy and did not eat his food. Matthew curtly replied that he was a bad boy last year and Santa came anyway. I threatened to throw all his toys away, including his GI Joe. To this threat, Matthew informed me that his mother would buy him some more when she got home. I thought of breaking his arm, but he was not my child and he knew from previous encounters that I would not hurt him.

My third attempt was to entice Matthew with something he liked, so I asked him what his favorite food was, expecting ice cream or candy. However, Matthew surprised me by saying tomato soup. I quickly heated some soup and put Matthew in his high chair. He just sat there and, rather boringly, looked at the ceiling. Remembering what my mother did when I was a child, I began to play games with Matthew's soup. I told him his spoon was a choo-choo train and made the appropriate sounds as it went into a cave (Matthew's mouth). Matthew seemed to like this game and happily ate the spoonful of soup. I thought I had solved the problem. However, by the third spoonful, Matthew suggested we play war in which he was the bad guy, I was the good guy, and the spoon was a tank. This all seemed fair to me, until Matthew splashed tomato soup all over me, Matthew, and his mother's ivory curtains.

Frustrated, after cleaning the war zone, I finally realized that the only way to change Matthew's mind was to make him want to grow up. I started by telling him all about the fun things he could do in school and how he could learn how to ride a bike. He could grow up to be a brave soldier or an air force pilot or a parachutist. I made up wild adventures about all the neat things Matthew could do if he decided to get big. Although Matthew appeared to be somewat interested in what I was saying, his eating did not improve. He would eat two or three bites and then bomb the rest of his plate. On the evening of the fifth day, while Matthew and I were watching TV, an advertisement for Wheaties came on showing Bruce Jenner with his Olympic gold medals. Matthew asked me what they were and so I began to tell him about the Olympics. I told him how the best athletes of the world compete in games in which the winner gets a gold medal, and Bruce Jenner had to eat a lot of food to get big enough to win one. Consequently, the next morning Matthew was up early. He headed straight for the cupboards, pulled out a box of Wheaties and told me, rather harshly, that he didn't like tomato soup anymore. Matthew also informed me that he wanted to get big enough to win a gold medal. Thus, I had no problem convincing Matthew to eat his meals the rest of the week. In fact, it was all I could do to get him away from the table. Matthew's mother was very pleased in his change of attitude when she returned. She tells me now that he never skips a meal and won't go a day without his Wheaties.

Possible Topics for Problem-Alternative Solutions Essay

1. *Ideas from Tasks 20 and 23 in Journal Sequence 2 on the possible causes or consequences of an event are particularly well-suited for this assignment. Remember, any question that can't be answered adequately in just one way is a good possibility to consider for this essay.*

2. *Despite widespread availability of contraceptives, the incidence of pregnancy among unmarried teenage girls is still rising alarmingly. Why? Write an introduction that sets up this problem in an engaging manner; then, in the body of your essay, offer several alternative explanations drawing wherever possible on personal experiences and observations. (Similar problems might be why the incidence of anorexia is rising despite the obvious danger of binge-purge eating; why young people take up smoking despite the warnings about heart and lung disease; why James Bond films are so popular; and so forth).*

3. *Recently there has been considerable discussion of merit pay for outstanding teachers. How many different ways can you think of to define an outstanding teacher? Remember Fritz Machlup's thesis (pp. 399–405) that students sometimes learn better from poor teachers; also recall your exploration of teaching in Journal Sequence 1.*

FIGURE 8-3   **Pablo Picasso, "Girl Before a Mirror"**
(Source: Picasso, March 14, 1932. Oil on Canvas, $64 \times 51\frac{1}{4}$. Collection, The Museum of Modern Art, New York. Gift of Mrs. Simon Guggenheim.)

4. *Observe the Picasso painting—"Girl Before a Mirror"—(Figure 8-3) and also the Renaissance portrait of Sir Thomas More by Hans Holbein the Younger (Figure 8-4). Why did Picasso decide to paint a portrait in such a strange way? In the introduction to your essay describe the Picasso portrait so that your reader will appreciate its strangeness (you may want to compare it to the Holbein portrait, which is obviously more realistic) and then ask your problem-question—"Why did Picasso paint this way?" The body of your essay will give several speculative explanations for the Picasso portrait. You might think that essays like this should be reserved for art historians since it is pointless for you to guess at things you know nothing about. On the other hand, your freedom from preconceptions might lead to some interesting speculations. This is a good assignment on which to practice using the pentad (pp. 175–179). How might the portrait in some sense be a reflection of Picasso's personality? How might the portrait have been influenced by the culture and environment of Picasso's time (early twentieth century)? How might the portrait have been influenced by the availability of new artistic tools or instruments? (For example, might the invention of the camera have influenced Picasso?) How might Picasso's purposes have required a new artistic style?*

ASSIGNMENT 3: QUESTION-EXPECTED, ANSWER-SURPRISING REVERSAL STRATEGY

A powerful strategy for organizing an essay is to begin with a conventional expected answer to a question and then, midstream, to reverse directions and give an unexpected, surprising answer. Read these brief essays by Ellen Goodman and Laura Straus, professional writers whose essays on the telephone and the rituals of death illustrate this strategy.

Hidden Consequences of the Phone*

by Ellen Goodman

My friends live in other places: other neighborhoods, other towns, other states. When we get together, it is often our fingers that do the walking from one home to the other.

FIGURE 8.4   Hans Holbein the Younger, "Sir Thomas More" (Source: Copyright © The Frick Collection, New York).

For us, the telephone is a meeting hall, a neighborhood, the way we keep our own small community together. We advise and consult each other by dialtone; we console and congratulate by area codes and digits.

By voice, we do the maintenance that keeps friendships alive, and sometimes families. If we have some piece of news to share, it goes out almost always, almost exclusively, by word of mouth.

This is called, in our culture, keeping in touch.

Yet I sometimes wonder whether there isn't a hidden cost to this piece of technology, too. I don't mean the costs of intrusion. It's true that the phone insults our quiet and insists its way into our privacy. But I will trade that for this lifeline.

Nor do I mean the cost that shows up on my bill. I rationalize that easily with friends from other area codes: Long distance is cheaper than planes or therapy . . . or disconnection.

But isn't it possible that this staple of modern life has had some odd consequences for us? Isn't it possible that the instrument has actually been an actor in our culture over a century?

John Staudenmaier, a Jesuit and visiting assistant professor at M.I.T.'s Center for Science, Technology and Society, talks about the birth of the phone in 1876 as "the first time in human history that we could split voice from sight, touch, smell and taste."

What does that mean to us? That we no longer have to be in the same room to talk to each other. That we can choose friends across space and keep friends over distance.

But doesn't it also mean that we can ignore the people who live in our hallway? In some ways, the same machine that offers us a handy shortcut through loneliness may also make it more likely for us to live alone.

"The hometown, the street and neighborhood has also been eroded particularly by the telephone," believes Staudenmaier, "because the real relationships in my life are not the people on my street and not the people in my apartment building. They can be strangers because I have 'real' friends connected by electronic rather than physical bodily connections."

It isn't just the phone that does this, I know. The car, the television set and manufacturing have also changed us so we live more in the wide world and less on our own block.

But I suspect that this odd and utterly routine ability to communicate by sound alone has altered another piece of our human psyche. We are more able now to protect and distance ourselves in human communication.

How many difficult conversations today take place by phone because we won't have to see someone's else tears? How skillfully have we learned to control our voices and hide our emotions? How often do we use the phone so we won't have to, literally, face each other?

I know a woman who bought a portable phone so that she could garden or scrub the sink or unload the dishwasher when her mother called. I know a man who regularly broke up with the women in his life by phone because it was so much easier.

We have all, at one time or another, retreated to a phone to share something personal while we are invisible. We are able to screen our messages, offer less, reveal less, feel less vulnerable. We can even hang up. The telephone is wonderfully efficient, and less intimate.

I am no Luddite, raging against electronics. In my home there are four extension phones, a hundred feet of cord and one teen-ager. I work by phone, send my column from one city to another by phone. I maintain—though I never make—friendships by phone.

Yet I think it's crucial to remember the limits, to remember the trade-offs of the technology we live with. The telephone company encourages us to reach out and touch someone. Funny, that's one thing we can't do by phone.

The Last Rite*

By Laura Straus

Well, it arrived today. Not that it came as a surprise. My mother had told me that she'd sent for a "living will," and she has since filled it out, got a witness and mailed it to me for safekeeping. My mother has stipulated in this document that she is not to be kept alive by artificial means, and that her body is to be donated to any individual or institution where it might be useful. Including research. Whatever is left is to be disposed of.

This means that there will be no grave for me to mourn at—not even any service or funeral. I have explained to her that a service is for the benefit of the living. I may have won on that point; she hasn't brought it up again—realizing, perhaps, that she'll have no control in this matter.

My mother is healthy. At 68 she golfs at least twice a week. Last month she bought her first-ever pair of tennis shoes, and I almost take it literally when she signs off a phone conversation saying that she has to "run"—to her WAR (Women Against Reagan) meeting, or to her volunteer work at a public-television station, or to the library to check out the latest novels.

She is on a fixed income since her retirement, and is always worried about becoming ill and needing long-term treatment. She doesn't want to buy a cemetery plot, nor does she want my sister and me to buy one for her. But her decision to have her body put to a "useful purpose" rather than be buried is not a financial one; it is a moral one based on a lifetime of "useful purpose."

I appreciate—am proud of—her social consciousness. But years ago I learned to appreciate the usefulness of death's rituals.

---

* From the *Los Angeles Times*, December 4, 1983. Reprinted by permission of the author.

One day when I was 16 my father peeked around the door to my room, where I was deep in a book. It was the anniversary of his father's death, and he was going to the cemetery. Would I like to come?

I thought for a moment only. He always went with his brothers and sisters, and they all would have breakfast afterward. I couldn't believe my luck. An outing with my busy father. Yes! I told him. You bet!

Because my grandfather committed suicide, his grave was originally outside the cemetery gates. (According to Jewish law, suicide is a sin, and such a sinner may not be buried with pious Jews.) But eventually the cemetery expanded, and my grandfather's grave wound up smack in the middle of the pious faithful. I'd never been there, but I knew the story and got a kick out of it. (I still do.)

That day only one uncle and his wife went with my father. The four of us stood at the grave in silence for quite a while. Then my father whispered to me: "Every day that I live past the age my father was when he died, I feel I have received a gift. I have already seen you and your sister live beyond the age I was when my father died."

I didn't say anything. At 16 I somehow knew that this was a moment to remember for the rest of my life.

"I used to think that we should all be cremated," he said. "But being able to come to this grave and know that my father's body is really here gives me great comfort."

At that impressionable age I silently signed an invisible pact with him—he would not be cremated when he dies. Nor would I.

That was also an age when I had a desperate need to put everything in order. I wanted things to be white or black. No grays. But as we left the cemetery my aunt stopped at another grave. And to my horror she began talking to her mother.

"It's all right," she said. "The kids are fine, I'm fine. No need to worry—everything you said has come true. But how I miss you."

I thought that she must have gone crazy. I looked to my father, and then my uncle, for confirmation. But they just stood by as if it were normal to talk to the dead. The idea was taking root: Maybe the presence of an actual body allows communication to continue in ways that memory doesn't serve.

Ten years later I was out of the country when my father had a fatal heart attack. I flew back for the funeral, and was relieved to find that I would not have to fight cremation. He had worked out all the details; he was buried, quite close to my grandfather.

Since then I have visited my father's grave. No, I don't speak to him. But I remember him speaking to me, and I feel comforted. There is a beautiful solemnity there that I've never experienced elsewhere. And I have a feeling that my father is near—closer than when I run the rat race of day-to-day life.

Now my mother has made an act-of-conscience decision. She hopes that her choice in death may have a positive effect on the lives of others. I, of course, will honor her decision. But I, too, will be affected by it. I will have no moments of quiet, beautiful solitude at a gravesite. I will have to find solace in her ideals.

Goodman begins by summarizing the obvious benefits of the telephone, followed by an unexpected question: "But isn't it possible that this staple of modern life has had some odd consequences for us?" Her answer is surprising, for she shows how our ability to keep in touch with friends by long distance may keep us from making friends in our own neighborhood. Suddenly the telephone becomes an actor in the depersonalization of American society.

Straus's strategy is a bit different, for she tells two contrasting stories. The first story is about her mother's modern liberal attitude toward funerals. "Don't bury me; just give my body to science and burn what's left." The second story is her own—about her memories of her father and her grandfather and the strange comfort she got from visiting their graves. The point of the second story, in effect, contradicts or reverses the point of the first story. The expected position, then, is the mother's liberal attitude; the surprising reversal is the author's own view.

What follows are several options for writing an essay that uses this thinking strategy.

Option 1: Giving a Surprising Answer to an Analysis Question

Write an introduction to your essay that arouses readers' interest in an analysis question. Typical questions might ask about the effect of some X on society such as the automobile, the birth control pill, or the computer. Or you might ask about the meaning of an image in a poem or the causes of a certain social phenomenon. Whatever you ask, the second part of your essay will give an ordinary, expected answer to your question—what we might call the popular view. After presenting the expected answers to your question, you will need a short bridging "yes ... but" paragraph preparing your reader for an unexpected answer. Your purpose at this point is to reverse the direction of your argument, surprising your readers with insights they hadn't anticipated. You will then move to the major point of your essay.

Option 2: Using Stories to Oppose a Popular Viewpoint

Using the Straus article as a model, create an essay in which you develop two attitudes toward something using scenes and stories to illustrate each attitude. The first attitude or point of view should be a common, popular one. The second attitude or point of view—the one you want readers to consider more deeply—should be an unexpected reversal of this popular view. Try to use Straus's technique of revealing each attitude through brief scenes and stories. Use details like Straus's mention of her mother's new tennis shoes and her volunteer work for public television (which help support Straus's portrayal of her mother as an up-to-date liberal woman, just the kind who would prefer cremation over out-of-date funerals and burials) or like the specific examples about her visits to her grandfather's and father's graves.

The following student essay illustrates Option 1.

Jekyll, Hyde, and Judy Blume

For several weeks last spring, our town boiled with the issue of censorship in the schools. In May, the decision came to rest on the school board's shoulders. Eyes flashing, the woman on the platform before the board read her statement. "These books should be taken out of the Junior High School library," she insisted. Another person came forward to give her opinions. She was a short, stocky eighth grader, who spoke with a slow, steady voice. "I've read the books," she said, "and I wouldn't say they ruined my values." The controversy was over a collection of books by Judy Blume, a children's and young adults' novelist. A small group of "concerned parents" had filed a complaint, calling Judy Blume's books pornographic, terribly written, and, most important of all, damaging to the values and attitudes of children. Because my mother was one of those selected by the school board to evaluate the books, my family had many hours of heated discussion about the effect of Judy Blume's books on young readers. Although there are many questions raised by the books, one was not dealt with in any detail. This is the question, "Do teenage readers imitate the actions of heroes in a book?"

Many people, including some of those who supported Blume, didn't really examine this question. They simply assumed that young readers would endorse the actions of a hero in a book. For example, in Judy Blume's book *Blubber*, a fat girl is mercilessly teased by the heroine and her friends. In one scene, Blubber is given her nickname when she gives a report on whales. Later she is disgraced and tormented by the group of girls when they lift up her skirt to point at the blubber on her legs. People who dislike Blume books argue that the heroine's actions condone teasing, and therefore children will think it is not wrong to tease and torment others.

All these parents' concerns are understandable, but I disagree with the assumption that young readers will automatically endorse the actions of the hero in a book. Adults seem to have a lack of faith in a young reader's ability to make decisions or to understand moral issues. As one of my younger sister's friends put it, "I know the difference between right and wrong, and it bugs me that people think I'm going to change my values just because of a book."

I think that Judy Blume's book *Blubber* brings to the surface both the Dr. Jekyll and the Mr. Hyde that exist in every kid. The Dr. Jekyll in us sympathizes with Blubber and wants the kids to stop teasing her, yet the Mr. Hyde sees that teasing someone gives an insecure kid a sense of power and belonging. Thus when reading *Blubber*, a young reader sees the swimming eyes of the poor teased girl but also understands the jeering voices of her tormentors. The reader, then, sees a global view of the situation. I think kids, after seeing this global view in a book, are more willing to see the complexity of an event in real life. Because kids will identify with Blubber as well as with the bullies, reading *Blubber* might make kids less apt to tease a fat girl in real life, not more apt to.

The opponents of Judy Blume wanted all her books replaced in the Junior High Library with goody-two-shoes books about ideal heroes and heroines. But who can identify with ideals? Teenagers like to read Judy Blume books because Blume's characters are realistic. They have mean streaks just like our own. But the books make us see the consequences of meanness; they awaken our Dr. Jekyll as well as make us acknowledge our Mr. Hyde. Look at adult libraries. They are filled with books in which the heroes and heroines have human faults. Books cannot be realistic if they do not. Think of characters like Hamlet, Odysseus, and King David, all of whom have faults. We learn most from books if we can see the hero or heroine face a problem with which we can identify and feel emotions like those we might feel. It is Judy Blume books, not goody-two-shoes books, that make us grow morally.

ASSIGNMENT 4: CONTRADICTION–QUANDARY STRATEGY

So far we have been discussing the problem-solution structure as one of the most frequent forms found in academic writing. The assignments so far in this chapter are intended to guide you toward essays that have both form and surprise. If you will look again at the attributes of a surprising thesis, as we described them in Chapter 7 (pp. 167–169), you will appreciate how much we have focused either on newness or on tension as a way of achieving surprise. The two-paragraph problem-solution essay achieves surprise primarily by bringing the reader new information—either by asking new questions that hadn't previously occured to the reader or by providing new answers to old, familiar questions. The "alternative solutions" assignment and the "surprising reversal" assignments all create tension by playing opposing solutions off against each other.

But surprise can also occur if a writer simply identifies a new problem for the reader without proposing a solution. This writing task—the "contradiction-quandary" assignment—lets you write a whole essay that simply sets forth a problem, one that you can't solve. In this assignment you will develop two sides of a dilemma. You begin by introducing a problem and then you complicate and deepen it. The conclusion of your essay then examines your problem in a more complex way emphasizing both the significance of your dilemma and your inability to resolve it. The purpose of the whole essay, therefore, is to describe a complex problem without offering a solution. The problem, in fact, may be unsolvable. The key to being able to write these essays convincingly is genuinely to feel a dilemma—to sympathize with two opposing world views simultaneously so that you are left with troubling, unresolved questions. In a sense, the "contradiction-quandary" assignment is the exact opposite of an argumentative essay of the kind you will be writing in Chapter 12. In an argumentative essay, you choose a position on an issue and defend it. In a "contradiction-quandary" essay, you should be unable to choose sides. You should, in short, feel caught in your dilemma.

We present below several alternatives for this assignment, all of which follow the contradiction-quandary model. Your instructor may tell you which option to choose; otherwise pick the option of your choice.

Option 1: Opposing Scenes

Choose two "focal" scenes from your life that suggest contradictory faces of topic X (a scene from your childhood showing your older sister as a happy cheerleader versus a scene from the present showing her screaming at her husband in alcoholic rage; or a scene from your childhood showing kids playing happily in a vacant lot versus a scene from the present in which the park is turned into a condo courtyard.) Present the two scenes in the first part of your essay. Then, in the last part, move up the ladder of abstraction a rung or so and identify the principles or values that are in conflict, analyzing why you are unable to resolve the dilemma. In the case of the vacant lot versus condo courtyard dilemma you need to move beyond saying "it's too bad there are no more vacant lots to play in," and weigh the good and bad of both open space and urban development. Or in the case of the alcoholic sister, you shouldn't just comment on the sadness of alcoholism, but again find a dilemma that puzzles you. Perhaps you might develop the issue of illness versus responsibility. Should your family be angry at her for her selfish drinking? Or should the family accept her drinking as an illness? Thus, your conclusion consists of open-ended musing on a defined problem that needs further exploration.

The essay you will write for this option has an interesting psychological effect on a reader since it must be read globally (see Chapter 2, pp. 64–65). The reader doesn't understand the full meaning of the conflicting scenes until coming to the final paragraph. The following student example illustrates this option.

It's 7 A.M. and another day of drudgery has begun. A low, sustained, mournful sound, as of sorrow, seems to be coming at me from everywhere. I shudder inside as I hear it. Why doesn't a nurse go see what Mrs. Smith wants? As I trudge into the room, carrying my cleaning supplies, the smell of stale urine and bowels overwhelms me. I want to open the window, to breath some fresh air, but the residents get chilled so easily. Holding my right hand over my mouth and nose, I head for the bathroom first. The smell attacks my throat like a guard dog. Oh, no! I think. God, I'm going to lose my breakfast. I wish Mr. Jones would stop using the trash-can as a toilet. The thought of having to put my hand in there to take out the garbage before disposing the remainder down the toilet, even with plastic gloves on, turns my stomach. I feel my skin crawling with germs. And the moist, greenish-yellow glob of slimy spit staring at me from the sink basin isn't in agreement with my already protesting tummy. Why won't he use the spit-can I gave him? And look at the wall. It's going to take me at least 20 minutes to clean off the dried chewing tobacco that he spit on it again—I'm already behind schedule. My Lord, there's snoose from the floor clear up to the towel-rack. It's the same old thing—yesterday, today, tomorrow.

As the door closes behind me, blocking out the crisp morning air, the smell of fresh brewed coffee is inviting. It's 7 A.M. and a few early risers have already gathered at the Strand Union Building. After taking off my coat, I settle into a booth and leisurely look over the day's schedule before getting a cup of coffee. I am no longer worried about the computer science test coming up this afternoon. I feel the previous hours of preparation will carry me through. Anxiously, I remove materials from my backpack that will help me determine my next quarter's classes. I feel excitement at the thought of the learning opportunities that lie ahead for me. Soon I have the table covered with class descriptions, time schedules, and graduation requirements. In the background I can hear the soft clammering of silverware and breakfast trays as the Sub slowly comes to life with more and more chattering students. The atmosphere is alive with the beginning of a new day. At the table beside me, papers rustle as four students study for mid-terms. The sounds of laughter fill the air when two students share a joke. I begin tidying up papers as my friend, Mary, will soon be joining me. We had promised to share our test triumphs over a cup of coffee.

I notice my husband tremble slightly as he motions for me to sit down. Dan has been laid off from the railroad for nearly two years. By careful budgeting we have managed to support ourselves with unemployment benefits, savings, grants, and a few odd jobs, but now our resources are nearly exhausted. Sadly, he asks me if I would quit school and return to work at the convalescent center. I'm enjoying college. I don't want to quit. I hated my job. Everyday I came home more and more depressed. I'm afraid if I were to return to work there I would go insane. I want a PhD. in psychology so badly I can taste it, but that's 8 years of schooling. I'm 36 years old. If I return to work full-time and become a part-time student, I'll be too old for employment when I graduate. With family obligations, if I work part-time and remain a full-time student, my G.P.A. will probably drop. Without a high G.P.A., I won't be able to get into a graduate school. I feel continuing my education is selfish, but I don't want to abandon it. On the other hand, I realize my family wants me to get a full-time job. Which need is more important—my need to develop as a person or my family's financial need?

Option 2: Opposing Viewpoints

This option focuses on a quandary caused by equally attractive but opposing viewpoints or theories. Your introduction will identify the problem and usually illustrate it with an example or scene. For example, the dilemma "Should American schools with many non-English speaking students be required to offer instruction in those students' native languages?" might be introduced with a description of a child brought to tears by a teacher insensitive to the needs of a non-native speaker, or a description of a child triumphantly translating an American newspaper story for her newly immigrated parents. The main body of your essay will be divided into two parts. The first part will explain one point of view or theory on this issue (perhaps the view that children forced to adapt completely to a new language will be both impeded in their educational growth and increasingly alienated from their family and cultural roots). The second part will explain an opposing point of view or theory (in this case the view that children who are unable to speak the language of the dominant culture will be handicapped throughout their schooling and therefore unable to be truly assimilated into American life). Your conclusion will point out in summary form just what the writer considers contradictory and troubling and will show the importance and significance of the quandary. An especially effective conclusion is the kind that points out the larger implications of a problem by relating it to a broader context of issues.

The Peter Elbow article on 'Contraries in the Teaching Process'' (pp. 406–419) has a lengthy introduction that follows this pattern very closely. The introduction sets up the dilemma of teachers having to choose between being supportive of students (rewarding effort with good grades) and being responsible for excellence in his or her discipline (giving low grades to maintain standards). Elbow describes both sides of this dilemma as a way of showing how complex the problem is. In the second part of his essay, he goes on to offer his own tentative solution. Unlike Elbow, you are not required to offer a solution to your dilemma; but, like Elbow, you need to show the complexity of your problem by spelling out both sides of the dilemma.

An illustration of this option—an opposing viewpoints essay—is the following student essay which poses two different viewpoints on how to discipline a child. (For another example, see the essay "A Cruel Dilemma?" pp. 13–14.)

Spanking—The Cure, or the Curse?

The supermarket is crowded and noisy, with throngs of people carefully maneuvering their carts around each other and through the aisles. A shopper politely avoids bumping another as she snatches wares from the shelf to put in her half-filled cart. An old, white-haired woman carefully inspects two cans, comparing them for the best buy. A young mother pulls her three-year-old son from a candy display; he has had enough candy for today. Then the boy shatters the murmuring calm of the store with a piercing scream, dropping to the floor and pounding his fists on his mother's arm in a temper tantrum. A few shoppers turn to see what the problem is, but the old woman just shakes her head slightly and continues inspecting her cans. The other shoppers return to their shopping; the young mother is left to her own devices for dealing with her unruly son. She feels her face becoming hot and flushed with embarrassment. She is not sure what she should do to control him.

If she were to ask the old woman for advice, the woman could tell her about how mothers handled these problems in the old days. Her three boys are grown now; they have families of their own. But she clearly remembers focusing her attention on an offending child, raising him to his feet, and delivering a spanking that would change the child's whole reason for crying. She never needed to get mad at her children, and she didn't have to spank them often. Her children learned quickly that their mom meant no when she said it, and that she would meet any challenge to her authority that they offered with an appropriate, and often painful, disciplinary measure. She remembers the embarrassment that she had felt because her children cried so loudly when she punished them in a public place. But the onlookers' faces had shown tacit approval of the firm grasp she took on the short hairs on the back of the child's neck as she had marched him to the car; both of them remained there until the child stopped crying. It would be a season before the child considered crying in the market again.

But if the young mother could ask her college child psychology professor, he would tell her to simply ignore the tantrum. She remembers how the owlish old man had lectured on the necessity of not "reinforcing" the child's behavior. The professor told the class that a temper tantrum was a child's way of demanding attention, and giving attention of any sort was a sure way of causing the child to have more frequent and severe outbursts. He had also given experimental evidence that a child who was spanked would be more likely to react with violence as an adult to an adverse situation, and a child who was dealt with in a non-violent manner would be more likely to resolve an adverse situation in adulthood in a peaceful manner. He had dismissed the traditional view of discipline, saying that the same man who wrote "spare the rod, spoil the child" had also written more violent prose, such as "beat your child with a rod, he will not die, and you will deliver his soul from Sheol". He had labeled the author, King Solomon, as a potential child abuser. The young woman is afraid of child abuse, yet she feels her anger rising each time the child screams.

The young mother hesitates; she knows that her own mother would have spanked her if she had acted like her son is acting. But she also knows that she would find no approval in the faces of the shoppers around her if she spanked her child. To her it seems that the wisdom of the past generations is in direct conflict with the knowledge of modern science, and she is caught in the middle. The need to do *something* and reluctance to cause her son pain are crushing in on her indecision. She decides not to give in to her son's demand for candy, but she can't stand the thought of his screaming in public. She picks up her wildly fighting son, and carries him to the car. The immediate situation has put her dilemma second in her mind. She will not let the child make a scene.

Option 3: A Mini-Research Essay

For this option you will need to use the library to find two articles that take opposing positions on the same issue. In the body of your essay you will summarize each of the articles in turn. (See the explanations for Microtheme 3 in Chapter 6, p. 140–145, for instruction on how to write a summary of an article as a paragraph for a research paper.) Suggested quandaries include these: What causes inflation? Does extrasensory perception really exist? Does watching violent TV shows lead to violent behavior? Should high school English classes teach grammar? Of course there are hundreds more. In each case your goal is to find two articles that argue opposing positions on the issue.

An alternative project would be to combine the use of an article summary with the use of other kinds of detail. For example, you could summarize Caroline Bird's "The Dumbest Investment You Can Make" (pp. 385–392) as one side of a dilemma. Then for the other side you could seek statistical data in the library that counters Bird's argument, or you could create your own argument.

The following student essay is a brief research paper exploring the dilemma—"Is a person's intelligence level primarily a result of his or her genetic structure or of the environment?"

Intelligence: Inherited or Learned?

Are some people born with more intelligence than others? My classmate Ann Jones believes they are. After studying for an accounting exam for eight hours, Ann felt confident that she was ready to "ace the test"; however, she was mistaken and got a low "C." The *coup de grace* that broke her spirit, however, was the person sitting next to her who sleeps everyday during class and yet did much better than Ann on the exam. He was simply born smarter, she believes. However, try to convince my other classmate Ken Goldman of this theory. When Ken was eight years old, he was given the Stanford-Binet Intelligence test. Although he doesn't recall taking the test, he will never forget the results. The results based on an interpretation of the test classified Ken as a borderline case of mild mental retardation. The ironic point of this example is self-evident as one looks at Ken's past high school record and current college board scores, which indicate Ken is near the top of his class. Ken believes that his hard work and good schooling have increased his intelligence level. He refuses to believe anyone is just born smart or dumb. These are two contradictory points of view about intelligence that have psychologists debating among themselves: Is intelligence inherited so that people's IQ's are determined by their genes, or is intelligence developed through environmental influences so that people's childhood environments mostly determine their IQ's? This essay reports on two contradictory answers to this question provided by Arthur Jensen, a supporter of the genetic position, and Arthur Whimbey, a supporter of the environmental position.

Arthur Jensen, Professor of Educational Psychology at the University of California, argues that "Genetic factors are much more important than environmental influences in accounting for individual IQ's" (Jensen, 235). Jensen bases his hypothesis on studies conducted on white North American and European populations. Jensen's strongest support comes from studies correlating IQ's of persons with varying degrees of genetic relationships to each other. For example, when identical twins, who develop from the same maternal egg and thus have identical genetic make-ups, are raised apart in different environments, these twins have a difference of only six or seven IQ points between them. In contrast, fraternal twins and siblings, raised together in the same environment, differ in scores of approximately twelve points. Jensen also defends his idea with studies involving experimental rats. Scientists can create strains of "bright" rats and "dull" rats such that "bright" rat offspring will learn to go through a maze much faster than their "dull" cousins, indicating that rat intelligence is genetic. These studies and others lead Jensen to conclude that 80 percent of the variance in IQ's in the general population is attributable to genetic differences and only 20 percent to environmental factors.

In sharp contrast to Jensen, many other psychologists believe that the environment is crucial in shaping a child's intelligence. They believe that in order to do well on IQ tests, one must possess a learned ability to form relationships with abstract and verbal concepts. These "thinking skills" are not innate talents, but can be taught in the home or in the classroom. Arthur Whimbey, a prominent educational psychologist, explains that children with low IQ scores have a deficiency in their ability to solve complex problems (Whimbey, 239). Whimbey traces poor thinking abilities to three causes: (1) inadequate attention to the details of problems to be solved; (2) inadequate utilization of prior knowledge that would help in solving the problem, and (3) absence of sequential, step-by-step analysis of the relationships among the ideas involved. With proper parent-child verbal communication, these problems can be overcome. Whimbey cites Rick Heber, director of the Milwaukee Project, as saying "Low IQ mothers create a distinct verbal-social environment that appears to be responsible for the perpetuation of low intelligence" (Whimbey, 241). These deficiencies in problem-solving, brought about by the child's environment, can be taught in compensatory programs such as Bloom and Broder's cognitive therapy. Whimbey believes that academic thinking skills of older students can be improved by this program which (1) demonstrates to the student the mental processes of analytical thinking, (2) requires extensive response from the student (orally) during problem solving, and (3) provides feedback and correction of the student's thinking. According to Whimbey, such therapy has been proven to increase student's competency in figural and verbal reasoning, reading comprehension, analytical thinking, and sequential deduction. Again he cites Rick Heber's compensatory education program where the IQ's of some children were raised by as much as thirty points. These studies strongly suggest that an individual's intelligence is directly influenced by the environment.

As we have seen, Jensen states that intelligence is inherited while Whimbey concludes that intelligence is shaped by environmental influences. Both psychologists back their arguments with research studies, and both seem to make strong cases for their positions. Unfortunately, neither writer attacks the studies cited by the other so that it is difficult for a non-psychologist to determine which studies have the most scientific merit. I am currently unable to take sides on this issue. However, it is very easy to see that this controversy is significant because the consequences of one side's being proven correct are enormous. Should Arthur Jensen's hypothesis prove correct, many social problems within our country may be intensified. For example, such findings could lead to increased racial prejudice since on the whole blacks score lower on IQ tests than whites, who in turn score lower than orientals. Couldn't Jensen's position lead to an increase in racism, maybe into a return to segregation of our educational system? Furthermore, Jensen's position could demoralize teachers, who would no longer keep trying to teach difficult concepts to certain students, saying to themselves, "Oh, well, they are just born dumb." On the other hand, if Whimbey's hypothesis is correct, our educational system will have to be changed. Presently, our educational system is geared for average and high IQ students but what about the low IQ student? Whimbey's position asserts that we could help these students if we changed their early childhood environment. We should start using cognitive therapy techniques in day care centers and then kindergarten. We should change our whole school system from the first grade through college to place greater emphasis on systematic problem-solving skills. If in fact Whimbey is correct, and the use of cognitive therapy works for all types of IQ's in children, then our society will be deeply enriched by more intelligent and productive individuals.

Works Cited

JENSEN, ARTHUR. "The Heritability of Intelligence." Reprinted in *Taking Sides: Clashing Views on Controversial Psychological Issues.* ed. J. Rubinstein and B. Slife. Guilford, Conn. Dushkin, 1980. 232, 234–238.

WHIMBEY, ARTHUR. "Something Better than Binet." Reprinted in *Taking Sides: Clashing Views on Controversial Psychological Issues,* ed. J. Rubinstein and B. Slife. Guilford, Conn. Dushkin, 1980. 233, 239–244.

ASSIGNMENT 5: FINDINGS-DISCUSSION ESSAYS

This task asks you to do analytical thinking in a sequence of two steps. The structure of your thinking and writing for this task is based on a conventional division in scientific writing between the Findings and Discussion sections of experimental reports. Let's begin our explanation of this task with an example. Suppose you were given the following assignment:

Observe the statistical table (on the following page) depicting death rates and causes of death from 1910 to 1966 in the United States. Then write a 350–450 word essay that answers this question: "Do data on death rates from selected diseases in the twentieth century show any meaningful patterns?" In the "Findings" section of your essay report whatever meaningful patterns you find in these data. Then, in the "Discussion" section speculate on the causes of these patterns, noting, if you wish, any issues or problems that you think these patterns give rise to.

The two example essays on p. 238 would both be good responses to this assignment. Please read them prior to continuing.

TABLE 8-1. Death Rates Per 100,000 in the United States, 1910–1966

Year	All causes	Cardio-vascular diseases	Malignant neoplasms	Certain diseases of early infancy	Influenza and pneumonia	Diabetes	Bronchitis and emphysema	Accidents	All Other
1910	1,468	287	76.2	73.0	155.9	15.3	—	84.2	776
1920	1,299	283	83.4	69.2	207.3	16.1	—	70.0	570
1930	1,132	328	97.4	49.6	102.5	19.1	—	79.8	456
1935	1,095	353	108.2	40.2	104.2	22.3	—	77.8	388
1940	1,076	407	120.3	39.2	70.3	26.6	—	73.2	340
1942	1,032	409	122.0	41.4	55.7	25.4	—	71.3	309
1943	1,087	439	124.3	41.3	67.1	27.1	—	73.4	315
1945	1,058	444	134.0	38.3	51.6	26.5	—	72.1	292
1948	989	437	134.9	42.1	38.7	26.4	—	66.9	243
1949	971	485	138.8	43.2	30.0	16.9	2.8	60.6	194
1950	964	494	139.8	40.5	31.3	16.2	2.8	60.6	178
1951	967	499	140.6	41.2	31.4	16.3	3.0	62.5	173
1952	961	499	143.4	40.9	29.7	16.4	3.1	61.8	168
1953	959	503	144.8	40.1	33.0	16.3	3.6	60.1	158
1954	919	485	145.6	39.4	25.4	15.6	3.6	55.9	149
1955	930	496	146.5	39.0	27.1	15.5	4.1	56.9	145
1956	935	501	147.8	38.6	28.2	15.7	4.6	56.7	142
1957	959	515	148.6	39.1	35.8	16.0	5.5	55.9	143
1958	951	516	146.8	39.8	33.1	15.9	6.2	52.3	141
1959	939	509	147.3	38.5	31.2	15.9	6.6	52.2	138
1960	955	515	149.2	37.4	37.3	16.7	7.6	52.3	139
1961	930	505	149.4	35.9	30.1	16.4	7.8	50.4	134
1962	945	515	149.9	34.5	32.3	16.8	9.2	52.3	135
1963	961	521	151.3	33.2	37.5	17.2	10.9	53.4	137
1964	940	509	151.3	31.5	31.1	16.9	11.1	54.3	135
1965	943	511	153.5	28.6	31.9	17.1	12.6	55.7	133
1966	954	520	154.8	26.1	32.8	18.1	—	57.3	146

Example 1

Findings

The table depicting death rates for various diseases between 1910 and 1966 reveals a significant pattern: Although the overall death rate has declined by more than 35 percent, the death rates for some diseases have declined more rapidly than this percentage while the death rates for other diseases have increased. A rapid decline occurs in the death rates for influenza and pneumonia, which dropped from 207.3 deaths per 100,000 population in 1920 to a low of 25.4 deaths per 100,000 in 1954—a decrease of 88 percent. A similar decrease occurs in the death rates from various childhood diseases (73 deaths per 100,000 in 1910 declining to 26.1 per 100,000 in 1966—a decrease of almost 75 percent).

On the other hand, death rates from heart and lung disease and from cancer have risen sharply. Death rates due to cardiovascular disease, for instance, have almost doubled, from 287 per 100,000 in 1910 to 520 per 100,000 in 1966. Similarly, deaths from bronchitis and emphysema, too low to be reported from 1910 to 1949, have now climbed steadily to 12.6 deaths per 100,000. And most significantly, cancer deaths have also risen steadily from 76.2 deaths per 100,000 in 1910 to 154.8 deaths per 100.000 in 1966—a 100 percent increase.

Discussion

These findings can be explained by medical and social history in the twentieth century. Thanks to the discovery of antibiotics and vaccines, death rates from such childhood killers as smallpox, diptheria, and whooping cough have declined rapidly. Similarly, better hospital care, better drugs, and increased knowledge of contagion have created the remarkable drop in death rates from flu and pneumonia. But these declines have been offset by frightening increases in death rates from heart and lung disease and cancer. To some extent these increases have simple statistical explanations: People who formerly might have died of small pox are now living long enough to die of heart attacks or cancer. But some of these increases must also result from our way of life—too much cholesterol and tobacco, too much stress, too much pollution, and too little exercise. Although the wonder drugs have wiped out some old diseases, we moderns are now creating new ways to die.

Example 2

Findings

The death rate tables show several predictable patterns as well as one puzzling one. The predictable patterns are these: The overall death rate has declined approximately 35 percent, but the death rates for some diseases have declined at a more rapid rate while the death rates for other diseases have increased. For example, death rates from influenza and pneumonia have declined approximately 79 percent from 1910 to 1966 while death rates from childhood diseases declined about 75 percent during the same period. On the other hand, death rates from heart disease and cancer have increased almost 100 percent. Even more dramatic percentage increases occurred with death rates from bronchitis and emphysema, which were too low to be reported until 1949, yet reached 12.6 deaths per 100,000 in 1965. (This is still a low absolute figure, however, compared to cancer's 154.8 deaths per 100,000 and heart disease's 520 deaths per 100,000.)

The puzzling pattern involves diabetes, the only disease that doesn't follow a primarily rising or falling curve. Its curve seems to be cyclical. The death rates from diabetes in 1910 and 1955 were nearly identical (15.3 and 15.6 deaths per 100,000), yet from 1935 to 1948 the death rate exceeded 22 deaths per 100,000 with a peak of 27.1 in 1943, after which it began declining rapidly. Since 1955, however, the death rate has again been increasing, standing at 18.1 in 1966 on an apparently rising curve.

Discussion

The predictable patterns are explained by advances in medicine coupled with changes in our life styles. Diseases cured by wonder drugs or better hospital care, such as many childhood diseases, flu, and pneumonia, have decreased dramatically. Since everyone must die, a decline in death rates from one cause must be balanced by an increase in death rates from another cause, and so the increases show in heart and lung disease and in cancer are at least partially explainable by laws of statistics. But death rates from these diseases also reflect a modern way of life where too much stress, unhealthy diets, industrial pollution, and lack of exercise all contribute to increased deaths from these new killers.

The puzzling pattern is the apparently cyclical nature of diabetes. Why was there a sudden increase in diabetes' deaths in the 1940s followed by a decline until 1955? Why has the rate of death from diabetes increased after 1955? Further research is needed to explain this phenomenon.

The difference between the Findings section and the Discussion section of these essays suggests two different modes of thinking—what we can call an "observing" mode, in which you report important data, and an "analyzing" mode, in which you comment on its meaning. What we want to do now is show you that the apparently simple skill of observing and reporting data (the Findings section) is much more complex than it at first seems. By distinguishing between the observing and the analyzing modes, we want you to think again about what happens when people write, that is, what happens when people turn mere information into meaning.

What we want to show you especially is that in the observing mode your mind does not act passively like a camera or tape recorder that merely collects data. Instead it works actively, selecting and shaping data to form a pattern. If different people see different patterns in identical data, then their "findings" will be different.

You should note first how the Findings sections of the two sample essays differ from the table itself. Whereas the table contains 270 individual pieces of data, the Findings section of each essay selects only a few numbers for discussion—numbers chosen not at random but chosen to illustrate a pattern that the writer finds in the data. Moreover, the writers have gone beyond the listed data to do their own calculation of percentage increases and decreases in death rates for certain diseases and in some cases have derived different figures. (For example, why does the first writer report an 88 percent decrease in the death rate from flu while the second writer reports a 79 percent decrease?)

Our point here is that the Findings section of these essays is not a simple reporting of facts but a reporting of patterns in the facts. Data remain meaningless—just a chaos of random information—until the mind imposes a pattern upon them. The Findings section has the purpose of reporting the patterns, thus converting formless data into forms with meaning. The Discussion section then goes on to explore questions about this pattern, questions concerning cause and effect, purpose, and significance.

The Purpose of Separating the Observing Mode from the Analyzing Mode

Our separation of the two modes into a Findings Section (observing mode) and a Discussion Section (analyzing mode) is based on two key sections of a conventional scientific report, which often has a Findings section distinct from a Discussion section. Outside of scientific writing it is far more common to blend the two modes. Certainly no essay in the arts or humanities would have separate sections labeled "Findings" and "Discussion," even though most essays would have some passages written in an observing mode and other passages written in an analyzing mode. Nevertheless, the distinction that scientists make between findings and discussion is an important distinction for problem-solvers in all disciplines to consider. By habitually going through an observing stage of thinking prior to an analyzing stage of thinking, you can train yourself to approach problems systematically. And since "observing" means not to soak up information like a sponge, but rather to seek patterns in the information, concentrating on an observing mode of thinking trains persons to "see" in new ways.

Our point is that the apparently simple act of observing is a skill students need to learn. Before one can learn to think analytically in, say, chemistry or music or sociology or literature, one needs to "see" in those disciplines. For example, an archeologist will see evidence of an ancient toolmaking culture where we might see only pieces of bone in a pile of rocks. A football coach will see a missed block in an end-around play, where an untrained observer might see only someone getting tackled for a two yard loss. A literary critic will see imagery patterns suggesting a poet's paradoxical attraction for death where her sociologist friend might see only flowery language. On the other hand, the sociologist will see white middle class attitudes toward personal space where the literary critic might see only a bunch of honkies at a cocktail party. In all these cases, the trained observer will be detecting meaningful patterns in what for others is formless data. When you take introductory college courses, therefore, you will be learning not only new knowledge and new ways of thinking and asking questions, but also new ways of "seeing." The "Findings" section you are asked to write for this assignment will help you appreciate how "seeing" is an important step, often neglected, in any complex thinking task.

Before moving to the writing assignments, let's illustrate the complexity of "seeing" by looking one more time at the death rate table and the earlier example essays. We can probably agree that the death rate table is a relatively simple piece of information, far simpler, say, than Shakespeare's *Hamlet* or a heart X-ray or statistical tables from the electron bombardment of metals in surface physics. And yet even here different observers will see different patterns in the data. The writers of example essays 1 and 2, for example, both agree on the rising pattern for cancer and on the declining pattern for infectious diseases. On the other hand, neither writer apparently finds a meaningful pattern in death rates from accidents, and only writer 2 describes the cyclical pattern of death rates from diabetes. (Did writer 1 not notice it or not find it significant?) Both writers assume that the absence of data about deaths from lung diseases prior to 1949 indicate that these rates were "too low to be reported," even though the table doesn't make this assertion. (Might it be possible that these data were lost or simply not reported, thus invalidating all their comments about these diseases?) However, despite slight differences in their perceptions, writers 1 and 2 "see" about the same things in the death rate table. But what about the following writer?

The death rate table shows that the rise in death rates from cancer isn't nearly as alarming as the media would have us believe. In 1935, 9.8 percent of all recorded deaths were due to cancer. In 1968, 16 percent of all deaths were due to cancer, an increase of only 6.2 percent, but even this figure is misleading because the overall death rate has dropped 35 percent since 1910. If we adjust death rate figures the way economists adjust real income for inflation, the rise in death rates from cancer is quite modest.

Writer 3 has a quite different perception of the patterns in the table than do writers 1 and 2, and yet all of writer 3's assertions can be supported by information in the table.

This problem with perception shows why scientists usually differentiate between "findings" and "discussion" in a scientific report. Scientists by nature move very slowly and cautiously from raw data to generalizations about the data. Accordingly, the results of a scientific experiment are typically reported at three levels of abstraction: raw data, usually displayed in graphs, tables, transcripts of interviews, photographs; a report of the meaningful patterns the scientist finds in the data (the prose portion of the Findings section); and an analysis of the meaning of those patterns (the Discussion section). Scientists generally keep these three levels of abstraction in separate compartments because controversy can arise at each level. For example, controversy will arise at the level of raw data if scientists try to replicate an earlier experiment and get significantly different results. The new data, if considerably different from previous findings, will cast doubt upon the entire earlier report. Disagreement can also occur at the level of the prose presentation in the Findings section. In this case scientists may agree that the raw data are accurate but disagree about the patterns found in the data. Finally, if scientists reach agreement on both the raw data and the patterns within the data, they might disagree on the significance of the patterns as explored in the Discussion section. It is, in fact, at the discussion level that scientists often carry on their most heated debates.

The prose portion of the Findings section—what we have been calling the observing mode of writing—is thus a crucial intermediate step between the raw data and the analytical discussion of the significance of the data. The necessity of writing a Findings section forces the writer to observe the data carefully and to seek to discover meaningful patterns within it. It also enables the writer to share his perception of the patterns in the data with the reader prior to discussing their meaning. In this way the Findings section ensures that writer and reader "see" the same thing. Only then can fruitful discussion continue.

Now it is your turn to practice "seeing" before you speculate. The following essay assignments vary in complexity. However, unless your instructor specifies a greater length, try to keep your essay between 400 and 600 words.

Option 1

Study Table 8-2—"Employed Persons by Sex, Race, and Occupation: 1972 and 1981,"—and then write an essay on either the topic

TABLE 8-2. Employed Persons, by Sex, Race, and Occupation: 1972 and 1981 [Civilians 16 years old and over. "N.e.c." means not elsewhere classified]

Occupation	1972 Total employed (1,000)	1972 Percent Female	1972 Percent Black and other	1981 Total employed (1,000)	1981 Percent Female	1981 Percent Black and other
Total	**82,153**	**38.0**	**10.6**	**100,397**	**42.8**	**11.6**
Professional, technical, and kindred workers	**11,538**	**39.3**	**7.2**	**16,420**	**44.6**	**9.9**
Accountants	720	21.7	4.3	1,126	38.5	9.9
Computer specialists	276	16.8	5.5	627	27.1	9.4
Engineers	1,111	.8	3.4	1,537	4.4	7.3
Civil	156	.6	5.2	190	1.6	7.9
Electrical and electronic	289	.7	5.2	380	3.9	7.6
Industrial	171	2.4	2.4	237	11.4	7.6
Mechanical	192	—	3.1	252	2.8	5.6
Lawyers and judges	322	3.8	1.9	581	14.1	4.6
Librarians, archivists, and curators	158	81.6	7.0	192	82.8	5.7
Life and physical scientists	232	10.0	7.8	311	21.9	10.6
Chemists	120	10.1	8.4	138	21.7	15.2
Personnel and labor relations workers	312	31.0	9.0	441	49.9	10.9
Physicians, dentists, and related practitioners	630	9.3	6.3	828	14.4	11.0
Dentists	108	1.9	5.6	130	4.6	6.2
Pharmacists	127	12.7	3.2	152	25.7	9.2
Physicians, medical and osteopathic	332	10.1	8.2	454	13.7	14.5
Registered nurses, dietitians, and therapists	956	92.6	8.1	1,654	92.6	12.7
Registered nurses	807	97.6	8.2	1,339	96.8	12.3
Therapists	117	59.1	4.3	251	70.5	12.0
Health technologists and technicians	319	69.5	11.1	643	72.3	14.9
Religious workers	293	11.0	10.6	337	11.9	7.4

TABLE 8-2 (*Continued*)

Occupation	1972			1981		
		Percent			Percent	
	Total employed (1,000)	Female	Black and other	Total employed (1,000)	Female	Black and other
Social scientists	143	21.3	5.7	314	33.8	8.0
Social and recreation workers	356	55.1	17.5	511	62.4	20.2
Teachers, college and university	464	28.0	7.2	585	35.2	9.2
Teachers, except college and university	2,852	70.0	9.2	3,197	70.6	10.1
Elementary	1,256	85.1	10.0	1,412	83.6	11.4
Pre-kindergarden and kindergarden	186	96.8	13.3	245	98.4	15.5
Secondary	1,118	49.6	8.3	1,231	51.3	8.0
Engineering and science technicians	835	9.1	5.2	1,141	18.8	9.9
Drafters	288	6.3	5.2	343	19.2	8.7
Electrical and electronic engineering technicians	166	5.5	6.1	275	11.3	9.1
Technicians, except health, engineering, and science	153	11.2	2.6	219	22.4	5.0
Vocational and educational counselors	134	50.0	11.9	188	53.7	18.1
Writers, artists, and entertainers	903	31.7	4.8	1,388	39.8	6.3
Athletes and kindred workers	79	30.8	6.4	135	43.0	7.4
Editors and reporters	164	41.4	4.3	205	50.2	4.9
Research workers, not specified	87	27.9	7.0	193	38.9	11.4
Managers and administrators, except farm	**8,081**	**17.6**	**4.0**	**11,540**	**27.5**	**5.8**
Bank officers and financial managers	430	19.0	2.6	696	37.5	5.5
Buyers, wholesale and retail trade	162	32.9	4.3	195	43.6	6.7
Health administrators	119	46.6	7.6	219	49.8	6.8
Managers and superintendents, building	137	42.6	8.8	161	50.9	9.3
Office managers, n.e.c.	317	41.9	1.0	504	70.6	4.0

Officials and administrators, public administration, n.e.c.	311	20.4	9.1	476	29.0	10.3
Purchasing agents and buyers, n.e.c.	366	21.2	3.6	264	30.3	6.1
Restaurant, cafeteria, and bar managers	498	32.4	8.9	727	40.3	9.9
Sales managers	574	15.7	1.6	720	26.5	4.6
School administrators	304	26.0	8.2	430	36.3	9.5
Sales workers	**5,383**	**41.6**	**3.6**	**6,425**	**45.4**	**5.4**
Hucksters and peddlers	231	73.0	6.1	170	79.4	7.6
Insurance agents, brokers, and underwriters	443	11.6	3.4	595	23.9	6.2
Real estate agents and brokers	352	36.7	2.6	562	49.8	3.0
Stock and bond sales agents	102	9.9	2.0	159	17.0	3.1
Sales representatives, manufacturing industries	401	6.8	1.5	416	20.0	4.1
Sales representatives, wholesale trade	700	4.7	1.4	971	11.9	2.9
Sales clerks, retail trade	2,359	68.9	5.0	2,431	71.2	7.7
Salesworkers, except clerks, retail trade	432	13.0	2.6	525	19.6	3.6
Salesworkers, services and construction	137	29.4	2.2	241	43.2	5.0
Clerical and kindred workers	**14,329**	**75.6**	**8.7**	**18,564**	**80.5**	**11.6**
Bank tellers	290	87.5	4.9	569	93.5	7.6
Billing clerks	149	84.6	6.7	153	88.2	10.5
Bookkeepers	1,592	87.9	3.6	1,961	91.1	6.3
Cashiers	998	86.6	8.0	1,660	86.2	11.8
Clerical supervisors, n.e.c.	200	57.8	10.1	250	70.8	10.8
Counter clerks, except food	331	73.9	6.4	360	76.4	10.3
Estimators and investigators, n.e.c.	350	43.4	4.9	540	54.6	10.6
File clerks	274	84.9	18.0	315	83.8	22.9
Insurance adjusters, examiners, and investigators	109	34.3	6.5	191	58.1	9.9
Mail carriers, post office	271	6.7	14.1	242	15.7	13.6
Office machine operators	679	71.4	13.1	966	73.6	17.5
Computer and peripherial equipment operators	199	37.8	10.2	564	63.8	15.8
Key punch operators	284	89.8	15.5	248	93.5	19.4
Postal clerks	282	26.7	19.6	269	37.9	26.4
Receptionists	439	97.0	7.7	675	97.3	8.6
Secretaries	2,964	99.1	5.2	3,917	99.1	7.2

TABLE 8-2. (*Continued*)

Occupation	1972			1981		
	Total employed (1,000)	Percent Female	Percent Black and other	Total employed (1,000)	Percent Female	Percent Black and other
Shipping and receiving clerks	453	14.9	13.7	525	22.5	14.7
Statistical clerks	301	70.9	8.4	370	80.3	15.1
Stenographers	125	90.4	8.0	74	85.1	13.5
Stock clerks and storekeepers	513	22.9	12.5	528	34.8	13.1
Telephone operators	394	96.7	12.8	308	92.9	17.2
Typists	1,025	96.1	12.0	1,031	96.3	17.8
Craft and kindred workers	**10,867**	**3.6**	**6.9**	**12,662**	**6.3**	**8.5**
Carpenters	1,052	.5	5.9	1,122	1.9	5.8
Other construction craftsworkers	2,261	.6	9.0	2,593	1.9	10.2
Brickmasons and stonemasons	176	—	14.2	152	—	12.5
Electricians	498	.6	3.2	684	1.6	7.9
Excavating, grading, and road machine operators	428	—	4.7	422	.5	12.3
Painters, construction and maintenance	430	1.9	10.0	471	5.7	10.2
Plumbers and pipe fitters	391	—	5.9	472	.4	7.6
Blue-collar worker supervisors, n.e.c.	1,419	6.9	6.0	1,816	11.3	7.6
Machinists and jobsetters	473	.6	6.2	668	4.0	8.5
Metalcraft workers	625	1.9	5.6	626	4.3	7.2
Sheet metal workers and tinsmiths	150	.7	4.7	157	3.2	6.4
Tool and die makers	184	.5	2.2	175	2.3	2.9
Mechanics, automobile	1,040	.5	8.5	1,249	.6	8.7

Mechanics, except automobile	1,746	1.0	5.3	2,159	2.5	8.1
Air conditioning, heating, and refrigeration	175	—	6.3	212	.5	7.5
Aircraft	124	—	3.3	123	3.3	13.0
Heavy equipment	719	.7	5.2	1,007	1.8	7.2
Radio and television	124	.8	6.5	109	3.7	6.4
Printing craftworkers	398	14.9	5.5	402	24.9	8.2
Compositors and typesetters	171	17.1	17.1	174	35.1	8.6
Printing press operators	142	4.9	4.2	166	11.4	7.8
All other craftworkers	1,855	9.4	7.4	2,028	15.3	9.2
Bakers	115	28.9	18.4	135	41.5	13.3
Crane, derrick, and hoist operators	150	1.3	16.0	143	.7	15.4
Electric power line and cable operators	102	—	3.9	117	.9	7.7
Stationary engineers	191	1.1	5.8	182	1.6	8.2
Telephone installers and repairers	312	1.9	4.2	326	9.8	9.2
Operatives, except transport	**10,388**	**38.6**	**13.2**	**10,540**	**39.8**	**16.2**
Assemblers	1,022	46.8	13.2	1,167	52.4	17.1
Checkers, examiners, and inspectors, mfg	688	48.5	8.8	800	53.8	13.8
Cutting operatives, n.e.c.	239	27.7	16.0	276	31.5	15.9
Dressmakers and seamstresses, except factory	133	97.0	9.1	117	97.4	15.4
Garage workers and gas station attendants	504	4.6	8.4	349	5.7	10.9
Laundry and dry cleaning operatives, n.e.c.	166	69.7	28.5	194	66.5	28.4
Meat cutters and butchers, except mfg	202	3.5	7.5	178	8.4	10.7
Mine operatives	144	.7	6.3	270	2.2	5.2
Packers and wrappers, exc. meat and produce	649	61.1	14.7	589	63.2	21.1
Painters, manufactured articles	179	14.6	14.6	166	16.9	13.9
Precision machine operatives	390	10.0	6.9	352	12.8	9.9
Punch and stamping press operatives	157	27.4	10.8	107	31.8	10.3
Sewers and stitchers	942	95.8	13.7	807	96.0	21.6
Textile operatives	426	55.2	15.8	360	61.0	26.7
Welders and frame cutters	558	3.6	10.1	728	4.7	13.2
Machine operatives	1,573	27.0	14.4	1,655	28.5	16.9

TABLE 8-2. (Continued)

Occupation	1972			1981		
	Total employed (1,000)	Percent		Total employed (1,000)	Percent	
		Female	Black and other		Female	Black and other
Transport equipment operatives	**3,223**	**4.2**	**14.8**	**3,476**	**8.9**	**15.5**
Bus drivers	253	34.1	17.1	360	47.2	21.1
Delivery and route workers	895	2.5	10.4	563	8.5	9.4
Forklift and tow motor operatives	304	1.0	22.1	369	5.7	22.0
Taxicab drivers and chauffeurs	167	9.0	24.1	164	9.8	28.7
Truck drivers	1,449	.6	14.4	1,878	2.7	13.9
Laborers, except farm	**4,242**	**6.0**	**20.2**	**4,583**	**11.5**	**16.5**
Construction laborers including carpenters helpers	948	.5	22.4	825	2.2	15.8
Freight and material handlers	765	5.9	22.1	753	9.7	18.5
Gardeners and groundskeepers, except farm	548	2.2	20.0	666	4.7	16.5
Stockhandlers	728	16.9	10.2	992	24.6	12.1
Service workers	**9,584**	**57.0**	**18.5**	**12,391**	**59.2**	**18.4**
Food service workers	3,286	69.8	13.9	4,682	66.2	14.0
Nurses aides, orderlies, practical nurses	1,513	87.0	24.6	1,995	89.2	24.3
Childcare workers	358	95.8	14.0	426	95.5	14.8
Firefighters, police	1,150	5.7	10.4	1,459	10.1	13.8
Domestic cleaners and servants	715	97.2	64.2	468	95.1	51.5

"Progress toward Job Equality for Women" or the topic "Progress Toward Job Equality for Racial Minorities." In the Findings section of your essay report the general trends that you find meaningful. Then, in the Discussion section, analyze the significance of these trends. Are women (racial minorities) making satisfactory progress toward job equality?

Option 2

Observe the three Beetle Bailey comic strips (Figure 8-5) and write an essay on the topic "stereotypes of women." In the Findings section, report the stereotypes of women that you think are contained in the comic strip. In the Discussion section, suggest what the presence of these stereotypes might tell us about contemporary American society.

Our students have found that the Findings section for this task is fairly easy to write but the Discussion section is difficult. A good procedure is to write a Dicussion section with a "problem-alternative solutions" shape or an "expected answer-surprising reversal" shape so that you juxtapose against each other several opposing possible answers to questions about the significance of sexual stereotyping in popular comic strips. Try to say something unexpected and hence surprising in your analysis.

Option 3: For Individuals or Small Groups

A mini-scientific experiment: Where do the bubbles come from?

- *Equipment needed: Several identical glasses; several cans of soft drink (same flavor, same brand) at room temperature; water at room temperature; ice cubes (not crushed ice).*
- *Procedure: You will be pouring liquid into the glasses under varying conditions and observing the amount of bubbles that form. Based on your observations, you will be trying to answer the following "analytic" questions: What are the bubbles? What causes them to form? Observe the amount of bubbles formed in each of the following five cases:*

1. *Pour water into an empty glass (water and glass at room temperature). Note the amount of bubbles, if any.*
2. *Pour soft drink into an empty glass (soft drink and glass at room temperature). Pour the soft drink within 15 seconds after opening the can or bottle. Note the amount of bubbles, if any.*
3. *Pour water (room temperature) into a glass containing three or four ice cubes. Note amount of bubbles, if any.*

FIGURE 8-5 **Women in Beetle Bailey Comic Strips (Source: Copyright © King Features Syndicate, Inc.)**

4. *Pour soft drink (room temperature, just opened as in Step 2) into a glass with three or four ice cubes (fresh ice cubes, not the same ones used for Step 3). Note the amount of bubbles.*

5. *Pour water (room temperature) into glass with three or four fresh ice cubes. Let ice cubes float in water for approximately one minute. Pour out water leaving ice cubes in glass. Pour soft drink (room temperature, just opened as in Step 2 and 4) into glass with these "used" ice cubes. Note the amount of bubbles, if any.*

Create a bar graph showing the amount of bubbles produced under each of the test conditions. (How you measure "amount of bubbles" is one of your problem-solving tasks.) Then, in the Findings section of your essay report the data from your graph that you think reveal a significant pattern. Finally, in the Discussion section create a theory about the formation of bubbles that accounts for your findings. The Discussion section will attempt to answer these questions: "What are the bubbles?" (air released from the ice? carbon dioxide from the soft drink?) and "What causes them to form in different amounts for each varying condition?" If you can't commit yourself to a theory, present some alternative hypotheses.

You get a bonus point if your theory explains why you always get so many bubbles when you make a root beer float (that is, when you pour the soft drink over ice cream instead of ice cubes.)

Option 4

Examine the painting by Drouais (Figure 8-6) and the advertisement from a recent magazine (Figure 8-7). Then write an essay on the topic—"the relationship between a culture's image of childhood and that culture's values." In the Findings section compare and contrast the Drouais painting and the advertisement at the level of physical details only (similarities or differences in clothing, in setting, in posture and facial expressions, in the objects the children are playing with, and so forth). Then in the Discussion section, speculate on what the painting and the advertisement might tell us about the different value systems of eighteenth century gentry in England and twentieth century middle class Americans. That is, if the two cultures imagine the "model child" in different ways, they probably have a different system of beliefs, values, and ideals. Try to analyze what those differences might be. Assume that you don't have any previous knowledge about either the eighteenth or the twentieth centuries. These two "pictures" are your only clues to the respective cultures.

FIGURE 8-6 Francois-Hubert Drouais, "The Comte and Chevalier de Choiseul as Savoyards" (Source: Copyright © The Frick Collection, New York)

FIGURE 8-7   An Advertisement for Levi's Jeans (Courtesy of Levi Strauss & Co.)

Option 5: An Article Review

Read an essay assigned by your instructor, either one of the essays printed in this text or another essay that your instructor chooses. In the Findings section summarize the article without including any of your own commentary (reread our discussion of summary writing in Chapter 6, pp. 140–145). Then, in the Discussion section analyze or evaluate the article. To stimulate analytic thinking, create some "analysis questions" such as the following: "What are the strengths and weaknesses of the author's argument?" "What are the implications of the author's argument?" "How do the author's ideas compare to X's ideas?" "How can I believe and doubt the writer's argument." "Do the author's ideas make sense in terms of my own personal experience." "Why is this article important?" This assignment models one of the most popular college writing assignments in many disciplines: the article review. Your job is first to summarize the article and then to evaluate it.

Issue-Defense Essays

Part III—Issue-Defense Essays—contains a journal sequence and four chapters. The journal sequence, which you should begin immediately, will help you discover and explore ideas for your issue-defense essays. You should do the first section of Journal Sequence 3 as you read Chapters 9, 10, and 11 and the second section when you begin writing your formal essays.

Chapter 9—"Issue-Defense Essays: Developing an Argument"—provides strategies for turning an initial idea into an effective argument. It will help you understand how to take a position on an issue and then to create a reasoned essay supporting and defending that position. Chapter 10—"Some Common Strategies of Argumentation"—will examine various kinds of claims that writers can make and suggest methods for supporting those claims. Chapter 11— "Issue-Defense Essays: Evaluating an Argument"—will help you analyze a finished essay by determining the strengths and weaknesses of its argument. Finally, Chapter 12 sets forth the formal essay assignments for Part III. It presents three basic assignment types, each focusing on a different argumentative strategy: a "supporting reasons" strategy, in which you develop arguments supporting your own position; an "opposition-refutation" strategy, in which you summarize your opponent's argument and then show its weaknesses; and a

"Rogerian strategy," in which you attempt to reach a non-threatening compromise between your original position and your opponent's. The final assignment lets you combine any of these strategies to create a longer, more complex issue-defense essay.

However, before we begin, we need to discuss briefly what we mean by an issue-defense essay and explain our basic strategy for helping you learn to write one.

WHAT IS AN ISSUE-DEFENSE ESSAY?

Our term "issue-defense" essay is similar to what other textbooks might call persuasive or argumentative writing. We have chosen the term "issue-defense" to highlight the key term *issue* because issues are the source of this kind of writing. By *issue* we mean a dispute or controversy in which participants must defend their points of view against opposing points of view. To put it another way, an issue is any question or problem that invites at least two plausible but opposing answers. An issue-defense essay, then, is really a sub-category of the problem-solution essay. However, it differs from the assignments in the previous chapter in that now you assume your readers will not necessarily agree with your solution. Instead of accepting your solution as new and useful information, your reader regards it as one of many possible solutions to a controversial issue. Thus the main body of an issue-defense essay is not an explanation of your solution so much as a defense of the adequacy and reasonableness of your solution.

By way of illustrating the difference between an issue-question and a more general information-question, let's look at the problem posed by Tim Andryk in his research on bighorn sheep (pp. 420–427): Is there a better way to live-capture bighorn sheep than using a dart gun with tranquilizers?" By posing the question this way, the writer assumes that the purpose of his essay will be informational—the writer will provide new knowledge, in this case a new way to live-capture bighorn sheep (using a net-gun). But suppose someone becomes angry that university researchers are out in the mountains capturing bighorn sheep at all. Leave nature alone, this person says. Such an attitude will raise not an information-question but an issue-question: "Should universities fund research on mountain sheep?" One person argues "no," another "yes," still another "maybe, under certain conditions." Thus whenever the same question can be answered different ways, we have a potential issue-question. Whenever a person writes an essay to defend one of several possible answers and imagines an audience that at least partially disagrees with that answer, he or she writes an issue-defense essay.

For Class Discussion

A good way to discover issues is to use the following trigger question: "When people discuss X, what do they disagree about?" For example, when people discuss "writing courses," what do they disagree about? Here are some possible responses: Should teachers require journals? Is a guided journal more effective than a freestyle journal? Does teaching question-asking improve a student's writing? What is the best sequence of assignments for a writing course? Should composition courses be pass/fail? All these (and there are dozens more) are issue-questions about the teaching of writing.

Try using the trigger question "When people discuss X, what do they disagree about?" to think of issues for the following topics. Try asking two or three issue-questions for each topic.

1. childraising
2. the economy
3. flowers
4. the college curriculum
5. computers
6. sports
7. feminism
8. the environment
9. old people
10. any topic of your choice

RESPONDING TO ISSUE-QUESTIONS: THE POWER OF "BECAUSE"

Chances are when you were a child the word *because* contained magical explanatory "powers."

Angela:	I don't want to watch TV anymore.
Jefferson:	Why?
Angela:	Because.
Jefferson:	Because why?
Angela:	Just Because.

Somehow *because* seemed decisive. It persuaded people to accept your view of the world; it asserted your own identity and caused others to change their minds. Later, as you got older, you discovered that *because* only introduced your arguments and that it was the reasons following *because* that made the difference. Still, the word *because* introduced you to the powers potentially residing in the adult world of logic.

For each of your essays in Part III we will ask you to summarize the structure of your argument in a writer's thesis statement containing several "because" clauses:

Mr. Rogers is a poor teacher because his courses are disorganized and because he shows little concern for students.

The Yankees will win the pennant because they have a shrewd manager and because they have the best pitching staff in baseball.

Although restaurant owners pay waitresses less than the minimum wage by arguing that tips will make up the difference, waitresses should be paid the minimum wage because tips are now fully taxable and because waitresses do a lot of work behind the scenes which does not result in extra tip income.

These sentences, taken from students' planning notes are writers' theses statements, which served as guides during the drafting of the essay. (For the distinction between "writers' thesis statements" and "readers' thesis statements," see Chapter 4, pp. 101–106.)

Of course all arguments do not need to contain the word *because*. Our language is rich in other ways of stating *because* relationships.

Mr. Rogers' courses are disorganized. As a result, he is an ineffective teacher.

Mr. Rogers' courses are disorganized; therefore, he is an ineffective teacher.

Being unable or unwilling to organize his courses, Mr. Rogers is an ineffective teacher.

Mr. Rogers' disorganized courses show that he is an ineffective teacher.

Even though arguments can be stated in various ways, inexperienced writers can often improve the focus of their issue-defense essays by summarizing the structure of their arguments in a single sentence with *because* clauses. The remaining chapters in this section will show you why.

For Class Discussion

As a class or in small groups, try creating some possible "writers' thesis statements" by writing reasons to support the following positions. Finish each sentence by adding *because* clauses. (Note how the apparently simple task of creating *because* clauses forces you to think of ideas.)

1.   **Issue-question:** Should writing courses be pass/fail?
       Position: Writing courses should be pass/fail because .... and because....
    Opposing position: Writing courses should not be pass/fail because ... and because....

2.   **Issue-question:** In good conscience can a feminist be a cheerleader?
       Position: It is not inconsistent for a feminist to be a cheerleader because ... and because ....
    Opposing position: It is inconsistent for a feminist to be a cheerleader because ... and because ....

3.   **Issue-question:** Should college basketball teams adopt a shot clock to prevent stalling?
       Position: College basketball teams should adopt a shot clock because ... and because ....
    Opposing position: College basketball should not adopt a shot clock because ... and because ....

THE PROCESS OF WRITING AN ISSUE-DEFENSE ESSAY

Throughout Part III we will urge you to use the following process for writing issue-defense essays:

1. Discover issues that interest you. The more you know about an issue and the more you can bring your own personal experiences or previous thinking to bear on it, the better. The first part of Journal Sequence 3 will help you discover ideas for issues.
2. After you have chosen an issue, brainstorm all arguments you can think of both for and against your position. The second part of Journal Sequence 3 will help you think through arguments, analyze your audience, and discover specific strategies and approaches.
3. After you have explored your issue in your journal, try to construct a framework for your essay by creating a writer's thesis statement with a series of *because* clauses. (You may have to write an initial draft to help you find an argument structure.)
4. Write a rough draft of your essay.
5. Analyze your argument by constructing, if possible, a loose syllogism for each of your "because" clauses. (Chapter 9 explains this procedure.) Creating these syllogisms can help you see the assumptions underlying

your argument and thus help you discover additional ways to support it. Then revise your draft.

6. Analyze your draft from a reader's perspective, trying to anticipate readers' objections (Chapter 11 provides help). Revise your draft using the kinds of advice we provide in Chapters 9, 10, and 11.

7. Exchange your draft with classmates getting as many peer reviews of your essay as you can.

8. Revise again and edit for style and the elimination of sentence errors. Make your essay ready for strangers.

Guided Journal: Sequence 3

Finding and Exploring Issues

This journal sequence differs a bit from Sequences 1 and 2 in that this time your journal writing is directly tied to your formal essays. The first section of this sequence—"Finding Issues"—helps you discover issues that you can use for essays. You can use this section most effectively if you do the tasks while reading Chapters 9, 10, and 11 on argumentation. We recommend one or two entries per day, approximately 15 minutes per entry. The second section—"Exploring Issues"—is a series of tasks designed to be completed before you write the drafts for each of your formal issue-defense assignments in Chapter 12. These tasks help you explore an issue in depth, giving you ideas you can use directly in your rough drafts.

FINDING ISSUES

As we explained earlier, an issue is any controversy or dispute in which reasonable people may take different positions. The exercises in this section will help you find issues that you can use in writing your own issue-defense essays.

Task 1

Keep an argument log.

Explanation

For the next few days be on the lookout for people arguing or disagreeing with each other about anything—arguments about living in the dorm, paying for a date, cutting classes, writing home for money; arguments about teachers, classes, politics, social issues, religion; arguments about what people should or shouldn't do; in short, any kind of argument or disagreement that you observe. Watch the editorials and letters to the editor sections of your local and school newspapers, which are a rich source of ideas for issues.

Set aside at least two blank pages in your journal for your argument log and make entries whenever you overhear an argument or get an idea for an issue. In your log make two entries for each argument:

1. A brief description of the argument itself, including a summary of opposing positions.
2. One or more questions that express the issue or issues being argued about. As you know, bull session arguments tend to get off track because opponents don't focus on the same question or because the question keeps shifting and changing. Your task here is to try to formulate several different questions that seem to have been at issue. You should see that each way of stating the question focuses the argument in a slightly different way.

Task 2

Explore ideas using this trigger question: "What do X and I disagree about?"

Explanation

A good way to generate ideas is to make a list of various people you know personally or know about through newspapers or your readings for a course: your mother, your roommate, a teacher, a person you are studying about in one of your courses, etc. Then ask yourself this trigger question:

"What do X and I disagree about?" (What do my mother and I disagree about? What do Senator Snorkle and I disagree about?)

Spend 15 minutes brainstorming arguments or disagreements you have with several persons on your list. You might try idea-mapping here.

Task 3

Explore ideas using this trigger question: "When people disagree about X, what do they disagree about?"

Explanation

Add to the following list three areas about which you have knowledge or personal expertise (i.e., computers, football, violin-playing, streetfighting, cooking).

- raising children
- garbage
- composition classes
- love
- politics
- your topic
- your topic
- your topic

Now take three words from this list (choose at least one of ours and one of yours) and brainstorm ideas using this trigger question: "When people disagree about X, what do they disagree about?" (When people disagree about garbage, what do they disagree about?) Either do three 5-minute freewrites or create an idea-map or other brainstorm sheet.

Task 4

Do 15 more minutes of brainstorming using the same trigger question: "When people disagree about X, what do they disagree about?"

Explanation

Choose as X either three more topics from the list in the Explanation of Task 3 or other topics of your choosing. Use freewriting, idea-mapping, or any other brainstorming technique that works for you.

Task 5

Reread now your argument log and your entries for Tasks 2, 3, and 4. Based on what you have recorded in those entries, ask five issue-questions. For each issue-question, list at least two opposing answers.

Explanation

From the raw material you have now written, you are ready to begin asking issue-questions that can become the focus of a formal issue-defense essay. As explained earlier, an issue-question is one that permits several opposing answers, each of which can be supported logically by reasonable persons. The best way to get a feel for issue-questions is to practice asking them and then to create several answers (claims) that assert different positions on the question. As long as you can write two or more opposing claims, you know you have focused on an issue. Here are some examples:

Issue-Question:	Should the federal income tax codes be simplified?
Claim:	The government should simplify its income tax codes.
Opposing claim:	The present income tax codes should be left as they are.
Issue-Question:	What causes inflation?
Claim:	Inflation is caused primarily by high interest payments on the national debt.
Opposing claim:	Inflation is caused primarily by demands for wage increases that outstrip increases in productivity.
Another opposing claim:	It is impossible to specify the exact causes of inflation.

Now in your journal ask at least five issue-questions and formulate two or more opposing claims for each one.

Task 6

Explore ideas using this trigger phrase: "X believes that . . . ; however, I believe that . . . .

Explanation

One way to sharpen your skill at asking issue-questions is to keep in mind specifically a person or group of people who hold views opposing yours. Try generating several more issue-questions, only this time use the following trigger question: "X believes that . . . ; however, I believe that . . . ." (In this trigger question X should be a real person or a real group of people with whom you have genuine disagreement.) After you have written an "X believes, however I believe" sentence, write out the corresponding issue-question. Here is an example:

"Joanna believes that Civil Engineering majors need to have a 5-year undergraduate curriculum; however, I believe it is still possible to get a good engineering degree in 4 years." Issue-Question: "Should our university expand its Civil Engineering degree to 5 years?"

Task 7

Discover issues by using the six types of arguments described in Chapter 10. Make an idea-map.

Explanation

Chapter 10 describes a heuristic (pp. 310–311) based on the following six categories of issue-questions: (1) Is X good or bad? (2) Should we do X? (3) Is X an instance of Y? (4) Does X resemble Y? (5) What causes X? (6) What are the consequences of X?

To use this heuristic, try playing mentally with your chosen topic, seeing how you can fit it into the six basic question types in ways that make sense. If you plug in words mechanically, you will often get pointless questions. For example, with the general topic "garbage," the question "Is garbage good or bad?" or "Should we have garbage?" seem silly. But if you continue to play flexibly, you might discover some intriguing issue questions: "Is the chemistry department's present system of disposing of toxic chemicals good or bad?" or "Should our city switch to a more automated system for collecting garbage?" Of course, you can't always make every topic fit all six classes of questions.

For this entry, use the six questions to think of potential issue-questions on a topic of your choice. Make an idea-map like the example shown on p. 311.

Task 8

Use the technique of "negative invention" to create an opposing claim and several alternative claims for one or two of the following generalizations:

- *Students learn the most from good teachers.*
- *Good leaders take strong positions on issues.*
- *Suffering is evil.*
- *Cramming for an exam is a poor study habit.*

Then jot down some ideas for supporting a position that at first seems unlikely or unusual.

Explanation

One way of achieving surprise in an issue-defense essay is to take an unexpected position. You might practice the following habit of mind: When confronted with a generalization whose truth at first seems obvious, try brainstorming ways to defend the "opposite case." This technique, which is really just an aggressive form of the believing and doubting game, is sometimes called "negative invention."

Generalization: Writing in a journal improves a person's creativity. (expected position)
Opposite Case: Writing in a journal can lessen or even destroy a person's creativity. (surprising position)
Generalization: Inflation hurts a nation's economy. (expected position)
Opposite Case: Inflation can help a nation's economy. (surprising position)

After stating the opposite case, you then brainstorm ways to support it, often discovering interesting insights you might not otherwise think of. Negative invention thus forces you to problematize experience, to think dialectically.

If at first you can't think of arguments to support the surprising opposite case, try this trick. Instead of creating just one "opposite case," which completely inverts the original generalization, try a series of "alternative cases," which only qualify the original generalization rather than totally oppose it. Often you can create alternative cases by systematically qualifying the original generalization one aspect at a time. For example:

Generalization: Writing a journal improves people's creativity.
Opposite Case: Writing in a journal hurts or even temporarily destroys people's creativity.
Alternative Case: Writing in a journal helps people develop only certain aspects of creativity, while it neglects other aspects.
Alternative Case: Writing in a journal helps only some kinds of people improve their creativity, but damages creativity in other types.
Alternative Case: Only some kinds of journal writing improve people's creativity; other kinds seem useless.

As you can see, thinking of alternative cases helps guard against the tendency to see only two sides to an issue. Rather, most issues allow for a whole series of somewhat different positions which blend into each other. For this entry, use negative invention to explore ideas opposing the "common sense" position expressed in the generalizations given at the beginning of this task. Use freewriting or idea-mapping.

EXPLORING ISSUES

The best way to write a short essay is to start exploring ideas well before its due date. This section of Journal Sequence 3 will help you approach your essays in this way. It will allow you to generate specific ideas for each of your essays before you write your first draft. We suggest you spend between one and two hours doing these brainstorming activities for each of your formal issue-defense essays. This section, therefore, isn't set up in the form of daily entries but rather in a sequence of eight tasks, all of which can be done in one or two sittings. To take full advantage of these pre-writing tasks, think of them as an efficient way of generating raw material rather than as an actual draft of your essay (much of what you write may never find its way into your drafts). After you have completed these tasks, you should find it much easier to begin composing an essay itself. Go through these eight tasks, therefore, for each issue-defense essay you write.

Task 9

Choose an issue which interests you (by now you should have a wealth of possibilities in your journal) and write it as a question. Then write out your own tentative answer to the question. This will be your beginning thesis statement or claim—the position you will try to defend in your essay. Finally, write out one or two tentative opposing answers to the question. These will be the possible claims of your opposition—a summary of the equally plausible positions you will be arguing against. At this time your thesis should state your position but not yet summarize your reasons—that is, you don't need to have "because" clauses at this time.

Task 10

Why are you interested in this issue? Your ideas here may prove useful in the introduction and conclusion of your essay. [Do a 5-or 10-minute freewrite.]

Task 11

What personal experiences do you have with this issue? (Personal experiences can include books or articles you've read, movies you've seen, lectures you've heard, as well as first hand experience.) Brainstorm as many actual personal experiences as you can think of. Relevant personal experiences can prove useful in any section of your issue-defense essay. Thinking of personal experiences may also help you clarify your feelings about your issue. [10–20 minutes].

Task 12

What reasons and evidence can you think of to support your position on this issue? Brainstorm every possible point you can think of in support of your position. You might want to use an idea-map here or else non-stop freewriting. Get as many ideas as possible on paper.

If you have trouble generating ideas for this question, you may have a topic that demands further research, either in the library or through interviews. If your claim can be supported with hard data such as statistics, testimony of experts, and so forth, make sure that you have collected (or will collect) these data. [30–45 minutes of journal writing, plus as much research as is necessary for your topic]

Task 13

What audience will you be writing your paper toward? What is your attitude toward that audience? How much do they know about your issue already? The more you consider your audience, the more you can adopt a strategy that will appeal to them. [5–10 minutes]

Task 14

What reasons and evidence can you think of to support claims that oppose your own position? Think about both the strengths of opposing positions and the weaknesses of your own position. Be brutal here. This will be useful when you need to summarize opposing positions and is crucial for helping you strengthen your own position. [20–30 minutes]

Task 15

Why aren't you convinced by these opposing arguments? If you had 5 minutes to rebut the arguments you cited in Task 14, what would you say? [15 minutes]

Task 16

Why is this an important issue? What are its broader implications and consequences? What other issues does it relate to? Thinking of possible answers to these questions may prove useful when you write your conclusion. [15 minutes]

After you have completed these pre-writing activities in the journal, you are ready to write your first draft, drawing on whatever material has proved useful and thinking of new material as you go along. After you have written a rough draft, you can create loose syllogisms for the main reasons of your argument, following the procedures suggested in Chapter 9. This may help you revise your essay. The general steps for composing and revising your issue-defense essays are discussed on pp. 259–260.

Issue-Defense Essays: Developing an Argument

WRITING TO CONVINCE: AN INTRODUCTION

In this chapter we'll be discussing processes of argumentation and writing-to-convince. While rhetoricians often class this sort of writing under the heading of "persuasion," we want to avoid that title. We avoid it because it promises more than we plan to deliver. Whereas persuasive writing includes appeals to reason (what the ancient Greek rhetoricians called *logos*), appeals to emotion (what they called *pathos*), and appeals to personal authority (what they called *ethos*), our primary focus is on the first element. While both *ethos* (establishing yourself as a trustworthy author) and *pathos* (stirring your audience's emotions to the point that they are ready to act on their convictions) are important elements, they are empty if detached from *logos*. By *logos* we mean a coherent structure of reasons and evidence in support of a claim. This chapter will help you learn how to create such a structure.

HOW HUMAN BEINGS DETERMINE A "STRUCTURE OF REASONS"

Let's begin by watching some minds at work. As you read the following problem, try to explain the reasoning processes that you observe. At the same time observe your own reasoning processes.

The police have just discovered the body of one Aristotle Ari "the Mule" Jones at a remote Florida airstrip known by police to be a drop point for drug smugglers. Coincidentally, Ari was nabbed here several years earlier unloading drugs from South America. Ari has been shot at close range with a .38. His wallet, containing several hundred dollars, remains undisturbed in his pocket. Since being released from prison several years earlier, Ari has managed to live in a large mansion, buy several expensive cars, dress tastefully, and entertain lavishly despite being unemployed.

Knowing this much about the case of Ari the Mule, how might you explain what happened here? Who might have killed Ari and why? The kind of reasoning you will have to use is commonly called *inductive* or *inferential* reasoning, which means that you go from given facts to a possible generalization that explains the facts. Hence, you can't be certain what happened to Ari; you can only conjecture, that is, make a reasonable guess, a plausible inference. Based on the information in the story, here are some possible explanations you might infer:

- Ari shot himself accidently while duck hunting.
- Ari committed suicide.
- Ari was mugged and then shot by the mugger when he put up a struggle.
- Ari is the victim of some kind of gangland slaying involving drug traffic.
- Ari is the victim of a senseless terror killing by young, alienated hoodlums.

Which of these inferences is the most convincing? Why? What thinking processes did your mind go through to answer these questions?

Now, let's continue with the saga of Ari "the Mule" Jones.

Inspector Bumble, Homicide's best man, has been put on the Jones murder case. "Why," he mumbles to himself, "did Aristotle die?" Overwhelmed by the question, he decides to call in world famous sleuth Shurlock Knowns, who is vacationing at nearby Disney World. Knowns is particularly renowned for using the deductive method to solve crimes, and Bumble, who never got through logic in college, is big enough to realize his weakness.

Standing at the scene of the crime, Bumble rehearses the facts of the case and repeats his question for Knowns. "Why did Aristotle die?"

Puffing his pipe contentedly, Knowns gazes into a nearby swamp. "Elementary, my dear Bumble," he intones finally. "You see, all men are mortal. Which is to say, all men die sooner or later."

Bumble raises his eyebrows, struck by Knowns' keen powers of mind. "What, he wonders, will he think of next."

"Now, we also know," Knowns continued, "that Aristotle was a man. That is, he belonged to that class of beings called 'man' that I earlier characterized as mortal. Personally," he interjected, turning on Bumble as though he were a truant schoolboy brought to him for a switching, "I prefer the earlier Greek designation for the class of man—'brutoi.' It means 'the dying ones.' Bit more graphic don't you think? Whatever, the important thing to keep in mind here is that *all* men are mortal, without exception."

Bumble is frowning by now. Where *could* Knowns be going with all this?

"So, you can readily see that because Aristotle was a man, and because all men are mortal, Aristotle too," he paused now for dramatic effect, removing the pipe from his mouth, "was mortal. In short, I deduce that Aristotle died because he was a man and because all men are mortal. Dying sooner rather than later is quite beside the point, don't you see. End of case. You are free to take the credit, Bumble. I ask only for my modest fee. In travelers cheques if you will, old man."

What sorts of differences in mental procedures can you describe between your own approach to the Jones case and Shurlock Knowns' approach?

If you have ever studied formal logic, you will know that we are poking fun here at a famous syllogism that appears in almost every textbook on logic:

All men are mortal.
Aristotle is a man.
Therefore Aristotle is mortal.

In fact, you may have sniffed "cheap shot" as we unfolded our parody. In point of fact, we have considerable respect for formal logic as a tool in argumentation, but we wish to emphasize some important issues about its applicability for teaching argumentation in a writing course. Among writing teachers there are several competing systems for helping students improve their skills at argumentation. Some writing textbooks lean heavily toward formal logic; others lean toward various systems of informal logic, particularly a legal model developed by Stephen Toulmin. You will best appreciate our own approach to argumentation if you understand briefly some differences between these competing systems.

FORMAL LOGIC: THE STRENGTHS AND LIMITS OF SYLLOGISTIC REASONING

Formal logic, traditionally taught in philosophy departments, examines the structure or form (hence *formal*) of arguments. Logicians generally identify two complementary structures of reasoning: *deductive* reasoning, which establishes conclusions with certainty if preceding premises are true, and *inductive* reasoning, which establishes conclusions only tentatively or probably. Formal logic courses generally focus most heavily on deductive reasoning.

Syllogistic Reasoning (Deduction)

The chief logical tool of deductive reasoning is the syllogism. A syllogism consists of three statements: A major premise, a minor premise, and a conclusion. In the "Aristotle" syllogism, "All men are mortal" is a major premise. It is a general statement about all the members of a class. "Aristotle is a man" is the minor premise. It is a more particular statement which asserts that a particular entity is a member of the class mentioned in the major premise. The conclusion, "Aristotle is mortal," combines the information in the two premises to conclude that what is true for all the members of a class is true for this particular member.

Given the two premises of Sherlock Knowns' syllogism, one is not simply 'justified' to draw the conclusion he draws, one is *driven* to accept it. One is similarly driven to accept the conclusion of *any* valid syllogism (a valid syllogism being one which contains no contradictions in its form). We can demonstrate this necessity graphically by using something called a Venn diagram in which we picture the information in a syllogism. A Venn diagram consists of a set of circles drawn inside or outside each other or intersecting each other. The circles represent classes or "sets" such as "mortals," "men," and "men named Aristotle." If we were to diagram Knowns' syllogism, it would look like the circles in Figure 9-1.

The circle representing "all men" is placed entirely inside the circle representing "all mortals" (since the major premise states that "All men are mortals"). The space outside the circle "men" but inside the circle "mortals" would represent all mortal beings which are not human. When we put Aristotle into the diagram, he's got to go inside the "man" circle ("Aristotle is a man"), which necessitates putting him inside the "mortal'" circle. You could no more put Aristotle into the "man" circle without putting him into the "mortal" circle than you could hit a bull's-eye without hitting the target. Thus the conclusion *must* be true if the premises are validly formed.

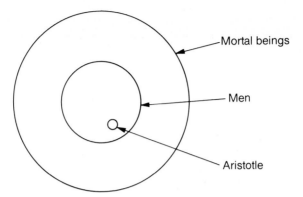

FIGURE 9-1   Venn Diagram of Valid Aristotle Syllogism

Conversely, a Venn diagram will also let you appreciate why some syllogisms are invalid. For example, the Aristotle syllogism is invalid when stated this way:

All men are mortal.
Aristotle is mortal.
Therefore Aristotle is a man. (See Figure 9-2).

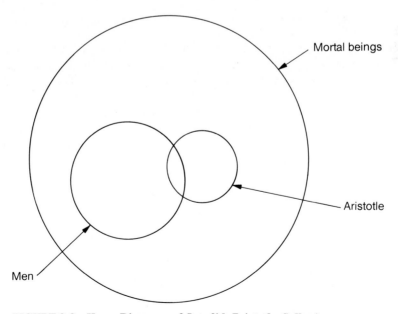

FIGURE 9-2   Venn Diagram of Invalid Aristotle Syllogism

Here the minor premise has been reversed. Instead of saying that Aristotle is a man—and thus belongs inside the man circle—it says only that he is mortal. Thus he fits anywhere inside the mortal circle. Aristotle may be a man, but he may also be a mouse, a frog, or any other kind of mortal being. The Venn diagram quickly helps you see whether the form of a syllogism is valid or invalid.

In sum, syllogistic arguments are tightly constructed with clear and absolute answers. If the form of the syllogism is valid, then we are driven to accept the validity of its conclusion. And yet we know in the real world that answers to arguments are seldom certain and clear-cut.

The Problem with Syllogistic Reasoning for Writers

The problem with syllogistic arguments, however, is that a valid argument isn't necessarily a *true* argument: for the conclusion of a valid syllogism to be true, the premises must also be true. Frequently a writer's problem is not demonstrating the validity of a syllogism but rather the truth of its premises. Let's illustrate this problem by continuing with the case of our departed friend Aristotle Jones.

Bumble is still standing there scratching his head when suddenly Sgt. Sharkey emerges from the undergrowth with Bluto Malcontent, a notorious local thug in tow. According to Sharkey, Bluto has been discovered hiding in the woods, a freshly fired .38 in his possession. His footprints, meanwhile, match perfectly those leading away from the body of Aristotle Jones. Bumble demands that Bluto account for himself.

"Certainly, my good man," replies Bluto. "I know what you're probably thinking right now, Bumble, but I've got conclusive, deductive proof that I'm innocent as a newborn babe. To wit: as you know yourself, Inspector B, there's a strict code of honor among thieves. And one of the first rules in that code is that 'No crook ever kills another crook.' Yuh with me so far?"

"OK, so, let it also be admitted that 'I'm a crook.' No, no, though I blush to admit it, it's true. As true of me as it is of the deceased Mr. Jones. Uhh, at least, so I'm told Mr. Jones is dead. At any rate, based on these two premises, we are driven to accept the inevitable conclusion (wanna get these handcuffs off me Sharkey?) that 'I would never kill another crook.'"

Here is Bluto's syllogism:

No crook ever kills another crook. [MAJOR PREMISE]
I am a crook. [MINOR PREMISE]
Therefore, I would never kill Aristotle Jones (who is also a crook). [CLAIM]

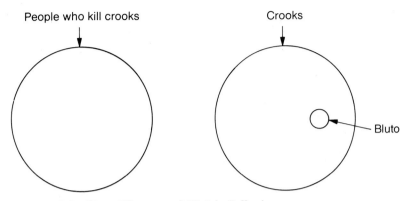

FIGURE 9-3   Venn Diagram of Bluto's Syllogism

Will Bluto's logic fool Sharkey? We hope not, for if Sharkey uncuffs Bluto, he will have been misled into mistaking the *validity* of an argument for the *truth* of an argument. Bluto's syllogism is *valid*, as a Venn diagram shows (see Figure 9-3). Note that the circle for "crooks" lies completely outside the circle for "people who kill crooks" ("No crook ever kills another crook"). Since Bluto is a crook, he necessarily is placed inside the circle of "all crooks" and outside the circle of "people who kill crooks." The syllogism is thus valid.

But valid syllogisms lead to true conclusions only if both premises are true. Now Bluto has conceded the truth of the minor premise, but the major premise is obviously false. We need only one example of a crook who has killed another crook to demonstrate that the major premise cannot hold true as a general principle.

In formal logic it is thus necessary to make an important distinction between an argument's validity and its truth. Courses in formal logic deal primarily with the validity of syllogisms. Written arguments, however, must deal with both the validity of an underlying argument and the truth of its premises. How do you persuade someone that the premises of an argument are true? This is often a writer's major problem and it often involves another kind of reasoning called *induction*.

Inductive Reasoning

The other form of reasoning studied in formal logic is inductive reasoning, which differs from deductive reasoning in that it cannot claim with certainty that its conclusions are true, only that they are probable or likely to be true. Typically an inductive argument claims that what is observably true for some members of a class is likely to be true for all members of the class.

All Doberman pinschers that I have observed have been evil-tempered.
Therefore this Doberman pinscher will be evil-tempered.

The sun has risen every morning in the past.
Therefore the sun will rise this morning.

It is this kind of reasoning that Bluto must use if he is to demonstrate that his premise "No crook ever kills another crook" is true.

No crook that I have ever known has killed another crook.
Therefore no crook ever kills another crook.

But it is easy to show that Bluto's argument is untrue. We need identify only one counter-example, one instance of a crook who has killed another crook, to falisfy the conclusion.

The Connection Between Inductive and Deductive Reasoning

So far we have implied that induction and deduction are quite different processes, but really they are closely related, two phases of the same complex mental process. When you yourself attempted to create an hypothesis about the murder of Aristotle Jones, you were doing inductive reasoning —moving from known facts to uncertain hypotheses that would account for the facts. But you were also doing a sequence of deductive calculations. If you briefly considered and then rejected the hypothesis that Jones was mugged, your mind probably created a loose syllogism something like this:

All victims of muggers are stripped of their cash.
Jones was not stripped of his cash.
Therefore Jones was not the victim of a mugger.

Even the most primary forms of inductive reasoning can be cast in syllogistic form:

Natural events that have happened consistently in the past will probably
    happen in the future.
The sun has risen consistently in the past.
Therefore the sun will probably rise in the future.

The distinction, then, between inductive and deductive reasoning isn't absolute. Both reasoning operations occur naturally whenever you think about a problem.

What We Will Borrow From Formal Logic

In the system for generating arguments that we will describe shortly, we will borrow the syllogism as a useful tool for developing a structured argument. We won't, however, explore the dozens of subtle variations among syllogisms or examine all the ways they can go wrong. In our view problems of logic are best dealt with like problems in grammar, on an individual basis, with the instructor taking a student through contradictions in his or her reasoning within a particular argument. In fact, we are continuously amazed at how accurate the mind is in manipulating ideas logically and intuitively without instruction in formal logic, just as the mind handles the arrangements of words into language without instruction in formal grammar.

In sum, we will borrow the syllogism as a way of helping writers think of ideas for supporting a claim. But we must always remember that a writer's problem in constructing an argument is far broader than the narrow issues of structural validity studied in formal logic. For these reasons, many writing teachers have turned toward "informal logic" as a way of helping writers.

INFORMAL LOGIC: THE STRENGTHS AND LIMITS OF TOULMIN'S LEGAL MODEL FOR ARGUMENTATION

Among the most influential systems of informal logic is one developed by philosopher Stephen Toulmin. Faced with some of the limitations of formal logic that we've outlined above and concerned with other, more subtle sorts of limitations, Toulmin developed a different logical model for use in the everyday world. Toulmin's method is based on a legal model of argumentation in which you imagine an adversary whose duty it is to question your reasoning whenever appropriate. You also imagine a judge or jury who will weigh your argument and your adversary's argument fairly and reasonably. If you speak only to your adversary, ignoring the jury, you are apt to become lost in a maze of nit-picking fine points; if you speak only to the jury, ignoring your adversary, you are apt to speak in vague generalities, thinking your case is airtight, only to have your adversary tear your argument to shreds when it is her turn to speak. Toulmin's model, then, involves a dramatic conflict between adversaries, as opposed to the uncontested world of eternal truths confidently assumed by formal logic.

According to Toulmin, there are six elements in an argument. The first three correspond roughly to the major and minor premises and the conclusion of a syllogism. Toulmin refers to these three elements as the Warrant

(W), the Grounds (G), and the Claim (C). The Grounds are all the facts and information at your disposal. (For example, if you wanted to argue that Aristotle is mortal or that Mr. Rogers is a bad teacher, you could "ground" your arguments on the observable information that Aristotle is a man or that Mr. Rogers' conducts his classes in a disorganized way.) Toulmin calls the Grounds "What you have to go on." A minor premise in a syllogism approximates a Ground. A Warrant, on the other hand, is a general sort of statement which licenses you to draw an inference from your Grounds (just as a search warrant licenses someone to search your house). Toulmin says that a Warrant is "How you get from your Grounds to your Claim." It approximates a major premise in a syllogism. (To coninue with the previous examples, your arguments will depend on the Warrant that all men are mortal or that disorganized teaching methods indicate a bad teacher.) Your Claim, meanwhile, is the inference that you have drawn and must justify. It is like the conclusion in a syllogism. (Aristotle is mortal; Mr. Rogers is a bad teacher.)

But Toulmin recognizes that in the real world, an argument's Warrant—the general statement that licenses the arguer to make a particular claim—is often open to question. You may therefore be required to provide a fourth element of an argument, Backing (B), to substantiate your Warrant. Thus Toulmin's system requires you not only to have evidence for your grounds (that is, some evidence that would make us admit that Aristotle is a man or that Rogers' teaching methods are disorganized), but also arguments *backing* our warrant (an argument showing that all men are mortal or showing that disorganized teachers are bad teachers).

The final two elements of Toulmin's logical model are ways of limiting our Claims. Toulmin calls these Qualifiers (Q) and Conditions of Rebuttal (R). With a Qualifier, we limit the force of our Claim to indicate the degree of its probable truth. We may say things like "very likely," "probably" or "maybe" to indicate the strength of the claim we are willing to draw from our evidence. A Condition of Rebuttal points out specific instances not covered by our Warrant (exceptions to the rule). Thus you might need to qualify your grounds by saying "Aristotle is *probably* a man" or "Rogers' courses *seem* disorganized to many students"; or you might need to qualify your warrants by saying "*Most* men are mortal" or "Disorganized courses are *often* the signs of a poor teacher." In either case you must then also qualify your claim: "Aristotle is *probably* mortal" or "Rogers' is *generally* not an effective teacher *for those students who thrive on well-organized courses.*" The conditions for rebuttal claim specific kinds of exceptions. "Aristotle is probably mortal *unless* he is a god or unless an immortality potion is discovered"; "Mr. Rogers is a bad teacher *unless* he is using the appearance of a disorganized course in a creative way to encourage students to think independently."

We can diagram Toulmin's model as follows:

GROUNDS

Aristotle is a man.

> WARRANT
>
> Because all men are mortal
>
> BACKING
>
> Evidence from observation and experience that all human beings eventually die

CLAIM

Aristotle is mortal.

QUALIFIER

Almost certainly

> REBUTTAL
>
> Unless modern medicine discovers an immortality drug
>
> Unless Aristotle is really a god

GROUNDS

Rogers' courses are disorganized.

> WARRANT
>
> Since organized courses are essential for good teaching
>
> BACKING
>
> Arguments showing that disorganized courses don't provide students with a sense of structure needed for effective learning

CLAIM

Rogers is a poor teacher.

QUALIFIER

for most students

> REBUTTAL
>
> Unless Rogers is using "disorganization" intentionally as a tool to stimulate creative thinking

GROUNDS

The Yankees have the best pitching staff in baseball.

> WARRANT
>
> Since pitching is the key to winning baseball games
>
> BACKING
>
> A statistical study showing the correlation between strong pitching and winning

CLAIM

The Yanks will win the pennant.

QUALIFIER

Probably

> REBUTTAL
>
> Unless their defense collapses

In looking at Toulmin's model, we get a clearer sense of what's required of a convincing argument. Whereas a syllogism assumes the truth, relevance, and plausibility of its premises, Toulmin's model shows us that considerably more justification is required of us. In turn, his model shows how tentative our claim must be when so many particulars of the case are taken into account.

What We Will Borrow from Toulmin

Our own model of argumentation is simpler and certainly less rigorous than Toulmin's. Instead of Toulmin's six terms, which many students at first find bewildering, we will use fewer and more generally familiar terms. By simplifying Toulmin's terms we will then be able to use a loose form of the traditional syllogism for displaying the structure of an argument instead of Toulmin's more precise but more complex display of six components to an argument. Note that almost any argument displayed in Toulmin's terms can also be displayed as a syllogism. Compare the following syllogisms with Toulmin's versions of the same arguments on p. 279.

All men are very likely mortal.
Aristotle is almost certainly a man.
Therefore Aristotle is very likely mortal.

Teams which have the best pitching staff usually win pennants.
The Yankees seem to have the best pitching staff.
Therefore the Yankees will probably win the pennant.

In many cases, teachers who fail to organize their courses are poor teachers.
Mr. Rogers fails to organize his courses.
Mr. Rogers is apt to be a poor teacher.

Note that Toulmin's Warrant is roughly equivalent to our major premise while his Ground is like our minor premise. However, we have added his Qualifiers into our major or minor premises, where appropriate, and hence into our Claim or conclusion. It is because we have added Qualifiers that we call our syllogisms "loose." Formal logic demands certainty and hence could hardly tolerate words like "probably" or "apt to" in a premise. But we will be using syllogisms mainly to help generate ideas, so our procedure is justified. Toulmin's terms of rebuttal (the *unless* component) is omitted from our syllogisms but is implied by the qualifier. By saying that the best pitching *usually* wins pennants, we have implied that sometimes it doesn't. As we shall see, writers should always explore ways their syllogisms could be falsified.

So while we will simplify Toulmin's model significantly, we are nevertheless influenced by his system. Particularly we are influenced by his legal model which suggests that no argument can be airtight and that no matter how good our case an opposing attorney will always cross-examine us and prepare a counter-argument. Whenever in our system we ask you to play the role of the opposing attorney or remind you that you are not preparing *proof* but rather the best argument you can to convince a jury, we are modeling our system on Toulmin's.

OUR OWN SYSTEM FOR PREPARING ARGUMENTS

In our model an argument consists of three main components: a claim, one or more reasons, and support for each of the reasons. Support for reasons can take two forms: either evidence—by which we mean facts, statistics, examples, or other empirical data—or a chain of other reasons. Figure 9-4 shows how these terms would look in a diagram:

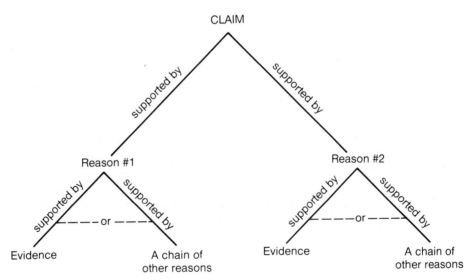

FIGURE 9-4   Diagram of Our Argumentation Model

Let us illustrate these terms briefly within the context of our model for structuring an argument. Suppose you wanted to argue that your home state should require all persons in a motor vehicle to wear seat belts. The issue-question is this: "Should the state require people to wear seat belts in cars?" Your *claim* is, "The state should require motor vehicle passengers to wear seat belts." Once you have established your claim, your next task is to develop *reasons* that will convince other people to agree with you. *Reasons* can be identified as statements within a "because" clause attached to your claim. Here are two reasons that might be used to support the preceding claim:

The state should require persons to wear seat belts because wearing seat belts saves lives and because the state has the right to regulate certain behaviors of persons using state-supported facilities.

Reasons by themselves will make your claim seem "plausible" but not yet convincing. You must now support each of your reasons. Most of the space taken up in an issue-defense essay is devoted to the support of the reasons. For example, in support of your first reason—that seat belts save lives—you could offer statistical data, expert testimony, and so forth about how seat belts have played an important role in the reduction of death and injury due to automobile accidents.

But not all reasons can be supported directly by evidence itself. Often reasons have to be supported by a chain of other reasons. For example, the second reason cited in the seat belt argument—that the state has the right to regulate certain behaviors of persons using state-supported facilities— why the state has the right to regulate those behaviors on state-supported a "reason" in your original seat belt argument, it is not a "fact" but a new claim which must itself be supported by new reasons. A writer would have to explain first what is meant by "certain behaviors" and then offer reasons why the state has the right to regulate those behaviors on state-supported facilities. We will return to this argument later to show more clearly how a "chain of reasons" passage differs from an "evidence" passage as a way of supporting a reason. For now, it is enough to note that a statement serving as a reason in one argument can become a claim in another, setting off a potentially infinite regress of reasons.

CONVERTING "BECAUSE" CLAUSES INTO LOOSE SYLLOGISMS

Knowing that you must find reasons and evidence to support your claims doesn't, in itself, help you do so. A good way to discover a strategy for supporting a claim is to construct for yourself a loose syllogism for each of your reasons. If you state your reasons as "because" clauses attached to your thesis or claim, you will discover that each "because" clause is usually the minor premise of a syllogism and that the major premise is unstated but implied.

Claims with "Because" Clauses

Aristotle is mortal because he is a man.

Mr. Rogers is a poor teacher because his courses are disorganized.

The Yankees will win the pennant because they have the best pitching staff in baseball.

Corresponding Syllogisms

All men are mortal [IMPLIED MAJOR PREMISE]
Aristotle is a man [STATED MINOR PREMISE: the "because" clause]
Therefore Aristotle is mortal. [STATED CLAIM]

Teachers whose courses are disorganized are poor teachers. [IMPLIED MAJOR PREMISE]
Mr. Rogers' courses are disorganized. [STATED MINOR PREMISE: the "because" clause]
Therefore Mr. Rogers is a poor teacher. [STATED CLAIM]

Teams with the best pitching staffs win pennants. [IMPLIED MAJOR PREMISE]
The Yankees have the best pitching staff. [STATED MINOR PREMISE]
The Yankees will win the pennant. [STATED CLAIM]

Not all arguments can be placed in syllogisms as readily as these can, so later we will suggest an alternative strategy if you are dealing with a particularly tricky argument. For now, however, get used to constructing syllogisms out of "because" clauses. With a little practice, you should be able to state the syllogistic structure that underlies most claims supported by "because" clauses. You can generally do so if you see that the major premise relates one class of things (X) to another class of things (Y). [X is a Y]. The minor premise then introduces a third class of thing (Z), which is related to the *first* item stated in the major premise. [Z is an X; therefore Z is a Y]. Sometimes you can construct a syllogism more easily if you place the major premise in the form of an "if . . . then" structure ("if something is an X, then it is also a Y"). Thus the Aristotle syllogism can also be stated this way:

If something is a man, then it is mortal.
Aristotle is a man.
Therefore Aristotle is mortal.

In the next section, we will show you how to use these syllogisms to plan a strategy for your essay.

For Class Discussion

Construct a loose syllogism implied by each of the following claims.
1. Writing courses should be pass/fail because the pass-fail system would encourage students to be more creative.

2. The *Orestean Trilogy* by Aeschylus is not really a tragedy because it ends with reconciliation rather than with death and suffering.

3. Cigarette smoking probably contributes to the creation of lung cancers because there is a strong statistical correlation between lung cancer and smoking.

4. Chemical Engineering is a better major than Music because it leads to higher paying jobs.

USING LOOSE SYLLOGISMS TO UNCOVER ASSUMPTIONS

Creating a syllogism helps you clarify your reasoning and discover the often unstated assumptions behind your reasons. Let's take an example.

The student who wrote the seat belt essay could initially think of only one main reason to support his claim that the state should require people to wear seat belts—seat belts save lives. He knew he had plenty of data to support that reason but couldn't think of anything else to say in the essay. Creating a syllogism helped show him what else needed to be said.

> If something saves lives, then the state should require it.
> Seat belts save lives.
> Therefore the state should require the wearing of seat belts.

Although he had plenty of data to support the minor premise, he saw that his major premise was questionable. If having your blood pressure taken regularly would save lives (by preventing strokes, for example) should the state therefore require you to check your blood pressure? Should the state make you take your vitamins? The writer now sees that he must devote a section of his essay to supporting the major premise. He must develop an argument showing why the state should intervene in the case of seat belts, but not in the case of blood pressure or vitamins. (We will see shortly how the writer develops this new section of the argument.) Our point is that constructing the syllogism helped the student think of material to put in the essay.

GETTING FROM A LOOSE SYLLOGISM TO AN ESSAY

The syllogism is simply a planning tool to help you see how to make your argument as convincing as possible. Each "because" clause in your writer's thesis statement can become a major section of your essay. In long arguments a writer might devote several paragraphs to a single "because" section or, conversely, in some highly compact arguments might place two or three "because" sections in a single paragraph. No matter whether the "because" section is long or short, the syllogism helps you plan out what you will need to say in it. Let's follow several writers from "because" statements to completed sections of an essay.

Ramona wants to write a letter to the chairperson of the philosophy department arguing that Mr. Rogers, a philosophy instructor, is an ineffective teacher. One of her reasons is this: "Mr. Rogers is an ineffective teacher because his courses are disorganized." As a planning guide, she constructs the following loose syllogism:

Teachers whose courses are disorganized are ineffective.
Mr. Rogers' courses are disorganized.
Therefore Mr. Rogers' is an ineffective teacher.

The purpose of constructing such a syllogism is to let her see the potential strengths and weaknesses of her argument. Once she has constructed a syllogism, she can ask herself a sequence of questions like the following:

1. Will my intended readers accept automatically the truth of my minor premise? If not, what evidence or chain of reasoning can I provide to support it?
2. Are there any qualifications I should add to the minor premise?
3. Are there any exceptions to the minor premise—times or occasions when it isn't true?
4. Will the reader accept the truth of my major premise? If not, how can I create an argument to support it?
5. Do I need to qualify the major premise?
6. What exceptions are there to the truth of the major premise?

In any argument it would be impossible to cover all these questions as if you had to prove beyond doubt the truth of both the major and minor premises. Often you can trust that your readers, reading "charitably," will grant you the truth of one of your premises right off. Your goal is to develop the strengths of your argument as convincingly as possible and *to be aware of its weaknesses.* Even if you don't have time to develop counter arguments to your readers' possible objections, you can at least anticipate those objections, acknowledging them in your essay. Ramona's planning notes based on the syllogism and the above list of questions is shown in Figure 9-5.

At the end of her notes, Ramona wrote for herself a set of directions about what her paragraph had to do:

1. Provide evidence that Rogers' courses are disorganized.
2. Counter possible objections that this disorganization is the result of creative teaching methods.

Here is how Ramona's paragraph finally looked when her argument was translated from planning notes to a prose essay.

Mr. Rogers is an ineffective teacher because his courses are so poorly organized. I have had him for two courses—Ethics and Introduction to Philosophy—and both courses exhibited the same confusion. He never provided a syllabus or explained his grading system. At the beginning of the course he never announced how many papers he would require, and he never seemed to know how much of the textbook material he planned to cover. For Introduction to Philosophy he told us to read the whole text but only covered half of it in class, and when one student asked (a week before the final) exactly what would be on it, he couldn't decide. The Ethics class had a different kind of confusion. He told us to read the text, which provided one set of terms for ethical arguments, and then he told us he didn't like the text and presented us in lecture a wholly different set of terms. The result was a whole class of confused, angry students. In Mr. Rogers' defense, it might be thought that he is trying to make us see that philosophy is not a tidy field of "right answers" but a field full of disagreements and controversy. Perhaps Mr. Rogers is using "disorganization" as a tool to deepen out thinking. But Mr. Rogers isn't experimenting with creative teaching methods; he is not helping us think through these problems in small group teams or anything like that. He teaches almost entirely through lecture and simply can't get his ideas into a coherent whole.

Most of this paragraph is devoted to supplying evidence in support of the minor premise. The writer decided that most readers would accept the truth of the major premise with one possible exception: perhaps Mr. Rogers is one of those creative teachers who purposely design courses that *appear* disorganized in order to throw a greater thinking burden upon students. The last part of the paragraph anticipates this objection and tries to counter it by asserting that Mr. Rogers is not one of those creative teachers.

A harder kind of "because" section to write is an argument that depends not so much on evidence as on a chain of supporting reasons. Let's return to the seat belt argument. That student knew that he would have little difficulty

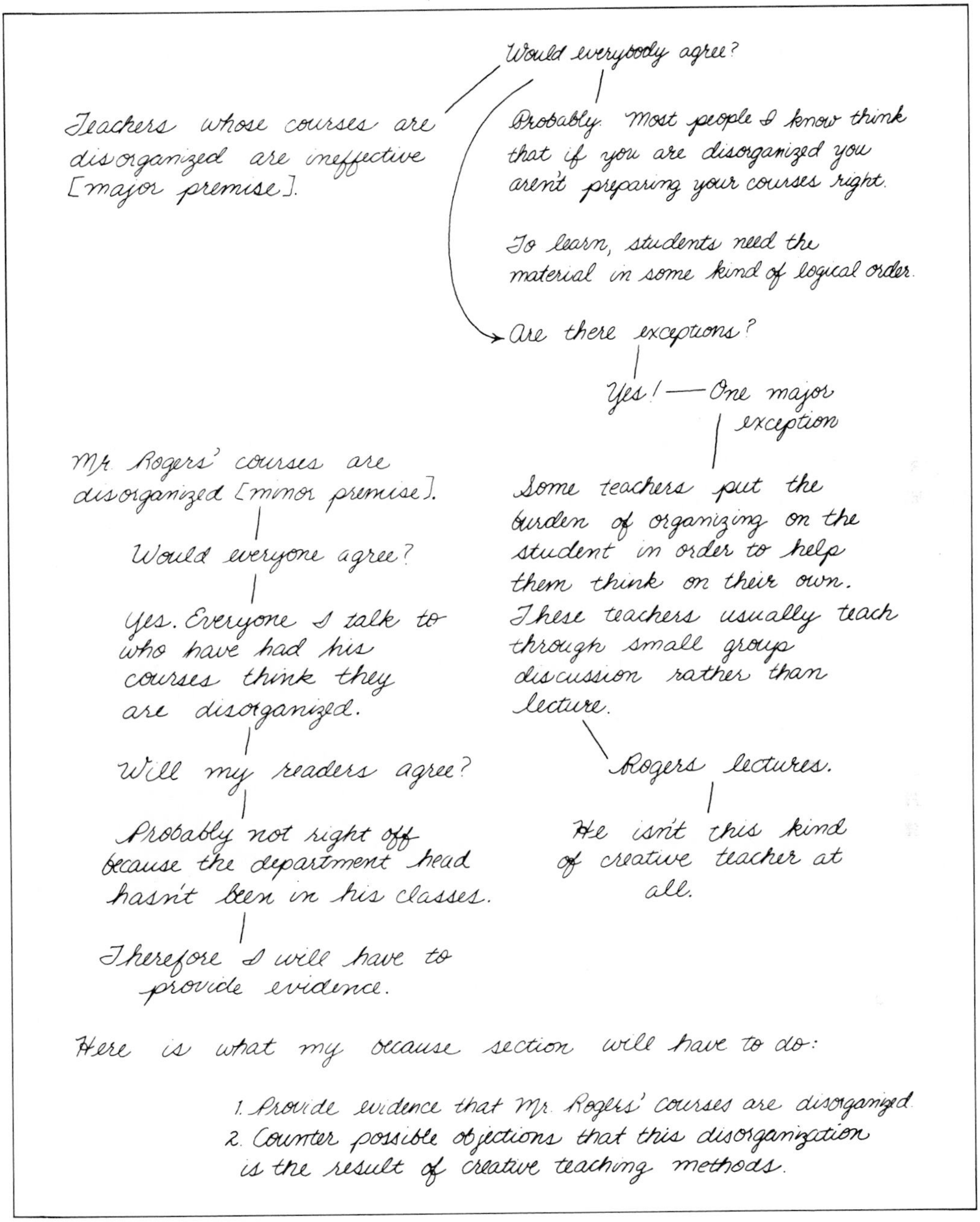

Would everybody agree?

Teachers whose courses are
disorganized are ineffective
[major premise].

Probably. Most people I know think
that if you are disorganized you
aren't preparing your courses right.

To learn, students need the
material in some kind of logical order.

Are there exceptions?

Yes! — One major
exception

Mr. Rogers' courses are
disorganized [minor premise].

Would everyone agree?

Yes. Everyone I talk to
who have had his
courses think they
are disorganized.

Will my readers agree?

Probably not right off
because the department head
hasn't been in his classes.

Therefore I will have to
provide evidence.

Some teachers put the
burden of organizing on the
student in order to help
them think on their own.
These teachers usually teach
through small group
discussion rather than
lecture.

Rogers lectures.

He isn't this kind
of creative teacher at
all.

Here is what my because section will have to do:

1. Provide evidence that Mr. Rogers' courses are disorganized.
2. Counter possible objections that this disorganization
is the result of creative teaching methods.

FIGURE 9-5 Ramona's Planning Notes for a Section of Her Argument

finding evidence to support the minor premise: "Seat belts save lives." But his major premise had him stumped. How could he argue that the state had the right to require seat belts without implying that the state would also have the right to require blood pressure checks or anything else that would save lives? He proceeded to make a list of several relevant differences between the seat belt case and other possible "do gooder" cases:

1. Driving is nearly always a public activity, done on state supported and controlled properties.
2. The connection between wearing seat belts and protecting lives is clear cut and immediate.
3. There's already a lot of legislation regulating our behavior on the highway, including laws which require seat belts to be installed in cars and, in some states, helmets to be worn by motorcyclists.
4. The wearing of seat belts is minimally disruptive. It doesn't cost us any more to wear them, they're already in place, the newer belt systems are designed for comfort, and so forth.

Each of these differences sets seat belt legislation apart from other less acceptable laws government might enact in the name of citizen safety. Together, they constitute some reasons for supporting seat belt legislation and for arguing that seat belt legislation is not an unreasonable infringement of citizens' rights.

Having worked out these differences, the student is ready to write a draft of the argument in essay form. Here is a portion the student's essay, picking up on his argument after he has shown that seat belts do indeed save lives.

But just because seat belts save lives does not necessarily mean that the state has the right to make us wear them. Certainly we don't want the state to make us put non-slip safety strips in our bathtubs or to get annual blood-pressure checks to prevent heart disease. But seat belt regulation governs our behavior on public roadways, not in the privacy of our homes, and the government is obviously responsible to make the highways as safe as possible. After all, we can sue the government for negligence if it disregards safety in its construction of highways. Forcing motor vehicle passengers to wear seat belts can thus be seen as part of their general program to make the highways safe. Moreover, the use of seat belts constitutes a minimal restriction of personal freedom. Seat belts are already standard equipment in cars, it costs us nothing to wear them, and they are now designed for maximum comfort.

There are also a number of precedents for seat belt legislation. Indeed, there are already government regulations requiring their installation in cars. To require their installation but not their use is silly. It is to require people to be potentially, but not actually, safe. In addition, a number of states, following the same sort of rationale as the one I've followed above, require motorcyclists to wear helmets. Such helmets are often costly and uncomfortable and, according to some cyclists, hurt the bikers' free spirit image. But because they protect lives and save millions of dollars in insurance and hospital costs, such objections have been overriden.

As you can tell, this section is considerably more complex than one that simply cites hard data as evidence in support of a reason. Here the writer must use an interlocking chain of other reasons, showing all the ways that a seat belt law is different from a safety-strip-in-the-bathtub law. Certainly it's not a definitive argument, but it is considerably more compelling than arguing strictly from a practical viewpoint of saving lives, without considering the thorny issues of principle raised by the assumptions behind the proposal. Although chain-of-reason arguments are harder to write than evidence arguments, many issue-defense essays will require sections like this.

SUMMING UP THE PROCESS OF DEVELOPING AN ESSAY: A CASE STUDY

To close out Chapter 9, let's follow one more student—you—this time starting at the very beginning when an idea for an issue-defense essay first strikes.

You've been assigned the task of writing an issue-defense essay. Stuck for a topic, you look back over your journal and then approach your teacher, who asks you what you care about, what in your life concerns or even angers you. Thinking it over, you remember paying your fees recently. The guy ahead of you, who was built like an upright freeezer, simply signed a little waiver based on the fact that he had a football scholarship. He then waltzed off to the business office to pick up a check. You, meanwhile, had to sign a large check, which would probably bounce, and beg for understanding because your loan hadn't yet come through. You're working three jobs and struggling to stay on the Dean's List. The more you think about it, the more aggrieved you feel. This just isn't fair.

"I want to write about athletic scholarships," you finally tell your teacher.

"What about athletic scholarships?" she asks.

"I don't think they're fair," you respond.

"Why not?" she queries.

You were afraid she'd ask this question. Writing teachers always do. All you can think of is that large, happy young man walking off to pick up his check. You tell her your story.

"Hmmm," she hums. "It's a place to start. Your personal experience helps me understand your feelings. I'm just not ready yet to agree that it's unfair. Why don't you go home and think about it for a while. Think of some reasons why other people ought to think athletic scholarships are unfair."

Several hours later, pen in hand, you begin exploring this idea in your journal. You go back to the scene at the registrar's office and try to figure out why you were irked and why you decided to justify your feelings by calling athletic scholarships unfair. Your first conclusion is that you can think of all sorts of reasons why the university ought to give you scholarship help, but you can't think of many reasons why the football player ought to get scholarship help. Colleges should give scholarships to scholars, based on their grades and their need for money, not to young hulks who knock down other young hulks. No reasonable person could dispute this. You go through the second sequence of journal assignments in Journal Sequence 3 trying to get a handle on this topic. Then you write a quick rough draft following your teacher's advice to get your ideas down on paper rapidly.

Looking it over, your English teacher hummms some more. A bad sign. She tells you you've come a long way. Another bad sign. She then tells you that you've got a lot of "assumptions" in your paper. She also objects to your characterization of football players as "mindless blocks of muscle tissue," one of your favorite phrases.

"Much of your argument rests on the assumption that the college pays for athletic scholarships out of state appropriations. I'm not sure that's true. You also assume that all football players are "mushwits," in your words, and that doesn't seem very plausible to me. I don't think you need to abandon your claim, but I do think you need to develop some of your reasons with evidence and perhaps qualify them a bit."

Back to the drawing board. You call up a friend on the college athletics committee and ask her where the money for athletic scholarships comes from. She tells you that most of it comes out of alumni donations earmarked for that purpose and from money generated by the athletic program. You wish you hadn't called her. You ask about the intelligence level of college jocks. Has she got any info on that? Anything showing what percentage of them are mushwits? Not exactly, she says, though she does have a study showing what percentage of all college athletes actually graduate from college. She promises to send the study and a copy of the athletic department budget over to you.

Looking over the material, you're at first depressed. Obviously your old argument will have to be changed. You still feel mad about the incident at the registrar's office, but some of your self-righteousness is gone. You've discovered that most of the money for athletic scholarships does come from outside sources. You also find that 55 percent of all college athletes somehow manage to graduate. Just when you were ready to make something of the 45 percent who don't graduate, you discovered that about 40 percent of *all* college students don't graduate. What to do?

You can either look around for some new reasons for calling athletic scholarships unfair, or you can go back to the evidence and think some more about it, or you can argue that athletic scholarships are fine. You decide to stick to your guns and go back to the evidence. You calm yourself by reminding yourself that so far the evidence does not prove that athletic scholarships *are* fair. So far the evidence simply won't support a claim as forceful as the one you want to make.

It is time now to get serious about applying some of the strategies discussed in this text. You need to commit yourself to a writer's thesis statement with some "because" clauses. Then you can construct some syllogisms which will help you see how to develop an argument. In considering the evidence, you decide to begin with the budget. You notice that although athletic scholarships come from outside sources, the university does subsidize the program to a considerable extent. Coaches' salaries, facilities, and much of the equipment are paid for by the university. Without that subsidy, athletic programs might not continue to exist. For sure, the program could not afford to pay all those scholarships.

You then return to the question of giving scholarships to people for playing football. OK, so they're not all dumb. But is that the point? They aren't given scholarships *because* they're smart or because they need the money. Although they are pretty much like the rest of the student population in terms of intelligence and need, they get scholarships and hardly anyone else does. Is a college education an appropriate reward for an athletic skill? How many other kinds of scholarships does your university give? Do athletes get a disproportionate amount of scholarship money? In considering fairness, that seems to be the real point—equality of opportunity. You then check out the financial aid office and discover that athletic scholarship monies are twice as plentiful as academic scholarship monies. Moreover, they are almost the only scholarships which are based entirely on skill, not need. Since many of the recipients could afford to pay a share of their academic costs, this seems a very inefficient way to distribute funds. You're ready to do your next draft.

After filling a page of scratch paper with various trial runs of a writer's thesis statement, you finally settle on the following sentence: "Athletic scholarships are unfair because they are given exclusively for athletic ability rather than for scholastic ability, because they don't take into acount a family's ability to pay, and because a large proportion of the money, contrary to popular belief, comes from general university funds that could be put into real scholarships for real scholars."

Each "because" clause in the thesis gives rise to a loose syllogism, which in turn helps you formulate a set of directions for the "because" sections that you must write:

First "Because" Section

Fair scholarships should be granted on the basis of scholastic ability only.
Athletic scholarships are not awarded for scholastic ability.
Therefore athletic scholarships are not fair.

Going through the list of questions on page 285 you identify music scholarships as a possible exception to the major premise. You also decide that both your major and minor premises will need support. You will be able to support your minor premise with evidence, but your major premise will require a chain of reasons for support. You then make up a set of directions for this section.

Directions for My First Section

1. I must show why fair scholarships should be awarded only for scholastic excellence.
2. I must show that athletic scholarships are given solely for athletic ability, not for scholastic excellence.
3. I must acknowledge objections that scholarships are often awarded on the basis of criteria other than pure scholarship—music scholarships for music performers, for example.
4. I must counter this objection by saying that these nonacademic scholarships are not justly distributed—athletes have a much better chance of free college education than do musicians.

Second "Because" Section

Scholarship aid should be based on financial need.
Athletic scholarships are not based on financial need.
Therefore athletic scholarships are not fair.

Directions for This Section

1. I must show why a fair scholarship program should be based on financial need.
2. I must provide evidence that financial need is not a factor in awarding athletic scholarships.

3. I must acknowledge objections that some scholarship programs are based on merit only, without consideration for financial need (the National Merit Scholarships, for example).
4. I must counter this objection by saying that these other merit scholarships are given for academic performance, which is the purpose of education.

Third "Because" Section

If athletic scholarships came entirely from sources that couldn't be used in any other way, then athletic scholarships would be OK.
But athletic scholarships are at least partly funded by general university funds. Therefore athletic scholarships are not OK.

Directions for This Section:

1. I must concede that athletic scholarships might be OK if they were totally paid for by non-university funds.
2. I must provide convincing evidence that athletic scholarships are largely subsidized by general funds. I can support this part with hard statistics.

You see that this argument now raises a lot of issues about athletics in general. The final paper that you write may or may not be all that conclusive. Certainly, however, it's more convincing than your initial argument. You've moved from explaining why you feel a certain way to convincing other people that the source of your feelings is not irrational. Along the way you had to articulate reasons for your feelings and to find evidence that those reasons were well grounded. Your reasons, then, guided you to certain forms of evidence and in turn gave meaning to that evidence.

For Class Discussion

1. What might be some weaknesses in the above argument as it is now being planned?

2. What might be some reasons for *supporting* athletic scholarships. Try creating a writer's thesis statement with two or three "because clauses" in support of athletic scholarships.

3. Choose one or two of the "because clauses" supporting athletic scholarships and try to construct a loose syllogism for each of them.

4. Finally, plan out a set of instructions for sections of an essay developing each of those "because" clauses.

CHAPTER 10

Some Common Strategies of Argumentation

Having set forth our own system for helping you create issue-defense arguments, let's step back for awhile and, in this somewhat more theoretical chapter, take a broader perspective on argumentative writing. We will begin by examining briefly some kinds of arguers and arguments to avoid. Then we will discuss a six-part classification scheme for claims that may help you understand more clearly how to generate reasons and evidence for different kinds of arguments. Finally we will provide some advice on how to increase the surprise and credibility of your own issue-defense essays.

ARGUERS AND ARGUMENTS TO AVOID

As you know, many "arguments" that at first seem like logical debate are really shouting matches masquerading as argument. You know the type. Silly debates on topics about which the disputants know little and feel much. The sorts of engagements where people toss the Principle of Charity out the window and try to win at any cost—asserting as facts statements they're unsure of, saying things they don't mean, citing vague authorities they've invented to suit their needs. We can learn little of value from clashes of ego such as this. But some interesting principles of argumentation can be learned from considering a couple of extreme cases of faulty arguers.

The two classes of disputants we will now consider argue for wrong reasons—either because they consider themselves always in the right or because they consider it impossible for anyone else ever to be right. They are known, respectively, as Fanatics and Skeptics. The assumptions they hold about justification call the very foundations of argumentation into question.

Fanatics are people whose standard test of any claim is simply to ask if it agrees with their beliefs. They do not waste their time pointing out flaws, errors, or inconsistencies in other people's arguments; they merely show how another argument deviated from their dogma. In name at least, their claim may rest on some authoritative text—the Bible, Freud's psychological system, the Communist Manifesto—but in fact, though they refuse to recognize it, it is often their interpretation of the authoritative text and not the text itself that supports their argument. Why is the Fanatic always right? Because he says so.

The Skeptic, on the other hand, dismisses the possibility that anyone could be proven right about anything (as opposed to a lower case "skeptic" who is simply difficult to convince). Because the sun has risen every day of recorded history is inadequate reason for the Skeptic to accept the claim that it will rise tomorrow. Short of absolute proof, which never exists, Skeptics accept no proofs.

In addition to there being people we must avoid arguing with or like, there are also certain sorts of statements that we should not take issue with: statements of fact and statements of opinion. We can see why if we remember two of our basic assumptions about arguments—(1) that more than one point of view is possible and (2) that one of the points of view is potentially more convincing than the others. Statements of fact are statements about which only one point of view is possible. Statements of opinion are statements which cannot be shown to be more or less convincing than any other statements. For a Fanatic, every claim is a statement of fact while for a Skeptic, every claim is an opinion.

Arguable claims are not always easily distinguished from facts and opinions and we must take great care in deciding which is which. A matter of taste or opinion is one which involves making a choice for which there are no agreed upon criteria. Some people like blue better than green, pizza better than salad, autumn better than spring, and while they might be able to tell you why they prefer one to the other (e.g., "Green's just too bright" or "It reminds me of Uncle Louie"), their explanation would not rely on evidence and justification so much as personal response. That doesn't mean that a nutritionist could not offer a reasoned judgment for preferring a salad to a pizza; or that an interior decorator could not offer a reasoned judgment for preferring a blue rug to a green one in a particular room. Many times a layperson offers opinions when an authority would offer a reasoned claim.

There may well be criteria for assessing something, but we just don't happen to know those criteria, and so we can only offer an opinion.

Consider the case of wine. Though most wine-drinkers simply drink what they like, it is possible for a wine expert to render a judgment about the quality of a particular variety of wine. A panel of wine experts, applying agreed upon criteria, could compare three glasses of Burgundy and render some sort of verdict on the wine which many people would accept. They would swirl the wine around in the glass and see what sort of "legs" it had. They would smell it for "bouquet." They would be on the alert for "corky" flavor. The ability to agree on what's important to look for and how to measure those qualities makes it possible for experts to judge wine. But if you asked a wine expert which was better, Burgundy or Chablis, he could only offer his opinion since there are not agreed upon criteria that could be applied to both.

Matters of opinion or taste, then, are matters in which the standards for judging are wholly personal. The second class of things we don't argue about is the class called "facts". Like most things which appear to be too obvious to require any definition, it is hard to define precisely what a fact is. The French mathematician, Poincaré, came up with a pretty good definition, though it requires a bit of clarification. Poincaré said that a fact is something which is "common to several thinking beings and could be common to all." In short, a fact is seen the same way by everyone who can possibly see it. No one who possessed a fact would disagree with anyone else in possession of it. Or at least, if there is a disagreement about a fact, it must be possible to settle that disagreement by reference to an authoritative source. If one person says it is 48 degrees outside, and another person retorts that it's really 53 degrees, they can settle that factual dispute simply by checking an accurate thermometer. The thermomoter is an authoritative source which makes the precise temperature "common to all" in Poincaré's phrase. A fact, then, is a statement that is verifiable by direct reference to empirical data.

But just when "facts" blend into "claims supported by facts" is a tricky problem. The statement from the last chapter that "Mr. Rogers' courses are disorganized" may seem like a fact, especially to someone who has suffered through several of Rogers' chaotic classes. In reality, however, it is a claim based on facts. The facts themselves would not be open to interpretation, that is, to any disagreement among persons with access to the empirical data. "Mr. Rogers did not give the class a syllabus for Philosophy 110," or "Mr. Rogers showed up nine minutes late for class on October 11"—these would be facts.

For Class Discussion

Various statements follow. Some are potentially facts because their truth can be verified by data; some are opinions because no criteria for judgment can be established; and some are arguable claims. Determine into which of the categories you would put each of the statements.

O 1. New York is a much more enjoyable city than Los Angeles.

F 2. The crime rate in L.A. is higher than the crime rate in New York.

C 3. New York is recovering well from its recent fiscal problems.

F 4. Students who take Math 123 pass/fail do as well on the final examination as students who take it for a grade.

5. The English Department should offer Freshman Writing on a pass/fail basis.

O 6. Math 123 is a waste of time.

C 7. Math 123 should not be a required course in the core curriculum.

8. Despite complaints from many parents of all races, forced busing should continue as a means to achieve school integration.

9. Forced busing has been a controversial issue in our city for many years.

10. Forced busing is bad for kids.

WHAT WE CAN ARGUE ABOUT: VALUE CLAIMS AND TRUTH CLAIMS

If we can't argue about facts and opinions, there are many kinds of claims that we can argue about. Most of these can be placed into two broad categories—value claims and truth claims.[1] That's not to say that every sort of arguable claim will fall under one heading or the other. To devise a scheme that might anticipate every possible argument would require us to construct a mind-boggling list. However, thinking about the nature of these two categories of claims and some of the issues that arise from them should deepen your thinking about argumentation. We'll settle for that.

These two major sorts of claims—value claims and truth claims— resemble opinions and facts respectively. A value claim resembles an opinion insofar as it designates degrees of preference. Unlike an opinion, however, value claims are the result of judgments based on criteria about which people are capable of agreeing. Thus the statement "Computer programming should be a required course for graduation" is a value claim while "Computer programming is fun" is an opinion. By the same token, truth claims resemble facts insofar as they are statements of the way things are (or were, or will be) rather than statements of preference. Facts can

---

[1] In this section we would like to acknowledge Jeanne Fahnestock and Marie Secor, "Teaching Argument: A Theory of Types," *College Composition and Communication* 34 (1983): 20–30. Although our classification scheme differs somewhat from the scheme proposed in their article, Fahnestock and Secor helped us rethink our own approach to argument.

always be confirmed or disconfirmed by agreed upon empirical measures. For example, the statement "The cost of living rose 8 percent from June, 1974 to September, 1976" can either be verified or not verified and is thus a potential fact. Truth claims, however, must be supported by reasoned argument and always presuppose the possibility that the claim could be false. The statement "Federal budget deficits are the primary cause of inflation" is a truth claim.

Value Claims: "X is Good/Bad"; "We Should/Should Not Do X"

We typically express value claims in either of two ways: "X is good or bad," or "We should or should not do X."

> Mr. Rogers is an ineffective teacher. [X is bad]

> *Moby Dick* is a better novel than *Jaws.* [X is better than Y, a variation of X is good]

> Our university should adopt a writing-across-the-curriculum program. [We should do X]

In supporting a value claim, a writer must first establish criteria on which to base judgment and then compare the thing to be evaluated against the criteria. Typically the major premise of a value syllogism cites a criterion, while the minor premise asserts that the thing to be evaluated meets (or does not meet) the criterion.

> Effective teachers organize their courses. ["organized courses" is the criterion for an effective teacher]

> Mr. Rogers does not organize his courses. [X fails to meet the criterion]

> Therefore Mr. Rogers is an ineffective teacher. [value claim]

> (Mr. Rogers is an ineffective teacher because he does not organize his courses.)

> A good novel explores life at a deep level. [criterion]

> *Moby Dick* explores life at a deeper level than *Jaws.* [X meets criterion better than Y]

> *Moby Dick* is a better novel than *Jaws* [value claim]

> (*Moby Dick* is a better novel than *Jaws* because it explores life at a deeper level.)

If a curriculum will help students develop thinking skills in their disciplines, then we should adopt it. [Developing thinking skills" is the criterion for an excellent curriculum]

A writing-across-the-curriculum program promotes the development of thinking skills. [X meets the criterion]

Therefore a writing-across-the-curriculum program should be established. [value claim]

(Our university should establish a writing-across-the-cirriculum program since such a program will promote the development of thinking skills.)

As these examples suggest, a writer conducting a value argument must be able to do three things: (1) establish criteria for the judgment; (2) defend the criteria (note that a person might object to the chosen criteria in each of our examples) and (3) defend the assertion that X meets or does not meet the criteria. In deciding upon criteria, you might consider the traits of an ideal member of the class (real or hypothetical), establish statistical averages for all members of the class (and assert that an excellent member should be above these averages), or derive criteria theoretically by analyzing the purposes of that class (and assert that an ideal member of the class achieves these purposes).

Generally an "X is good or bad" argument is somewhat easier to write than a "We should do X" argument because it involves fewer steps. In a "We should do X" argument you must first predict the consequences of doing or not doing X and then argue that those consequences are good or bad. It follows, then, that a "We should do X argument" is really an "X is good or bad" argument with an extra step attached—determining the consequences of X.

In evaluating the consequences of a given act—"Are the consequences of X good or bad?"—you can often make comparisons to the consequences of an alternative act or to the consequences of not acting at all. For example, in evaluating the consequences of an MX missile system, we can compare those consequences to the consequences of building a satellite missile system instead; or, we can compare the consequences of building an MX missle system to the consequences of maintaining the status quo. The criteria we apply to claims of value based on consequences are usually expressed as "costs and benefits." Thus, in the argument that "the state should require the wearing of seat belts" (pp. 286–289), the student writer first predicted the consequence of requiring seat belts—saving lives—and then evaluated whether the benefit of saving lives outweighed the cost of government intrusion on our freedoms.

There are special difficulties based on consequences, and those should be acknowledged at the outset. (1) All arguments of consequence are based on predictions, which can be particularly risky sorts of inference given that the future is never as knowable as the past. (2) Costs and benefits are frequently difficult to assess relative to one another because they belong to different classes (for example, fiscal costs versus psychological benefits). (3) What will be a cost for one group of people (higher social security taxes for workers) will sometimes be a benefit for another group of people (better social security benefits for the elderly). Indeed, arguments of consequence are so problematic that we'd be tempted to avoid them if they weren't among the most frequent and essential kinds of arguments that educated persons must make in a free society.

For Class Discussion

To sharpen your thinking about value claims, examine the following list. What criteria could be used to defend each of these claims? How could you demonstrate that the X in each claim meets or does not meet the criteria? Could you restate any of these claims to make them more defensible? Can you convert one or more of these claims into a tentative writer's thesis statement by adding two or three "because" clauses?

1. Robert Redford is an outstanding director. [Hint: What are the criteria for an outstanding director? Does Redford meet those criteria?]
2. The U.S. should not intervene in Central American affairs. [Hint: What would be the consequences of intervening or not intervening in Central American affairs? Are those consequences good or bad?]
3. America should invest more money in education.
4. The Punk Rock movement is immoral. [Hint: What are the criteria for labeling something "immoral"?]
5. Jim Rice is a better ballplayer than Carl Yastrzemski.
6. Solar power is a more promising energy alternative than nuclear power.
7. American high school curricula should place more emphasis than they do now on job skills.
8. Professional athletes are overpaid.
9. Computers dehumanize society. [Hint: Try rewording this claim into an "X is good/bad" format.]
10. Elwood Lunt is a great teacher.

Before moving on to truth claims, we need to comment on a couple of difficulties with value claims that some of the previous examples may have raised for you. In responding to number four, for example, you may be able to outline a reasonable argument pro or con for yourself, but in talking to others you may find it particularly difficult to reach any sort of consensus. This is because moral judgments are a particularly problematic sort of value claim. The norms for evaluating moral questions usually exist prior to any particular moral claim. These norms are derived from ethical systems such as Christianity, existentialism, or the values of an upwardly mobile middle class. Many persons subscribe, consciously or unconsciously, to such systems and hence have a set of assumptions which they bring to bear on any moral question.

Thus, for example, a fundamentalist Christian might decide that Punk Rock is immoral because of its lewd song lyrics (underlying premise: "lewdness is bad"). An existentialist, on the other hand, might champion Punk Rock's morality on the grounds that it forces the middle class to examine its values (underlying premise: questioning of an inherited value system is good). But an existentialist might just as well criticize Punk Rock because its followers do not live "authentically," that is, because they are caught up in faddish group values (underlying premise: following group values is bad). It is possible, therefore, that the Christian fundamentalist and the existentialist might both argue against Punk Rock, but for entirely different reasons.

Another difficulty associated with value claims concerns the differences between criteria and measures. If we decide, for example, that an important criterion for good teaching is that a good teacher promotes student learning, we may then decide to evaluate teachers according to how well their students learn. But that raises a serious question about measurement. How do we measure how much students learn from a particular teacher? Grades? Standardized tests? Student testimony? How can we control for all those variables, such as entry level knowledge or other courses taken by students which might affect their learning in any given class, and so forth? We may decide that measuring learning *can* be done, but certainly most people would agree that student learning is harder to measure than, say, student satisfaction. In considering your criteria, take care that you have some confidence in your ability to measure those criteria. By the same token, don't accept something as a criterion merely because it's easy to measure. (For example, don't claim Nolan Ryan is the best pitcher in baseball solely because his fastball has been clocked as the fastest in baseball or that a piece of writing is ineffective because some computer counted an above average frequency of "to be" verbs.)

In some cases, persons will have difficulty establishing criteria because there will be widespread disagreement about the purposes of a given class. We might have some difficulty determining, for example, just what a film director is supposed to do or be. And because we are often uncertain about the purpose of what we are evaluating, we disagree about how to weigh given criteria. For example, in evaluating a piece of writing, some people might weigh the "quality of ideas" more heavily than "organization of ideas" or "correctness of the sentence structure" though they would agree that all these criteria are important.

Finally, it is important to derive your criteria from the smallest relevant class in which you can place your subject. We call this "the apples and oranges law." It's much harder to evaluate an apple and an orange as members of the class "fruit" than it is to evaluate two oranges relative to the class "oranges." By the same token, it's easier to evaluate "chemistry teachers" than to evaluate "teachers" in general or "science fiction movies" rather than "movies" in general. In short, don't stop with a particular class as the basis for your norm until you're satisfied that there's no smaller sub-class which would provide a clearer and fairer norm.

Truth Claims

There is no neat division between questions of truth and questions of value. Indeed, most arguments of value involve making truth claims also. Confusion between the two sorts of claims can, however, be damaging. For example, consider the claim that "Men are better at math than women." Some might take that to be simply a value claim. ("X is better than Y.") It is, but it also implies an important truth claim. If one were to skip over the complex question of truth underlying this claim, one would be guilty of sloppy reasoning. One can make the factual statement that "Beyond the fifth-grade level, American males score higher on standardized tests of mathematical reasoning than American females." This fact would appear to support the value claim that men are better at math than women. But in leaping to evidence to support our value claim, we have ignored the whole difficult truth question "What are the causes of American males having a higher average score than American females on standardized math tests?" What we might discover when we sort out the answer to the latter question is that women score lower than men on standardized math tests not because they are innately inferior mathematicians but because of cultural conditioning. Often, then, issues about truth crop up inside larger issues about values so that a reason offered in a values argument is simultaneously a truth claim that needs its own supporting structure of reasons and evidence. Chain of reasons arguments thus frequently link together values claims and truth claims.

Whereas we suggested two major sorts of value claims, we will now suggest four major sorts of truth claims: (1) "X is an instance of (belongs to the class) Y." (2) "X resembles Y." (3) "X causes Y." (4) "X is a consequence of Y."

For Class Discussion

Below are listed several examples of truth claims, including at least one from each of the four categories mentioned above. Can you recognize what sort each of them is? What reasons and evidence might you use to support these claims? How might you modify these claims to make them more defensible? After you've finished reading the discussion of truth claims that follows, come back to this exercise and test yourself again on them.

1. The Ford Thunderbird is not really a sports car.
2. Passage of the ERA would increase wages for nurses, secretaries, and people in other occupations held predominately by women.
3. Conditions surrounding the current international monetary crisis resemble conditions prior to the Crash of 1929.
4. Genetic factors, rather than the environment, cause women to score lower than men on standardized math tests but higher than men on verbal tests.
5. New Journalism is really fiction.
6. The "trickle down" theory of economics is simply nineteenth century laissez faire economics dressed up in twentieth century clothing.
7. If all behavior in rats can be explained by operant conditioning, then all behavior in humans can also be explained by operant conditioning.
8. Selling off public lands would help the U.S. government reduce the national debt.
9. Since gun control works in Japan, it will work in the United States.
10. Dabbing whale blubber behind your ears will make you more attractive to the opposite sex.

X is an Instance of Y

The first of the four major truth claims can be cast in the form "X is an instance of (belongs to the class) Y."

Ronald Reagan is not a fiscal conservative.

The philosophy underlying small group learning is the philosophy of secular humanism.

Formal logic is more nearly mathematics than humanities.

In defending such claims, we must be able to describe the characteristics that define class "Y" and show that X possesses those characteristics.

In a syllogism showing the structure of this argument, the major premise usually identifies a characteristic of class Y, while the minor premise asserts that X possesses or does not possess that characteristic.

Fiscal conservatives support balanced budgets. ["Supporting balanced budgets" is a defining characteristic of the class "fiscal conservatives."]

Ronald Reagan has not supported a balanced budget.

Therefore Ronald Reagan is not a fiscal conservative.

(Ronald Reagan is not a fiscal conservative because he has not supported a balanced budget.)

As you can see, supporting this kind of truth claim seems similar to supporting a value claim. However, in a truth claim the writer's purpose is not to evaluate class Y. The characteristics of class Y are simply treated as defining traits. Thus, in claiming that "Ronald Reagan is not really a fiscal conservative," we aim only to define fiscal conservatism, not to approve or disapprove of it. We may go on later to conclude that not being a fiscal conservative is good or bad, but then we've moved beyond a truth claim to a value claim.

Arguments about truth issues, however, sometimes get muddled by their closeness to related value issues. For example, in a recent controversy at a local high school, a woman teacher accused male teachers and administrators of being sexist. Her basic value claim was that "sexist behavior is bad." It turned out, however, that her male adversaries had no argument with this claim. Instead, they argued that her definition of sexism was inadequate. The real issue did not concern a value question (Is sexism good or bad?) but a truth question (Is such and such a behavior sexist?) For example, is it "sexist" for a wrestling coach to require one of his wrestlers to forfeit a match rather than wrestle a female opponent? Is it sexist for administrators not to grant a male teacher maternity leave when his wife has a child? While most people would agree with the value claim that "Sexist behavior is bad," there is less universal agreement about how to define sexism, and about truth claims associated with that definition.

X Resembles Y

Claiming that "X resembles Y" is often similar to claiming that "X is an instance of (belongs to the class) Y." One could say, for instance, that "Ronald Reagan resembles fiscal liberals in his actions toward federal debt," a claim which is simply a bit more tentative than saying that he *is* a fiscal liberal with regard to federal debt. But there are two sorts of resemblance claims which are significantly different and deserve special treatment: analogies and precedents.

If you claim that "the fiscal problems facing the federal government are analogous to the fiscal problems facing a private family," you are no longer fitting a particular case to a general principle; rather, you are comparing two areas of experience. Your purpose in doing so is to use an area that is fairly easy to understand (the way a family governs its financial decisions) to help you make sense of a more complex area (the way a federal government should manage its decisions). Thus this analogy might lead you to make the following claim of resemblance: "Just as a family will go bankrupt if it continually spends more than it makes, so the federal government will go bankrupt if its expenses exceed its revenue."

Such arguments are often very powerful and yet very dangerous. Whereas defining X as an instance of Y is a "definitive" action, analogies are only "suggestive." An analogy can only be a starting point. Any analogy has to accept at the outset that there are important differences between the two things being compared as well as similarities. We call these differences "disanalogous" elements. One can think, for instance, of many differences between a family and the federal government. For example, the federal government, unlike a private family, prints its own money and does most of its borrowing from its own members. Perhaps these differences negate the claim that family debt and federal debt are similar in their effects. It is thus essential that an argument based on analogy acknowledge important disanalogies. Here is how one student qualified his claim that gun control laws will work in America because they work in Japan. His syllogism was the following:

Laws that work in Japan will probably work in the U.S.

Gun control laws work in Japan.

Therefore they will probably work in the U.S.

After providing evidence of the low incidence of murder and manslaughter in Japan, which he attributed largely to gun control, the student then added the following qualification.

Of course, it is possible that the low murder and manslaughter rate in Japan is not caused by the gun control laws. Perhaps instead Japanese citizens accept gun control laws because they are by nature a non-violent society unlike the U.S. with a history of violence. There can be no certainty of which comes first in this chicken/egg relationship. We must acknowledge, therefore, that a comparison with Japan is not conclusive, only suggestive. But just as a crackdown on speeding and drunk driving has noticeably cut traffic deaths in the U.S. so might a crackdown on handguns reduce the number of deaths from firearms.

Here the student qualifies the argument from resemblance by identifying possible disanalogies between Japan and the United States. But even as he qualifies his analogy, he goes on to cite another—cracking down on guns would be like cracking down on drunk driving. Indeed, whatever the limitations of analogies, they are one of the most fundamental sorts of claims that one encounters in argumentation, and they are frequently among the most psychologically persuasive strategies a writer can use.

A precedent is somewhat different from an analogy. A precedent is a completed event from the past that is held to be similar to an unfolding event in the present. The reasoning which governed decisions in the preceding event is thus held to be applicable in the present situation. Arguing from precedent is particularly common in our legal system. If, for example, a judge rules that a certain case can serve as a precedent in an undecided case (just as a motorcycle helmet law might be considered a precedent for a seat belt law), that ruling will go a long way toward determining the outcome of the undecided case.

X Causes Y

A third major category of truth claims asserts that one thing causes another thing.

The invention of the automobile soon caused people to redesign their cities.

Variances in intelligence are caused more by the environment than by genetic makeup.

Well designed writing assignments impact on the increase in students' thinking skills. [... cause an increase in thinking skills]

A basic design error by a team of engineers caused the tower to collapse.

Whenever we answer the question "What are the causes of (or what caused) X?" we make causal claims. Unlike other truth or value claims, however, causal claims often can't be supported by "because" clauses that fit neatly into syllogisms with major and minor premises. In many causal claims, "because" isn't at issue so much as "how." (How does a writing assignment increase thinking skills? How did the design error lead to the collapse of the tower?) Often in a cause-and-effect argument a writer does not put member X in class Y (the major thinking operation that occurs in a syllogism) but instead argues that X causes Y to happen, which in turn causes Z to happen. Syllogisms will be relevant mainly when one is trying to determine the assumptions behind the claim that X causes Y. We will return to this point and illustrate it after we describe causal arguments in more detail.

Causal arguments are always thorny. Just as it is easy and often tempting to make "false analogies" which mistake relationships of resemblance for relationships of identity, it is not uncommon to mistake relationships of association for causal relations. Just because X and Y commonly occur together does not mean that one causes the other. To say that X causes Y is to say a good deal more than X and Y commonly occur together or even that X commonly precedes Y.

In arguing causal relationships, we must also avoid the temptation to talk about **the** cause of a given effect. In the world of human affairs, causation is seldom this simple. Most phenomena in human affairs have multiple causes. Seldom will a single cause fully explain a given effect. And seldom will one cause always yield a given effect. Take, for example, the problem of determining the causes of the Civil War. Most of us have studied them in some detail, learning that there were three, five, eight, or eleven or more, depending on who taught us. But still, if we ask the typical American what caused the Civil War, he or she will respond with something like "The North's opposition to slavery." They are in effect saying that slavery was the necessary and sufficient cause of the war; that is, without the slavery issue the Civil War would never have occurred and that the slavery issue alone was enough to trigger the war. Given a minute to think back to their school days, most would probably begin to hedge and qualify their claim, but the human tendency to assert a single cause for a given effect is very strong. Most of us prefer the simple to the complex. But there's a fine line between the simple and the simplistic and in causal arguments, it's easy to cross that line.

In creating causal arguments, therefore, one must be aware of complexity. With this in mind, let's return to the relationship between causal arguments and syllogisms mentioned earlier. Causal arguments, like other arguments, can regularly employ the word *because*, but the *because* often has a slightly different meaning than it does in other arguments. Let's look at two pairs of sentences.

Getting the flu caused me to flunk math.

I flunked math because I got the flu.
[CAUSAL ARGUMENT—"X causes Y"]

Mr. Rogers' disorganized courses show that he is a poor teacher.

Mr. Rogers is a poor teacher because his courses are disorganized.
[VALUE ARGUMENT—"X is bad"]

Both sets of "because" statements can also be placed in syllogisms.

Students who get the flu flunk math.
I got the flu.
Therefore, I flunked math.

People whose courses are disorganized are poor teachers.
Mr. Rogers' courses are disorganized.
Therefore, Mr. Rogers is a poor teacher.

In the Rogers example, the syllogism is useful because the major premise makes a plausible generalization about all members of a class: it establishes a criterion for good teaching (organized classes) that may be universally true for all teachers. But in the flu example, the major premise seems silly as a general principle because obviously all students who get the flu don't flunk math. The word *because* in the second sentence of the flu example is really a *how* word signalling a cause, not a *why* word signalling a reason as we have been using the term *reason* in other kinds of arguments.

Now this is admittedly a subtle distinction, but it has a useful point for writers. Sometimes in creating a causal argument you won't find syllogisms helpful as planning devices. Instead you will want to create a map of possible causal chains. Let's illustrate with another example. Consider two quite different strategies you might use for arguing that smoking causes cancer. One is a *why* argument that could profitably use a syllogism; the other is a *how* argument that wouldn't use syllogisms. Here is the *why* argument:

If X and Y are highly correlated statistically, then X is quite likely a contributing cause of Y.

Smoking is highly correlated with cancer.

Thus smoking is quite likely a contributing cause of cancer.

(Smoking probably causes cancer because there is high statistical correlation between smoking and cancer.)

Here the major premise cites a general principle which allows us to make the cause-and-effect assertion. Such arguments are naturally structured syllogistically. Someone attacking this argument would try to show why the statistically significant correlation isn't conclusive in this case.

But we could create a quite different kind of argument linking smoking to cancer, an argument that wouldn't have a syllogistic structure but a "chain of causes" structure. Such an argument would go something like this: Smoking causes chemical A to be deposited in the lungs; this chemical causes X kind of cells to quit producing substance B; without substance B another kind of cell produces too much of substance C which causes the nucleus of cells with a Z structure to alter their DNA code; and so forth. Eventually a clearcut chain of events could be identified, each event causing the next. If no scientists doubted the validity of every link in the chain, then we could establish with reasonable certainty that smoking causes cancer. Because scientists have so far been unable to produce such a "chain of causes" argument, some proponents of the tobacco industry still claim that no cause-and-effect linkage between smoking and cancer has been conclusively established.

To summarize our point: If you are conducting a causal argument, you may find that our advice about constructing syllogisms won't be helpful. In that case, plot out a set of "chained causes" and show your readers how A leads to B, which leads to C, and so on. At anytime, however, when the assumptions behind your reasoning that A causes B are in doubt, then a syllogism will be useful.

X is a Consequence of Y

In making our final sort of claim, the claim that "The consequences of X are Y, Z, etc." we are simply reversing our causal claim. We are asking "What will be the effects of a given event or phenomenon?" Usually, the phenomenon or event in question is a novel one or one which has been proposed but not yet enacted. If, for example, a hay field is about to become a shopping mall, the first questions that arise concern the possible consequences of that action. What will happen to the environment? What will happen to the existing sewer and road facilities? How about the tax base? Before we can begin to evaluate consequences, and thus shift from a truth argument to a value argument, we have to come to some agreement about what those consequences will be. Two people who agree that the shopping center will generate new revenues may well disagree about the amount of revenue to be generated and about which negative costs to consider in computing net revenues. In cases of this sort, people commonly take a step back and look for precedents which might provide them with guidelines for estimating consequences. And, barring precedents, they must plot out hypothetical causal chains showing how A will lead to B which in turn will lead to C and D.

Because a consequence argument is the reverse of a causal argument, many of the observations we made about causal arguments will apply to consequence arguments also.

For Class Discussion

1. Create a "causal chain" to show how the first mentioned item below could eventually lead to the last one.

a.	invention of the automobile	redesign of cities
b.	invention of the automobile	changes in sexual morality
c.	invention of the automobile	deterioration of the environment
d.	invention of the automobile	the Ford Foundation contributes a million dollars to a college liberal arts program
e.	invention of the automobile	some consequence that no one else in your class will think of

USING THE "CATEGORIES OF ARGUMENT" AS A HEURISTIC

In Chapter 7 we discussed different kinds of heuristics, which we defined as procedures for discovering ideas. The six categories of arguments described in the preceding section might help you think of ideas for your issue-defense essays. Many of our students like to use the categories as starting points for an ideas map. Suppose you were given the general area "teacher evaluations" and were instructed to write an issue-defense essay on that topic. Your first step would be to think of some issue-questions and subsequent claims. Figure 10-1 shows how the six categories of arguments might help you get started.

As the idea map shows, the categories of argument helped this writer think of issues that might lead to an issue-defense essay. Such an argument, of course, would often end up combining ideas from various branches. Here are two examples of writer's thesis statements that might emerge from the idea map in Figure 10-1.

The university should not use student evaluation forms to measure teaching effectiveness because this method is really just a popularity contest and because it consequently encourages teachers to focus on being well-liked rather than on teaching what needs to be taught.

The university's current student evaluation form is ineffective because it is geared toward lecture classes only and because it doesn't reward teachers who require lots of writing in their classes.

BRINGING SURPRISE AND CREDIBILITY TO YOUR ARGUMENTS

While it is true that all truth and value claims are at least potentially arguable, it does not follow that all of them are worth arguing about. By the same token, it's not enough to be right in an argument if you aren't also credible (believable). In this brief section, we'll discuss ways in which you can assure yourself not only of a strong argument, but of a surprising and credible one as well.

Some issue-defense essays begin life with a severe handicap: the subject has been done to death. The essay's topic is a well-established staple of TV news and weekly magazines. Such topics come to us so readily because they are everywhere. Thus, when we first start brainstorming for issues, it is only natural that many of us come up with the same "big issues" at the top of our

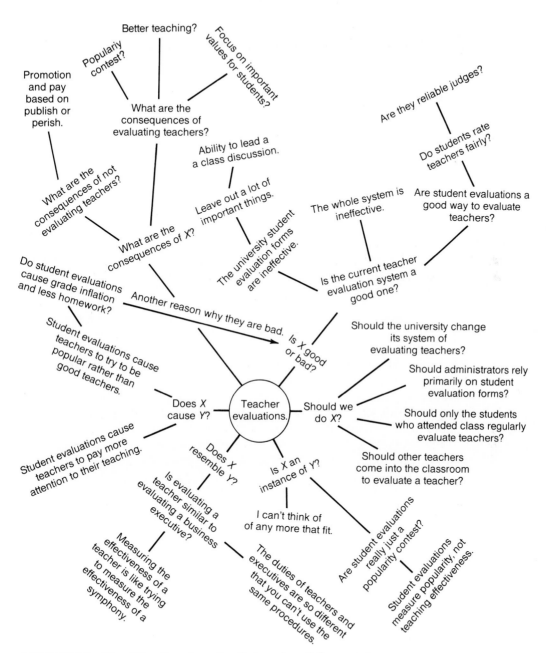

FIGURE 10-1   Idea Map Based on the Categories of Argument

lists: abortion, gun control, the legal drinking age, and so forth. All of these issues are potentially fine subjects for an essay, but unfortunately students often treat them unsurprisingly because they just rehash commonplace ideas already well known to the reader.

How might a student salvage a surprising essay out of these oft-treated subjects? A student choosing the "big issues" has basically two options: to do enough research to bring new information and insights to the reader, often by treating the topic from an unexpected angle; or to give your ideas surprising particularity by basing your argument on personal experience. For example, an abortion essay that draws on the writer's own personal involvement with the issue—perhaps the writer has had an abortion or has chosen not to have one or can otherwise bring personal experience to bear on the issue—will have a much better chance of surprising a reader than will an essay that repeats conventional arguments. In both cases, the writer will be able to create surprise by focussing on particulars unfamiliar to the reader.

If you decide to avoid the ready made "big issues," just what sorts of conflicts prove fruitful to explore? One of the most interesting kinds of issue-defense essays is one that challenges the *status quo*. Such challenges are, by their very nature, surprising to most people insofar as the *status quo* is a product of popular beliefs. According to the philosopher Chaim Perelman, there is in human thought a sort of "law of inertia" which inclines people to resist changing their minds. When certain ideas and beliefs become habitual, we don't really have to think about them any more. They no longer "trouble" us. To challenge one of these habitual notions is to rouse people from their slumber.

When someone says "Dogs are man's best friend," you can almost feel yourself nodding off into sleepy assent. But if you hear some freethinker assert that "the ony thing dumber than a dog is a dog owner," you start up, pulled from your dreams of doggy fidelity, ready to demand justification for so abnormal a view. So if no one in your audience finds your claim in any way remarkable or new, they will be unlikely to read, let alone argue with, your essay.

There is one important exception to the above proviso. There are instances when one might attempt to convince someone to do something that everyone agrees is a good thing to do. The key word here is *do*. Often times, people will assent in theory to the soundness or worth of a particular notion, but not act on that conviction. Few people, for example, would argue with the claim that poor study habits lead to bad grades. Any writer who sets out to prove that poor study habits are bad is doomed to die unread. But if you write an appeal to students to *change* their study habits and show them specifically *how* to do this, you've still got a chance to write a decent persuasive essay.

What will help make it decent is another element of surprise—the writer's ability to give the topic some "presence." An argument is said to have presence when it contains the sorts of details and experiences which allow the reader or listener to experience the truth of the statement directly. In our earlier example of the student who thought athletic scholarships were unfair, the scene at the registrar's office would give "presence" to his case. When *Time* magazine simply published the pictures of all the American dead on a randomly selected day in the Vietnam War, it lent great presence to the case against continued involvement in the war. If your essay is to convince people to act, the failure to give your argument presence will almost surely doom it. But it's also true that presence can lend force to any sort of argument.

The concept of presence is related to what we called *pathos* at the beginning of Chapter 9, *pathos* being the writer's power to make an audience empathize with her point of view. In turning now to the importance of credibility for an argument, we turn to the third element of classical argumentation, *ethos*. *Ethos* refers to character, in this case the character or personality which we infer from the writer's prose. Does the writer sound like a trustworthy person? Of course, it's not enough simply to sound trustworthy (like those TV doctors hawking liver pills), but if your argument is to get a fair hearing, it's a good place to start.

To be sure, the most important way to establish your credibility is to create a reasonable case based on reasons and evidence (*logos*). But it is also true that how you present your case, in terms of your tone and voice (*ethos*), also has an effect on your audience and their willingness to accept your claims. Thus you should be willing to grant the truth and force of an opposing argument and to credit your opposition with a full measure of intelligence and humanity. Some people cause us to disagree with them simply because they present their cases so abrasively that we can't stand the thought of being allied with them. Abusive and insensitive arguments give rise to an enormous number of stupid debates wherein people exchange accusations rather than ideas. For some handy examples of such debates, peruse the "Letters to the Editor" section of almost any newspaper.

A key, then, to being a credible speaker is to sound fair-minded and trustworthy. Sometimes, of course, the temptation to vent your anger, take a cheap shot, or get a good laugh at the expense of the opposition will prove too much for even the saintliest of writers. The question you must ask is whether such gambits are necessary to your argument or only to your ego. Good arguments are not without passion; passion and reason can complement each other. But the passion must be controlled to be effective. Raging or mocking speakers may be entertaining, but seldom do we trust them.

CONCLUSION: AN ARGUMENT IN ACTION

By way of concluding this chapter, we'll take a look at a sample argument taken from a recent essay by columnist Ellen Goodman. Though it's a short argument, about the same length as many of the arguments you are asked to write in college, it is far from simple. It contains a number of distinct claims, some of which are stated as reasons for accepting other claims. Like many arguments, it depends less on hard data for evidence than on a coherently linked chain of reasons. And, like many arguments, it begins by assessing an opposing argument (you will be asked to do this regularly in the assignments in Chapter 12). It is part of an ongoing conflict between the value of freedom of speech and the evil of pornography and is thus rooted in a particularly knotty kind of problem—how to reconcile two opposing values. Let's examine the structure of this argument using some of the terms set forth in Part III.

Minneapolis Ordinance Broad and Dangerous*

by Ellen Goodman

Just a couple of months before the pool-table gang rape in New Bedford, Mass., Hustler magazine printed a photo feature that reads like a blueprint for the actual crime. There were just two differences between Hustler and real life. In Hustler, the woman enjoyed it. In real life, the woman charged rape.

There is no evidence that the four men charged with this crime had actually read the magazine. Nor is there evidence that the spectators who yelled encouragement for two hours had held previous ringside seats at pornographic events.

But there is a growing sense that the violent pornography being peddled in this country helps to create an atmosphere in which such events occur. As recently as last month, a study done by two University of Wisconsin researchers suggested that even "normal" men, pre-screened college students, were changed by their exposure to violent pornography.

After just ten hours of viewing, reported researcher Edward Donnerstein, "the men were less likely to convict in a rape trial, less likely to see injury to a victim, more likely to see the victim as responsible." Pornography may not cause rape directly, he said, "but it maintains a lot of very callous attitudes. It justifies aggression. It even says you are doing a favor to the victim."

If we can prove that pornography is harmful, then shouldn't the victims have legal rights? This, in any case, is the theory behind a city ordinance that recently

---

* © 1985, The Boston Globe Newspaper Company/Washington Post Writers Group, reprinted with permission.

passed the Minneapolis City Council. Vetoed by the mayor last week, it is likely to be back at the Council for an overriding vote, likely to appear in other cities, other towns. What is unique about the Minneapolis approach is that for the first time it attacks pornography, not because of nudity or sexual explicitness, but because it degrades and harms women. It opposes pornography on the basis of sex discrimation.

University of Minnesota Law Professor Catherine MacKinnon, who co-authored the ordinance with feminist writer Andrea Dworkin, says that they chose this tactic because they believe that pornography is central to "creating and maintaining the inequality of the sexes .... Just being a woman means you are injured by pornography."

They defined pornography carefully as, "the sexually explicit subordination of women, graphically depicted, whether in pictures or in words." To fit their legal definition it must also include one of nine conditions that show this subordination, like presenting women who "experience sexual pleasure in being raped or ... mutilated . . . ."

Under this law, it would be possible for a pool-table rape victim to sue Hustler. It would be possible for a woman to sue if she were forced to act in a pornographic movie. Indeed, since the law describes pornography as oppressive to all women, it would be possible for any woman to sue those who traffic in the stuff for violating her civil rights.

In many ways, the Minneapolis ordinance is an appealing attack on an appalling problem. The authors have tried to resolve a long and bubbling conflict among those who have both a deep aversion to pornography and a deep loyalty to the value of free speech.

"To date," says Professor MacKinnon, "people have identified the pornographer's freedom with everybody's freedom. But we're saying that the freedom of the pornographer is the subordination of women. It means one has to take a side."

But the sides are not quite as clear as Professor MacKinnon describes them. Nor is the ordinance.

Even if we accept the argument that pornography is harmful to women—and I do—then we must also recognize that anti-Semitic literature is harmful to Jews and racist literature is harmful to blacks. For that matter, Marxist literature may be harmful to government policy. It isn't just women versus pornographers. If women win the right to sue publishers and producers, then so could Jews, blacks, a long list of people who may be able to prove they have been harmed by books, movies, speeches or even records. The Manson murders, you may recall, were reportedly inspired by the Beatles.

We might prefer a library or book store or lecture hall without Mein Kampf or the Grand Whoever of the Ku Klux Klan. But a growing list of harmful expressions would inevitably strangle freedom of speech.

This ordinance was carefully written to avoid problems of banning and prior restraint, but the right of any woman to claim damages from pornography is just too broad. It seems destined to lead to censorship.

What the Minneapolis City Council has before it is a very attractive theory. What MacKinnon and Dworkin have written is a very persuasive and useful definition of pornography. But they haven't yet resolved the conflict between the harm of pornography and the value of free speech. In its present form, this is still a shaky piece of law.

One of the first things we should notice here is how patiently Goodman develops her case. She refrains from making her own argument until she has thoroughly summarized the issue and the counter-argument. This procedure, which is typical of many argumentative essays, departs from a traditional rhetorical prescription to begin with your own thesis. What advantages can you see to Goodman's decision to wait until the last part of the essay to present her own position?

In her opening, Goodman suggests a link between a notorious gang-rape case in Massachusetts (one which she'd commented on in an earlier column) and a depiction of a rape scene in *Hustler* magazine. But note how she stops short of making any claim of a causal connection between the two events. In lieu of any evidence which would link the two causally, she settles for a suggestion of resemblance between the two events. She uses the conjunction of the two events primarily to give "presence" to the more general claim that pornography is harmful. However, for the claim that pornography is harmful, she offers empirical evidence from a scientific study. This section of her argument could be paraphrased: "Pornography is bad [value claim] because it causes men to develop a more callous, unsympathetic view of women [reason] as shown in a University of Minnesota study [empirical evidence]." This "because clause," offered as a reason in support of the value claim, is itself a truth claim in the form X (pornography) causes Y (unsympathetic view of women).

Although Goodman will, by the end of the article, oppose the censorship of pornography, at this point she is acknowledging the strength of the case against pornography. This opposing argument, which evolves from the University of Minnesota study, can be summarized as follows: "Women should be able to sue pornographers [a value claim in the form 'we should do X'] because pornography is a violation of women's rights [a truth claim in the form 'X is an instance of Y']." This truth claim in turn is supported by the previous argument linking pornography to a callous attitude toward women. From the initial evidence that pornography causes men to view women less sympathetically, the Minnesota writers build up a compelling argument to outlaw pornography altogether.

In responding to this argument, Goodman first predicts the consequences of the proposal to censor pornography [a truth claim in the form "the consequences of X are Y"] and then argues that the costs of these consequences outweigh the benefits. She believes that the proposed ordinance, no matter how carefully it is defined, would not be able to limit censorship to cases of pornography. The ordinance would become, in her view, a precedent for the censorship of other forms of controversial literature. She offers no hard data in support of this contention; rather, she describes a plausible causal chain by showing how an ordinance against pornography on the grounds of its damage to women could lead to ordinances against written materials that are damaging to Jews, Blacks, or others. Her argument might be paraphrased as follows: "This ordinance should not be passed [value claim that we should not do X] because the ordinance would lead to infringements of legitimate expressions of freedom of speech [reason in the form of a truth claim about consequences]."

Like most issues growing out of proposals for change, this one involves a number of uncertainties. The costs and benefits of the proposed ordinance cannot be assessed fully before the fact. Moreover, the costs and benefits certainly affect different groups differently. Certainly, too, the conflict centers on two different sorts of values which are difficult to weigh against each other. But the necessity of making a judgment overrides all those uncertainties. However tentative our judgment, a reasoned argument is preferable to a coin flip.

For Class Discussion

1. As a class, find several newspaper essays by local or syndicated editorial writers like Goodman. Using the concepts from Part III, analyze those arguments. Compare the procedures used by two or three different writers.
2. Examine a number of different ads from magazines. Assuming that all ads are attempts to persuade you to buy a particular product, ask *why* the ad claims you should buy the product. Translate the ad into a claim and a reason. Do the admakers offer any evidence? Can you think of any evidence which might support their arguments?

CHAPTER 11

Issue-Defense Essays: Evaluating Arguments

In learning how to form convincing essays from questions of truth and value, you are well on your way to understanding how to go about assessing other people's arguments. As we shift now from developing arguments to evaluating arguments, we are really simply shifting our point of view. The criticism which we must learn to apply to other people's arguments must also be applied to our own. Being a proponent of one point of view generally entails being an opponent of another point of view, and persuasive arguers will invariably wear both hats.

Assessment of any argument begins in the Principle of Charity. Any good critical reading must first discover the significant points the writer is making. Quibbling over minor errors or willfully ignoring strong points misdirects your response and renders it trivial. A strong argument is an argument which confronts rather than ignores significant points. If you fail to confront the strengths of your opponent's argument, you will create what logicians refer to as a "strawman," a made-up opponent with a head full of straw who says all the things you wish that a really stupid opponent might say rather than what your opponent really said. Following the Principle of Charity is one way of guarding against strawman arguments and the unenlightening sorts of conflicts which generally follow such practices.

A QUESTION STRATEGY FOR ASSESSING OTHER PEOPLE'S ARGUMENTS

Because the analysis of other people's arguments is such an extremely complex business, we have compiled a set of questions to assist you in giving a full and charitable reading to any persuasive statement. Depending on the argument posed by a writer or speaker, some of these questions will be more relevant than others. Indeed, some may not be at all relevant in certain circumstances, since no general formula can anticipate every individual circumstance. But in any sort of persuasive case, at least one or more of these questions should raise crucial issues to the surface and clarify differences between your point of view and alternative points of view. If, after considering another's argument question by question, you find yourself more in agreement than disagreement with the other's point of view, the Principle of Charity suggests that you re-examine your own point of view and perhaps change it. To do so is not necessarily to "capitulate" to the other side; it is simply to be convinced by the other side. Because argumentation assumes such a possibility (only Fanatics and Skeptics reject the possibility), you should not feel that it is a sign of weakness to do so.

Again, in order to simplify the procedure and make it easier to apply, we have divided the questions to be addressed into six categories. These categories are adopted from the familiar 5W's of journalism with the added "How?" question. You may find, in your own application of the heuristic, that other good questions come to the fore. That's fine. Our list is intended to be suggestive rather than exhaustive.

1. *What* claim(s) is the writer making? Relate this question back to the classifications in Chapter 10 to see not just what specific claims the writer is making, but what *sorts* of claim they might be. Also, see if you can make a distinction between major and minor claims (and concentrate on the former).
2. *What* reasons and/or evidence does the writer offer in support of his or her claims? Are the links between the claims and the reasons/evidence clear? Is the evidence proportional to the claim?
3. *Who* is making the argument or being cited as an authority? What sort of credentials do they have? Be careful here. Don't dismiss a convincing case just because the person is not an authority. By the same token, don't dismiss an argument just because the person making that argument has a personal stake in its outcome. You should only challenge peoples' credentials if their testimony's weight rests solely in their good name rather than reasons or evidence.

4. To *Whom* is the argument being addressed? Can you conceive of an audience that would not agree with the writer's criteria or assumptions? Pay particular attention to this question when considering values arguments involving moral questions.

5. *When and Where* was the evidence gathered? Was it gathered fairly and completely? Has anything occurred between the time the argument was made or the evidence gathered to change its truth or forcefulness? Be especially alert in dealing with arguments by analogy (for example, an argument about United States foreign policy in Central America based on comparisons with Vietnam). Be careful, too, to guard against the so-called genetic fallacy, the tendency to believe that the way something *originally was* is the way it *ought* to be (for example, let's not change the Constitution lest we betray the Founding Fathers).

6. *Why* is this position preferable to some other position on the issue? According to the Law of Parsimony, the least complex explanation is often the most preferred. The longer the chain of reasons in an argument, the more possibility there is for error. Note that this criterion is especially applicable when you are faced with at least two possible explanations for a phenomenon, neither one of which can be conclusively proven to be correct (for example, is the human personality the product of sunspots or parental influence?) How far do you have to go to fetch evidence to make your case?

7. *How* does the speaker propose to act on his claim? It's not always mandatory, unless a proposal is made, that the writer be able to show how one might act on his claim. But generally, it strengthens a claim to do so. Hence, if a person argues in favor of merit pay for teachers, he should be prepared to demonstrate how merit might be measured.

This list of questions, while hardly exhaustive, will go a long ways toward helping you evaluate arguments that you encounter in college and later in your professional life.

For Class Discussion

Use this list of questions to evaluate Fritz Machlup's argument that students often learn more from poor teachers than from good ones (see his essay on pp. 399–405.

A BRIEF LOOK AT SOME MAJOR LOGICAL FALLACIES

In Chapter 9 we used a loose form of syllogism to help you see the main logical structure of your arguments. Logicians study problems in logic in one of two ways: either through formal fallacies, in which there is a flaw in the structure of a syllogism, or through informal fallacies, which comprise other ways that arguments can go wrong. We have excluded a study of formal fallacies from this text on the grounds that they are not particularly useful for writers. However, because informal fallacies can occasionally crop up in anyone's writing and because advertisers and hucksters often try to exploit them, it is a good idea to be familiar with some of the most frequently encountered kinds of informal fallacies.

Post Hoc, Ergo Propter Hoc

A survey of drug addicts confirmed that all of them drank milk as children. Therefore milk leads to drug addiction.

For years I suffered from agonizing abdominal itching. Then I tried taking Jones pills. Within weeks my abdominal itching ceased. The specific ingredients in Jones pills work wonders.

In our view, one of the most prevalent logical fallacies is the *post hoc, ergo propter hoc* ("after this, therefore because of this") fallacy. The error involved here is to mistake sequence for cause. Remember, proving cause involves more than establishing the conjunction of two events in an invariable sequence. You've got to be able also to establish *how* one thing causes another. For example, you can't point to an increase in government spending and a subsequent decrease in unemployment and say the first thing caused the second without evidence that the first event set in motion particular events and created specific conditions which brought about the second. If one thing follows another consistently, you've got a *prima facie* (on the face of it) case for causality, and certainly you could hypothesize a causal connection. But you can't claim causality until you've tested your claim and identified specific links between the two events.

Hasty Generalization

The food-stamp program supports mostly free-loaders. Let me tell you about my worthless son-in-law.

Midsummer Night's Dream and *As You Like It* both have plots that move from court to forest and then back to the court. This must be the pattern for all of Shakespeare's comedies.

Closely related to the *post hoc* fallacy is *hasty generalization*, a fallacy that's been touched upon in several different places in the text. Hasty generalizations result from basing claims on insufficient or unrepresentative evidence. Establishing that government spending *once* led to decreased unemployment does not warrant the claim that it always will. Or establishing that the chemistry department places more emphasis on research than on teaching does not mean that the history or the psychology departments do also. Making general claims on the basis of a small sample is always dangerous. Stereotypes, as you will recall, are often the result of hasty generalizations that harden into assumptions.

False Analogy

You can't force a kid to become a musician any more than you can force a tulip into becoming a rose.

I'm too old to go back to school. You know you can't teach an old dog new tricks.

We've also discussed the dangers of mistaking analogical relationships for truth or identity relationships. To say that one thing resembles another is to say simultaneously that it's similar *and* different. To mistake an analogy for identity is to make a "false analogy." For example, if you see an analogy between twentieth century America and ancient Rome, that analogy can form the basis of an hypothesis that America will decline, but it cannot be used to "prove" that America will decline. Similarly, the oft noted parallels between the lives and deaths of Presidents Lincoln and Kennedy "prove" nothing—except, perhaps that if you look long enough at any two complex phenomena you can come up with plenty of similarities between the two things.

False Division

Differences in IQ are caused by environment or they are caused by the genes.

Either you support a pro-choice attitude toward abortion or you are an anti-feminist.

As we have tried throughout this text to suggest, particularly in Chapter 2, it is almost always a mistake to reduce complex matters of choice to two alternatives. In logical terms, this habit is known as "false division, as in that classic saying of the sixties—"America: Love it or Leave It." The "false division" fallacy omits the possibility of more than two positions—either a middle ground, a synthesis, or a new way of representing a problem so as to eliminate the dilemma. People responding to criticism tend also to reduce their opposition's position to an act of betrayal and thus to set up a false division. "You're either with me or against me," "Fish or cut bait," and "My way or the highway" are all familiar phrases used to falsely divide our choices into black and white extremes and to pull the middle ground out from under our feet.

Ad Hominem (Against the Person)

Don't trust Dr. Strong's views on the development of social values. She's a communist.

Don't pay any attention to Fulke's views on pornography. He get's paid by *Reader's Digest.*

Sometimes when people can't find fault with an argument, they will attack the arguer, substituting assertions about that person's character (which are irrelevant to the argument) in place of an analysis of the argument itself.

Appeals to False Authority/Bandwagon Appeals

If a great football coach like Rock Knookne supports Senator Fribble, Fribble must be OK!

How can abortion be wrong if millions of people support its legalization?

Both of these fallacies ask us to accept as support for an argument the fact that influential people already support it (either a famous person or that most influential of people—a crowd). But unless the supporters are themselves authorities in the field, their support is irrelevant.

Non Sequitur

Senator Jones opposed abortion. She will therefore support school prayer.

George will be a good father because he has a great sense of humor.

A *non sequitur* occurs when two statements linked in the grammatical form of a traditional claim-reason sentence (that is, using words like *because* or *therefore*) don't in fact connect logically. *Non sequitur* means *it does not follow*, an appropriate name because the claim of a *non sequitur* argument does not follow from the reasons. Often non sequiturs can be repaired by filling in some missing steps and/or properly qualifying a claim. For example, in the claim about George you'd have to spell out the missing connections between a good sense of humor and effective parenting and qualify your prediction that George will be a great father with a "probably".

Circular Reasoning

Billy Williams doesn't belong in the Hall of Fame because he wasn't a great ballplayer. If he were a great ballplayer, he'd already be in the Hall of Fame.

Marijuana is injurious to your health because it harms your body.

"Circular reasoning" occurs when you state your claim and then, usually after rewording it, you state it again as your reason. Sometimes circular reasoning can be tricky to spot: "A communist country, too, would benefit from allowing free speech because a society needs the advantages of having everyone able to speak his or her mind openly." It might take two readings here to appreciate that the "reason" given is simply a restatement of the claim.

Although logicians have identified and labeled many additional kinds of informal fallacies, these are the most frequently encountered ones. Practice spotting them whenever you read or listen to an argument.

THE NUMBERS GAME: DEALING WITH DATA

One of the characteristic differences between argumentation today and argumentation in the past is our increased reliance on and belief in numbers. Whereas in ancient times speakers relied primarily on logical proof and the invocation of shared principles to convince an audience to accept their point of view, writers and speakers today rely more on statistics, charts, graphs, and various manifestations of numbers to make their points. Whereas an opponent of abortion in older times might simply have invoked the principle "Thou shalt not kill" and then amplified that principle by citing horrors that occurred in the lives of women who aborted their offspring, a latter-day opponent of abortion will have to confront statistical or quantitative issues such as biological data about the day-by-day development of the fetus, the percentage of abortions which result in death for the mother, the comparative death rates for mothers who legally or illegally abort offspring, the economic costs associated with aborting or not aborting an offspring, the increase or decrease in unwanted pregnancy which follow changes in abortion laws, and so on. While one may argue with the appropriateness of such statistical arguments, one cannot argue with the pervasiveness of data in argumentation. Whether we want to or not, we need to be able to deal with numerical forms of evidence.

Before moving on to a discussion of arguments based on data, we need to say a word about our infatuation with data itself. We speak of "hard" data as though they were eternal and unquestionable truths. In contrast to hard data, which are based on extensive gathering of information in response to precisely formulated questions, soft data may be a rough estimate based on limited sampling and/or in response to less precise questions. Whereas soft data often seem one step removed from opinion, hard data often seem factual.

But are hard data "factual"? One could, for instance, ask a hundred students to rank professors A and B on "overall effectiveness as a teacher" (on a scale, say, of 1 to 10 with 10 the highest), and find that A scored 8.2 while B scored 5.8. What do these "hard" data mean? Do they mean that A is a better teacher than B? Do they necessarily even mean that students think that A is a better teacher than B? Do we have any certainty what criteria students are using when they evaluate "effectiveness"? Are they all using about the same criteria? What if A teaches consistently through lecture and multiple choice exams while B teaches through small group discussion interspersed with lots of writing assignments? Do the "hard" data mean that students think A is a better teacher than B or that lecturing is a better teaching method than small group discussions? What if *every* student ranked A as either 8 or 9 on the scale, while 50 percent of all students ranked B as 10 while the other 50 percent ranked B between 1 and 4?

The point being made is that while some data can be considered more trustworthy than other data, no data are "hard" in quite the way that word suggests. In some sense, all numbers are "soft." You can't pick them up or eat them or build houses out of them. Any number system is "made up" and meaningful only in relation to other numbers. All that "2" means is twice as many as "1," half as much as "4." While numbers can be applied to almost anything in the world, none of them refers directly to anything outside the system of numbers. What all this means is that numbers must be *made* meaningful and one makes them meaningful by viewing them in the context of other numbers. Hence, a billion is a big number if you're talking about people, but a small number if you're talking about atoms. Numbers alone, then, won't settle arguments and one of the greatest dangers which people fall prey to is to rely too much on numbers and not enough on analysis to make numbers significant. (Numbers, in abundance, can also be extemely boring unless you have created a context to make them meaningful, hence the unpersuasiveness of long strings of figures. In this regard, recall the old George Carlin routine where George, playing a manic DJ, abruptly announces "And now for some baseball scores: 8 to 3, 4 to 1. Hey! and here's an upset, 6 to 5!")

MAKING NUMBERS MEANINGFUL: CHARTS, TABLES, AND GRAPHS

One of the most common ways of making numbers meaningful is to "picture" them in graphs, charts, or tables. A chart is quite literally a picture of numerical values. A pie chart, for example, gives you an immediate sense of how big a portion of the whole each part claims. Figure 11-1, for example, is a pie chart showing how big a piece of the federal budget pie goes to various areas. In a table, on the other hand, numerical data can be expressed much more complexly than in a pie chart, but their significance in relation to other numbers is not so visually highlighted. Somewhere in

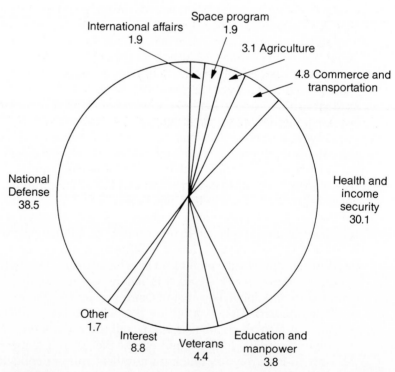

FIGURE 11-1 Federal Budget, Percent Distribution by Function: 1968–1972

between is a graph, in which the numbers are "pictured" in the form of a line or lines drawn on a grid of squares called "scale units." Since graphs are the most common—and most commonly misunderstood—form of data presentation, we'll look at them a bit more closely.

In reading a graph, as in reading a table, we read from the "outside-in." We look for a title to the graph which tells us what two values are being related. We then look to see which value is represented on the vertical axis and which one is represented on the horizontal axis. We check to see what quantity each scale unit represents for each of the two values. Then we look at the line to see what it tells us about the relationship between the two values.

When the line goes straight out from the bottom left of the graph to the upper right, the line is telling us that an increase in one value is matched by an increase in the other value. Likewise, if a line starts in the upper left corner and descends toward the lower right corner, we know that an increase in the value plotted on the horizontal axis is matched by a decrease in the value plotted on the vertical axis. Squiggly lines which go up and down indicate a variable relationship between the two values.

While it takes a fair amount of time to say all this, one can see this at a glance if one is familiar with the logic of graphs. This, in fact, is the power of graphs. They can give instant presence to a complex relationship. The more dramatic the movement of the line (also called the "slope" of the line), the more weight the graph can give to statements relating the two values.

But graphs can be deceiving. Let's take a look at a graph more closely to see how they are made and what sorts of things one should be careful of in interpreting them. Arranged in tabular form, Table 11-1 shows some data on the profitability of Squiggle Pen Company, manufacturers of cheap ballpoint pens.

TABLE 11-1.   Monthly Net Profits for Squiggle Pen Co. 1982—First 3 Quarters

Month	Net Profits (in thousands of $)
Jan.	1.0
Feb.	2.0
Mar.	3.0
Apr.	4.0
May	4.0
June	5.0
July	6.0
Aug.	8.0
Sept.	12.0

One can, by looking at the table, get a general sense of Squiggle's profit pattern, but it takes a while and the impact is thus diminished. Now let's take a look at a graphic display of the information as compiled by Luther Squiggle, president of the firm. (See Figure 11-2.)

Looking at this graph, one can see that Squiggle Pen is headed for the stars. Just look at that line, taking off like an F-16. But before you grab your checkbook and ring up your broker, let's analyze the graph. One of the trickiest features of graphs is that they often suggest more about relationships than we have any right to infer. It would appear from looking at this graph that as time passes on the horizontal axis, profitability increases on the vertical axis. Our tendency is to say that the passage of time *results* in an increase in profit. In fact, all we can say is that during the time period depicted in the graph, profits did increase. We cannot legitimately infer that profits will continue to increase over time. No permanent or necessary relationship between the two values has been established, though the picture presented by the graph tends to "fix" that relationship and make it appear permanent.

The graph presents *a* picture of Squiggle's profitability, but not *the* picture. To fully understand this graph, we need to have a sense of the larger picture, of other numbers and other graphs. The assumption we made above was that this particular picture of Squiggle's profits was typical or representative of the larger picture. But the smaller the particular picture we look at in a graph, the more risky it is to make inferences about the bigger picture. If, for example, we looked at a graph which represented Squiggle's profits over the life of the company, our steeply rising line might turn out to be a mere "blip" upward in an inexorably descending line. If we looked at profits for the last quarter of 1982, we might see a precipitous drop. If we looked at the same graphs for 1980 and 1981, we might see the same pattern, which would indicate that the apparent steady ascent is merely part of a cyclic pattern of rises and falls, with every January being a low-sale month (after shoppers have bought their Christmas stocking stuffers) and every September a high-sale month (when students return to school).

Another important consideration to keep in mind when interpreting graphs is the quantity assigned to each square. However truthful one must be in picturing the correct quantities graphically, *how* one presents those quantities, the proportion represented by each square, is usually a matter of choice and can profoundly influence a reader's perception of the relationship being pictured in the graph. If Squiggle, for example, had chosen not to let each square on the vertical axis represent $1,000, his company's rise in profitability might not look quite so astonishing. If each of the squares were instead to represent $5,000, it would appear to be a less remarkable change, barely creeping up to the second square. (See Figure 11-3). Hence, one can easily distort or overstate a rate of change on a graph by carefully

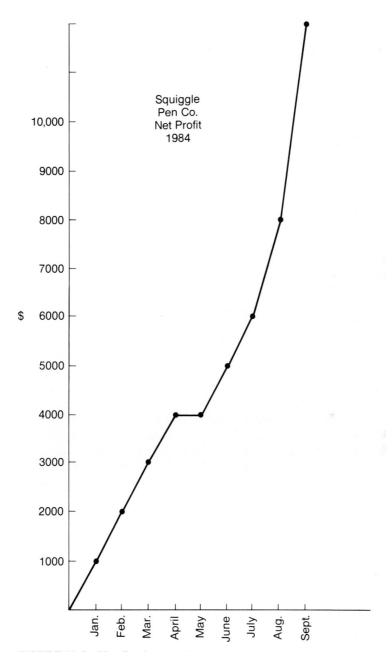

FIGURE 11-2   Net Profits, Squiggle Pen Company, 1984

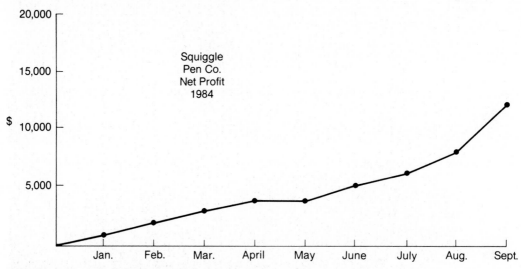

FIGURE 11-3   Net Profits, Squiggle Pen Company, 1984

selecting the quantities one assigns to each scale unit on either the horizontal or vertical axis.

Number Traps to Beware of

In addition to these basic sorts of questions about tables, charts, and graphs, one should always be on the lookout for common numbers traps. For example, beware of "hidden factors," things which influence the picture you're seeing, but which aren't mentioned explicitly when a series of numbers are displayed. The discovery of hidden factors requires that you know something about the phenomenon being shown in a chart, table, or graph. First, you often need to know how the values being related on a graph were derived. In the case of Squiggle, for instance, you might want to question why the graph only depicts the first three quarters and ends in September. It could be that September, when school buyers traditionally seek out cheap pens, is always an up month for Squiggle. You might also want to know how net profit was computed, since there are various bookkeeping procedures which allow companies to hide losses or understate gains (for example, you need to know whether or not net profit includes sale of land or equipment, or a tax write-off). Or what about inflation, a major hidden factor in many economic pictures? If inflation was running at a high rate during 1982, so that Squiggle felt justified in doubling the price of his pens in July, then Squiggle's profit picture might have to be re-evaluated.

Another trap you can fall into occurs when you are interpreting data from surveys or polls. Say you see a chart relating degree of favorable response to Senator Phogbound across all income levels of the respondents. It may show that Phogbound is headed for a landslide victory. However, the chart may once again be deceiving. What questions were asked of respondents which drew this almost unanimously favorable response? If the respondents were saying yes to questions like "Do you support Senator Phogbound's courageous stand against waste in government?" you might begin to question his true voter support since the wording of the question almost insured a positive response. You might also want to know how many people were questioned and how people were selected for the poll. Did the pollsters visit only one county in the state, a county that went heavily for Phogbound in the last election? Did they question only members of his political party? Did they question six people or six thousand? Though accurate projections can be made on the basis of very small samples, the accuracy of those projections depends upon the sample being representative of the whole. Moreover, the margin for error decreases as more people are questioned. Finally, who did the polling? Polls done by nationally respected firms and disinterested parties tend to be more accurate than those done by interest groups.

Finally, you need to be especially careful in interpreting data that can be reported either as raw numbers or as percentages. Politicians who enthusiastically report that more Americans are working today than ever before may be conveniently forgetting to mention that the percentage of unemployment is higher than since the Depression. In other words, we may have more employed persons because the population has grown, not because the economy is better. Similarly, the increase in the size of the defense budget can be made to sound huge if raw numbers are displayed, but much more moderate if the defense budget is displayed as a percentage of the gross national product. Thus, in order to comprehend the significance of absolute numbers, you often need to see them both in relation to other absolute numbers and in relation to percentages. For example, "40 percent of the American population would survive nuclear war" doesn't sound quite as grim as saying "130 million Americans would die in a nuclear war." You need to see the numbers both ways to get a comprehensible picture.

In sum, arguments relying on data, and visual displays of data, demand a knowledge of the sources of those numbers and the context within which those numbers are meaningful. You can always choose to express the same data in a number of ways, and *how* you say it with numbers is as important as *what* you say. Whenever you are given numerical evidence of any kind, ask yourself two questions: "Where did the numbers come from?" and "In relation to what other numbers are these numbers significant?"

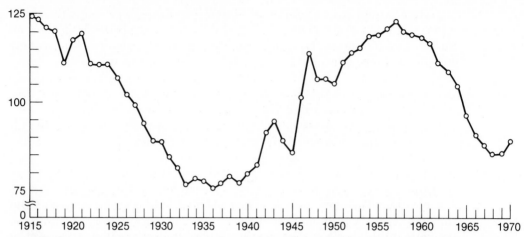

FIGURE 11-4   Fertility Rates, American Women, 1915–1970 (Rate per 1,000 females, ages 14–44)
Source: Reprinted with permission of John Wiley & Sons, from *Handbook of Graphic Presentation*, 2nd ed., by Calvin Schmid and Stanton Schmid, 35. Copyright 1979 by John Wiley & Sons.)

For Class Discussion

1. Examine the preceding graph (Figure 11-4) showing fertility rates for American women between the ages of fifteen and forty-four. The graph shows the number of births per thousand women during each year.
   a. Discuss possible hypotheses that might explain the changes in fertility rates for the period shown.
   b. As a class determine what sorts of supplementary data you might need to confirm your hypotheses.
   c. What hypotheses might you form about fertility rates prior to and after the time period shown on the graph? What would you hypothesize about the fertility rate in 1850? In 1865? In 1980? Why?

2. *For Baseball Fans Only*. Since statistics are so vitally important to the sport of baseball, and since many of you baseball fanatics learned math in order to calculate batting averages, we include one challenge for baseball fans. Printed on page 333 are two pairs of statistics. They show the lifetime totals for two short-stops and two outfielders from approximately the same eras (early 1940s to mid-1950s for the first pair, late 1950s to mid-1970s for the second pair.) To help give you some sense of what these statistics "mean," we should point out that shortstop A's homerun total is the second highest and his RBI total is fourth highest *among all*

shortstops who ever played the game. (None of shortstop B's totals would put him in the top ten for his position.) On the other hand, outfielder A is in the top 20 in homeruns, the top 40 in hits and the top 60 in runs on the all-time list *for all players* regardless of position. (Outfielder B is not in the top 100 in any category.) One of the two shortstops is frequently mentioned as a candidate for the Hall of Fame; the other is never mentioned. Both outfielders are mentioned as potential Hall of Famers, though as of this date neither has been elected. (Note: Defensively, the candidates are relatively well-balanced. All were at least average at their position.)

Looking over their stats, select which one of each pair is, in your judgment, the most worthy of selection. Be able to defend your choice before the other baseball fans in the class. On what do you base your judgment in particular? What factors other than the statistics shown might influence you to change your vote? How big a role do you think statistics should play in the evaluation of baseball players?

You might be surprised when you learn the identity of the players. (The answers are printed in the *Instructors Manual* for this text, so ask your teacher.) Once you know the answers, do any new factors enter into your judgment that you had not yet considered?

Shortstops	Games	Hits	Homeruns	Runs	Runs Batted In	Walks	Batting Average	Stolen Bases
Shortstop A.	1720	1859	247	1001	1174	692	.286	25
Shortstop B.	1661	1588	38	562	562	650	.273	149

Outfielders	Games	Hits	Homeruns	Runs	Runs Batted In	Walks	Batting Average	Stolen Bases
Outfielder A.	2488	2711	426	1410	1475	1045	.290	90
Outfielder B.	1463	1325	275	826	851	652	.260	21

CHAPTER 12

Assignments for Issue-Defense Essays

When you write an issue-defense essay, you defend a position on an issue, all the while trying to show a tolerant awareness that there are reasonable positions opposing yours. Sometimes in an issue-defense essay you will address an audience directly opposed to your position. More often, however, you will assume that you can't sway those directly opposed to you; hence you address a group of "neutral," undecided people who have yet to make up their minds on the issue. You must be aware, therefore, that this audience will also be considering opposing arguments, much as a jury considers the arguments of both the defense and prosecuting attorneys.

A time-honored classical model for argumentation contains the following sections:

1. An *introduction*, in which you engage your reader's attention, introduce your issue, give it "presence," and state your own position.
2. *Background and preliminary material*, in which you place your issue in a current context, perhaps by summarizing historical events leading to the issue, by referring to recent events that have brought the issue to public attention, or by telling of a personal experience that makes the issue important to you. You would also use this section to define key terms or clarify needed concepts.

3. A *summary of opposing views*, in which, through the Principle of Charity, you objectively lay out arguments opposing your position. This section not only helps the reader understand the issue more clearly, but establishes you as a fair-minded, rational writer willing to admit to the complexity of the issue.

4. *Discussion of the strengths and weaknesses of the opposing views*, in which you concede to strong points in your opponent's argument and point out its weaknesses.

5. *Presentation of arguments supporting your own position*, in which you make the best case possible for your views using evidence and chains of reasons. This is usually the longest part of your essay.

6. *Anticipation of possible objections that your audience might make to your position*, in which you show again an awareness of the complexity of your issue and acknowledge again that your position can never be the whole truth.

7. *Rebuttal of objections to your argument, including a concession to those weaknesses that seem insurmountable.* Here you respond to anticipated objections, buttressing your position "in advance," as it were.

8. A *conclusion*, in which you place your argument in a larger context, perhaps summarizing your main points and showing why this issue is an important one.

Of course, this classical model can be modified in various ways. Often, for example, you might choose to present your own position first, before you summarize the opposition and examine weaknesses in opposing views. But a full-scale defense of a position would generally include all these traditional elements somewhere in the essay.

The first two assignments for this chapter will help you develop two complementary strategies of argumentation needed for the above classical method: (a) a strategy for supporting your own position, and (b) a strategy for summarizing an opposing view and showing its weaknesses.[1] The third assignment in this chapter will describe a somewhat different and more modern argumentation strategy, sometimes called Rogerian argument, which grows out of the kind of Rogerian listening you have already practiced. Finally, the last assignment will leave you free to write a longer, more complex issue-defense essay using whatever strategies and shapes that best fit your purpose.

---

[1] We are indebted for our discussion of the first two assignments in this chapter to Kenneth Bruffee, whose book *A Short Course in Writing*, 2nd ed. (Boston: Little, Brown, 1980) contains the assignments upon which we have modeled ours. Our more general indebtedness to Professor Bruffee is gratefully acknowledged in the Preface.

Assignment 1: Supporting Reasons Strategy

Write a multi-paragraph essay in which you develop two or more reasons in support of your thesis or proposition. Each of your reasons should be summarizable in a "because" clause attached to your claim to form a writer's thesis statement. If you have more than two reasons, develop your most important reason last. Your opening paragraph should introduce your issue and give it presence. Prior to presenting your own thesis, you might briefly summarize a view opposing yours to help clarify the issue for your reader. A good concluding strategy is to place your issue inside a larger context of issues—the strategy we call the "web conclusion" (Chapter 4, pp. 108–109).

Discussion

The strategy for writing supporting reasons essays is discussed at length in Chapters 9, 10, and 11. A good way to improve your skill at composing supporting-reasons essays is to develop a writer's thesis statement which contains your claim followed by a series of two, three, or four "because" clauses that summarize your supporting reasons. How you turn a "because" clause into a section of an essay is the subject of Chapter 9. Journal Sequence 3, especially the eight tasks in the second section (pp. 266–268), will help you explore ideas for your essay. The key here is to develop a clear position with clear supporting reasons, each of which can be developed either by evidence or by a chain of other reasons.

One key to the success of your essay will be your introduction, which will typically have the following shape:

- Has a good lead to grab attention—often a personal experience, quote, startling statistic, memorable scene, or other device to give presence to the essay.
- Explains issue and gives background. You may choose to present the issue as an issue-question.
- Briefly summarizes an opposing view.
- Has a "yes, but ..." or "however" transition.
- Ends with a reader's version of your claim or thesis.

Note that although we suggest you summarize an opposing argument in your introduction, you do not need to evaluate its strengths or weaknesses. Simply by summarizing the argument, however, you accomplish two things: you clarify the issue for your reader and you demonstrate your objectivity and fairness.

Although we have called this assignment a multi-paragraph essay, some instructors will prefer to restrict you to four paragraphs—one for the introduction, two for the body, and one for the conclusion. If you have two supporting reasons (two "because" clauses in your writer's thesis statement), then you will use one body paragraph to develop each reason. If you have three or more supporting reasons, you will summarize your minor reasons in the first body paragraph and use the second body paragraph to develop your main reason. The following student examples of supporting reasons essays employ this more restricted pattern.*

Rapelje Station

A short Burlington Northern freight train rumbles out of the station at Billings, Montana. It consists of one engine, two empty box cars and a caboose. One hour later the train is crawling slowly up the branch line tracks to its destination: Rapelje, a struggling town of less than one hundred people, only thirty-eight rail-miles from Billings. Despite the short distance, the train takes four hours to get there. The rusty rails dip and bend, barely supported on old rotting ties; if the train exceeds eight or ten miles per hour it will derail. After picking up one loaded car at the Rapelje Grain Company elevator, the train leaves the two empties and heads back. Half way home the train lurches and suddenly stops; a fatigued rail has finally broken and the engine is on the ground. Over the last few years this sort of scene has become commonplace. Only two trains a month run to Rapelje and little track maintenance is done between trips. Usually only one or two cars are picked up, which means the railroad can't make enough to pay for each trip, let alone for the cost of track maintenance. Now the Burlington Northern has petitioned the ICC for permission to abandon the Rapelje line, citing unprofitability and poor track condition as the main reasons. The railroad has the figures to back up its claims, and seems to have a good case for abandonment. But the BN is not presenting all the facts and should not be allowed to abandon the Rapelje branch line.

First, the BN should not be permitted to follow through with its plan because the railroad is the primary means of commerce for the town. Rapelje is a farming community set in the heart of some of Montana's finest wheat country and was built around the railroad during the homestead years of the early 1900s. The railroad encouraged the town's growth by promising a means of transporting both people and goods to the distant main line at Billings. Once on the main line, farmers had access to markets all over the country, from the cattle markets in Chicago to the grain terminals on the west coast. Today the railroad is still the most economical means of transporting grain to the buyers. Though there is one country road which now goes to Rapelje, giving truckers access to the town, a large part of it is rough and unpaved, and it features a steep pass. It's a difficult fifty mile round trip from the nearest main highway for any trucker. Should

---

* For additional examples of supporting reasons essays—including some unsuccessful ones—see the Appendix, pp. 442–447.

Rapelje ever find itself without rail service, it would be forced to depend on expensive and inconsistent truck service, and could be without any service at all during bad winter weather.

The second reason Rapelje should continue to receive rail service is that, contrary to what the BN would have the ICC believe, the profit potential for that branch line is excellent. I have seen the Rapelje railroad shipping records dating back to the 1930s. For decades the Rapelje line saw thousands of tons of grain and cattle shipped on trains that ran two to three times a week. Today the amount of wheat leaving the area is not any less than twenty years ago. But in its efforts to become a modern, main-line railroad, the Burlington Northern has decided that branch line service is not worth the effort, and has allowed both the service and the road bed to deteriorate. Trains to Rapelje are now irregular, infrequent, and short on cars, leaving the elevator without a shipping schedule it can depend on. In order to get the best price for its product, the grain company must arrange large-quantity sales in advance and be able to meet the buyer's shipping deadlines. These sales often fall through before the railroad supplies the needed cars, so the grain must be slowly shipped out by truck at an unprofitable rate; or, if truck service is not available and the elevator is full, the surplus grain simply rots on the ground. But the railroad records do not reflect the abundant shipping potential, only the infrequent and low-revenue service. Though there's often enough grain in Rapelje to fill twenty jumbo hopper cars, Burlington Northern rarely sends more than one or two smaller cars to the terminal.

If the ICC were to refuse the Burlington Northern permission to abandon the Rapelje line, then the railroad would be forced to operate the line in a more financially and morally responsible manner. Leaving Rapelje without a feasible shipping alternative would show callous inconsideration for a town which the railroad helped to build. Without a dependable and economical way of shipping, the farming economy of the area would surely weaken. Higher truck rates and less dependable service may force some struggling farmers out of business. Eventually major track maintenance will have to be done, and when that time comes, the railroad would be wise to reinvest in this short line to accommodate sufficient traffic to again be profitable. Considering the extent of the repairs needed, it is not likely that the Rapelje line would show a profit for the first few years after renovation. But since no other form of shipping can compete with the railroad in this area, the potential for consistent, long-range income for the BN should justify a relatively low maintenance cost. Renovation and a return to regular service may not be the best thing for the railroad, but it could still be profitable, and it would certainly be a source of stability for the farming economy of Rapelje.

Gambling on Stocks

Easy money—everybody wants it—but aside from a few lottery winners, Reader's Digest Clearing House winners and other such lucky souls, most people never get it. Even so, it's hard to resist the fantasy of the big killing; that's why there are gambling casinos, supermarket sweepstakes, and bookies; and that's why there's a stock market. Now some people might tell you that putting money in the stock market is not gambling at all. They would say that it's investing—putting money into the economy, building the country, creating jobs, and so forth. These same people would probably tell you that a careful, hard-working and aware investor can make good money in the stock market. The truth is, however, that the majority of the people who "invest" in the stock market don't care at all about anything except making some bucks. Unfortunately, they would have just as good a chance if they put their money in a slot machine or on a horse race. The stock market is gambling, pure and simple.

First of all, the stock market is gambling because its profits and losses depend on future events, and no one knows what the future is going to bring—in any area. Only two years ago, practically everyone thought the price of oil was going to keep on rising and rising. Now there is a big oil glut, and anybody who got into oil stocks a couple of years ago has some real losses. In the same manner, video games, both home games and arcade games, appeared to obsess teenagers and children so much that they would never go out of style. It hardly seemed likely that in a year or so after the craze began, Mattel's Intellivision Division and the Atari Division of Warner Communications would be deeply in the red. In contrast, the recording industry was in its fourth year of a bad slump. Hardly anyone would be caught dead buying Columbia Records stock, but now it is booming. Utility stocks (electric companies, gas companies, telephone companies) have long been called "widows and orphans" stocks because of their supposed safety and stability. You just buy them and hold them, and they pay good dividends year after year. Then came nuclear power and the breakup of the phone company. These two events have totally changed the nature of utility stocks. Electric companies who invested in nuke plants found themselves faced with long delays and cost over-runs (take the now infamous bankruptcy of the nuclear power plants under construction in Washington, for example); their stocks plummeted and the widows and orphans were just out of luck.

The most important reason that playing the stock market is like throwing dice in a Las Vegas Casino, however, resides in basic human psychology. Because one has to go against his own emotional response, losing becomes almost a sure thing. The only way to make any money in the stock market is to buy low and sell high—something that is extremely difficult. For one thing, nobody knows what "low" or "high" are until it is too late. When stock prices are down and appear very cheap, it is usually because conditions are terrible. Everyone is selling because the economy is bad, business is bad, and things look like they are just going to get worse. In the summer of 1982, many people thought the U. S. was heading into a second depression. Most people gave up and sold their stocks in despair. And then what happened? In August of 1982, stocks began to soar, and they kept going up for ten months. But only the few hardy souls who bought stocks at their miserable lows, when everything seemed at its blackest, made any big money. Ironically, now that the recovery is underway and the economy is booming, the stock market has dropped over one hundred points, ignoring completely all the good news about falling unemployment and rising profits. In other words, just when it seems to be time to buy, it's time to sell. Most people cannot handle this. They sell when they see everybody else selling, and they buy when they are convinced it is safe to do so. This kind of behavior is logical; the problem is, it doesn't work.

Clearly, the only way most people will make money in the stock market is through pure luck. It's just like backing the right horse or putting your money on the right number. The theory that you might as well throw darts at the stock market page is true—so why do thousands of people pretend otherwise? Why do they spend so much time and money trying to choose the "right" stocks? The answer is that there is a multi-million dollar industry out there that wants them to think that the market is not a gamble at all. There are hundreds and hundreds of brokerage houses, money managers, market letter writers and bank trustees that want the public to believe that careful study and analysis can pay off. Smith Barney "makes money the old-fashioned way"—they fool you. There are also publications that live by their stock market advice—*The Wall Street Journal, Forbes, Money, Fortune, Barrons,* and many others. The constant blitz in the media and in the financial industries has convinced the public of the need for useless services. And the public has gone along with the idea that an informed, aware, educated and prudent investor can achieve stock market success. The public is being taken for a ride.

For Class Discussion

1. Working as a whole class or in small groups, compose the writer's thesis statement for each of these student essays. (A writer's thesis statement for a supporting reasons argument would be the writer's position followed by "because" clauses.)

2. Create a loose syllogism for each of the "because" clauses.

3. Describe the writers' strategies for developing each "because" clause. Do they use evidence? A chain of reasons? Do they concentrate mainly on supporting the minor premise or the major premise for each "because" clause?

Assignment 2: Opposition/Refutation Strategy

Write a multi-paragraph essay in which you summarize a position opposing yours and then show the weaknesses of that position. Each of the reasons in your opponent's argument should be summarizable in "because" clauses attached to your opponent's claim. Your essay should have four sections. The opening section—your introduction —should introduce your issue, give it presence, and briefly summarize your own position. This section should conclude with a purpose statement indicating your intention to show weaknesses in an opposing argument. Your second section should summarize an opposing view, following the Principle of Charity. Each of the reasons supporting your opponent's position should be clearly highlighted. The third section should concede to the strengths of this opposing view and then point out its weaknesses. You should attack, in turn, each of the reasons summarized earlier. Finally, your last section should conclude the essay by placing your issue within a larger context of issues.

Discussion

The conclusion for this essay is the same kind of "larger context of issues" conclusion that you used in the supporting reasons argument. The introduction for this essay, however, differs slightly from the strategy used previously. Because the body of this essay deals with weaknesses in your opponent's position rather than with strengths of your own position, you should summarize *your own position* in the introduction. You can then conclude the introduction with a purpose statement showing that your essay will point out weaknesses in an opponent's position. (Since your thesis statement would normally support your own position rather than point out weaknesses in your opponent's position, a purpose statement here is an effective substitute for a thesis statement. See Chapter 4 for a discussion of the difference between a thesis statement and a purpose statement, both of which are common methods of focussing an essay.) A typical introduction for this essay will have the following shape:

- Has a good lead to grab attention—often a personal experience, quote, startling statistic, memorable scene, or other device to give presence to the essay.
- Explains issue and gives background. You may choose to present the issue as an issue-question.
- Briefly summarizes *your own position* on the issue.
- Has a transition noting that everyone doesn't agree with you.
- Ends with a purpose statement showing that you plan to summarize and then attack an opposing position.

The second section of your essay (generally a single, well-developed paragraph) summarizes your opponent's position. The key here is completeness and fairness. If you summarize only the weakest parts of your opponent's argument, you will have created a "strawman" that is easy to knock down. Summarize the strongest opposing arguments you can devise. To find opposing arguments, you can either read essays opposing your position or you can interview people, including fellow classmates, who disagree with you. Be sure that the opening sentence of this section tells readers you are summarizing opposing views; otherwise, readers may think you are arguing your own position.

The heart of your essay will be the third section, which focuses on the weaknesses of the argument that you summarized in the second section. Many students initially go astray in this third section because they want to present their own position rather than attack the weaknesses of the opposition. The third section will be successful only if you deal point by point with the arguments raised in the second section. Let's therefore discuss in more detail ways of attacking an opposing position.

Discovering Weaknesses in Your Opponent's Argument. In creating opposition/refutation arguments, the writer needs to understand the argument of the opposition and to be able to search for its weaknesses. One way to do so, of course, is to search an argument for obvious logical fallacies of the kind we discussed in Chapter 11.

But the arguments that are most challenging are those that are logically sound and that we therefore disagree with because we disagree with the argument's basic premises or with the persuasiveness of evidence. An effective way to examine such arguments is to construct your opponent's syllogism for each of his or her major "because" sections. You can then begin to isolate ways of attacking the argument. Do you accept the minor premise but disagree with the basic principle identified in the major premise? Or do you accept the major premise but disagree with arguments supporting the minor premise? The more you appreciate the structure of the opposing argument, the more you can develop ways to attack it.

As an example, we will use an issue that created heated debate in one of our recent Freshman English sections. Students were asked to write a "committee" problem-solution essay (a simulated grant proposal) as a group project. After each group's proposal was evaluated, the group as a whole got a specified number of points for the essay, depending on its grade. They then divided the points up among group members according to the contributions of each member of the group. The class was strongly divided on the value of this assignment.

As an illustration of how to refute an opponent's argument, let's assume that you wish to write an opposition/refutation essay that opposes the writing of group essays like this "committee" grant proposal. Your task, then, will be to show weaknesses in the arguments of those who support group essays. Here is the general issue:

> **Issue question:** Are group essays valuable assignments for Freshman English?

> **Your position:** Group essays are a waste of time in Freshman English.
>
> **Countering position:** Group essays are valuable assignments for Freshman English.

Your opponents (those who support group essays) have developed a number of reasons showing why group essays are valuable, and you have summarized those reasons in your second section. Here is an excerpt from that section—your summary of one of their reasons:

Writing group papers is valuable because the process of thinking and writing in groups prepares students for the kind of writing that they will encounter in the world of work. For example, much writing in science, engineering, business, and industry is done by teams or committees.

This part of your opponet's argument is based on the following implied syllogism:

Valuable assignments imitate writing situations encountered in the world of work.
Group essays imitate writing situations encountered in the world of work.
Therefore, group essays are valuable.

Now here are some examples of both ineffective and effective strategies for rebutting this argument.

1. My opponent says that writing group essays prepares students for the world of work. Hah! This is a bunch of baloney. The assignment is so stupid it wouldn't prepare anybody to do anything. It just wastes everyone's time. Our group just sat around shooting the bull.

This argument is ineffective: The argument is circular because the assertion "the assignment is stupid" is what this essay is trying to prove; it can't therefore use that assertion as evidence. The remaining evidence (our group just sat around shooting the bull) doesn't by itself refute the opponent's position. Don't groups in the real work world also sit around shooting the bull at times? Didn't this group eventually complete their group essay? Maybe part of what this writer calls "shooting the bull" was more productive than the writer admits.

2. My opponent says that writing group essays prepares students for the world of work. But this isn't so. The assignment hasn't helped me at all.

This argument is also ineffective. Because the writer hasn't yet entered the world of work, he can't yet be certain that learning about group writing won't help him in the future.

3. My opponent says that writing group essays prepares students for the world of work But this isn't so. The assignment hasn't helped me at all. I also took a poll of fellow classmates, and three out of four agreed that the assignment didn't help them either.

Although better than the second argument, this argument remains ineffective. This writer has a better sense of what may constitute evidence, but the poll she cites would only support the point "Many students in our class didn't think group writing was helpful." The poll cannot support the point "Group writing will not help us in the world of work" because none of those interviewed has yet lived out the future.

4. My opponent says that writing group essays prepares students for the world of work. My opponent's argument depends on our accepting as "fact" our teacher's assertion that group writing is common in the world of work. I don't believe it is. I am majoring in elementary education and decided to take a survey of present elementary teachers. I interviewed a dozen teachers at Irving and Longfellow grade schools, and none of them has ever written a group paper nor even heard of anyone else writing a group paper. Thus, for my profession at least, group writing doesn't seem common at all. Unless my opponent could demonstrate that at least half of this class could really expect to do frequent group writing in their careers, this assignment is not worth the time and trouble.

This argument is far more effective because it casts doubt on an assumption behind the opponent's minor premise that group writing imitates writing situations encountered in the world of work. If group writing isn't really common in the world of work, then an exercise to give you that skill is irrelevant. To counter-attack this argument, believers in group writing would now have to demonstrate that such writing really is common.

5. My opponent says that writing group essays prepares students for the world of work. I agree with my opponent that group writing occurs frequently in the world of work. I also accept my opponent's assumption that assignments that prepare us for the world of work are valuable. However, the circumstances under which we do group writing in Freshman English are so different from the circumstances under which scientists or business people do group writing that the two experiences are not comparable, and hence the one doesn't prepare you for the other. In the business world people have common goals, common interests, and flexible enough time schedules to permit successful group meetings. They have an intrinsic interest in succeeding as a group. In our class, however, the groups are entirely artificial. Some of us want to be in college; some of us don't. Some of us want to get A's; some of us plan to flunk out anyway. Nobody in our group really wants to write a group paper. We are motivated only by grades, not by common interests. Moreover, our schedules are so inflexible

that we can't hold group meetings without interfering with other parts of our lives. This situation makes us dislike group writing, and thus the process we go through is entirely different from what would happen in a real work situation. Freshman English courses cannot teach students how to do successful group writing for the world of work unless they can create the kind of environment that occurs in the world of work. That certainly didn't happen in this class.

This is an effective argument. It accepts the opponent's criterion for judgment but denies that the specific case matches the criterion.

The direction of this argument can be indicated by returning to the opponent's syllogism:

Valuable assignments imitate writing situations encountered in the world of work. [The argument accepts this criterion.]

Group essays imitate writing situations encountered in the world of work. [The argument denies this link between the specific case and the criterion. The argument claims that group essays do not imitate writing situations in the world of work because the group processes in Freshman English are not comparable to group processes in a real work situation.]

Therefore, group essays are valuable. [The argument claims group essays are not valuable since the minor premise of the syllogism is false.]

6. My opponent says that writing group essays prepares students for the world of work. I concede that a lot of real world writing is done in groups and that group practice in Freshman English will probably be of some help in later life. However, I do not accept my opponent's criterion that a valuable assignment is one that directly imitates writing situations encountered in the world of work. I asked several businessmen what bothered them most about student writing. Not one of them complained that students didn't know how to write in groups. Rather, they complained that students didn't know how to spell or punctuate or write short clear sentences or compose a simple memo. This group assignment took an enormous amount of time—at least four complete class meetings and much valuable study time. This time would have been better spent on the basics. Perhaps English teachers could teach group writing in an advanced course on technical communication. But in Freshman English they should spend that valuable time on the basics. Our class hasn't spent nearly enough time reviewing punctuation or studying spelling rules. Instructors should teach us to walk before we take on some strange kind of dance movement like group writing.

This is an effective argument that accepts the matching of the specific case to the criterion but denies the criterion itself.

The direction of this argument can also be indicated by returning to the opponent's syllogism:

Valuable assignments imitate writing situations encountered in the world of work. [This argument denies this criterion by claiming that other kinds of more general assignments, such as studying the basics, would be more valuable. It uses the brief interview with business people to support the point that basics are more important than group writing.]

Group essays imitate writing situations encountered in the world of work. [The argument accepts this assertion by acknowledging that group writing really is common in the world of work and that practicing group writing as freshmen will help develop this skill. The author's objection is with the major premise, not the minor premise.]

Therefore, group essays are valuable. [The argument denies this conclusion because it denies the criterion established in the major premise.]

The following student example illustrates the opposition/refutation strategy:

Who Should Choose Essay Topics, Student or Teacher?

It's a crisis every writing student faces at one point or another. A basket full of crumpled papers lies in the corner. At the desk a weary student doodles on another wordless sheet of paper. Seconds dutifully tick from the tarnished clock on the cluttered shelf and still the student's pen scratches meaninglessly across the paper. "I've been here for two hours and I *still* haven't thought of a topic for my next English paper," he mutters. Then in sheer frustration he blurts out, "I wish the teacher would just give us a subject!" Yes, the familiar crisis of not being able to think of a topic for that next English paper. Should writing teachers just assign students a topic on which to write and end all this frustration and paper waste? Although I often wish they would, I sincerely believe that they should not assign specific topics. I usually prefer to select my own subject because it's almost always something that concerns, fascinates or puzzles me and something for which I desire an answer. I also seem to write better papers—both mechanically and stylistically—if I've chosen the theme. (Besides, I kind of enjoy doodling sometimes.) There are others, however, who disagree with my view. I have to admit, they have strong reasons to support their position. But I can still find weaknesses in their arguments.

Students who dislike choosing their own topics have several major arguments. First, they say that the main purpose of a writing course is to teach the fundamentals of clear, concise, well organized writing. The student can apply these principles regardless of the topic or who chooses it. He can write on anything from why journals are an effective teaching tool to chicken toenails and still apply the principles of proper grammar, colorful detail, paragraph construction and so forth. Second, the opposition points out that the teacher is more capable of providing help to the students because he is more familiar with the subject. He may, in fact, be an expert on the assigned topic. Thus, he can give the students helpful hints and insights on how to "attack" the subject. For instance, a young lady recently sought help from her writing instructor on an essay concerning several Beetle Bailey comic strips. She was having a great deal of difficulty knowing just how to analyze the subject, but after a few suggestions and possible interpretations from her instructor, she had no problem writing the paper. (Incidentally, she received an 'A' on the essay.) Finally, students in favor of teacher-assigned-topics point to the amount of time wasted trying to think of a topic. They claim that this time could be better spent editing and revising drafts. Our instructor often reminds his classes that a 'C' paper is often an 'A' paper turned in too soon. Many times an individual *had* to turn in a paper "too soon" because he had to spend so much time finding a topic that there was not time left to revise it.

Although I must concede that these are strong arguments and that I've shared similar views many a time, I can still find flaws in the arguments. My first objection is that a paper's topic and who chooses it *does* affect the student's application of writing fundamentals. If the individual is not interested in the assigned topic, he tends to care less about what he is saying and how he is saying it. Almost as if out of rebellion for having to write on something he did not select, he will simply write a paper he can "turn in"—often disregarding its quality. For example, a graphic design major in another class had to write an essay on why a young man, visiting her parents' home, should not belch at the supper table. Not surprisingly, she found the topic ridiculous and repulsive, and she hardly even tried to apply the rudiments of writing. She refused to use subtopic sentences, colorful language, flawless punctuation and so on. Needless to say, she received a wonderfully low grade. She admits, however, that if she had been allowed to write on her topic preference—why Pop art became so popular during the last half of this century—she would have taken more pride in what she was writing and how she was stating it. My second argument is that not only do we (as students) realize that teachers can provide more hints on writing the paper if he assigns the topic, we *use* this knowledge to our "advantage." If we can convince the teacher to partially explain how he would organize the paper, we then have a clearer idea of what he expects to read in our papers and we figure we can probably get a slightly higher grade. That is, we often use the instructor's ideas as our own. So, we have to do little to no personal thinking on the topic, and we never really learn the process of "thinking through" our own essay content. This does not help us learn how to write our own ideas in a way that others can understand, which is the basic purpose of writing. My final argument is that time spent generating topics is never wasted. Although the student may use only one of the topics he has listed for the paper he is currently writing, the other subjects are always optional themes for later papers. One student, for instance, had generated a number of possible topics for her issue/defense paper, but it wasn't until the opposition/refutation essay that she used her idea of discussing why programmed math instruction is not an effective method. Yet she *did* eventually use the topic. Furthermore, I question whether students would (or do) really use that saved time to revise their essays. Perhaps I'm just not a member of the "dedicated majority of students", but I know I'd much rather be skiing during that saved time than editing a paper.

I believe this issue of whether or not teachers should assign topics is related to a larger societal issue. I feel that our society is becoming too dependent upon having someone to tell us what to write, say, believe and think. Creative writing and thinking is apparently losing importance in our society, and I believe this may be partially responsible for our comparatively stagnant culture. A MSU history professor recently lectured that Japan, for example, is continually developing a rich, full culture because of its abundant "human resources" in creativity, while he stated that the United States is lacking in cultural richness. Perhaps we simply need to try to reintroduce the importance of creative thought and writing through such a trivial matter as having students select their own topics for papers. This certainly is not the only solution to cultural growth, but it is a beginning.

Assignment 3: Rogerian Strategy

Write a multi-paragraph essay that refrains from presenting your position until the conclusion. The opening section introduces the issue, provides needed background, and ends with a purpose statement indicating that the essay will present a compromise or synthesis between the writer's view and the opponent's view. The tone is warm and non-threatening. The second section summarizes the views of the opposition in a sympathetic manner. The opening of the third section creates a bridge between writer and opponent by pointing out major areas of agreement that writer and opponent share in common. After examining this "common ground," the third section then points out areas of disagreement, but stresses that these are minor compared to the major areas of agreement already discussed. Finally, the last section presents the writer's position, which, if possible, should be a compromise or synthesis indicating that the writer has shifted his original position (or at least his sympathies) toward the opposition's view and is now asking the opposition to make a similar shift toward the writer's new position.

Discussion

Rogerian argument, named for the psychologist Carl Rogers (whose article on "listening" you first read during Journal Sequence 1), is based on the assumption that argumentative essays are usually threatening. Because persuasive arguments try to change people's minds, they tend to demand a change in people's world views, to get readers, in a sense, to quit being their kind of person and start being your kind of person. Psychologists have shown that persons are often not swayed by a logical argument if it somehow threatens their own view of the world. Because Rogerian argument is a way of reducing threat, it is a particularly useful strategy for issues that involve a strong emotional element. Although Rogerian argument uses reason just as much as traditional argument, its persuasive strategy is psychological as well as logical.

Under Rogerian strategy, the writer's job is to show that his or her position is not threatening to the opposition *because both writer and opponent share many basic values.* Instead of attacking the opponent as wrong-headed, the Rogerian writer makes the opponent feel intelligent and valued. The Rogerian writer always "listens" carefully to the opponent and refrains from stating his or her own position until demonstrating that the opponent's position is understood. Finally, the writer seldom asks the opponent to accept all of the writer's ideas, but just to shift somewhat toward the writer's views. As a precedent, the writer demonstrates how he or she has already shifted toward the opponent's views, so that the conclusion of Rogerian strategy is ideally a compromise between—or even better, a synthesis of—the opposing positions. (A compromise is a middle ground that neither party particularly likes; a synthesis is a new position that both parties like better than their original positions.)

The key to successful Rogerian argument, besides the art of listening, is the ability to point out areas of agreement between the opposing positions. For example, if you support a woman's right to choose abortion and you are arguing with someone completely opposed to abortion, your best hope is not to change the opponent's view but simply to dispel some of your opponent's misconceptions that pro-choice people are baby-killing murderers. After summarizing your opponent's position in a sympathetic light, you can then stress how many values you and your opponent really share. Depending on what you really believe, you might say, for example, that you too value children, that you too are appalled by people who treat abortion as a form of birth control with no more moral significance than a pulled tooth, that you too agree that an easy acceptance of abortion might lead to a lessening of the value a society places on life, and finally that you too agree that accepting abortion lightly can lead to lack of sexual responsibility. After building bridges like these between you and your opponent, you are then ready to introduce gently your "however ...."

Your opponents will be more prepared to consider the areas where you and they disagree if you have already shown the larger, more important areas where you do agree.

Thus, when you finally get to your own position at the end of your argument, your reader will be more prepared to appreciate it and respond. You will have approached your opponent, not as a boxer ready to deck him, but as a potential friend ready to listen and compromise. Most importantly, you must enter Rogerian argumentation with the same openness as you expect of your opponent: that is, you too must risk change. This is why your last section, ideally, represents a shift in your position, just as much as you hope for a similar shift from your opponent.

Here is an example of a Rogerian argument written by a student. Since Rogerian argument is usually aimed directly at the persons opposing your position, this student chose to write her essay as a letter.

Ms. Beth Downey, Owner/Manager
Downey's Music
Grayfish

Dear Mrs. Downey:

I would just like to comment on the success of "Downey's Music" in Grayfish and say that, as owner and manager, you have done a wonderful job. I'm sure that you have the most extensive classical music, music teaching books, piano and acoustic guitar inventory of any store in a 100 square mile area. After working for you for three years, I have encountered music teachers and classical music lovers coming as far as 70 miles to buy their music from Downey's. All have had nothing but compliments for you and for the store. However, I would once again like to bring up the subject of introducing an inventory of electronic music equipment to the store. Since Grayfish is mainly a tourist town, many times a week I have people from touring bands, visiting Canadians, and also locals coming into the store looking for such things as electronic keyboards, electric guitars, and amplifiers. I know that you have qualms about this idea, but I believe that I have a suggestion that we could both agree on.

First, let me restate your reasons for objecting to such a move. You have already stated that if a change will benefit the store, the initial investment is well worth the expense in the long run (i.e., when pianos were added to the inventory). Therefore, I assume that cost is not a factor at this time. However, you feel that the "kind of people" that electronics may draw could possibly offend our present clientele. You feel, as well as others, that the people who are drawn by electronics are often long haired, dirty, and give a bad impression. This would in effect change the store's image. Also, you are afraid that the noise caused by these instruments could turn classical music lovers away from the store. The sounds of electronic instruments are not always pleasing, and since most of our clientele are older, more refined persons, you feel that these sounds will force some to go to other stores. Mainly, however, you are worried about the result that the change in the store's image could have upon a community the size of Grayfish. Many people in this area, I realize, feel that electronic music means heavy rock music, while this in turn means alcohol and drugs.

Basically, I agree with you that Grayfish needs a "classical" music store and that the culture that your store brings to Grayfish greatly enhances the area. I also love classical music and want to see it growing and alive. I also have some of the same fears about adding electronic music to the inventory. I enjoy the atmosphere of Downey's, and I have always enjoyed working there, so I don't want to see anything adverse happen to it either. On the other hand, I feel that if a large electronic music section were added to the store with sound-proof rooms a "sit and try it" atmosphere, and a catalog inventory large enough to special order anything that a customer may want that is not in the store, it would help immensely in the success of the store. With the way that Downey's is built, on two levels, it would be very easy to accommodate the needs of both departments. Even now we are only using about half the floor space available, while the rest is empty storage area. By building sound-proof rooms on the lower level, we could easily double the in-use floor area, increase our tourist clientele, have the music business in *all* areas cornered for approximately 60 square miles, and could also add practice rooms for our present customers to use when they are choosing music.

I know that you are wrestling with this idea of such a drastic changeover, so I would like to propose a solution that I feel we could both agree on. My solution is to start slowly, on a trial basis, and see how it works. I suggest that we start with a few small electronic keyboards, a few electric guitars, and one or two amps. In this way, we could begin to collect the information and literature on other electronic equipment that may be added later on, see how the community responds to such a move, find out how our present clientele reacts, get a feel for the demand in this field, and yet still be a small home-town music store without a great investment in this electronic area. I still feel that a large addition would be more successful, but I also believe that this little test may help prove to you, or disprove to me, that electronic music instruments in this area are in high demand. I honestly feel that electronics could produce fantastic profits for the people who get in the business first. I would love it if these "people" could be the owners and workers at Downey's Music.

Sincerely,

Mary Doe

Assignment 4: A Longer Essay Using a Combination of Strategies

Write an issue-defense essay of an approximate length specified by your instructor. Use any combination of strategies appropriate to your chosen audience and purpose.

Discussion

This essay is your chance to show what you have learned about argumentation. You are now free to remove the weights from your ankles and write an essay without the restrictions of a prescribed shape. Some instructors may require that you use library research in preparing this essay. Many will want you to include all of the sections common to classical argumentation (the eight parts mentioned at the beginning of this chapter). It is also possible to combine traditional argumentation with some of the strategies of sympathy and empathy highlighted in Rogerian argumentation. Whatever strategies you choose, this is your opportunity to write a major college essay.

PART IV

Story-Based Essays

It is unusual to end a writing text for college students with a discussion of descriptive and narrative writing, which we think is the heart of storytelling. Usually, texts begin with descriptive and narrative writing and end with, say, argumentation or the research paper. The traditional arrangement assumes that narrative and descriptive writing is the easiest kind of witing to do and that the academic research paper is the ultimate goal for college writers. In contrast, we end with storywriting because we think good narration and description is the hardest sort of writing to do well, and yet may well be the most important in terms of our humanity.

Writing stories is important because as human beings we need to tell stories, and indeed the world would probably be a better (or at least a more comprehensible) place if we told more of them. Story forms are more fun and easier to read than other forms of writing. They're also more memorable. In ancient times, civilizations used to store their most important knowledge in story forms called myths (which translates literally as "plot"). If you read the Bible, for example, you'll find a wealth of parables and tales which embody the knottiest and densest sort of theology in story form. And to appreciate the economy of these stories, all you have to do is survey the thousands of scholarly books that have been written about these "simple" stories. Although these books attempt to explain the meanings of the stories in essays governed by thesis statements, a story is always larger than a thesis statement, its meaning always more complex and elusive than a thesis-based essay can encompass.

We have therefore chosen "Beyond the Thesis Statement" as the subtitle for our chapter on story-based essays. Recall again Blake's statement that you first encountered in Chapter 2: "To generalize is to be an idiot." Thesis statements, by definition, are generalizations. And the whole purpose of writing thesis-governed essays (such as the problem-solution essays or issue-defense essays you have written earlier) is to support a thesis, which is to say, to answer a question for readers who don't already share that answer or agree with that answer. Thesis statements imply world views in conflict; no single thesis statement can ever be the whole truth. Blake's point is that generalizations extract us from the concrete world of particulars. Generalizations are not truth but only someone's interpretation of truth, and an interpretation can never do justice to *all* the particulars. But, as we shall try to explain in Part IV, stories allow us to get at truth in a different way.

This part of the text will give you a chance to develop your own skills as a storyteller. You can use stories in a variety of ways as a writer: to create "presence" in the introduction of an essay; to illustrate ideas presented in thesis-based essays, thereby increasing their depth and complexity; or to create essays "beyond the thesis statement"—essays that are themselves stories, either "true" stories that tell about your own personal experiences or about other people's lives, or fictional stories that you invent.

This section has one chapter, which includes the formal assignment for Part IV, and a journal sequence, which will help you explore ideas for a story you will write. You should begin the journal sequence right away, doing the tasks as you read and discuss Chapter 13.

Story Essays: Beyond the Thesis Statement

STORYWRITING AS A NATURAL ACTIVITY

As we switch over now from persuasive writing to the writing of story-based essays, many of us may breathe a collective sigh of relief. The rigors and complexities of persuasive writing are immediately evident to almost everyone who has to engage in it. It's an activity fraught with peril and Latin rules and library research. Many of us avoid controversial topics in large part because we don't wish to engage in the tiresome business of argumentation. And, indeed, we *can* avoid writing persuasive essays, so long as we are willing to accept a passive role in our society. Occasions which call for a persuasive response, however crucial those occasions may be to our welfare, don't typically arise on a daily basis. Hence our sense that persuasive writing is an "unnatural act."

But storytelling seems at first glance to be both a completely natural (unavoidable some would say) and effortless act. We're all storytellers and storylisteners, and few of us don't enjoy doing it, whether in the form of day-dreams, gossip, rationalizations, conversations, TV shows, novels, or short stories. Much of our earliest learning comes to us in the form of stories and fairy tales. We measure our intimacy with other people in part by how much of their "story" they've passed along to us. Some psychologists who study the phenomenon of conscious processes say that we structure our very consciousness with stories, ongoing narratives which give continuity to our experiences and help us put those experiences in context. In reading this book, for instance, you make all sorts of decisions about what to retain and what to ignore on the basis of how that information fits into the ongoing story of your class, your progress as a writer, and your life-long interests.

This feeling that storywriting is somehow a more natural act than argumentation or other modes of writing is both a curse and a blessing. It's a blessing in that most of us are less afraid of writing stories than of writing other forms of prose. None of us is a stranger to the process, after all, and we are as prone to associate story with pleasant personal memories as we are prone to associate argumentation with school writing and personally uncomfortable situations.

By the same token, however, this assumption that we all know how to write story can also be a curse. It blinds us to the underlying complexity of storytelling and our need to think about the task at hand. After all, we tell ourselves, even a five-year-old can tell a story (indeed, five-year-olds often *insist* on telling stories). But the number of five-year-olds who can tell a *good* story is, in our view, probably not much greater than the number who can put together a convincing argument.

Part of the reason we are blind to the difficulties of effective storytelling has to do with the uncritical way we typically take it in. Whereas persuasive writing is clearly aimed at a judgmental audience, storywriting seems just as clearly aimed at a receptive audience. We rarely *write* persuasively to intimate friends, but we constantly recount stories to friends and family members. As a consequence, we're all pretty tolerant of each other and the media when it comes to the quality of a story we'll sit through.

So our first task in this brief chapter is to convince you to take storywriting more seriously. Not more grimly, because that sense of pleasure in story is one of its great strengths. But we do want you to be more consciously aware of what it is you're doing in writing a story. And the reason this section on story is so much briefer than the previous section on argumentation is not because it is proportionately simpler. On the contrary, while one can formulate a number of useful principles which apply almost universally to argumentation, the principles of story are much more elusive. There simply aren't as many things to say about story which would hold true universally as there are to say about persuasive writing.

STORYWRITING AND THE CONSTRAINTS OF A THESIS

While we tend to associate story with childhood, simplicity and various forms of pleasure, it is additionally a form which people turn to when their subject defies the sort of clear hierarchical ordering called for in most essay writing. When our point is too complex or subtle for a thesis statement, when our feelings toward our subject are finally, unalterably contradictory, we might well turn to story to help our readers understand the wholeness of our experience with its ambiguities and complexities. To put it another way, problem-solution essays and issue-defense essays are rooted in thesis statements—one-sentence summary answers to questions. But stories usually don't work this way. They aren't answers to questions; they are ways of remaining open to questions.

As an illustration, suppose you are asked to write a persuasive essay on a complex and troubling human issue—let's say something like euthanasia for severely deformed or retarded infants. You might decide early on to commit yourself to a conservative thesis ("Neither passive nor active euthanasia of infants can be justified") or to some sort of liberal thesis ("Infant euthanasia is justified if the infant has no chance for a meaningful human life"). But whatever position you choose, unless you are an unyielding Fanatic, you will surely recognize problems with your position—the more you try to believe it, the more you will come to doubt it. Although the necessity of writing a persuasive essay forces you to *choose* a position, the complexity of the issue—its significance in terms of real human lives—makes you increasingly unwilling to choose. Once you realize that *no* thesis statement can capture what you really want to say about infant euthanasia, your best option may be to refuse to write a persuasive essay and instead turn to story.

For example, you could make up a story (in which case you would become a fiction writer), or you could tell a true story—what actually happened to your cousin Elaine, whose baby was born with *spina bifida*. Such stories could tell the "truth" you want to convey in a deeper, more complex way than could a thesis-based essay because a story can root the reader in the real world of people suffering, choosing, and living with consequences. One character in your story could take a conservative position, a second person a liberal position, and out of the dramatic conflict you could show that neither position is satisfactory.

The way you shape your story could give it different meanings. You could show a family brought together in humility and suffering, learning the meaning of love—the deformed, mute child as a catalyst for a family's growth toward wisdom. Or you could see truth in a very different way: You could show a family torn apart by bickering and anger, crushed financially by medical expenses and psychologically by a pointless commitment, forced on them by an outdated morality, to keep alive a mindless vegetable. If you were skillful enough you could keep both viewpoints juxtaposed in the same story—a mother with one view, a wise, old grandmother with another—or you could have both views held simultaneously and paradoxically by a single character. Moreover, you could show changes in perspective over time—a morally certain person who makes a decision easily and then comes to doubt it—structuring your story with flashbacks so that a scene immediately after the birth of the child is contrasted with a scene several years later. Our point is that story can free you from the tyranny of the thesis statement; it allows you to tell your truth "from all sides now" without becoming Blake's fool committed to a single generalization. Whereas the thesis statement commits you to a world view—fixes you, freezes you—a story can keep you flexible and paradoxical.

In sum, we approach story not as an alternative to or escape from the dialectic thinking we have emphasized throughout this text. Story, for us, is not a simple linear, one-thing-after-the-other sequence which makes no pretense at synthesis. Story, good story anyway, always involves some sort of tension or conflict between antithetical ideas, attitudes, characters, points of view, or alternatives for action. The dialectic of story is, however, often resolved quite differently from the dialectic of essay. Unlike a thesis-governed essay, which aims at offering a solution that seems *most* workable, the story writer may be concerned only that the story is plausible and true to the complexity of life. The resolution of story is apt to be more psychological than logical.

WHO USES AND DOESN'T USE STORY AND WHY

Obviously novelists, screenwriters, bards, and entertaining party guests all use story. But who else uses story as a mode of understanding and explanation? In other words, who are the "serious" practitioners of story one might encounter even in a college classroom? The answer that we propose is this: Anyone who is trying to understand a unique phenomenon that takes place in time is a potential story-user. Fairy tales, it will be remembered, always begin with "Once upon a time...," clearly signalling both the importance of "onceness" and of "time" to story. But clearly that concern is not restricted to writers of fictional narrative. Each of us will use story to save and to "fix" what happens once and only once in our lives. Maybe we all undergo various rites of passage or "stages of personality development" such as those described in introductory psych texts. Maybe our own development bears a great similarity to the universal structure of development described in the texts. But none of us is willing to simply substitute those structures for our autobiography. Story allows us to preserve what is unique *as well as* what is universal about our development.

At first glance, this sense of onceness and uniqueness that is native to story may seem antithetical to scientific writing where the focus is on the quantitative formulation of the experience and the use of universal laws to explain particular occurrences. At the extremes of science, in the realm, for example, of experimental science, this is indeed true. To many empirical scientists, storytelling is not part of their professional work since it seems an imprecise, nonobjective way of comprehending experience. The empirical scientist, after all, forms hypotheses on the basis of certain universal scientific laws. These laws in turn assume the uniformity of the material to which they are applied. Hence, a scientist can predict that water will come to a boil as soon as it reaches 212 degrees F. The scientist usually doesn't concern herself with the "onceness" of any particular batch of water—whether it came from rainfall or meltoff or underground spring, or whether it came from the Snake or the Chattanooga River.

If the scientist had to take all these things into account, science wouldn't get very far. It would be forever bogged down in particulars. Particular circumstances only come into play when a scientific law doesn't account for an experience, when nature and experience somehow defeat scientific laws. If the water doesn't boil at 212 degrees, for example, it may be because it is being heated at a great altitude where water boils faster. This latter fact is really an amendment to the law, itself a universal law, rather than a particular circumstance.

Empirical science for the most part deals with law-governed phenomena and matter which uniformly follows its laws. Any experience which can't be anticipated or predicted by such laws is not a good candidate for strict scientific study. For the storyteller, on the other hand, unpredictability is joy. And, conversely, a story which is "predictable" is usually pretty bad.

But science doesn't turn its back completely on unique, temporal experiences. The so-called "human sciences" or social sciences and even some of the life sciences based on observation of animal behavior will focus on unique temporal events insofar as they both confirm and defy the norms and laws of its science. And when they do so, they will often use story to structure their understanding of the event. Ethnographers, sociologists, social psychologists, psychiatrists, anthropologists, archaeologists, folklorists, even lawyers, business consultants and economists turn to story to account for and to explain complex and/or unpredictable events.

Faced with the puzzle of animals communicating in an almost human way, of a whole society that continues to persist in spite of its inhumane social institutions, of a choir boy turned mass murderer, professional observers from various fields will turn to story, be it in the form of a case history, a field study or a legal brief, to comprehend the event. Through story, they can identify some sort of causal sequence which ties the unlikely event back to some normal set of initial conditions which gave rise to the event. How did that monstrous thing called Nazi Germany arise out of a thoroughly civilized nation? How did the long moribund Giants resurrect themselves to win the pennant in 1951? Whatever the answers, no set of laws, principles or statistics will be wholly adequate to account for them. Before we can do so, we have to know their stories, the unique chain of causes and effects, and the singular cast of extraordinary characters that constitutes them.

As a mode of explanation, story offers the serious practitioner some other advantages beyond those already discussed. Topics that the average reader might find dull at best can come alive when cast in story form. People who plodded dutifully through required science courses will suddenly find themselves totally engrossed in Jane Goodall's accounts of primate society and communication, Lewis Thomas's stirring tales of life among microorganisms, or Loren Eisley's narrative adventures about evolutionary processes. We as readers begin to share with the scientist not just the knowledge that they've acquired, but the drama of coming to know that knowledge—the puzzlement and frustration of the early stages, the excitement of a solution beginning to form, the joy of an hypothesis confirmed.

Besides being more pleasurable to read (and hence more likely to be read) than standard essays, stories are more memorable than other modes of writing. First of all, story is memorable because it tends to be so visual. We "picture" stories more readily than we do essays, and pictures tend to stay with us longer than ideas, particularly if the pictures are tied to a narrative. Beyond their visual power, stories are relatively easy to reconstruct because in story "one-thing-*leads*-to another." (That is very different from "one-thing-*after*-the-other.") The power of continuity and suspense pulls us through a story almost irresistibly, both when we're reading and when we're recalling it. Oral cultures stored their most vital truths in stories—myths, fables, parables—in part because of the mnemonic power of story. And who of us hasn't continued to remember a teacher's stories long after we've forgotten the specific information contained in their lectures.

If, in turn, a writer's goal is to gain not only intellectual comprehension of a subject, but a sympathetic understanding as well, story is a natural means of gaining that desired sense of identification with a subject. To use a term from the previous section, story has a great deal of presence. We tend to project ourselves into the narrative situation and test our own reactions to events against those of the characters depicted. Any writer attempting to convince an audience that a given subject, however abnormal or foreign it may appear, has a bearing on their own lives is well advised to present his case in story form.

WHAT ARE STORIES MADE OF?

In order to get beyond talking about "this story" or "that story" to the point that we are able to talk about Story, we must identify the formal elements common to all stories. Having a formal grasp of story in turn gives us a wider sense of possibility about our own stories. We can begin to recognize some alternative ways of constructing our story once we are aware of the materials which all storytellers have at their disposal.

To begin with the most general way of talking about the constituent elements of story, we can say that there's a *what* and a *how* to story. The "what" in this case consists of what the story is about. Included under this heading would be the characters, the settings, and the events depicted. You can make a list of all these items in any order you wish without fear of distortion because these "whats" are essentially static and separable. But when you come to the "how" of story, primarily plot and point of view, you can't alter sequence or arrangement without distorting story. For example, if you are writing about a murder, you might choose to reveal the murderer's identity early in the work or late. That's a decision about plot, and that decision shapes your readers' whole attitude toward the characters and the focus of their attention. Likewise, your decision to tell the story from the detective's point of view or from the murderer's point of view has an ongoing, constant effect on your readers' relationship to your story.

From our discussion so far about the formal elements of story, you might conclude that we're talking mostly about fictional stories. That's really not the case at all. Any story, true or fictional, will contain all of these elements. We're simply unused to taking non-fiction narratives as seriously as we take fictional ones and hence haven't developed a vocabulary for talking about them. So, for now, we borrow the vocabulary of fiction to help you understand your own stories. Let's look briefly here at the elements of story named above and see what sorts of options you have in constructing your story.

Character

In any given story taken from actual experience, the writer has to decide which characters to include and which to focus on. Invariably, you won't want to include all characters involved in an experience primarily because each character has to be introduced to your reader and that's a cumbersome process. A Hollywood film may get away with a "cast of thousands," but a writer has to select characters according to the importance of the role they play in the story because each one costs words and time. One possibly helpful way of thinking of character in making your selection is to decide who forwards the action and who frustrates the action. Anyone who plays a major role in either movement should be included. Additionally, some characters are important for what they represent more than what they do. Even though they might be outside the action proper, such characters might represent alternatives or ideals for characters in the story. Whatever the case, the important thing to remember about character is to be sure your reader knows why they're there and who they are.

Events

Remember, the events depicted aren't the same as plot. A plot points toward a connection of events, a rationale for their relationship to one another. But "events" are not necessarily purposive. How many of the events experienced do you want to include in your story? Again, there will undoubtedly be more events to relate than you have time or space to depict in your written version. How can you select which events to include? In part, of course, that decision hinges on your decision about plot, but some events will suggest themselves less because they fit neatly into any overall pattern than because they dramatically reveal something about character or setting. You might, for example, tell an anecdote or two about one of your major characters by way of introducing that character to your reader. You could do the same sort of thing by way of showing your reader what a particular place was like. Events may suggest themselves because they are very visual, colorful, or funny. In the end, you should include only those which either contribute to your plot, or, at the very least, don't detract from the plot. But at the outset, you ought to consider events "for their own sake"—vivid memories which might well become vivid scenes.

Setting

Of all the elements of story which you control, setting is probably the one over which you have the most control. A "story" can consist of a dialogue between two people with little if any sense of where it takes place. Or, story can take its deepest meaning from the place in which it's set. For example, when New Journalist Tom Wolfe writes about contemporary American tastes, he often does so in the form of stories in which the details overrun the characters. In Wolfe's essay about a Black Panther fundraiser at composer/conductor Leonard Bernstein's apartment, we're more aware of Leonard Bernstein's living room than we are of Leonard Bernstein's actions. As with events, details of setting will suggest themselves according to what they reveal about the subjects of the story.

Point of View

Point of view usually indicates either physical perspective, the vantage point from which things are observed, or attitude. Thus, point of view might be detached or intimate, friendly or hostile, general or particular. Many of you will choose to write your stories from your own point of view, using the first person singular "I" voice. But some of you may wish to write about events from the third person point of view, particularly if you are not a major character in the story you are telling. You may wish to write about an event in the past tense or the present. You may wish to keep the narrative voice discretely out of sight, letting the characters do the talking, or you may wish to offer a running commentary and judgment on the scenes depicted. In every case, your decision about point of view moves the reader closer or further away from your story and radically affects how they judge the events described.

Plot

As already indicated, plot is the *pattern* of events depicted. One of the most overlooked choices available to storywriters concerns the sequence of their story. Too often, storytellers will simply recount events in the order of their original sequence. As a result, the story often takes on the plodding "and then" tone of a simple chronicle. By shifting events forward and backward, we can rearrange them so that they are side by side other events which through contrast or similarity bring out the important features of both events. In thinking about plot, a writer has to think also of the "pacing" of the story. How much time should be given to each scene? Again such a decision should be made more on the basis of the scene's contribution to the final outcome than to its historical time or significance. In some stories, an old man's teasing remark to his granddaughter might get more attention than the old man's entire career, depending on where the writer is headed. In considering plot, the writer is really considering the stages by which some sort of change takes place. Each stage, as part of a causal nexus, reveals to us in part *why* things are the way they finally are. As we noted before in discussing causal arguments, few complex human events can be explained by a simple, single cause or chain of causes. Hence stories of complex human events may shift from one parallel causal chain to another, moving back and forth in time in the process, in order to be true to the complexity of the event.

Theme

In discussing the previous five elements of story, we have not yet mentioned one element commonly included by most commentators on story—theme. Theme is usually defined as being synonymous with the "meaning" of the story. Thus, the theme of a particular war story might be "man's inhumanity to man." It is, in short, the generalizable significance of the story, a significance it shares with other similar stories. For our purposes, however, we identify theme as that principle of selection which causes you to shape your plot and choose your point of view the way that you do. If your theme is, say, "man's inhumanity to man," you might choose to structure your plot so that the death of the central character is foretold early on, lending a sense of doom to the account. In some sense, then, plot and theme aren't really separable, especially from the writer's perspective as she actively constructs her story. While events can exist apart from their significance, a plot cannot exist apart from a theme.

For Class Discussion

1. Now that you've had a chance to consider the formal elements of story, we invite you to check your understanding of those elements by considering the following story that one of our students, Tracy, wrote about her grandfather. What decisions has she made about each of the discussed elements in structuring this story, and what, in your view, are the effects of those decisions?

Grandpa Zi: peace among the ruins

One afternoon when I was five, I attempted an awesome experiment. "Grandpa," I announced. "I'm gonna make you into a beautiful lady." With those words, I descended upon him and began to busily brush, tease, and primp his thinning white hair. At the end of my labors, Grandpa's locks were haphazardly caught up in several large, pink, plastic curlers while a garish red bow graced the top of his head. Throughout this torture, sat Grandpa, carefully trying to ignore the tugs and pinches created by the industry of my clumsy young fingers. Upon seeing his reflection in a mirror, his usually forbidding features folded into a wide grin, and between rumbles of laughter he gruffed, "I betcher hankerin' for a spankin'!" His mock ferocity didn't scare me, but familiar with the rules of our "game," I ran from him, trailing shrieks of laughter behind me. Later I returned to listen to my Grandpa Zi blow strange old-fashioned songs through his battered harmonica, and eventually I curled up on a rug near his chair, and drifted into the contented sleep of a tired but happy child.

Today, nearly fifteen years later, Grandpa seldom listens to the sounds of his large and vibrant family; sitting almost motionless in his chair he hears only the bland, perfectly modulated voice of a narrator who, on a "Talking Book for the Sight Impaired," dutifully drones out an issue of *Time* or a Zane Grey novel. His film-covered eyes stare vacantly ahead, his floppy ears enveloped by a huge set of earphones. Only his full, heavy lips move, busily gathering saliva which he spits upon the carpet. At the sound of his spitting, our heads jerk toward him simultaneously, and I can see the hostility in my family's eyes, a burning emotion which is mirrored in my own. Unified by disgust, we crash into a familiar wall of resentment so dense that the emotional impact of striking it carries the pain of a physical blow.

The "wall of resentment" which isolates Grandpa from our family has not always existed; it has risen, "stone by stone," during these past two years in which we have shared his home. Our move, which was intended to be only temporary, was prompted by the death of my grandmother who had dutifully but somewhat begrudgingly catered to Grandpa's every whim and need. It was evident that without Grandma, Grandpa was incapable of living alone, yet my parents rebelled against placing him in County Rest Home, a dismal refuge where dark, endless corridors reek of ammonia and urine, and where grim silent patients sit hunched in their wheelchairs, totally withdrawn into themselves. Feeling that removing Grandpa from his familiar, comforting environment would increase his sense of loss, my parents decided, reluctantly, to close their own spacious home, and gingerly squeezed our large family into Grandpa's small house.

It soon became apparent that caring and providing for a selfish 88-year-old man would not be an easy task, for the mere day-to-day routine proved to be exhausting. From the time we fix his special breakfast in the morning to our final ritual of the day—setting out a glass of freshly squeezed orange juice, a laxative, medicine, and a spoon in a precise formation, awaiting "the old Sire's" attention—we are rewarded for our efforts only by his constant, autocratic criticism and profound lack of expressed gratitude. It is not unusual to enter a bathroom and find excrement smeared on the various fixtures, or to be called into Grandpa's room to empty one of the "piss-cans" that he keeps by his bedside. Grandpa will frequently appear for dinner in torn jockey shorts or a sagging union suit, and after slobberingly gobbling his food, usually with the help of his fingers, he will laboriously rise and lumber away, flatulating loudly with each step. The revulsion that has resulted from Grandpa's rudeness and crudity have gradually made the gentle man who cheerfully endured the indignity of a little girl's playful fantasy indistinguishable from the isolated, often offensive burden who sits in his lonely chair.

Even though I have often been a full participant in building the "wall of resentment" directed at my difficult, implacable grandfather, I am haunted not only by memories of the Grandpa Zi I adored as a child, but also by a more recent memory of a Grandpa who, for all of his demands and commands, is strangely vulnerable. I didn't truly recognize the growing frailty of my grandfather until I witnessed a confrontation between him and evidence of his own mortality. This "confrontation" came when Grandpa, after attending a son-in-law's memorial service, asked to see the newly installed gravestone which he will share with Grandma. Guided by one of his sons, he hobbled across the rough lawn, breathing the grunting, rasping breath of the very old. Bending slightly, he ran his gnarled hand slowly across the inscription, tracing the letters of his name that were deeply hewn into the cold, grey granite.

Although I do not know what thoughts were in Grandpa's mind when he viewed his own monument, I couldn't help thinking how difficult it must be for him to witness proof that he is indeed at the end of life, especially when that life has been characterized by failure and futility. Although he worked nearly continuously from the age of 15 until retiring from the "Milwaukee Road" a seasoned veteran, he has nothing to show for his years of labor, but is instead dependent upon the state for his pension, a wealthy son for his home, and a tired and overworked daughter for his care. The son of a stern but foolish Prussian immigrant, Grandpa lacked a deep and sustaining love during both his childhood and his adult life. Although he married twice, both marriages can be deemed failures. His first wife left him, taking their three children with her, and although his second wife, my grandmother, was faithful to him for nearly 46 years, she loved another man, and died wishing that she had spent her life with *him*, and not with my abusive, crude grandfather. Although once a robust and massive man, his oversized skin hangs in long folds around his bent frame, and his days drift by in a hazy drug-induced haze. Tired of struggling with a harsh and pain-racked existence Grandpa longs only for the quiet release of death, and speaks fondly of the day when he will "go up on the hill with Mama."

Even though Grandpa's continued life with my family is a constant source of pain and humiliation for us, his presence offers us, as a family, a chance to participate in his waiting for death and achieve what St. Paul called "charity." We must learn to recognize that he is indeed a fellow creature, with wants and needs which are crucial to him, and who is bound to us through our mutual suffering. In doing so, we must render to Grandpa the love, honor, and compassion that is due him. If we can see beyond the inconvenience and frustration Grandpa promotes within our family, and if we can quell the burning animosity which leads to the "wall of resentment," we have a chance to render comfort where it's truly needed, and contentment where it's truly desired. By creating an atmosphere in which Grandpa is allowed to await his longed for "escape" amid the loving care and concern that can be given only by his family, we are, in effect, smoothing the lines of worry from his brow and whispering "Peace. Peace. All is well." Perhaps by giving peace to a world-weary old man, we can attain it ourselves.

2. Review two other stories in this text: John Ramage's story of Dr. P., p. 49–51, and Tim Andryk's story of the live-capture of bighorn sheep, p. 424–427. Ask the same questions about these stories. How do each of them handle character, plot, setting, point of view, and theme?

3. Prior to class, prepare to tell a story from your family. It could be one of those recurring stories that family members love to tell whenever they get together or whenever someone in the family wishes to characterize what sort of people belong to your family. Or it could be a story about your family told from your own unique perspective. In groups of five, tell your stories aloud to each other. Can you recognize any similarities or patterns in the stories? Keeping in mind the formal elements of story discussed earlier, discuss whether these oral stories have character, plot, setting, point of view, and theme.

4. Prior to class watch one or more prime time action TV dramas (not sitcoms but good guy/bad guy adventures) and take notes on plot, character, setting, and theme. Can you identify any common patterns to the types of heroes, heroines and villains featured? Can you see any similarity among the stages of the plot? Assuming that these programs are popular for a reason, what might you conclude about the sorts of story that will have broad appeal?

YOUR ASSIGNMENT FOR THIS CHAPTER: TELL A STORY

It is now time for you to write a story of your own. Our assignment this time is about as open-ended as an assignment can be: Write a story. It can be a story based on your own personal life or, if your instructor allows, a fictional story. We recommend that you limit your story to 3–4 pages, but that too is a decision for your instructor to make.

From our discussion so far, you probably have a reasonably good idea of what we mean by "story," even though we purposely haven't defined the word. In rough terms, a story is an attempt to recreate through language a sequence of events happening once in time. Perhaps the first thing to keep in mind, then, as you write your story is that stories create alternative worlds. When you hear a story, you live for a time in another place, another setting. You encounter new people, often people whose assumptions, motivations, and values are different from your own, and these new people and places are described fully enough for you to "be there" in your imagination. This is why stories depend so heavily on details—the way things looked, sounded, felt, tasted, smelled. Second, stories convey meaning through the selection and arrangement of details. This selection and arrangement we have called "plot," which is usually quite different from a simple, chronological, "and then" structure.

To put it another way, story is a meaningful use of *description* and *narration*. *Description* attempts to reproduce for readers a particular scene—as when you describe a room or a duck pond or the expression on a loved one's face. *Narration* attempts to reproduce for readers an event as it unfolds through time, as when you narrate the action of a basketball game or the sequence of actions during a drug bust or a teenager's first date. *Story* occurs when description and narration are combined through a shaping vision that conveys the writer's understanding of the significance or point of the experiences that make up the story's content.

Let's return to Tracy's story of her grandfather as an illustration. The story begins with a happy episode—a little girl playing make-believe games with her Grandpa. Had the story simply continued with happy episodes, one after the other, it would soon have lost its interest. But the story shifts suddenly, unexpectedly, to a different point of view, throwing the writer's relationship to her grandfather in entirely new light. By creating an obstacle—new scenes showing a flatulent, tyrannical, ungrateful grandfather—Tracy creates conflict, difficulty. How will she resolve this conflict? What understanding of her grandfather will Tracy and her readers possess when the story ends?

Thus, when a story is particularly good, readers begin to ask something besides "And then?" They begin to ask more thoughtful questions such as "Why?" or "What am I coming slowly to see and feel?" When a story begins to provoke this higher level response from readers it has become a "plot." In addition to curiosity, a plot requires intelligence and memory. A plot which offers an understanding of a complex event or personality requires us to go back and link together the sequence of events into an illuminating pattern. Ideally, everything in the story will contribute to the story's explanation of meaning. The best sorts of story, then, have a clear criterion by which events or characters or descriptions are chosen for inclusion or are excluded. They must contribute to the reader's ability to answer the "Why?" question posed by the story. Whereas the bad story simply records everything that happens, the good story selects things which have explanatory power.

With this much explanation, we now leave you on your own to write your own story. If you have done Journal Sequence 4, you have already explored many ideas for a story. The following list of suggestions may further spark your imagination. Remember that your story must contain both narrative and description and that the scenes and events you choose must add up to something—a theme, a meaning, a guiding purpose.

1. Write a story that focuses primarily on a person's character. Your job is to convey to the reader the personality of another human being (see John Ramage's "Dr. P.").

2. Write a story that focuses primarily on the accomplishment of a difficult event or exciting action. Here the focus is on adventure and suspense more than character (see Tim Andryk's story about capturing bighorn sheep).

3. Write a story about a memorable event that changed your life or contributed significantly to your maturity.

4. Tell your story about "education" from the Tasks 1–13 in Journal Sequence 1.

5. Write a story that makes heavy use of setting to convey theme or character.

6. Write a story that uses conflict/reconciliation between two characters.

7. Write a story that conveys a complex attitude toward something or someone (Tracy's story about her grandfather).

8. Write a story that begins by juxtaposing two scenes (this is the opening technique Tracy used).

9. Write a story about a time in which you were misunderstood because no one listened to your story.
10. Write a story that captures the "range of variation" in something: the many faces of a friend, the richness of a certain summer (see the range of variation heuristic, p. 182).
11. Write a story that makes your reader feel horror. Or joy. Or fear. Or a sense of the meaninglessness of life. Or a sense of love and reconciliation.
12. Write a story that will preserve for the next generation in your family something important from your own generation.
13. Write a story that will make readers laugh.
14. Write a story that will make readers understand what it feels like to be laughed at, humiliated, embarrassed.
15. Write a story that will make your readers feel caught in a dilemma.

Guided Journal: Sequence 4

Writing Stories

In this section of the journal, we'll be helping you develop your story-telling abilities. You'll be exploring three sources of story—memory, observation, and awareness of conflict—and three major elements of story—theme, plot, and character.

Some of the writing you will be doing in the following tasks will be quite personal while other writing will be relatively impersonal. This movement back and forth between the personal and the impersonal is the dialectic of story writing. You must tap into moods, feelings, and sentiments of your personal life and yet focus and shape those emotions through craft. Without craft, strong emotions can turn flabby as a drunk's confession. Without a sense of personal investment on the part of the writer, the prose will turn bloodless as a clam.

This journal sequence is divided into two parts. The first part will help you explore ideas for a story of your own. You should begin it as you read Chapter 13 on story-based essays. The second part is a series of exercises to help you develop your craft as a story-writer. You should do these exercises while you are in the early stages of writing your own story. Some of the skills you develop from your journal writing can then be transferred directly to your own story.

EXPLORING IDEAS FOR STORIES

In this part of the journal you will explore ideas out of your personal life that might become material for a story. It is important not to settle in too soon on exactly the story you want to write. Live for a while with lots of ideas.

Tasks 1 and 2

Look over your previous journal entries and make a log of possible "seed-ideas" for stores you might like to write—either real ones based on your personal experience or fictional ones. Enter ideas under these three columns (feel free to add new ideas later as they occur to you):

Characters   Action/events   Themes

Explanation

Most writers keep journals both as a source of ideas and as a place to practice writing bits and pieces of drafts of stories. Your journal so far is a potential source of many stories. In the "character" column write down people who might figure in your story either as a main character or as a "bit player." Under action/events list incidents from your life that might make good stories—a camping trip, a disastrous subway ride, an embarrassing moment. Under "themes" list ideas or purposes you might want to develop into a story—living with shyness, the way gardening has shaped my life, the way divorce changed my mother. Here are some examples of what John chose based on ideas he explored in Journal Sequence 1.

Characters	Action/events	Themes
Dad, Mom, Uncle Art, Aunt Dorothy, Julio and Frankie, Eddie Butler, Crazy Pete, my sister and her kids.	Sledding, the big snow storm, the trip to the Nampa State School, fishing and working, the time I hit Frankie with the rock.	The difference between my childhood and my children's childhood; my affection for my parents; living with value conflicts.

Tasks 3 and 4

Here we've listed numerous items which could trigger memories for most of us. In response to each item, jot down a word, a phrase or an image to serve as a memory cue for later. If you draw a blank on any of the items, skip over them and come back to them later. Do your best to respond to as many as possible.

1. *Your first house/other houses*
2. *Your first close friend*
3. *The joys and sorrows of friendship*
4. *Your favorite childhood past time*
5. *Your best/worst memories of childhood*
6. *Family get-togethers*
7. *Your first teacher/most memorable teacher/favorite teacher*

8. *Your first romantic interest*
9. *Memories associated with dating/relationships with the oppo-site sex*
10. *The most fair/unfair punishment you ever received*
11. *Your place in the high school social scale*
12. *Your most memorable confrontation with temptation/evil*
13. *Major family moves*
14. *Major family changes (divorce, change in economic status, brother or sister leaving, etc.)*
15. *Starting college*
16. *The death of someone close*
17. *Your first job*
18. *Town or neighborhood "characters"*
19. *Your relationships with brothers, sisters, parents*
20. *Personal triumphs/failures/regrets/successes/mistakes*
21. *People you most respect/least respect*
22. *Fears in your life*
23. *Childhood heroes and heroines*
24. *The place you felt most secure when growing up*
25. *Bullies and villains in your life*
26. *The most dangerous thing you ever did*
27. *The most unusual thing about your growing up years*
28. *Feelings about your physical self*
29. *The most difficult decision you ever had to make*
30. *Others?*

Explanation

This inventory should help trigger lots of memories, some of which might eventually find their way into a story that you will write. Don't worry about developing your ideas here; just jot down a word or phrase to help you recall your memories later.

Task 5

Look over your list of responses and choose three which evoked particularly strong reactions (powerful feelings, lots of images and associations). Freewrite 5 minutes on each of these three items, exploring the network of images, feelings, and ideas that each evokes.

Explanation

The purpose of this freewriting is to help you discover why certain memories are powerful to you. Such a discovery may help you find a theme for your story, a way of selecting and ordering details to create meaning.

Task 6

Choose a "focal scene" from your life—something that you might like to include in a story. A focal scene is one where many strands of experience, feeling, and value come together—a scene richly packed with meaning for you. Such scenes can often become a focus for a story. (Choose a scene with persons and at least some action. Imagine yourself taking a photograph or motion picture of the scene.) Take notes on the scene using the journalist's questions:

- *Who: List the people in the scene and jot down little thumbnail sketches about them.*
- *Where & When: Jot down notes about the setting—when and where the scene occurs, descriptions of the place.*
- *What: Take notes about the action in the scene—what are people doing? What is happening?*
- *How: Describe the manner in which the action is occurring, various people's attitudes toward the scene.*
- *Why: Why has this scene occurred? Why are the people doing what they do? Jot down notes exploring the motivation, goals, and purposes of people involved in the scene.*

Explanation

This entry will help you develop a scene that may become part of a story. If you later choose to abandon this scene, you will nonetheless create other ones for whatever story you choose to write. The journalist's questions are a good way to jog your memory and to cause you to think about your scene objectively, piece by piece.

Task 7

Writing rapidly nonstop for 15 minutes, describe your scene (from Task 6) for a classmate.

Explanation

Your task now is to create an "other world" for readers. As you write your scene, imagine details that appeal to all the senses. Have sight words and sound words. Try also to have some touch words and maybe even smell or taste words.

Tasks 8 and 9

Choose a character that you think might figure prominently in a story you want to write. This could be a character from the scene you described in Task 7, or it could be a new character. Using free-writing or idea-mapping, explore this character using either the "particle/wave/field" heuristic or the "range of variation" heuristic in Chapter 7, pp. 179–182.

Explanation

Either of these heuristics will help you see your character from a variety of perspectives and perhaps trigger ideas that could be included in your story. The "particle/wave/field" heuristic gives you three useful perspectives. From the particle perspective, describe your character and explore what makes him or her unique, different from every other person in the universe. From the wave perspective, imagine your character changing over time. Describe a typical hour or day in your character's life. How is your character changing? What was he or she like a year ago? As a child? (Much of the material for Tracy's story of her grandfather was first recorded when she was using the wave perspective in her journal.) From the field perspective, imagine your character in relationship to a scene or setting. What backgrounds does your character most belong in? Can you best picture your character working in a noisy factory? Riding a subway late at night? Dancing in a singles bar? Changing a baby's messy diapers in a cramped apartment bedroom?

The other heuristic you might use is the "range of variation" heuristic, which asks you to imagine the various moods or faces of your character. If you had, say, six different photographs that you could take of your little sister, each photograph showing us a different side of her personality, what would you take? Your little sister snuggled in bed with a teddy bear? Your little sister stamping her feet in a temper tantrum? Your little sister, dirt-smudged, wearing a baseball cap, helping you change the oil in the Chevy? Explore as many different views of your character as possible.

Task 10

Reread your description of a scene in Task 7 and your exploration of a character in Tasks 8 and 9. Then imagine ways that you could include either your scene or your character in a story to achieve conflict. Make an idea-map or other kind of notes to yourself.

Explanation

By *conflict* we mean *tension* or *opposition*: a clash between two or more characters, a contrast of personalities within one character, a scene from your happy past juxtaposed with a scene from your unhappy present, your view of yourself versus someone else's view of you, and so forth. Stories often depend on some kind of conflict or obstacle to overcome. The obstacle in Tim Andryk's bighorn sheep story is finding out how to capture the sheep without getting killed or injuring the animals. The conflict in Tracy's story is how to resolve her conflicting attitudes toward her grandfather. The conflict in John Ramage's story of Dr. P. is the conflicting values systems of Ramage, all the math majors in the course, and Dr. P. himself.

Review your scene and your character and search for potential conflicts, either within what you have already written, or within what is potentially there if you juxtapose what you have written against something else. The next two entries will also help you explore conflict.

Task 11

As a way toward appreciating values conflicts as a source of story, try the following exercise. Carefully consider the following inventory of values and attributes. Place a check on the line between the attributes or values which reflect the degree to which you value one over the other. Thus if you think you are more rational than intuitive, place your check close to "rational" on the line. Whenever in doubt, put your mark in the middle. If possible, try to think of people in your life whose position on each scale would be very different from yours. Maybe you can build a story out of this conflict.

Your position on this line	Person different from you?
Intuitive _____ Rational	_____
Imaginative _____ Analytical	_____
Self-Aware _____ Knowledgeable about external world	_____
Skeptical _____ Trusting	_____
Judgmental _____ Compassionate	_____
Loyal to principles _____ Loyal to friends	_____
Independent _____ Sociable	_____
Serious _____ Whimsical	_____
Good with people _____ Good with things	_____
Tactful _____ Honest	_____
Extravagant _____ Thrifty	_____

Your position on this line	Person different from you?
Principled _____ Flexible	_____
Affectionate _____ Reserved	_____
Impulsive _____ Disciplined	_____
Good Leader _____ Good follower	_____
Competitive _____ Supportive	_____

Explanation

The point here is to think about your own values and about people whose values seem quite different from yours. Effective stories often have characters with widely conflicting values.

Task 12

If you were forced to choose between the following conditions, which would you choose for yourself? Jot down a brief description of yourself in reference to each choice.

- *Security/Freedom*
- *Success/Tranquility*
- *Comfort/Challenge*
- *Respect of Others/Love of Others*
- *On Top/Behind the Scenes*

Explanation

Again, our purpose here is to have you think of your own values as a way of deepening your approach to story telling.

Task 13

Looking over your journal so far, freewrite now about a story you might like to write. In your freewrite explore several possibilities for stories. Begin your freewrite with this starter: "Here are some things I might like to write a story about:"

Explanation

Your freewrite may help you articulate ideas that could become the basis for a story.

Task 14

It is now time for you to make some decisions about a story you want to write. For this entry write a series of "notes to yourself" about a formal story you want to write.

Explanation

By "notes to yourself" we mean a sort of plan or outline for the story you want to write. The purpose here is to help you focus your thinking, not to commit you to something that you can't change. Here are Tracy's "notes" to herself about her story of her grandfather in Chapter 13.

I want to write about how I feel about my grandfather, contrasting my present disgust (at least it feels like disgust) with the warm memories I have of Grandpa when I was a little girl. I think I'll start my story with that scene from my journal about my fixing up his hair like a girl's when I was about 5-years-old. That will be a warm, happy scene. Then I will switch immediately to a scene from the present, trying to show what Grandpa is like now. I want to hit my readers with the contrast so I will try to paint a picture that will make them feel the same sort of resentment I feel. I'm not sure what I will do next. Somewhere I will need to give my readers the background about how our family came to live in Grandpa's house. I know somewhere in the story I also want to include the part about how Grandma loved another man. I also want to tell my memories of watching Grandpa trace his name on the gravestone. I don't know how I will end my story.

SOME SKILL-BUILDING EXERCISES

As you are writing the draft of your story, you should also practice some of the skills good story writers need in order to perfect their craft. The following tasks are designed to get you to observe things and then to interpret your observations by putting them into the context of a story. Our hope is that these skills will then transfer to the story that you are writing on your own.

Task 15

Find a public place where you can sit and observe people interacting —a cafeteria, cafe, bar, game arcade, shopping mall, library, TV room, courtyard, wherever. Locate a person to focus on. Pretend that you are an actor who will soon play the part of this person. Record any observation of the person which would help you play the part.

Explanation

Our purpose here is to help you develop your skill at observing minute details. Here's a checklist that you might find helpful in directing your powers of observation.

1. Age. (What clues are provided? Can you see the hands? the back of the neck?)
2. Dress. (Notice details: what style of shoes? are there laces? how are they tied? Is the clothing conventional or strange? Based on the clothes this person is wearing, what do you think this person's closet looks like?)
3. Gestures. (Notice particularly the eyebrows, the curve of the mouth, the use of fingers during hand gesturing, the movement of the eyes.)
4. Features. (Hair, eyes, complexion, build, hands, etc. If you had to identify this person positively in a police line-up, what are the distinguishing characteristics?)
5. Walk. (You may have to wait quite a while until the person gets up.)
6. Habits. (Gum, cigarettes, cigar, manners, etc.)
7. Subject's reaction to other people.
8. Other people's reaction to your subject.
9. Other. (Reading material? canes? umbrellas? brief cases? backpacks?)

Task 16

Review your description of your human subject, trying to interpret the significance of each element of your description. For example, do the hand and facial gestures indicate someone who's nervous? emphatic? timid? From the person's clothing, would you say they are rich or poor? nonconformist? urban? rural? Then write a brief hypothetical biography of your subject. In your bio, you might include what the person does for a living or what his or her major in school is. Marital status and family background could certainly be significant. You might also consider how happy the person is, what pressures the person might be under, his or her self-concept and feelings toward others, and so on. What sorts of stories can you imagine the person in? (e.g. murder mystery? romance? tragedy? farce? science fiction?)

Explanation

Our point is that the way a person looks and moves often tells us something about that person's values and style of life. You can bet that a person wearing a "Pete's Tavern" bowling shirt and driving a pickup with a gunrack in back is probably operating out of a different value system from a bearded fellow with a backpack, sandals and ten-speed racing bike. But these are obvious cases. The skilled storywriter can indicate differences in people by the way they hold their coffee cups, by the shine on their shoes, by the way they talk to their children, by the music on their radios. Your job in this task is to go from observation to generalizations. How can a person who looks and acts like the person you observed become a character in a story?

Task 17

You are standing on a street corner and three people drive by in their cars. Describe the scene (people and cars) as each drives by. Choose three people out of the following list of possibilities:

- *a subscriber to The Wall Street Journal*
- *a subscriber to Hot Rod Magazine*
- *a subscriber to Rolling Stone*
- *a subscriber to Playboy*
- *a subscriber to Parents Magazine*
- *a subscriber to Guns Magazine*

Explanation

Use your imagination to describe car and driver in a way that indicates a value system and life style that seems plausible for a reader of each magazine. Make your descriptions appeal to as many senses as possible.

Task 18

Choose a room or setting that, for whatever reason, is important to you. Choose in turn some focal point in that place, a center of attention, the part that best expresses the mood of the whole. Now, we're going to ask you to attempt to draw that scene. (Don't worry—no one but you will ever have to see your sketch.) Draw it in the following way. First, stare at the scene you intend to draw, paying particular attention to the relationships of shape and size. To help you see these more clearly, you might form a cylinder with your hand and peer through the resulting hole. This enhances your attention by limiting the scene. Put pencil on paper and lifting it from the paper as seldom as possible, keeping your eyes on the scene at all times, slowly but steadily draw what you see. Remember, this is more an exercise in seeing than in drawing, so don't get discouraged with whatever you produce.

Explanation

By asking you to draw the scene you are observing, rather than describe it in words, we are really asking you to *look* at it with the artist's eye, that is, to notice it, to really see it. Perhaps you have never really *looked* at a scene before in exactly the same way that this drawing exercise forces you to do.

Observing scenes is a skill needed for creating "setting" in a story. Setting is one of the most important (and most frequently overlooked) aspects of story. Whereas when we interpret the physical characteristics of a person we come up with a personality or character, when we interpret the characteristics of a place we come up with a mood or tone. How you choose to integrate that setting into your story is, of course, totally up to you. An austere cathedral may be the setting for a murder, a marriage, or a religious conversion. In each case, however, the setting colors the event in a different way. The murder might seem even more outrageous in such a setting while the marriage might seem colder, more formal. In either case, the setting is an important dimension of meaning and we need to be conscious of that dimension.

Task 19

Now describe the same scene in language as vividly as possible. Use words that appeal to all the senses. Make this scene "another world" for your readers.

Explanation

Don't just *list* everything (e.g., "On the east wall is a dresser. Above the dresser is a round mirror.") *Describe* the objects and elements of the scene that strike you as important. (In the southeast corner of the room sits 'Aunt Julia's' dresser. It's blonde oak, low with a round mirror attached at the back. Aunt Julia's legacy. No one would buy it, I suppose, unless they were striving for a camp effect. It's got that raffish air of the Salvation Army survivor. A litter of nieces' and nephew's coy, fat baby pictures are tucked into the mirror frame.")

Task 20

After reviewing your description, freewrite on the mood and feeling of your scene as though it were to become the setting of a story. What kind of events could take place in this setting? What kind of people belong here? What other kinds of settings might be appropriate in the story in order to create tension or conflict?

Explanation

Our point here is that good story tellers use setting to enhance plot and character. The way the setting is described contributes to the unfolding meaning of the whole story. What kind of characters or actions would be appropriate if you were to use the scene you just described as a setting for part of a story?

Readings About Thinking, Writing, and Learning

Part V is a short anthology of readings related to thinking, writing, and learning. All of these articles have been referred to frequently throughout the text both as models of writing and as sources of ideas for you to consider and react to.

The first article in the collection is Caroline Bird's "The Dumbest Investment You Can Make," which makes a persuasive economic argument against going to college. We begin Part V with this article in order to stimulate in you a sense of contrariety, a sense of a problem. Since you or your parents or someone else is investing a considerable sum of money to send you to college, this article should "problematize" your decision to postpone entry into the world of work. We hope this article will stimulate what we call in Chapter 2 "dialectic thinking."

The next article—Carl Rogers' "Communication: Its Blocking and Its Facilitation"—explains an important skill for anyone setting out to problematize experience—the ability to listen to other points of view, to adopt temporarily the world view of another person. Rogers' thesis is that the ability to listen carefully to another's argument—so carefully that you could summarize it for that person to his satisfaction—will go a long way toward making people rational problem-solvers instead of mutually deaf antagonists.

The third article—Fritz Machlup's "Good Learning from Poor Teachers" —has the surprising thesis that students often learn effectively from poor teachers because they are forced, out of necessity, to learn material on their own. This article will perhaps encourage you to take charge of your own learning. Many of the learning strategies explained in this text, especially the use of writing as a way of seeing and knowing, can help you become a more effective student.

We have included the fourth article—Peter Elbow's "Embracing Contraries in the Teaching Process"—for several reasons. First, it is a model of the dialectic process described in Chapter 2. Second, the article can help you appreciate some of the problems that teachers take home with them. If teachers are required, day after day, to see the world from their students' perspective, it is sometimes useful for students to see the world from a teacher's perspective. Third, in our effort to help you problematize experience, this article should get you thinking more deeply about the role of grades in an educational environment.

The final three essays are all by a graduate student in Wildlife Management, and all concern a new way to capture bighorn sheep. The author, Tim Andryk, has written the same "topic" three ways for three different purposes. The first version is a two-paragraph problem-solution essay exactly like the kind assigned for Task 1 in Chapter 8. The second version, which Andryk wrote with colleagues, is a scientific report. The last version is written as an adventure story for a popular audience. We discuss these three versions at length in Chapter 5 to illustrate the relationship of detail to a writer's audience and purpose.

The Dumbest Investment You Can Make*

Caroline Bird

College isn't supposed to be for the money. College catalogues never mention high earnings as a goal, and money gets a low priority when parents, students, and alumni are asked to choose among expectations of college or, indeed, among lifetime goals.

This low priority doesn't mean that college students don't care about money. Quite the reverse. They don't talk about money and college or even money and jobs in the same breath, because, as sociologist David Gottlieb reported in *Youth and the Meaning of Work*, an exhaustive investigation of student attitudes, "an adequate income is expected." For many years, a majority of entering freshmen polled by the American Council on Education have agreed with the statement: "The benefit of college is monetary." Some of the first-generation college students are quite willing to come out and say so. "As far as I'm concerned, college is strictly for the money," a blue-collar student at a community college told us. But most will deny that money is their only motive for going.

It's a good thing for colleges that students think they are getting something more out of their education than increased income. For if students hoped only for money, and each student had a banker with a computer at his elbow, enrollments would drop much further below expectations than they did during the enrollment recession of the mid-1970s. I say this only because I persuaded a

* From Caroline Bird, *The Case Against College* (New York: David McKay, 1975), pp. 62–74. Reprinted by permission of the author.

young banker in Poughkeepsie, New York, Stephen G. Necel, to compare college as an investment in future earnings with other investments available in the booming money market of 1974.

For the sake of argument, Steve and I invented a young man whose rich uncle undertook to give him, in cold cash, the cost of a four-year education at any college he chose—and he didn't have to spend the money on college. He could invest it, save it, or blow it—but he had to explain why. After bales of computer paper had been filled with figures, we had our mythical student write to his uncle: "Since you said I could spend the money foolishly if I wished, I am going to blow it all—on Princeton." We concluded that in strictly financial terms, college is the dumbest investment a young man can make.

In the course of our statistical workout, we discovered that an investment in potential future earnings does not compare very precisely with other forms of investment, but one figure stands out as clearly valid and significant: A Princeton graduate of 1956 could expect to earn 12.5 percent on the comparatively modest cost of four years at that institution then, but a member of the class of 1976 could expect to realize only a 9.5 percent return of his investment. As human capital economists and government statisticians patiently pointed out to us, the calculations we made required heroic assumptions. We freely admit as much. But we feel that our assumptions are just as valid as those behind the calculations that have been used for more than a generation to convince taxpayers as well as students that college is worth it—"even" in money.

"A college education is among the very best investments you can make in your entire life. It will lead to an enormous payoff in increased earnings, in brighter job prospects, and in a host of intangible cultural and social benefits for which you always will be grateful."

That's what Sylvia Porter said when a 9.4 percent hike in college costs was reported by the College Scholarship Service for 1974–75.

That bit about "enormous payoff in increased earnings" was especially appealing to the class of 1976 bracing for a senior year that was going to cost an unexpected 36 percent more than their freshman year. Sylvia Porter is one of the most widely read and most credible of American economists, and when she talks about "enormous payoff in increased earnings" she ought to know whereof she speaks.

Newsmen had been equally encouraging a few weeks earlier, when the Census Bureau reported that as of 1972 a man who completed four years of college could expect to earn $199,000 *more* between the ages of twenty-two and sixty-four than a man who had only a high-school diploma. Of course, everyone was earning more money, in dollars, than ever before, and headlines applauded the big numbers: COLLEGE MAN CAN EXPECT LIFETIME EARNINGS OF $601,000.

Headlines scream the conventional wisdom because their writers have time for little else. But an enterprising desk man who took a sharp pencil and a compound interest table to these two reports, issued little more than a week apart, could have supported a headline which would have attracted much wider attention:

PRINCETON DOESN'T PAY OFF IN EARNINGS
1972 High School Graduate Ahead
If He Banks the Cost of College
and Goes Right to Work

If a male Princeton-bound high-school graduate of 1972 had put the $34,181 his diploma would eventually cost him into a savings bank at 7.5 percent interest compounded daily, he would have at the retirement age of sixty-four a total of $1,129,200 or $528,200 more than the earnings of a male college graduate and more than five times as much as the $199,000 extra he could expect to earn between twenty-two and sixty-four because he was a college, rather than merely a high-school, graduate.

Okay, you say. That's Princeton—just about the most expensive college in the 1974–75 list put out by the College Scholarship Service of the College Entrance Examination Board. How about a state-supported college?

The payoff on the lower investment in a public college education is, of course, higher to the student because other people—in this case the taxpayers—are putting up part of the capital for him. Even so, the return is not as much higher as it sounds, because the biggest part of the investment in college is the earnings a student foregoes to attend. These costs he bears himself.

Preserving his college money as capital isn't much fun for the frugal high-school graduate. He can't spend more than he earns as a high-school graduate, while the college graduate with whom we are comparing him gets to live it up with the extra money he earns. And the difference—particularly as both grow older—is considerable. If the college graduate banks the yearly difference, at the 7.5 percent savings bank rate, that difference alone would grow to $1,222,965 at age sixty-four, which amounts to $93,765 more than the high-school graduate of 1972 would accumulate by banking the cost of a Princeton education. Figured this way, a Princeton degree is worth $93,765. The joke is that the Princeton graduate has to wait until he's sixty years old before his bank account pulls ahead. The advantage of his college education comes at the very end of his earning life.

When the Princeton graduate is young, the difference between his earnings and that of a high-school graduate is less than the interest on the money he has spent for college would earn in the savings bank. As of 1972, a male college graduate earned only $96 more than a high-school graduate of the same age during his first year out of college—this is nowhere near the $3,423 in interest that the high-school graduate could draw out if he had invested the cost of college in the savings bank. During his second year out of college, the college graduate, now twenty-three, earns $558 more than the twenty-three-year-old high-school graduate. He doesn't reach the "average" advantage in earnings of college graduates over high-school graduates—a difference of $4,823—until he is thirty-five years old.

The big advantage of getting your college money in cash now is that you can invest it in something that has a higher return than a diploma. The options are enticing. A Princeton-bound high-school graduate of 1972 who likes fooling around with cars better than immersing himself in books could have banked his $34,181 and gone to work at the local garage at close to $1,000 a year more than the average earnings reported by the Census for high-school graduates eighteen years old, and the chances are that he could have moved up in income faster than the average high-school graduate, too. Meanwhile, as he was learning to be an expert auto mechanic, his money would be ticking away, compounding itself at the bank. When he gets to be twenty-eight, he will have earned $7,199 less, from age twenty-two, than if he had graduated from college, but he will have $73,113 in his passbook—enough to buy out his boss, go into the used-car business, or acquire a new-car dealership. As an enterpriser, he could thenceforth expect to take home more than he could have expected as a college graduate, and if he had the wit to get into Princeton, and a genuine interest in cars, he should be more likely to succeed than the average man in the business.

Supposing, on the other hand, he has the money, but neither the wit nor the interest for Princeton. After all, about a third of the high-school graduates from families with incomes of $15,000 or more *don't* go to college. Suppose he banks his Princeton money and travels around, supporting himself at odd jobs, as so many privileged young people like to do. At twenty-eight, when he's tired of pickup jobs, he can take out his $73,113 and buy a liquor store, which will return him well over 20 percent on his investment as long as he's willing to mind the store. (He might, of course, get fidgety sitting there, but he has to be extraordinarily dim-witted to *lose* money on a liquor store, and for the moment we are talking only about dollars.)

But suppose at twenty-eight he still isn't sure what he wants to do and is willing to go on living on a high-school graduate's income. At thirty-eight, he has $156,391 in the bank and he's still ahead of the college graduate, who at age thirty-eight has made and very probably spent $48,166 more than his noncollege counterpart. If he wants to quit working and loaf full time, he can probably find a place to invest his $156,391 for a return sufficient to keep him in the modest circumstances to which he has become accustomed.

If all this forbearance sounds inhuman, consider a more likely comparison. Suppose that neither the high-school graduate nor the Princeton graduate saves anything before attaining annual earnings of $12,000. The high-school graduate will not be able to start saving until he is forty-five, the age at which his income rises to $12,000. The college graduate will have started savings at the age of thirty, but he will never be able to catch up with the bank account of the high-school graduate who started his college money earning interest when he was eighteen.

Any fair comparison between the return on investing in college and investing in a savings bank requires unnaturally long-headed calculations of future gains. Most people, and especially young people, aren't willing to sacrifice much now for uncertain prospects in the remote future.

Bankers are different. They bet every day on the chance that tomorrow will come, and they bet with numbers. They regularly calculate how much they are willing to give you today for your promise to pay in the future. A classic tool of the banking trade is a table that gives the present value of money due in the future, a specific instance of which is the merchant's "discount for cash." This discount rate depends on the interest the money could earn if you had it now.

Discounting for net present value shrinks those impressive lifetime earnings to thinkable sums. In 1972, for instance, the $601,000 a twenty-two-year-old college graduate was projected to earn was worth only $165,000 when discounted at 7 percent. And because so much of the lifetime earnings of a college graduate come late in life, the net *present* value of his lifetime earnings shrinks faster than the net present value of money compounding in a savings account. In 1972, for instance, the $416,000 a high-school graduate could expect to earn was worth $104,000 when discounted at 7 percent. That means that the difference—$61,000 —is all a college degree was worth in dollars to an eighteen-year-old on the day he received his high-school diploma in 1972. This may sound technical, but collegebound high-school graduates have to be bankers or specialists in judging investment to prefer a bird in hand to a bigger bird in a faraway bush.

How you come out, of course, depends on how you figure. If you count the extra dollars a college graduate earns in toto and compare it with the amount that accumulates if he invests in a savings bank instead of in his education, the savings bank wins. If the college graduate puts the extra he makes every year into a savings account as he makes it, college wins, at the very end. If you take the value of all these future piles at the age of eighteen by discounting them for the wait involved, the way a banker would do, college loses to the savings bank.

What about inflation? Earnings follow the price level, while money in the savings bank does not. Those who advise a young man to invest in education almost always talk about the bright future ahead for those who are prepared to take advantage of an expanding economy. But what if it isn't going to expand? What if roller coaster inflation-depression is ahead? In 1974 some of the most sophisticated investors were advising their clients to keep their money in cash—or in the near cash of treasury bills and other money-market instruments —rather than locking it in to *any* investments. Money in the savings bank keeps options open in a time of troubles or change.

What's ahead, after all, is anyone's guess. Inflation may increase everyone's dollar earnings, but an over-supply of college graduates could narrow the advantage they have in income, too. The fifty-three-year-olds who in 1972 were earning $7,044 more than high-school graduates were twenty-two-year-olds in 1941 when a diploma was something exceptional in the job market and therefore worth more.

The decline in return for a college degree within the last generation has been substantial. In the 1950s a Princeton student could pay all his expenses for the school year—eating club and all—on less than $3,000. When he graduated, he entered a job market which provided a comfortable margin over the earnings of age mates who had not gone to college. Everything that the Sylvia Porters of the day said about the dollar value of a college education was true.

There are several reasons why the return on the investment in college may continue to decline in the future.

The number of college graduates has increased to the point where many of them are doing jobs that simply do not produce the added value that would lead to higher salaries. The gap between the income of the college educated and noncollege educated will surely begin to narrow very soon.

The return on investment in education has to be less in the future because growth rates are slower than they were, reducing the proportion of jobs for which higher education is needed. All through the 1950s and 1960s great organizations like IBM were expanding. They needed to take in lots of people with potential for advancement. But by 1974 these organizations were no longer recruiting future managers in the numbers anticipated at a time when they thought they would continue to expand.

Rates of return and dollar signs on education are a fascinating brain teaser, but it should be obvious by now that there is a certain unreality to the game. Quite aside from the noneconomic benefits to college—and these should loom larger once the dollars are cleared away—there are grave difficulties in assigning a dollar value to college at all. The economists who developed the concept are the first to state its limitations.

First, there is no real evidence that the higher income of college graduates is due to college at all. As we shall see in greater detail later, college may simply attract people who are slated to earn more money anyway—those with higher I.Q.'s, better family backgrounds, and a more enterprising temperament. Statisticians try to disentangle I.Q. test scores, educational background of parents, income of parents, and other characteristics of the collegebound from the influence of their education itself by formidable mathematical maneuvers called "regression analyses." They differ among themselves about the specific results. But no one who has wrestled with the problem is prepared to attribute all of the higher income of college graduates to the impact of college itself.

Dael Wolfle, one of the first economists to calculate the dollar value of college, thought that college itself accounted for about three-fourths of the difference in lifetime income between college and high-school graduates. Harvard professor Christopher Jencks, in his report *Inequality: A Reassessment of the Effect of Family and Schooling in America*, finds that education in general accounts for less than half of the difference in income in the American population. "The biggest single source of income differences seems to be the fact that men from high-status families have higher incomes than men from low-status families even when they enter the same occupations, have the same amount of education, and have the same test scores."

It looks as if a substantial proportion of the advantage of the college educated is due not to any benefit that college confers, but to plain, old-fashioned class distinction: the upper-class intonation, acquired in the nursery, associated with Harvard graduates at a time when a most Harvard graduates had upper-class parents; the "background" rather than the schooling of the new vice-president at the bank. Jencks estimates that "an extra year of schooling seems to do about twice as much for a student from the middle-class background as for a student from a working-class background."

Does it matter what kind of college you attend? Early studies relied on the incomes reported by alumni and noted that the prestigious colleges seemed to have a higher proportion of high earners, but the recent consensus seems to be that it doesn't matter. And there is now very serious doubt that if good colleges do give you a better chance of high income, the credit goes to the quality of education you get there. If Harvard men do, in fact, earn more—and maybe they don't—it may be because employers have been unduly impressed with a Harvard degree.

One thing that is quite obvious and easy to document is that the money a college graduate earns depends a great deal on the courses he takes. Since engineers earn more than teachers, an engineering degree is going to be worth more in future earnings than a degree in education. The charges to the student are the same, so the return on an engineering degree has to be higher. (Maybe it shouldn't be, though, since the cost to the college of providing an engineering education is higher than the cost of educating a teacher.)

How much college is worth in future earnings depends on who you are and, particularly, what you look like. Blacks pay the same tuition as whites, but since they earn less, they enjoy a lower return on their investment in college. In 1969 blacks still earned only about three-fourths of the pay of whites with the same amount of schooling, and since blacks are out of work more frequently and longer than whites at every level, their lifetime earnings would be only half as much as that of their white counterparts on the basis of 1960 statistics. This doesn't mean, of course, that it isn't worthwhile for a black to go on in school. College improves the earnings expectancy of blacks by about the same percentage that it improves the earnings expectancy of whites, but since tuition, room and board, and books cost both races the same, the investment is worth less to blacks than to whites. Blacks often make a bigger sacrifice to go and get less out of it in money. One of the factors making blacks bitter is increasing educational attainment which increases their income *expectancy* faster than employers upgrade them in jobs. College hardly affects the gap between the earnings of black and white men. In 1969 black male high-school graduates averaged 79 percent of the pay of their white counterparts, compared with 78 percent for graduates with four years of college. College did a little better by black women, narrowing the race differential from 91 percent of white pay for high-school graduates to 97 percent for four-year college graduates.

Sex makes so much difference on the whole that the return on the education of all females simply hasn't been published by the Census Bureau. They would have to calculate the lifetime income of women who work full-time year round, and have always worked, and compare it with the return of similarly employed males.

The Census Bureau didn't make this comparison on the basis of 1972 data, on the assumption that there would be little demand for this data because it affected so few. The male statisticians accept the general premise that women do not invest in college in the hope of higher full-time, year-round, lifelong earnings, but in the hope, perhaps, of performing more adequately as mothers and attracting higher-earning if not otherwise "better" fathers for their legitimate children. Data is available for 1966 and shows that four years of college boosted the lifetime earnings of women by 31 percent, compared with a boost of 49 percent for men.

Collegebound students can draw one very practical conclusion from these calculations. Averages may fascinate economists and social scientists. Averages may persuade legislators to spend on colleges. But the average income advantage of college graduates does not represent a bankable investment for any individual. The dean of the economists studying human capital is Jacob Mincer of the National Bureau of Economic Research and Columbia University. He states flatly that "for, say, 20 to 30 percent of students at any level, the additional schooling has been a waste, at least in terms of earnings." For one reason or another, whether it's I.Q. or race or sex or ambition, or temperament, or charm, or social class, or home environment, or some inextricable combination of everything that could conceivably bear on success, college fails to work its income-raising magic for almost a third of those who go. An even higher proportion of those who earned $15,000 or more in 1972—58 percent to be precise—reached that comfortable bracket without the benefit of a college diploma, 30 percent made it with just a high-school diploma, and another 12 percent had even less education. Christopher Jencks says that financial success in the United States depends a good deal on luck, and the most sophisticated regression analyses have yet to demonstrate otherwise.

Communication: Its Blocking and Its Facilitation*

Carl R. Rogers

1.   It may seem curious that a person whose whole professional effort is devoted to psychotherapy should be interested in problems of communication. What relationship is there between providing therapeutic help to individuals with emotional maladjustments and the concern of this conference with obstacles to communication? Actually the relationship is very close indeed. The whole task of psychotherapy is the task of dealing with a failure in communication. The emotionally maladjusted person, the "neurotic," is in difficulty first because communication within himself has broken down, and second because as a result of this his communication with others has been damaged. If this sounds somewhat strange, then let me put it in other terms. In the "neurotic" individual, parts of himself which have been termed unconscious, or repressed, or denied to awareness, become blocked off so that they no longer communicate them-selves to the conscious or managing part of himself. As long as this is true, there are distortions in the way he communicates himself to others, and so he suffers both within himself, and in his interpersonal relations. The task of psychotherapy is to help the person achieve, through a special relationship with a therapist, good communication within himself. Once this is achieved he can communicate more freely and more effectively with others. We may say then that psychother-apy is good communication, within and between men. We may also turn that statement around and it will still be true. Good communication, free communica-tion, within or between men, is always therapeutic.

2.   It is, then, from a background of experience with communication in counseling and psychotherapy that I want to present here two ideas. I wish to state what I believe is one of the major factors in blocking or impeding communication, and then I wish to present what in our experience has proven to be a very important way of improving or facilitating communication.

3.   I would like to propose, as an hypothesis for consideration, that the major barrier to mutual interpersonal communication is our very natural tendency to judge, to evaluate, to approve or disapprove, the statement of the other person, or the other group. Let me illustrate my meaning with some very simple examples. As you leave the meeting tonight, one of the statements you are likely to hear is, "I didn't like that man's talk." Now what do you respond? Almost invariably your reply will be either approval or disapproval of the attitude expressed. Either you respond, "I didn't either. I thought it was terrible," or else you tend to reply, "Oh, I thought it was really good." In other words, your primary reaction is to evaluate what has just been said to you, to evaluate it from *your* point of view, your own frame of reference.

4.   Or take another example. Suppose I say with some feeling, "I think the Republicans are behaving in ways that show a lot of good sound sense these days," what is the response that arises in your mind as you listen? The overwhelming likelihood is that it will be evaluative. You will find yourself agreeing, or disagreeing, or making some judgment about me such as "He must be a conservative," or "He seems solid in his thinking." Or let us take an illustration from the international scene. Russia says vehemently, "The treaty with Japan is a war plot on the part of the United States." We rise as one person to say "That's a lie!"

5.   This last illustration brings in another element connected with my hypothesis. Although the tendency to make evaluations is common in almost all interchange of language, it is very much heightened in those situations where feelings and emotions are deeply involved. So the stronger our feelings, the more likely it is that there will be no mutual element in the communication. There will be just two ideas, two feelings, two judgments, missing each other in psychological space. I'm sure you recognize this from your own experience. When you have not been emotionally involved yourself, and have listened to a heated discussion, you often go away thinking, "Well, they actually weren't talking about the same thing." And they were not. Each was making a judgment, an evaluation, from his own frame of reference. There was really nothing which could be called communication in any genuine sense. This tendency to react to any emotionally meaningful statement by forming an evaluation of it from our own point of view, is, I repeat, the major barrier to interpersonal communication.

6.   But is there any way of solving this problem, of avoiding this barrier? I feel that we are making exciting progress toward this goal and I would like to present it as simply as I can. Real communication occurs, and this evaluative tendency is avoided, when we listen with understanding. What does that mean? It means *to see the expressed idea and attitude from the other person's point of view, to*

sense how it feels to him, to achieve his frame of reference in regard to the thing he is talking about.

7.   Stated so briefly, this may sound absurdly simple, but it is not. It is an approach which we have found extremely potent in the field of psychotherapy. It is the most effective agent we know for altering the basic personality structure of an individual, and improving his relationships and his communications with others. If I can listen to what he can tell me, if I can understand how it seems to him, if I can see its personal meaning for him, if I can sense the emotional flavor which it has for him, then I will be releasing potent forces of change in him. If I can really understand how he hates his father, or hates the university, or hates communists—if I can catch the flavor of his fear of insanity, or his fear of atom bombs, or of Russia—it will be of the greatest help to him in altering those very hatreds and fears, and in establishing realistic and harmonious relationships with the very people and situations toward which he has felt hatred and fear. We know from our research that such empathic understanding—understanding *with* a person, not *about* him—is such an effective approach that it can bring about major changes in personality.

8.   Some of you may be feeling that you listen well to people, and that you have never seen such results. The chances are very great indeed that your listening has not been of the type I have described. Fortunately I can suggest a little laboratory experiment which you can try to test the quality of your understanding. The next time you get into an argument with your wife, or your friend, or with a small group of friends, just stop the discussion for a moment and for an experiment, institute this rule. "Each person can speak up for himself only *after* he has first restated the ideas and feelings of the previous speaker accurately and to that speaker's satisfaction." You see what this would mean. It would simply mean that before presenting your own point of view, it would be necessary for you to really achieve the other speaker's frame of reference—to understand his thoughts and feelings so well that you could summarize them for him. Sounds simple doesn't it? But if you try it you will discover it one of the most difficult things you have ever tried to do. However, once you have been able to see the other's point of view, your own comments will have to be drastically revised. You will also find the emotion going out of the discussion, the differences being reduced, and those differences which remain being of a rational and understandable sort.

9.   Can you imagine what this kind of an approach would mean if it were projected into large areas? What would happen to a labor-management dispute if it was conducted in such a way that labor, without necessarily agreeing, could accurately state management's point of view in a way that management could accept; and management, without approving labor's stand, could state labor's case in a way that labor agreed was accurate? It would mean that real communication was established, and one could practically guarantee that some reasonable solution would be reached.

10.   If then this way of approach is an effective avenue to good communication and

good relationships, and I am quite sure you will agree if you try the experiment I have mentioned, why is it not more widely tried and used? I will try to list the difficulties which keep it from being utilized.

11.   In the first place it takes courage, a quality which is not too widespread. I am indebted to Dr. S. I. Hayakawa, the semanticist, for pointing out that to carry on psychotherapy in this fashion is to take a very real risk, and that courage is required. If you really understand another person in this way, if you are willing to enter his private world and see the way life appears to him, without any attempt to make evaluative judgments, you run the risk of being changed yourself. You might see it his way, you might find yourself influenced in your attitudes or your personality. This risk of being changed is one of the most frightening prospects most of us can face. If I enter, as fully as I am able, into the private world of a neurotic or psychotic individual, isn't there a risk that I might become lost in that world? Most of us are afraid to take that risk. Or if we had a Russian communist speaker here tonight, or Senator Joe McCarthy, how many of us would dare to try to see the world from each of these points of view? The great majority of us could not *listen;* we would find ourselves compelled to *evaluate,* because listening would seem too dangerous. So the first requirement is courage, and we do not always have it.

12.   But there is a second obstacle. It is just when emotions are strongest that it is most difficult to achieve the frame of reference of the other person or group. Yet it is the time the attitude is most needed, if communication is to be established. We have not found this to be an insuperable obstacle in our experience in psychotherapy. A third party, who is able to lay aside his own feelings and evaluations, can assist greatly by listening with understanding to each person or group and clarifying the views and attitudes each holds. We have found this very effective in small groups in which contradictory or antagonistic attitudes exist. When the parties to a dispute realize that they are being understood, that someone sees how the situation seems to them, the statements grow less exaggerated and less defensive, and it is no longer necessary to maintain the attitude, "I am 100% right and you are 100% wrong." The influence of such an understanding catalyst in the group permits the members to come closer and closer to the objective truth involved in the relationship. In this way mutual communication is established and some type of agreement becomes much more possible. So we may say that though heightened emotions make it much more difficult to understand *with* an opponent, our experience makes it clear that a neutral, understanding, catalyst type of leader or therapist can overcome this obstacle in a small group.

13.   This last phrase, however, suggests another obstacle to utilizing the approach I have described. Thus far all our experience has been with small face-to-face groups—groups exhibiting industrial tensions, religious tensions, racial tensions, and therapy groups in which many personal tensions are present. In these small groups our experience, confirmed by a limited amount of research, shows that this basic approach leads to improved communication, to greater acceptance of

others and by others, and to attitudes which are more positive and more problem-solving in nature. There is a decrease in defensiveness, in exaggerated statements, in evaluative and critical behavior. But these findings are from small groups. What about trying to achieve understanding between larger groups that are geographically remote? Or between face-to-face groups who are not speaking for themselves, but simply as representatives of others, like the delegates at Kaesong? Frankly we do not know the answers to these questions. I believe the situation might be put this way. As social scientists we have a tentative test-tube solution of the problem of breakdown in communication. But to confirm the validity of this test-tube solution, and to adapt it to the enormous problems of communication-breakdown between classes, groups, and nations, would involve additional funds, much more research, and creative thinking of a high order.

14.   Even with our present limited knowledge we can see some steps which might be taken, even in large groups, to increase the amount of listening *with,* and to decrease the amount of evaluation *about.* To be imaginative for a moment, let us suppose that a therapeutically oriented international group went to the Russian leaders and said, "We want to achieve a genuine understanding of your views and even more important, of your attitudes and feelings, toward the United States. We will summarize and resummarize these views and feelings if necessary, until you agree that our description represents the situation as it seems to you." Then suppose they did the same thing with the leaders in our own country. If they then gave the widest possible distribution to these two views, with the feelings clearly described but not expressed in name-calling, might not the effect be very great? It would not guarantee the type of understanding I have been describing, but it would make it much more possible. We can understand the feelings of a person who hates us much more readily when his attitudes are accurately described to us by a neutral third party, than we can when he is shaking his fist at us.

15.   But even to describe such a first step is to suggest another obstacle to this approach of understanding. Our civilization does not yet have enough faith in the social sciences to utilize their findings. The opposite is true of the physical sciences. During the war when a test-tube solution was found to the problem of synthetic rubber, millions of dollars and an army of talent was turned loose on the problem of using that finding. If synthetic rubber could be made in milligrams, it could and would be made in the thousands of tons. And it was. But in the social science realm, if a way is found of facilitating communication and mutual understanding in small groups, there is no guarantee that the finding will be utilized. It may be a generation or more before the money and the brains will be turned loose to exploit that finding.

16.   In closing, I would like to summarize this small-scale solution to the problem of barriers in communication, and to point out certain of its characteristics.

17.   I have said that our research and experience to date would make it appear that breakdowns in communication, and the evaluative tendency which is the

major barrier to communication, can be avoided. The solution is provided by creating a situation in which each of the different parties come to understand the other from the *other's* point of view. This has been achieved, in practice, even when feelings run high, by the influence of a person who is willing to understand each point of view empathically, and who thus acts as a catalyst to precipitate further understanding.

18.   This procedure has important characteristics. It can be initiated by one party, without waiting for the other to be ready. It can even be initiated by a neutral third person, providing he can gain a minimum of cooperation from one of the parties.

19.   This procedure can deal with the insincerities, the defensive exaggerations, the lies, the "false fronts" which characterize almost every failure in communication. These defensive distortions drop away with astonishing speed as people find that the only intent is to understand, not judge.

20.   This approach leads steadily and rapidly toward the discovery of the truth, toward a realistic appraisal of the objective barriers to communication. The dropping of some defensiveness by one party leads to further dropping of defensiveness by the other party, and truth is thus approached.

21.   This procedure gradually achieves mutual communication. Mutual communication tends to be pointed toward solving a problem rather than toward attacking a person or group. It leads to a situation in which I see how the problem appears to you, as well as to me, and you see how it appears to me, as well as to you. Thus accurately and realistically defined, the problem is almost certain to yield to intelligent attack, or if it is in part insoluble, it will be comfortably accepted as such.

22.   This then appears to be a test-tube solution to the breakdown of communication as it occurs in small groups. Can we take this small scale answer, investigate it further, refine it, develop it and apply it to the tragic and well-nigh fatal failures of communication which threaten the very existence of our modern world? It seems to me that this is a possibility and a challenge which we should explore.

Poor Learning from Good Teachers*

Fritz Machlup

Most professors at colleges and universities think they know a good teacher when they see one, or rather when they have observed him closely for a long time, or seen him perform in the classroom, in seminars, and in departmental meetings. They may also have heard that he has received excellent evaluations from his undergraduate students; that some of them rave about his personality and his brilliant, exciting, and witty lectures; that most of them praise his lucid exposition, his fine rapport with students, his availability to all who seek extra help or a sympathetic ear; and that all mention his fairness in setting and grading examinations. Yet, in my view, many of these good teachers actually do a poor job of teaching—in the sense that the learning that results from their performance is sometimes worse than that produced by notoriously poor teachers. If this statement sounds paradoxical, or just plain silly, consider the arguments in its support.

A Paradox?

Like most paradoxes, the assertion that a good teacher is not always one who teaches effectively reveals a problem of definition. If a good teacher is defined as one who produces or induces real learning in the sense of substantial improvements in students' achievements, clearly my statement would be self-contradictory. If, however, a good teacher is defined by those criteria enumerated in the preceding paragraph—those characteristics generally emphasized

* Fritz Machlup is a former President of the Association and Professor of Economics at New York University. This article is reprinted with permission from *Academe*, October, 1979, 376-380.

in the judgments of colleagues and students—then it can and will happen that good teachers fail badly.

My point is that the mentioned characteristics do not ensure good results in terms of students' achievements, of their tested knowledge and comprehension of the subject taught. *The teacher's performance that prompts witnesses to say he is a good teacher is not always equivalent to good teaching if good teaching is what produces good learning.*

Teacher Evaluation by Colleagues and Students

Since some of the things I intend to say may be taken to be disparaging of the customary teacher evaluations, I wish to state my position regarding these polls. I favor regular evaluations of the teacher's performance by the students. Not only do they give students a sense of participation in the affairs of the institution, but they give the teacher an opportunity to learn what parts of his teaching practices are appreciated and in what respects he should try to improve. However, I do not support the practice of taking high marks of the teacher by the students as justification of decisions for promotion, tenure, and salary raises. It is reasonable to trust the students' judgment of poor performance and to consider this in decisions about the teacher, but their judgment of good or outstanding performance should be discounted if not completely disregarded. Students cannot be judges of the content of what they are taught. What goes over well is not necessarily what ought to be learned.

There is a substantial amount of evidence to the effect that favorable evaluations of teachers by students are unreliable. Much of that evidence is based on experiments which proved that students prefer vague discussions to rigorous arguments, and favor the learning of routine procedures over analysis of basic concepts. Among many reported experiments is that of a lecture that was carefully designed to include an abundance of wrong, vague, and absolutely nonsensical statements presented vigorously by a scintillating orator: he received the highest ratings from his audience.

Evaluations of a teacher by his colleages, though taking account of the formal ratings by the students, rely more on informal oral reports from selected students and still more on impressions gathered in faculty meetings, seminars, discussions, and other such occasions. By and large, most professors believe they are good judges of their colleagues' qualifications as teachers. Yet, too many cling to the hypothesis that a good teacher can be expected to teach well. They presuppose that a colleague who has intelligence, clarity of expression, ability to explain complex issues, and a mastery of his subject will automatically do a good job of teaching. I call this the naïve hypothesis.

The Naïve Hypothesis and the Failure of Its Test

A group of economists in a major university wanted to test the naïve assumption that there is a close correlation between the quality of teachers, as judged by the customary traits, and the average achievement of their students, as judged by the numerical scores they received on their final examination. The opportunity was afforded in a large elementary course in economics taught in ten sections by different instructors, with uniform assignments and a uniform final examination graded by uniform standards.

The instructors apparently had very unequal qualifications. Some were senior professors with many years of teaching experience, some had been teaching for only a few years, some were complete novices. Some were great wits, others were hopeless dullards; some knew the literature of their subject, others were not well read at all; some were broadly educated, others were narrow technicians; some were interested in the affairs of the nation and the world, others had parochial interests. Weighting all these differences, a group of colleagues ranked the instructors with regard to their apparent qualifications as teachers. To support the hypothesis that better teachers get better results, the average grades achieved in different sections of the course should have corresponded to the rankings. The findings were devastating to the naïve hypothesis. To the surprise of the analysts comparing the distributions and averages of the numerical grades, the variances of section averages from the course average were insignificant. There was no correlation between teacher quality and teacher success.

As is the habit of economists, good or bad, they were not embarrassed by the failure of their expectations or predictions; they quickly formulated an alternative hypothesis: Students compensated for differences in teacher quality through differential investment in out-of-class study time. The poorer the lectures to which they were exposed, the more studying the students must have done to supplement the little they had gotten out of the classroom activities.

The New Hypothesis and the Absence of Its Test

The new hypothesis may be dramatized in a more elaborate model: A good teacher, by presenting his material in an exciting way (so that the students cannot help being attentive) and with extraordinary lucidity (so that the students hardly notice the inherent complexities of the subject and grasp easily even the most subtle interrelations among its components), gives the students a feeling of comprehension and mastery of the subject; the result is that they can safely neglect the reading required and recommended for the course and allocate their time to their more demanding courses and extracurricular activities. An inept teacher, on the other hand, by presenting the same material in a dull manner so that the students fall asleep or let their thoughts wander and with so little expository skill as to leave the students adrift and unable to see how things hang together, gives the students a feeling of uncertainty and makes them sense a need for clarification, which they may try to find in the assigned readings and problems. Thus, the bad teachers' students spend much more time reading and studying for the course than they would if they comprehended what their instructor taught.

The hypothesis is plausible and believable. In a nutshell, the students in the section of the "good teacher" skimp on their reading or problem-solving, while those in the section taught by the "bad teacher" devote more time to studying. This hypothesis is, of course, in need of testing. Unfortunately, no survey of the students' actual reading-and-studying time was made. Such a survey would have been needed for a test of the new hypothesis, particularly since not only the hypothesis itself but also the validity of the grade comparisons that had given rise to it can be challenged on several grounds. Three such challenges may be addressed here:

1. Was the grading really based on uniform standards? On this there can be little doubt, since the section teachers did not grade the examination papers of their own students, but each instructor graded the answers to one question in the papers of all students in all sections of the course.
2. Were the sections comprised of different kinds of student, say, selected according to scholarly standing, particular background (mathematics, for instance), or prospective fields of concentration (majors in economics, physics, engineering)? No, students had been assigned at random, though with consideration of their schedules for other courses.
3. Would this consideration—the avoidance of conflicts with other courses —introduce a bias in the composition of particular sections? For example, would a conflict with courses in mathematics or physics scheduled for certain days and hours increase the share of mathematics and physics students in the sections scheduled for a nonconflicting time? Yes, this might well be the case, and the findings were not checked for this possible bias. If, because of conflicts in schedule, the sections taught by the presumably bad teachers had a heavier concentration of presumably brighter students (i.e., students taking more difficult courses), this would weaken or replace the hypothesis of compensatory investment in reading and problem-solving.

Thus the statistical findings were inconclusive. The new hypothesis, not yet refuted, still invites appropriate testing, which, I submit, would be well worth doing.

My Proposal

Even though the hypothesis may in the end prove exaggerated, if not false, its mere formulation suggests a policy. Fear not that I will urge teachers to stop being lucid, brilliant, witty, helpful, and enthusiastic. Instead, the solution is to make good classroom work and intensive out-of-class study complementary. As long as students can learn from the fine lectures, discussions, and lab work all that they need for doing well on the examinations, there will be some students—of all degrees of intelligence and ambition—who will skimp on their studying.

The only technique for changing this is to set examinations that test the students' book learning, homework, and comprehension of materials not covered in class. Students should not be able to regard class attendance as an alternative to doing their homework. Lectures and assignments should complement each other: the lectures should be more enlightening and more comprehensible to students who have done their reading and exercises, and the reading and exercises should be more helpful in light of what was learned from the work in class. And, I repeat my prescription, the examinations should test chiefly the comprehension of material *not* presented by the teacher.

Testing and Reading, Reading and Testing

At a time when restive students and pliant instructors have reduced the weight of examinations and graded courses, a word should be said for the place of tests in education at all levels, from the lowest to the very highest. Examinations can serve a variety of purposes,, most of them not connected with my present argument. They may be used to screen students in several respects; to judge their achievement, their readiness for more advanced studies, their comparative qualifications for different disciplines or occupations; to certify their attainments or standing and to recommend them for positions, promotions, or awards; to provide incentives for students to review their notes, reading assignments, and exercises in a more comprehensive, coordinated manner; to help students realize where their comprehension is inadequate and where more study is needed; and so forth. Different educators will give different weights to these possible uses of examinations. For my present argument I wish to emphasize only one role of testing the students' progress: its role as an integral part of the learning process.

In a sense, education consists of an endless succession of tests, chiefly self-administered by the student. At every stage in reading, writing, doing numbers, in all forms of reasoning, the learner proceeds (usually without knowing it) in a sequence of tests. The act of comprehending the second sentence of an argument is an implied test of the comprehension of the first. If the third sentence is not fully grasped, the student has failed his test and must go back to square one. To learn how to learn is largely to learn how to test oneself. Most people need some guidance in learning how to learn, and the greatest help they can receive consists of tests administered by others, particularly by teachers. The rebellion of students and some of their teachers against tests and against grades is in effect a rebellion against learning.

The amount of learning in the classroom is limited, because it takes only a third of a work week and especially because the listener cannot test himself at every successive step. The student cannot go back to an earlier stage of the argument when he finds, at some point of a lecture, that his grasp is imperfect. In reading at his own pace, he can stop, go back a few paragraphs, and reread for better comprehension. He stops for a self-administered test; he sees that he cannot give himself an A—even an A minus is not good enough—and he tries again. Reading for full comprehension leads to real learning. And the same is true for problems and exercises.

The importance of reading in all education, but especially at college, cannot be exaggerated. Its position has been undermined at far too many academic institutions. It can only be restored with teacher-administered tests. Those splendid lectures and interesting discussions in the courses given by the good teacher may do more harm than good. For, to the extent that they satisfy the students' intellectual appetites and contain all that the students need to know in order to do well on the examinations, they reduce the students' need and urgency to read and do other homework. The students miss out on a chance which good teaching—that is, strong inducements to read and solve problems—should have provided.

The Proposal Restated

Every *good* teacher can become a really *effective* teacher if, to his fine qualities as lecturer, expositor, discussion leader, adviser, and sympathetic friend of students, he adds the simple technique prescribed: to make reading and other homework indispensable for students attempting to pass his course. It is especially important that his lectures be not repetitive of assigned reading materials, not substitutes for reading, but truly complementary with reading; that many classroom discussions be based on assigned reading or exercises but in a way that the student who had skimped on his homework feels that he is at a serious disadvantage; that examinations during and at the end of the term test the successful comprehension of the materials read by, or problems assigned to, the students—a comprehension, of course, that does not depend on memorizing.

What to Read and What to Teach?

The decision to make reading indispensable for full comprehension of the lectures and for success in the examinations does not by itself answer the question of the optimal division of labor between home-and-library work and classroom work.

In selecting which materials to assign for reading and which to present orally, the instructor may be aided by one major principle: Never lecture on anything that the students can find in acceptable and accessible published sources. Guidelines for making choices include the following:

- Elucidate what the published sources leave obscure.
- Elaborate on what the published sources leave seriously incomplete.
- Present different aspects or dissenting views and, if the class size permits, invite discussion of the differences.
- Adopt the principle of comparative advantage by selecting for oral presentation those topics (relevant to the course) on which you have special competence.

- Relate, if possible, the issues assigned for reading (or the problems assigned for exercises) to current affairs, recent findings, new publications.
- Tie together the information conveyed by published sources and earlier lectures in order to give the students a comprehensive picture of the subject.

The classical goal of a university education has been to prepare the student for a lifetime of self-directed learning. In practice this means a lifetime of reading and problem solving; if college does nothing else, it should implant in the student's taste system an unquenchable thirst for the printed word.

Some Side-Effects

I like to think that my suggestions, if generally adopted, would prove fatal to bad teachers. If course examinations were based exclusively on outside study and graded for the comprehension of assigned reading and exercises, students would find the bad teachers' classes unhelpful and therefore they would not attend. But the good teachers would continue to attract students since their lectures and discussions would be enlightening, stimulating, perhaps even exciting. In self-defense some bad teachers might decide to include in their examinations questions calling for regurgitation of orally presented material. As a firm believer in academic freedom, I see no way of preventing such a practice. Thus, after all, my plan is not an effective remedy for bad teaching; its adoption, however, can transform a "good teacher" into an effective one.

Embracing Contraries in the Teaching Process*

Peter Elbow

My argument is that good teaching seems a struggle because it calls on skills or mentalities that are actually contrary to each other and thus tend to interfere with each other. It was my exploration of writing that led me to look for contraries in difficult or complex processes. I concluded that good writing requires on the one hand the ability to conceive copiously of many possibilities, an ability which is enhanced by a spirit of open, accepting generativity; but on the other hand good writing also requires an ability to criticize and reject everything but the best, a very different ability which is enhanced by a tough-minded critical spirit. I end up seeing in good writers the ability somehow to be extremely creative and extremely critical, without letting one mentality prosper at the expense of the other or being halfhearted in both. (For more about this idea see my *Writing With Power* [Oxford University Press, 1981], especially Chapter 1.)

In this frame of mind I began to see a paradoxical coherence in teaching where formerly I was perplexed. I think the two conflicting mentalities needed for good teaching stem from the two conflicting obligations inherent in the job: we have an obligation to students but we also have an obligation to knowledge

* Peter Elbow teaches and directs the writing program at the State University of New York at Stony Brook. He is the author of *Writing Without Teachers* (Oxford, 1973) and *Writing With Power* (Oxford, 1981). He also has written *Oppositions in Chaucer* which, like the essay that appears here, examines the principle of getting closer to the truth by pursuing contraries. An earlier version of this article was presented at the meeting of the Modern Language Association in New York City, December 1981. Professor Elbow thanks the many readers of earlier drafts for their help. Reprinted from *College English*, April 1983. Copyright © 1983 by the National Council of Teachers of English. Reprinted by permission of the publisher and the author.

and society. Surely we are incomplete as teachers if we are committed only to what we are teaching but not to our students, or only to our students but not to what we are teaching, or halfhearted in our commitment to both.

We like to think that these two commitments coincide, and often they do. It happens often enough, for example, that our commitment to standards leads us to give a low grade or tough comment, and it is just what the student needs to hear. But just as often we see that a student needs praise and support rather than a tough grade, even for her weak performance, if she is really to prosper as a student and a person—if we are really to nurture her fragile investment in her studies. Perhaps we can finesse this conflict between a "hard" and "soft" stance if it is early in the semester or we are only dealing with a rough draft; for the time being we can give the praise and support we sense is humanly appropriate and hold off strict judgment and standards till later. But what about when it is the end of the course or a final draft needs a grade? It is comforting to take as our paradigm that first situation where the tough grade was just right, and to consider the trickier situation as somehow anomalous, and thus to assume that we always serve students best by serving knowledge, and vice versa. But I now think I can throw more light on the nature of teaching by taking our conflicting loyalties as paradigmatic.

Our loyalty to students asks us to be their allies and hosts as we instruct and share: to invite all students to enter in and join us as members of a learning community—even if they have difficulty. Our commitment to students asks us to assume they are all capable of learning, to see things through their eyes, to help bring out their best rather than their worst when it comes to tests and grades. By taking this inviting stance we will help more of them learn.

But our commitment to knowledge and society asks us to be guardians or bouncers: we must discriminate, evaluate, test, grade, certify. We are invited to stay true to the inherent standards of what we teach, whether or not that stance fits the particular students before us. We have a responsibility to society—that is, to our discipline, our college or university, and to other learning communities of which we are members—to see that the students we certify really understand or can do what we teach, to see that the grades and credits and degrees we give really have the meaning or currency they are supposed to have.[1]

A pause for scruples. Can we give up so easily the paradigm of teaching as harmonious? Isn't there something misguided in the very idea that these loyalties are conflicting? After all, if we think we are being loyal to students by being extreme in our solicitude for them, won't we undermine the integrity of the

---

[1] I lump "knowledge and society" together in one phrase but I acknowledge the importance of the potential conflict. For example, we may feel *society* asking us to adapt our students to it, while we feel *knowledge*—our vision of the truth—asking us to unfit our students for that society. Socrates was convicted of corrupting the youth. To take a more homely example, I may feel institutions asking me to teach students one kind of writing and yet feel impelled by my understanding of writing to teach them another kind. Thus where this paper paints a picture of teachers pulled in two directions, sometimes we may indeed be pulled in three.

subject matter or the currency of the credit and thereby drain value from the very thing we are supposedly giving them? And if we think we are being loyal to society by being extreme in our ferocity—keeping out *any* student with substantial misunderstanding—won't we deprive subject matter and society of the vitality and reconceptualizations they need to survive and grow? Knowledge and society only exist embodied—that is, flawed.

This sounds plausible. But even if we choose a middle course and go only so far as fairness toward subject matter and society, the very fact that we grade and certify at all—the very fact that we must sometimes flunk students—tempts many of them to behave defensively with us. Our mere fairness to subject matter and society tempts students to try to hide weaknesses from us, "psych us out," or "con us." It is as though we are doctors trying to treat patients who hide their symptoms from us for fear we will put them in the hospital.

Student defensiveness makes our teaching harder. We say, "Don't be afraid to ask questions," or even, "It's a sign of intelligence to be willing to ask naive questions." But when we are testers and graders, students too often fear to ask. Towards examiners they must play it safe, drive defensively, not risk themselves. This stunts learning. When they trust the teacher to be wholly an ally, students are more willing to take risks, connect the self to the material, and experiment. Here is the source not just of learning but also of genuine development or growth.

Let me bring this conflict closer to home. A department chair or dean who talks with us about our teaching and who sits in on our classes is our ally insofar as she is trying to help us teach better; and we can get more help from her to the degree that we openly share with her our fears, difficulties, and failures. Yet insofar as she makes promotion or tenure decisions about us or even participates in those decisions, we will be tempted not to reveal our weaknesses and failures. If we want the best help for our shortcomings, someone who is merely fair is not enough. We need an ally, not a judge.

Thus we can take a merely judicious, compromise position toward our students only if we are willing to settle for being *sort of* committed to students and *sort of* committed to subject matter and society. This middling or fair stance, in fact, is characteristic of many teachers who lack investment in teaching or who have lost it. Most invested teachers, on the other hand, tend to be a bit passionate about supporting students or else passionate about serving and protecting the subject matter they love—and thus they tend to live more on one side or the other of some allegedly golden mean.

But supposing you reply, "Yes, I agree that a compromise is not right. Just middling. Muddling. Not excellence or passion in either direction. But that's not what I'm after. My scruple had to do with your very notion of *two directions*. There is only one direction. Excellence. Quality. The very conception of conflict between loyalties is wrong. An inch of progress in one direction, whether toward knowledge or toward students, is always an inch in the direction of the other. The needs of students and of knowledge or society are in essential harmony."

To assert this harmony is, in a sense, to agree with what I am getting at in this paper. But it is no good just asserting it. It is like asserting, "Someday you'll thank me for this," or, "This is going to hurt me worse than it hurts you." I may say to students, "My fierce grading and extreme loyalty to subject matter and society are really in your interests," but students will still tend to experience me as adversary and undermine much of my teaching. I may say to knowledge and society, "My extreme support and loyalty to all students is really in your interests," but society will tend to view me as a soft teacher who lets standards down.

It is the burden of this paper to say that a contradictory stance is possible —not just in theory but in practice—but not by pretending there is no tension or conflict. And certainly not by affirming only one version of the paradox, the "paternal" version, which is to stick up for standards and firmness by insisting that to do so is good for students in the long run, forgetting the "maternal" version which is to stick up for students by insisting that to do so is good for knowledge and society in the long run. There is a genuine paradox here. The positions are conflicting and they are true.

Let me turn this structural analysis into a narrative about the two basic urges at the root of teaching. We often think best by telling stories. I am reading a novel and I interrupt my wife to say, "Listen to this, isn't this wonderful!" and I read a passage out loud. Or we are walking in the woods and I say to her, "Look at that tree!" I am enacting the pervasive human itch to share. It feels lonely, painful, or incomplete to appreciate something and not share it with others.[2]

But this urge can lead to its contrary. Suppose I say, "Listen to this passage," and my wife yawns or says, "Don't interrupt me." Suppose I say, "Look at that beautiful sunset on the lake," and she laughs at me for being so sentimental and reminds me that Detroit is right there just below the horizon—creating half the beauty with its pollution. Suppose I say, "Listen to this delicate irony," and she can't see it and thinks I am neurotic to enjoy such bloodless stuff. What happens then? I end up *not* wanting to share it with her. I hug it to myself. I become a lone connoisseur. Here is the equally deep human urge to protect what I appreciate from harm. Perhaps I share what I love with a few select others—but only after I find a way somehow to extract from them beforehand assurance that they will understand and appreciate what I appreciate. And with them I can even sneer at worldly ones who lack our taste or intelligence or sensibility.

Many of us went into teaching out of just such an urge to share things with others, but we find students turn us down or ignore us in our efforts to give gifts. Sometimes they even laugh at us for our very enthusiasm in sharing. We try to show them what we understand and love, but they yawn and turn away. They put their feet up on our delicate structures; they chew bubble gum during the slow

---

[2] Late in life, I realize I must apologize and pay my respects to that form of literary criticism that I learned in college to scorn in callow fashion as the "Ah lovely!" school: criticism which tries frankly to share a preception and appreciation of the work rather than insist that there is some problem to solve or some complexity to analyze.

movement; they listen to hard rock while reading *Lear* and say, "What's so great about Shakespeare?"

Sometimes even success in sharing can be a problem. We manage to share with students what we know and appreciate, and they love it and eagerly grasp it. But their hands are dirty or their fingers are rough. We overhear them saying, "Listen to this neat thing I learned," yet we cringe because they got it all wrong. Best not to share.

I think of the medieval doctrine of poetry that likens it to a nut with a tough husk protecting a sweet kernel. The function of the poem is not to disclose but rather to conceal the kernel from the many, the unworthy, and to disclose it only to the few worthy (D. W. Robertson, *A Preface to Chaucer* [Princeton, N.J.: Princeton University Press, 1963], pp. 61 ff.). I have caught myself more than a few times explaining something I know or love in this tricky double-edged way: encoding my meaning with a kind of complexity or irony such that only those who have the right sensibility will hear what I have to say—others will not understand at all. Surely this is the source of much obscurity in learned discourse. We would rather have readers miss entirely what we say or turn away in boredom or frustration than reply, "Oh, I see what you mean. How ridiculous!" or, "How naive!" It is marvelous, actually, that we can make one utterance do so many things: communicate with the right people, stymie the wrong people, and thereby help us decide who *are* the right and the wrong people.

I have drifted into an unflattering portrait of the urge to protect one's subject, a defensive urge that stems from hurt. Surely much bad teaching and academic foolishness derive from this immature reaction to students or colleagues who will not accept a gift we tried generously to give (generously, but sometimes ineffectually or condescendingly or autocratically). Surely I must learn not to pout just because I can't get a bunch of adolescents as excited as I am about late Henry James. Late Henry James may be pearls, but when students yawn, that doesn't make them swine.

But it is not immature to protect the integrity of my subject in a positive way, to uphold standards, to insist that students stretch themselves till they can do justice to the material. Surely these impulses are at the root of much good teaching. And there is nothing wrong with these impulses in themselves—only *by themselves*. That is, there is nothing wrong with the impulse to guard or protect the purity of what we cherish so long as that act is redeemed by the presence of the opposite impulse also to give it away.

In Piaget's terms learning involves both assimilation and accommodation. Part of the job is to get the subject matter to bend and deform so that it fits inside the learner (that is, so it can fit or relate to the learner's experiences). But that's only half the job. Just as important is the necessity for the learner to bend and deform himself so that he can fit himself around the subject without doing violence to it. Good learning is not a matter of finding a happy medium where both parties are transformed as little as possible. Rather both parties must be maximally transformed—in a sense deformed. There is violence in learning. We can not learn something without eating it, yet we can not really learn it either without letting it eat us.

Look at Socrates and Christ as archetypal good teachers—archetypal in being so paradoxical. They are extreme on the one hand in their impulse to share with everyone and to support all learners, in their sense that everyone can take and get what they are offering; but they are extreme on the other hand in their fierce high standards for what will pass muster. They did not teach gut courses, they flunked "gentleman C" performances, they insisted that only "too much" was sufficient in their protectiveness toward their "subject matter." I am struck also with how much they both relied on irony, parable, myth, and other forms of subtle utterance that hide while they communicate. These two teachers were willing in some respects to bend and disfigure and in the eyes of many to profane what they taught, yet on the other hand they were equally extreme in their insistence that learners bend to transform themselves in order to become fit receptacles.

It is as though Christ, by stressing the extreme of sharing and being an ally—saying "suffer the little children to come unto me" and praising the widow with her mite—could be more extreme in his sternness: "unless you sell all you have," and, "I speak to them in parables, because seeing they do not see and hearing they do not hear, nor do they understand" (saying in effect, "I am making this a tough course *because* so many of you are poor students"). Christ embeds the two themes of giving away and guarding—commitment to "students" and to "subject matter"—in the one wedding feast story: the host invites in guests from the highways and byways, anybody, but then angrily ejects one into outer darkness because he lacks the proper garment.

Let me sum up the conflict in two lists of teaching skills. If on the one hand we want to help more students learn more, I submit we should behave in the following four ways:

1. We should see our students as smart and capable. We should assume that they *can* learn what we teach—all of them. We should look through their mistakes or ignorance to the intelligence that lies behind. There is ample documentation that this "teacher expectation" increases student learning (Robert Rosenthal, "Teacher Expectation and Pupil Learning," in R. D. Strom, ed., *Teachers and the Learning Process* [Englewood Cliffs, N.J.: Prentice-Hall, 1971], pp. 33–60).

2. We should show students that we are on their side. This means, for example, showing them that the perplexity or ignorance they reveal to us will not be used against them in tests, grading, or certifying. If they hide their questions or guard against us they undermine our efforts to teach them.

3. Indeed, so far from letting their revelations hurt them in grading, we should be as it were lawyers for the defense, explicitly trying to help students do better against the judge and prosecuting attorney when it comes to the

"trial" of testing and grading. ("I may be able to get you off this charge but only if you tell me what you really were doing that night.") If we take this advocate stance students can learn more from us, even if they are guilty of the worst crimes in the book: not having done the homework, not having learned last semester, not *wanting* to learn. And by learning more—even if not learning perfectly—they will perform better, which in turn will usually lead to even better learning in the future.

4. Rather than try to be perfectly fair and perfectly in command of what we teach—as good examiners ought to be—we should reveal our own position, particularly our doubts, ambivalences, and biases. We should show we are still learning, still willing to look at things in new ways, still sometimes uncertain or even stuck, still willing to ask naive questions, still engaged in the interminable process of working out the relationship between what we teach and the rest of our lives. Even though we are not wholly peer with our students, we can still be peer in this crucial sense of also being engaged in learning, seeking, and being incomplete. Significant learning requires change, inner readjustments, willingness to let go. We can increase the chances of our students being willing to undergo the necessary anxiety involved in change if they see we are also willing to undergo it.

Yet if, on the other hand, we want to increase our chances of success in serving knowledge, culture, and institutions I submit that we need skill at behaving in four different ways:

1. We should insist on standards that are high—in the sense of standards that are absolute. That is, we should take what is almost a kind of Platonic position that there exists a "real world" of truth, of good reasoning, of good writing, of knowledge of biology, whatever—and insist that anything less than the real thing is not good enough.
2. We should be critical-minded and look at students and student performances with a skeptical eye. We should assume that some students cannot learn and others will not, even if they can. This attitude will increase our chances of detecting baloney and surface skill masquerading as competence or understanding.
3. We should not get attached to students or take their part or share their view of things; otherwise we will find it hard to exercise the critical spirit needed to say, "No, you do not pass," "No, you cannot enter in with the rest of us," "Out you go into the weeping and gnashing of teeth."
4. Thus we should identify ourselves primarily with knowledge or subject matter and care more about the survival of culture and institutions than about individual students—even when that means students are rejected who are basically smart or who tried as hard as they could. We should keep our minds on the harm that can come to knowledge and society if

standards break down or if someone is certified who is not competent, rather than on the harm that comes to individual students by hard treatment.

Because of this need for conflicting mentalities I think I see a distinctive distribution of success in teaching. At one extreme we see a few master or genius teachers, but they are striking for how differently they go about it and how variously and sometimes surprisingly they explain what they do. At the other extreme are people who teach very badly, or who have given up trying, or who quit teaching altogether: they are debilitated by the conflict between trying to be an ally as they teach and an adversary as they grade. Between these two extremes teachers find the three natural ways of making peace between contraries: there are "hard" teachers in whom loyalty to knowledge or society has won out; "soft" teachers in whom loyalty to students has won out; and middling, mostly dispirited teachers who are sort of loyal to students and sort of loyal to knowledge or society. (A few of this last group are not dispirited at all but live on a kind of knife edge of almost palpable tension as they insist on trying to be scrupulously fair both to students and to what they teach.)

This need for conflicting mentalities is also reflected in what is actually the most traditional and venerable structure in education: a complete separation between teaching and official assessment. We see it in the Oxford and Cambridge structure that makes the tutor wholly an ally to help the student prepare for exams set and graded by independent examiners. We see something of the same arrangement in many European university lecture-and-exam systems which are sometimes mimicked by American PhD examinations. The separation of teaching and examining is found in many licensing systems and also in some new competence-based programs.

Even in conventional university curricula we see various attempts to strengthen assessment and improve the relationship between teacher and student by making the teacher more of an ally and coach. In large courses with many sections, teachers often give a common exam and grade each others' students. Occasionally, when two teachers teach different courses within each other's field of competence, they divide their roles and act as "outside examiner" for the other's students. (This approach, by the way, tends to help teachers clarify what they are trying to accomplish in a course since they must communicate their goals clearly to the examiner if there is to be any decent fit between the teaching and examining.) In writing centers, tutors commonly help students improve a piece of writing which another teacher will assess. We even see a hint of this separation of roles when teachers stress collaborative learning: they emphasize the students' role as mutual teachers and thereby emphasize their own pedagogic role as examiner and standard setter.

But though the complete separation of teacher and evaluator is hallowed and useful I am interested here in ways for teachers to take on both roles better. It is not just that most teachers are stuck with both; in addition I believe that opposite mentalities or processes can enhance each other rather than interfere with each other if we engage in them in the right spirit.

How can we manage to do contrary things? Christ said, "Be ye perfect," but I don't think it is good advice to try being immensely supportive and fierce in the same instant, as he and Socrates somehow managed to be. In writing, too, it doesn't usually help to try being immensely generative and critical-minded in the same instant as some great writers are—and as the rest of us sometimes are at moments of blessed inspiration. This is the way of transcendence and genius, but for most of us most of the time there is too much interference or paralysis when we try to do opposites at once.

But it is possible to make peace between opposites by alternating between them so that you are never trying to do contrary things at any one moment. One opposite leads naturally to the other; indeed, extremity in one enhances extremity in the other in a positive, reinforcing fashion. In the case of my own writing I find I can generate more and better when I consciously hold off critical-minded revising till later. Not only does it help to go whole hog with one mentality, but I am not afraid to make a fool of myself since I know I will soon be just as wholeheartedly critical. Similarly, I can be more fierce and discriminating in my critical revising because I have more and better material to work with through my earlier surrender to uncensored generating.

What would such an alternating approach look like in teaching? I will give a rough picture, but I do so hesitantly because if I am right about my theory of paradox, there will be widely different ways of putting it into practice.

In teaching we traditionally end with the critical or gatekeeper function: papers, exams, grades or less institutionalized forms of looking back, taking stock, and evaluating. It is also traditional to start with the gatekeeper role: to begin a course by spelling out all the requirements and criteria as clearly as possible. We often begin a course by carefully explaining exactly what it will take to get an A, B, C, etc.

I used to be reluctant to start off on this foot. It felt so vulgar to start by emphasizing grades, and thus seemingly to reinforce a pragmatic preoccupation I want to squelch. But I have gradually changed my mind, and my present oppositional theory tells me I should exaggerate, or at least take more seriously than I often do, my gatekeeper functions rather than run away from them. The more I try to soft-pedal assessment, the more mysterious it will seem to students and the more likely they will be preoccupied and superstitious about it. The more I can make it clear to myself and to my students that I do have a commitment to knowledge and institutions, and the more I can make it specifically clear how I am going to fulfill that commitment, the easier it is for me to turn around and make a dialectical change of role into being an extreme ally to students.

Thus I start by trying to spell out requirements and criteria as clearly and concretely as possible. If I am going to use a midterm and final exam, it would help to pass out samples of these at the beginning of the course. Perhaps not a copy of precisely the test I will use but something close. And why not the real thing? If it feels as though I will ruin the effectiveness of my exam to "give it away" at the start, that means I must have a pretty poor exam—a simple-minded task that can be crammed for and that does not really test what is important. If the exam gets at the central substance of the course then surely it will help me if students see it right at the start. They will be more likely to learn what I want them to learn. It might be a matter of content: "Summarize the three main theories in this course and discuss their strengths and weaknesses by applying them to material we did not discuss." Or perhaps I am more interested in a process or skill: "Write an argumentative essay on this (new) topic." Or, "Show how the formal characteristics of this (new) poem do and do not reinforce the theme." I might want to give room for lots of choice and initiative: "Write a dialogue between the three main people we have studied that illustrates what you think are the most important things about their work." Passing out the exam at the start—and perhaps even samples of strong and weak answers—is an invitation to make a tougher exam that goes more to the heart of what the course is trying to teach. If I don't use an exam, then it is even more crucial that I say how I will determine the grade—even if I base it heavily on slippery factors: e.g., "I will count half your grade on my impression of how well you motivate and invest yourself," or "how well you work collaboratively with your peers." Of course this kind of announcement makes for a tricky situation, but if these are my goals, surely I want my students to wrestle with them all term—in all their slipperiness and even if it means arguments about how unfair it is to grade on such matters—rather than just think about them at the end.

When I assign papers I should similarly start by advertising my gatekeeper role, by clearly communicating standards and criteria. That means not just talking theoretically about what I am looking for in an A paper and what drags a paper down to B or C or F, but rather passing out a couple of samples of each grade and talking concretely about what makes me give each one the grade I give it. Examples help because our actual grading sometimes reflects criteria we do not talk about, perhaps even that we are not aware of. (For example, I have finally come to admit that neatness counts.) Even if our practice fits our preaching, sometimes students do not really understand preaching without examples Terms like "coherent" and even "specific" are notoriously hard for students to grasp because they do not read stacks of student writing. Students often learn more about well-connected and poorly-connected paragraphs or specificity or the lack of it in examples from the writing of each other than they learn from instruction alone, or from examples of published writing.

I suspect there is something particularly valuable here about embodying our commitment to knowledge and society in the form of documents or handouts: words on palpable sheets of paper rather than just spoken words-in-the-air. Documents heighten the sense that I do indeed take responsibility for these standards; writing them forces me to try to make them as concrete, explicit, and objective as possible (if not necessarily fair). But most of all, having put all this on paper I can more easily go on to separate myself from them in some way—leave them standing—and turn around and schizophrenically start being a complete ally of students. I have been wholehearted and enthusiastic in making tough standards, but now I can say, "Those are the specific criteria I will use in grading; that's what you are up against, that's really me. But now we have most of the semester for me to help you attain those standards, do well on those tests and papers. They are high standards but I suspect all of you can attain them if you work hard. I will function as your ally. I'll be a kind of lawyer for the defense, helping you bring out your best in your battles with the other me, the prosecuting-attorney me when he emerges at the end. And if you really think you are too poorly prepared to do well in one semester, I can help you decide whether to trust that negative judgment and decide now whether to drop the course or stay and learn what you can."

What is pleasing about this alternating approach is the way it naturally leads a teacher to higher standards yet greater supportiveness. That is, I feel better about being really tough if I know I am going to turn around and be more on the student's side than usual. And contrarily I do not have to hold back from being an ally of students when I know I have set really high standards. Having done so, there is now no such thing as being "too soft," supportive, helpful, or sympathetic —no reason to hold back from seeing things entirely from their side, worrying about their problems. I can't be "cheated" or taken advantage of.

In addition, the more clearly I can say what I want them to know or be able to do, the better I can figure out what I must provide to help them attain those goals. As I make progress in this cycle, it means I can set my goals even higher—ask for the deep knowledge and skills that are really at the center of the enterprise.

But how, concretely, can we best function as allies? One of the best ways is to be a kind of coach. One has set up the hurdle for practice jumping, one has described the strengths and tactics of the enemy, one has warned them about what the prosecuting attorney will probably do: now the coach can prepare them for these rigors. Being an ally is probably more a matter of stance and relationship than of specific behaviors. Where a professor of jumping might say, in effect, "I will explain the principles of jumping," a jumping coach might say, in effect, "Let's work on learning to jump over those hurdles, in doing so I'll explain the principles of jumping." If we try to make these changes in stance, I sense we will discover some of the resistances, annoyances, and angers that make us indeed reluctant genuinely to be on the student's side. How can we be teachers for long without piling up resentment at having been misunderstood and taken advantage of? But the dialectical need to be in addition an extreme adversary of students will give us a legitimate medium for this hunger to dig in one's heels even in a kind of anger.

This stance provides a refreshingly blunt but supportive way to talk to students about weaknesses. "You're strong here, you're weak there, and over here you are really out of it. We've got to find ways to work on these things so you can succeed on these essays or exams." And this stance helps reward students for volunteering weaknesses. The teacher can ask, "What don't you understand? What skills are hard for you? I need to decide how to spend our time here and I want it to be the most useful for your learning."

One of the best ways to function as ally or coach is to role-play the enemy in a supportive setting. For example, one can give practice tests where the grade doesn't count, or give feedback on papers which the student can revise before they count for credit. This gets us out of the typically counterproductive situation where much of our commentary on papers and exams is really justification for the grade—or is seen that way. Our attempt to help is experienced by students as a slap on the wrist by an adversary for what they have done wrong. No wonder students so often fail to heed or learn from our commentary. But when we comment on practice tests or revisable papers we are not saying, "Here's why you got this grade." We are saying, "Here's how you can get a better grade." When later we read final versions as evaluator we can read faster and not bother with much commentary.[3]

It is the spirit or principle of serving contraries that I want to emphasize here, not any particular fleshing out in practice such as above. For one of the main attractions of this theory is that it helps explain why people are able to be terrific teachers in such diverse ways. If someone is managing to do two things that conflict with each other, he is probably doing something mysterious: it's altogether natural if his success involves slipperiness, irony, or paradox. For example, some good teachers look like they are nothing but fierce gatekeepers, cultural bouncers, and yet in some mysterious way—perhaps ironically or subliminally—they are supportive. I think of the ferocious Marine sergeant who is always cussing out the troops but who somehow shows them he is on their side and believes in their ability. Other good teachers look like creampuffs and yet in some equally subtle way they embody the highest standards of excellence and manage to make students exert and stretch themselves as never before.

For it is one's spirit or stance that is at issue here, not the mechanics of how to organize a course in semester units or how to deal in tests, grading, or credits. I do not mean to suggest that the best way to serve knowledge and society is by having tough exams or hard grading—or even by having exams or grades at all. Some teachers do it just by talking, whether in lectures or discussions or conversation. Even though there is no evaluation or grading, the teacher can still

---

[3] Since it takes more time for us to read drafts and final versions too, no matter how quickly we read final versions, it is reasonable to conserve time in other ways—indeed I see independent merits. Don't require students to revise every draft. This permits you to grade students on their best work and thus again to have higher standards, and it is easier for students to invest themselves in revising if it is on a piece they care more about. And in giving feedback on drafts, wait till you have two drafts in hand and thus give feedback only half as often. When I have only one paper in hand I often feel, "Oh dear, everything is weak here; nothing works right; where can I start?" When I have two drafts in hand I can easily say, "This one is better for the following reasons; it's the one I'd choose to revise; see if you can fix the following problems." With two drafts it is easier to find genuine strengths and point to them and help students consolidate or gain control over them. Yet I can make a positive utterance out of talking about what *didn't* work in the better draft and how to improve it.

demonstrate her ability to be wholehearted in her commitment to what she teaches and wholehearted also in her commitment to her students. Thus her talk itself might in fact alternate between attention to the needs of students and flights where she forgets entirely about students and talks over their head, to truth, to her wisest colleagues, to herself.[4]

The teacher who is really in love with Yeats or with poetry will push harder, and yet be more tolerant of students' difficulties because his love provides the serenity he needs in teaching: he knows that students cannot hurt Yeats or his relationship with Yeats. It is a different story when we are ambivalent about Yeats or poetry. The piano teacher who mean-spiritedly raps the fingers of pupils who play wrong notes usually harbors some inner ambivalence in his love of music or some disappointment about his own talent.

In short, there is obviously no one right way to teach, yet I argue that in order to teach well we must find *some* way to be loyal both to students and to knowledge or society. Any way we can pull it off is fine. But if we are teaching less well than we should, we might be suffering from the natural tendency for these two loyalties to conflict with each other. In such a case we can usually improve matters by making what might seem an artificial separation of focus so as to give each loyalty and its attendant skills and mentality more room in which to flourish. That is, we can spend part of our teaching time saying in some fashion or other, "Now I'm being a tough-minded gatekeeper, standing up for high critical standards in my loyalty to what I teach"; and part of our time giving a contrary message: "Now my attention is wholeheartedly on trying to be your ally and to help you learn, and I am not worrying about the purity of standards or grades or the need of society or institutions."

It is not that this approach makes things simple. It confuses students at first because they are accustomed to teachers being either "hard" or "soft" or in the middle—not both. The approach does not take away any of the conflict between trying to fulfill two conflicting functions. It merely gives a context and suggests a structure for doing so. Most of all it helps me understand better the demands on me and helps me stop feeling as though there is something wrong with me for feeling pulled in two directions at once.

I have more confidence that this conscious alternation or separation of mentalities makes sense because I think I see the same strategy to be effective with writing. Here too there is obviously no one right way to write, but it seems as

---

[4] Though my argument does not imply that we need to use grades at all, surely it implies that if we do use them we should learn to improve the way we do so. I used to think that conventional grading reflected too much concern with standards for knowledge and society, but now I think it reflects too little. Conventional grading reflects such a single-minded hunger to *rank* people along a single scale or dimension that it is willing to forego any communication of what the student really knows or can do. The competence-based movement, whatever its problems, represents a genuine attempt to make grades and credits do justice to knowledge and society. (See Gerald Grant, et al., *On Competence. A Critical Analysis of Competence-Based Reform in Higher Education* [San Francisco: Jossey-Bass, 1979]. See also my "More Accurate Evaluation of Student Performance," *Journal of Higher Education*, 40[1969], 219-230.)

though any good writer must find some way to be both abundantly inventive yet tough-mindedly critical. Again, any way we can pull it off is fine, but if we are not writing as well as we should—if our writing is weak in generativity or weak in tough-minded scrutiny (not to mention downright dismal or blocked)—it may well be that we are hampered by a conflict between the accepting mentality needed for abundant invention and the rejecting mentality needed for tough-minded criticism. In such a case too, it helps to move back and forth between sustained stretches of wholehearted, uncensored generating and wholehearted critical revising to allow each mentality and set of skills to flourish unimpeded.

Even though this theory encourages a separation that could be called artificial, it also points to models of the teaching and writing process that are traditional and reinforced by common sense: teaching that begins and ends with attention to standards and assessment and puts lots of student-directed supportive instruction in the middle writing that begins with exploratory invention and ends with critical revising. But I hope that my train of thought rejuvenates these traditional models by emphasizing the underlying structure of contrasting mentalities which is central rather than merely a mechanical sequence of external stages which is not necessary at all.

In the end, I do not think I am just talking about how to serve students and serve knowledge or society. I am also talking about developing opposite and complementary sides of our character or personality: the supportive and nurturant side and the tough, demanding side. I submit that we all have instincts and needs of both sorts. The gentlest, softest, and most flexible among us really need a chance to stick up for our latent high standards, and the most hawk-eyed, critical-minded bouncers at the bar of civilization among us really need a chance to use our nurturant and supportive muscles instead of always being adversary.

Three Bighorn Sheep Essays

Tim Andryk*

These essays by Tim Andryk are three different versions of the same topic—a new way to capture bighorn sheep. The first version is a two-paragraph problem-solution essay. The second is a scientific essay that he wrote with colleagues. The third and final version is an adventure story written for a popular audience.

Two-paragraph Version

How We Learned to Capture Big Horn Sheep

As researchers trying to track the seasonal movements of bighorn sheep from one grazing range to another, my colleagues and I needed to attach radio collars to some of the sheep so we could follow them from the air. We first tried shooting them from a helicopter with a dart gun. However, the constant, forceful winds characteristic of this east front of the Rockies area made accurate shooting nearly impossible. Consequently, we missed many sheep. On other occasions we made only poor hits so that the sheep did not receive the full injection of the tranquilizer and did not go down. The paltry success of our darting operation could not justify the expensive air time of the jet-powered helicopter. Our bighorn sheep study seemed doomed. How could we live-capture these sheep now that the dart gun had proven ineffective?

A net-gun was the answer to our live-capture problem. Previously the net-gun (a bazooka type gun that shoots a 9 × 9 foot net) had been used on coyotes,

*Tim Andryk is a graduate student in Wildlife Management at Montana State University.

antelope, and other animals of the plains country. Researchers felt that the net-gun required wide open terrain which allowed a helicopter time enough to approach a fleeing animal within range (10–15 feet) for a successful shot. Nevertheless, I felt the enhanced maneuverability of the powerful jet helicopter, the semi-open terrain of the capture area, and the escape tendency of bighorn sheep to run uphill justified a capture attempt using the net-gun. On my first shot with the net gun-we captured and radio-collared three sheep. Using the net-gun, we captured four more sheep during the same afternoon. Our ability to capture two or more sheep simultaneously, made possible by the inclination of bighorn sheep to flee in a tightly packed group, greatly increased the efficiency of our capture operation. The net-gun was an extraordinary success.

Scientific Essay

Comparison of Mountain Sheep Capture Techniques: Helicopter Darting Versus Net-gunning*

A mixture of etorphine (a Schedule II narcotic that is extremely toxic to humans) and xylazine hydrochloride or acetylpromazine is one of the most effective drug combinations available for use in dart-delivery systems to capture mountain sheep (*Ovis canadensis*) (Thorne 1971, Heimer et al. 1980, Jessup et al. 1980). A new technique, a recoil-less rifle firing a 5.8-m triangular net with 15-cm mesh (Coda Net Gun, Coda Enterprises, Mesa, Ariz.) was recently tested on coyotes (*Canis latrans*) and 5 ungulate species in western Canada (Barrett et al. 1982) and may prove more effective. This paper describes the relative efficiencies of these approaches for capturing Rocky Mountains bighorns (*O. c. canadensis*) in remote areas.

Methods

Mountain sheep were captured from 1 population in the Gallatin Range of southwestern Montana and 2 in the Sawtooth Range of north central Montana. Darted sheep were captured using M99 (1 mg etorphine/ml, Lemmon Co., Sellersville, Pa.)—Rompun (xylazine hydrochloride, available in 20 and 100 mg/ml concentrations, Haver-Lockhart, Shawnee, Kans.) mixtures in 5-cc darts fired from a modified 28-gauge shotgun by a veterinarian who was certified to use M99. Dosages for $1 > 8$-year old female and 4 males, 2–3 years of age, were 5.0–5.2 mg M99 combined with 12.0 mg Rompun. Dosages for 4 females, estimated ages 2–8+ years, were 4.0 mg M99 and 8.0 mg Rompun. A 6-year-old male and a 2-year-old female were redarted following glancing hits and may have received higher dosages. Drugged animals were injected with penicillin and BoSe (Burns-Biotec, Omaha, Neb.) as a precaution against infection and

* Tim Andryk wrote this article with Lynn Irby, Daniel Hook, John McCarthy and Gary Olson. Reprinted from *The Wildlife Society Bulletin*, Vol 11, No. 2, Summer 1983 with permission of the author and publisher. Copyright © 1983 by The Wildlife Society.

capture myopathy, and were revived using intravenous injections of M50–50 (1 mg diprenorphine/ml, Lemmon Co., Sellersville, Pa.) at the same dosage as M99. No drugs were administered to sheep captured using the net-gun. Netgun captures included 9 females (<1–10+ years) and 3 males (<1–5 years). Blood samples from all darted and 2 net-gunned individuals were examined for evidence of capture myopathy (abnormal levels of creatinine phosphokinase, lactic dehydrogenase, serum glutamic oxaloacetic transaminase, serum glutamic pyruvic transaminase, cortisol, potassion ions, and glucose) by David Jessup, California Department of Fish and Game, Sacramento.

All captures were effected using a jet-converted Bell B2 helicopter. The same pilot was used for darting and net-gunning. Darted sheep were pursued along open, snow-covered slopes for pass shots or were forced into rocky areas for standing shots. The most effective approach for net-gunning involved hazing sheep slowly downslope then forcing them to run uphill on steep, open slopes where their flight speed was reduced without causing them to deviate from a straight flight path. A more detailed description of net-gunning procedures is given by Barrett et al. (1982).

Results and Discussion

During February and March 1982, 16 shots were required to capture 10 sheep, 6 from the Gallatin Range and 4 from the Sawtooth Range, using M99-Rompun mixtures. Approach times (times from the beginning of the approach to firing) varied from 5 to 14 min ($\overline{X} = 9.3$ min for 6 timed approaches) The longest approaches, 13.5 and 14.0 min, involved individuals that were redarted following a glancing shot and included the total elapsed time between the beginning of the first approach to the firing of the second dart. All approach times included periods of low intensity hazing as well as high intensity pursuit. Hits were made at distances of 8–15 m. Darted sheep dropped 7–12 min following successful hits ($\overline{X} = 9.2$ min for 6 timed shots). Immobilization times (times required to reach the animals, attach radios, collect blood, and inject M50-50) varied from 10 to 30 min. Most of the variation was due to differences in times required for the person with the blood collection kit to reach immobilized animals. All sheep revived and ran within 2 min (and most in <1 min) after M50-50 was injected.

Although no dehabilitating injuries or signs of extreme respiratory or circulatory distress were noted at the time of release, and preliminary blood analyses indicated that no serious capture stress problems occurred (D. Jessup, unpubl. data), 3 animals from the Gallatin Range, 2 > 8-year-old females and a yearling male, died within 2 months of capture. These deaths could have been directly linked to capture stress but were more likely due to malnutrition or predation. The remaining animals were alive and apparently healthy through September 1982.

Twelve sheep from the Sawtooth Range were captured using the net-gun during March and April 1982. Approach times varied from 1 to 10 min for all shots and 1 to 5 min ($\bar{X}$ = 3.2 min) for successful shots. These times included low intensity hazing as well as the intense pursuit immediately preceding firing. Sheep were captured in 9 of 13 shots. Multiple captures were made on 4 occasions. On 2 of these, 3 were entangled but 2 escaped before workers could reach the net. On 1 occasion 3 of 3 and on another 2 of 4 entangled animals were captured. Four individuals were captured in 25–50-cm snow and 8 on bare grassy slopes. Shots made at distances >3 m were unsuccessful. The sheep were down within a few seconds following a successful shot. Immobilization times varied from 2 to 20 min depending primarily on the number of animals caught per shot and whether or not blood samples were drawn. All individuals stood and ran as soon as they were released.

Barrett et al. (1982) reported the deaths of 2 of 3 net-gunned Dall sheep (*O. dalli*) males from presumed capture myopathy. No obvious symptoms of severe stress or injury were noted in the 12 animals we captured. Blood parameters for the 2 animals sampled indicated no serious capture myopathy problems (D. Jessup, unpubl. data). Only 1 animal, a 3-year-old female, died in the 6 months following capture. Her death occurred 2–3 months after she was released. Animals that escaped from the net were apparently unharmed.

Both techniques met our objectives for location and sex ratios of captured animals. Neither technique resulted in mortality at capture sites. As long as a careful, experienced pilot-gunner team and a jet-powered helicopter are used, the dangers incurred during flights were considered equivalent for both techniques (S. Duffy, pers. commun.).

Each technique did have technical advantages and disadvantages. Optimal situations for net-gunning (open, steep slopes and shots at ranges of 1–3 m) were more limited than for darting. Entangling running animals in nets increased opportunities for broken bones but eliminated the possibility of mortality due to poor dart placement, overdosing, bloating, injury or predation during the recovery phase, or infection at injection sites (Harthoorn 1965:23–34; 1976: 254–255). Drugged animals were more easily handled, but 2 people were able to control an undrugged adult male in the net sufficiently well to take blood samples and attach a radio. Net-gunning might prove better for capturing lambs because problems with overdosing and poor dart placement are avoided. Darting potentially provides greater opportunities for capturing specific animals in tightly bunched groups because a dart can be more accurately aimed. Use of etorphine precludes the possibility of helicopter malfunction due to a net becoming entangled in the rotor (Barrett et al. 1982) but exposes personnel to the danger of possible death through etorphine absorption through the skin or a cut.

The major difference in desirability of the 2 techniques may be economic rather than technical. Although the initial purchase price of the net-gun and nets ($2,900 in 1982) is approximately 10 times that of powder-charged dart-delivery system ($300 in 1982), etorphine and its antagonist are expensive and subject to tight restrictions on purchase and use. Each shot with etorphine costs approximately $20 (1982 prices) if an animal is missed and $40 if it is hit, as M50-50 is sold at the same price as M99 and administered at the same dosage. The blank cartridges used to propel the net cost approximately $.20 each. Net-gunning also required approximately 8 min less helicopter rental time per captured animal than did darting due to shorter approach times, reduced times between hits and immobilization, and multiple captures. The differences in approach times may have been an artifact of the more limited situations in which the net gun was used, but the other time savings were real.

Overall, the net gun was the more efficient of the 2 techniques for accomplishing our objective, placement of radio transmitters on mountain sheep in remote wintering areas. Researchers who need to collect extensive measurements or tissue samples and those working in terrain in which open slopes are distant from sheep groups may find darting more desirable.

Acknowledgments—The cooperation and assistance of Glenn Erickson, Montana Department of Fish, Wildlife, and Parks; Richard Kinyon, Conrad Veterinary Hospital; and Murray, Mark, and Steve Duffy, Central Helicopters, were greatly appreciated. The net gun was provided by Bart O'Gara, Montana Cooperative Wildlife Research Unit. Funding was furnished by the Foundation for North American Wild Sheep, Montana Department of Fish, Wildlife, and Parks, and the United States Forest Service.

Literature Cited

BARRETT, M. W., J. W. NOLAN, AND L. D. ROY. 1982. Evaluation of a hand-held net-gun to capture large mammals. Wildl. Soc. Bull. 10: 108–114.

HARTHOORN, A. M. 1965. Application of pharmacological and physiological principles in restraint of wild animals. Wildl. Monogr. 14. 78pp.

———. 1976. The chemical restraint of animals. Bailliere Tindall, London, U.K. 416pp.

HEIMER, W. E., S. P. DUBOIS, AND D. G. KELLEYHOUSE. 1980. A comparison of rocket-netting with other methods of capturing dall sheep. Pages 601–614 *in* W. E. Hickey, chairman, Trans. N. Wild Sheep and Goat Counc., Salmon, Idaho.

JESSUP, D. A., W. CLARK, AND B. HUNTER. 1980. Animal restraint handbook. California Dep. Fish and Game, Sacramento. 37pp.

THORNE, E. T. 1971. The use of M99, etorphine and acetylpromazine in the immobilization and capture of free-ranging Rocky Mountain bighorn sheep. Pages 127–131 *in* E. Decker, ed. N. Am. Wild Sheep Conf., Colorado State Univ., Fort Collins.

Version for Popular Audience

All in the Name of Science?

It was cold for a March day, I thought, as I listened to the whirr of the helicopter blades while we flew over the snow-laden peaks. Mark Duffy (the pilot), Dick Kinyon (a veterinarian skilled in the use of dart-guns), and I were looking for bighorn sheep to shoot with tranquilizer darts so we could attach radio-collars to them. The first sheep we saw were a group of four rams, supporting an impressive arsenal of large, light brown, curled horns. They frantically lunged through the knee-deep snow as we buzzed over them in an attempt to herd them into a clearing, away from the cliffs. Once they were in the open, Mark deftly rolled the powerful, jet-engine modified helicopter to our left and I felt exhilaration as we swept down on them, approaching within 20 feet. My stomach twisted as the roaring winds jarred and shook the helicopter. Consequently, it was difficult for Dick to aim the dart-gun; the first dart sailed wide to the right and disappeared in a puff of snow. I shouted above the din of the rotor blades that we could get in one more shot before the sheep reached the cliffs. With a right side roll the helicopter swung around and we zipped in for a second shot. The second dart hit the last ram, but glanced off his rump without delivering the full injection of the drug. As a result, the ram managed to reach the cliffs and started climbing down before he passed out on a rock ledge.

The ridge above the ledge was too steep to land on. The helicopter hovered a few feet above the ground while Dick and I leaped out into a cloud of swirling snow, landing hard on the rocks and frozen ground. We raced to the edge and started to inch our way down an icy rock chimney to get to the ram. We had to reach him quickly since he was starting to slide off the ledge. As my toes dug into the frozen snow for a hold, I peered over my shoulder at the view. I felt like I was teetering on the edge of the world; the vastness of the drop below me swallowed up my view. My only thought was how disappointed my parents would be if my toehold broke. We finally reached the ram as he was about to slide over the edge. Dick grabbed the ram and pulled him back, and I grabbed Dick and pulled him back.

There we were, huddled on a small rock ledge, on the cliff side of a mountain, while the relentless wind tried to dust us off. I wondered what in the world these stupid sheep were doing wintering up here in this land of snow, ice, and hazardous cliffs. With my gloves off, my hands became numb with cold, and I could not fasten the radio-collar around the ram's neck. The freezing wind burned our faces and the tears on our cheeks turned to ice.

Although we finally managed to attach the radio collar to this ram, inject an antidote into the ram's neck, and make the perilous ascent back up the ice chimney to the safety of the helicopter, the rest of the day was a series of failures. Our darts missed the targets when we fired at a group of ewes and lambs, and when we finally located another ram, the dart glanced off the ram's shoulder. With our helicopter continually buffetted by high winds, we risked disaster with every maneuver. Frustrated and out of darts, we flew back to where the trucks waited. We had just spent over $1,000 in helicopter time and had managed to radio-collar only one bighorn sheep.

As a wildlife graduate student at Montana State University, my master's thesis depended on attaching radio-collars to at least ten members of this bighorn sheep population. This sheep herd was transplanted in 1976 into a remote mountain area on the east side of the Rockies in northern Montana. Prior to my research project the success of the transplant was unknown. My objectives were to determine the population's status and trend, seasonal ranges, and critical areas. Subsequently, I was to draft plans for minimizing the impact of mineral exploration and development on bighorn sheep in this area. To accomplish these objectives, I needed to have radio-collared sheep so I could locate them from the air and follow their movements. These sheep resided in an isolated area that was inaccessible from the ground. Therefore, initially my colleagues and I decided to try darting the sheep from a helicopter in order to collar them. Helicopter darting is a common method for live capturing bighorn sheep in remote mountain areas. However, the constant, forceful winds of this area seemed to make helicopter darting ineffective.

I suggested we next try shooting a net-gun from the helicopter to live-capture these bighorn sheep. A net-gun is a rifle that fires a 19 × 19 foot net from a large funnel mounted on the front of the gun. Previously, this gun had been used on coyotes, antelope, and other animals of the plains country. Researchers felt that the net-gun required wide-open terrain, which would allow a helicopter time enough to approach a fleeing animal within a range of 10 to 15 feet for a successful shot. Nevertheless, I was desperate; funding and time were running out and my bighorn sheep study was in jeopardy. I needed to dispatch these radio-collars soon, before the bighorn sheep concentrations dispersed from their winter range.

Gary Olson (a state biologist) replaced Dick Kinyon in the helicopter on our net-gun capture attempt two weeks after the dart-gun fiasco. The mountains were still blanketed by glistening white snow, as we hummed over the ridges and peaks searching for bighorn sheep. The net-gun felt light in my arms in relation to its awkward shape. We soon located a group of 15 ewes and lambs. Mark skillfully maneuvered the helicopter down on the fleeing sheep, and I nervously aimed and squeezed the trigger. Boom! The gun exploded and the net sailed out over the sheep. I was surprised by how little kick the gun had. In the blink of an eye, three sheep went down, entangled in the net and thrashing frantically in a twisted heap of brown and white fur. While we circled above looking for a place to land, I felt sorry for the sheep as I watched them desperately fight for their freedom.

The helicopter touched down and Gary and I leaped out. Adrenalin surged through my body as we dashed through the snow toward the net. By the time we reached it, two ewes had practically worked their way free. I dove for one (a dive that would have made Pete Rose proud). Grabbing the ewe by her horns, I dragged her out of the net, and flipped her on her back with a move I had seen Tarzan use on a lion. Gary did likewise, and we sat on top of the sheep awaiting the arrival of the radio-collars.

Ten minutes later the helicopter arrived and Lewis Young (a U.S. Forest Service biologist) hopped out with the radio-collars. Lewis distributed the collars, then jumped on the lamb remaining in the net and attached a collar to it. I was so excited I forgot about the sharp horns of the ewe under me, and as I leaned over to snap the radio-collar together around her neck, she bucked her head backwards into my face. I felt fire on my left cheek, as bright red blood spurted over the bleached white fur of the ewe and the glistening snow.

Undeterred, I securely fastened her radio-collar and checked her age. Then I rolled off; she scrambled to her feet, and made a dash for the sanctuary of the cliffs. Gary and Lewis finished their sheep and all three of us watched them gracefully pick their way up the cliff. Later that night in the hospital, I wondered if my health insurance covered something as extraordinary as being horned by a bighorn sheep.

We continued using the net-gun for capture and quickly dispatched the remaining radio-collars. However, our capture operation was not without further incident. On one occasion we located a group of four rams hiding in the cliffs. After the third pass with the helicopter, one of the rams bounded up over the cliff and dashed across the snow-covered ridgetop. We quickly swept down on him, and with a loud blast I sent the net sailing. Immediately the ram dropped in a puff of snow. While kicking and rolling in the net, though, he moved dangerously close to a steep avalanche chute which extended down the side of the mountain. I had to reach him quickly.

It was too steep to land in the vicinity of the downed ram so I leaped from the helicopter as it hovered a few feet above the ground, and sprinted for the ram. My quick approach startled him and he struggled closer to the edge. I jumped on him and grabbed hold of his large, yellowish horns as we frantically wrestled in the net. With a powerful lunge of his hindquarters, the ram bowled both of us over the edge. As we started sliding down the avalanche chute, I desperately shoved the ram's horns toward a stunted limber pine growing on the side of the chute. Smack! The ram's left horn hooked the tree perfectly, and with a sudden jerk we stopped sliding. Emitting an immense sigh of relief, I let go of the ram (who was completely immobilized as he hung by his horn hooked around the tree) and stomped out a ledge in the snow to work on.

Gary Olson arrived quickly, and we worked the net free and attached a radio-collar to the ram. Still, one problem remained; we could not get the heavy ram unhooked from the tree. After many futile attempts to work the horns free, we decided to chop the small tree down. It brought a chuckle from us as we watched the powerful ram run up and over the ridge with the tree still in his horns! It took him three days to work the tree free.

The net-gun was my study's salvation. I attribute its remarkable success to the enhanced maneuverability of the modified helicopter (jet-engine added), the skill of our pilot Mark Duffy, the semi-open terrain of bighorn sheep winter range, and the tendency of bighorn sheep to flee in a tightly packed group when threatened. This live-capture operation, though, was not as easy as it looked on paper. As my father remarked, we took some dangerous risks. Nevertheless, I wouldn't trade this exciting experience for the world, and if the situation arose I would jump at the opportunity to do it again.

The Writing Community: Working in Groups

THE INTERACTIVE CLASSROOM

In Chapter 2—"Problematizing Experience: A Discussion of Reasoning for Writers"—we tried to show how certain principles of reason could be helpful to a writer. In this Appendix, we will extend some of those same principles of reason to the process of learning itself. Whereas in Chapter 2 you were asked to think about being a better writer, here you will be asked to think about being a better student of writing. Our task will be to assist you in creating an environment that is best suited to improving your writing skills.

As one might expect, there are a number of different theories about what constitutes the best learning environment for writers. And depending on how a writing teacher expresses the goals for a course, some of these classroom approaches can be more helpful than others. Thus, while many writing instructors stress the importance of studying writing as a "knowledge" subject focusing on principles, theories, examples, and so forth, others stress the importance of the process of learning how to learn. Consequently the knowledge-oriented teacher may tend to rely upon the lecture method or on class discussions led by the instructor, while the process-oriented teacher will stress classroom projects and group work to involve students actively in the material. The danger of the knowledge-centered approach is that students may lapse into passivity. The danger of the process-centered approach is that students might continually reinvent the wheel and lose the benefit of their instructor's knowledge.

Because each of these teaching methods has its strengths and weaknesses, it is impossible to claim that any one method is best for all students in all circumstances. Our own approach to classroom teaching, as you can probably predict from the kind of text we've written, borrows from both approaches. We call our own approach the "interactive method," but of course many other teachers use similar techniques with different names. Teachers using this approach have their students sometimes working in small independent groups, sometimes listening to the instructor, and sometimes discussing subjects with the instructor as a class. While students generally spend less than one third of their class time listening to the instructor, the instructor's influence is felt at every step of the learning process insofar as he or she will structure and explain group tasks, respond to the groups' findings, and assist groups who have trouble dealing with tasks.

In this setting the acquisition of knowledge or content is important, as it is in the lecture system, but teachers try as much as possible to make the knowledge their students' own by having students discover the knowledge for themselves, thereby learning how to learn. Let's examine some of the underlying philosophical differences between the two approaches by introducing an example.

SOME PHILOSOPHICAL DIFFERENCES BETWEEN THE LECTURE APPROACH AND THE INTERACTIVE APPROACH

Suppose a teacher wanted the class to study the criteria for an outstanding essay. A number of writing researchers have published lists of criteria for "good writing." In the lecture method, an instructor might reproduce a list of the experts' criteria on a ditto, pass it out to students, and explain its features through lecture. In the interactive method, however, a teacher might want students to go through the same sort of reasoning processes that writing specialists went through to develop the list in the first place. (In Exercise 2 at the end of this Appendix, we take you through the steps involved in the interactive development of grading criteria. It takes two or three classroom hours with some outside homework time. Your instructor may have you do these tasks as a group project. If not, you can imagine how the process would work.)

The initial differences between the approaches are thus easy to highlight. In the lecture setting you study a well-established set of criteria for good writing and then have time to move on to other material (the lecture method can cover in 30–45 minutes what can take 2–3 hours in the interactive method.) This efficiency is one of the major advantages of teaching through lecture.

In the interactive method, however, you go through a series of problem-solving tasks that mirror the process by which writing theorists themselves arrive at criteria. But while you read only a few essays and concentrate your energies for only a few hours on the issue, writing theorists have read thousands of essays and spent hundreds of hours thinking about the issues and discussing them with colleagues. Nevertheless, the processes are similar, and like all processes, they take time. Thus any process-oriented classroom has to sacrifice some "content" to make space for student interaction. Before you decide which method you personally prefer— lecture or interactive—you should consider some philosophical implications in the difference between the approaches.

As interactive learners you do not see experts' criteria until the very end, after you have developed your own criteria. When you finally get an opportunity to compare your group's criteria with those of the experts, there are two possibilites: either your group's list is similar to the experts' list or it is different. If your list is similar, then you have the satisfaction of knowing that you thought your way toward the same solution to a problem as did the experts. This new knowledge is "yours" because you have a stake in it; you didn't passively memorize it but rather helped create it.

But what if your criteria are significantly different from the experts'? It is here that teachers in an interactive setting face their greatest dilemma. Their tendency, perhaps, is to assert that the experts' criteria are better because they are "professionals" and you are merely students. But this is an unreasonable appeal to authority and should raise the hackles on the back of any reasonable student's neck. The only way that the experts' criteria can be shown to be better than yours is for the teacher to establish reasonable criteria for the criteria themselves, that is, to create a reasonable argument showing why the experts' list is better. If you are not convinced, then you, in turn, can create your own reasonable argument that your criteria are better.

This is how knowledge is built up in any social community—by the dialectic clashing of opposing views, as we discussed in Chapter 2. The primary objection that we ourselves have against the straight lecture approach to teaching is that lectures model a world view where authority reigns. Interactive learning, on the other hand, models a world of conflicting views—not a world where every view is equally valid, but where certain views can attain the status of reasonable positions because they can be supported with sound arguments while others cannot.

By emphasizing a world of opposing views, interactive learning mirrors the processes of reasoning which were outlined for individual thinkers in Chapter 2. The interactive classroom enacts or dramatizes these mental scripts for reasoning. Not only do you pose contrary or alternative points of view for yourself, but others in your group provide them for you and for others. And while the instructor plays a leading role in the classroom, the direction of learning is also determined by the parts students play and the conflicting ideas they help to generate. In addition to simply soliciting information from teachers, you are asked to pose your own points of view to your teachers, points of view buttressed by the collective wisdom of the class, and to defend those points of view against the critical questioning of your instructor.

Let's move on now to some of the practical advantages of and basic procedures for successful interactive learning. If your teacher chooses to use group work in class, then the following discussion may help you make those group sessions more productive. But because there are many other ways to teach writing than through group work, we recognize that all teachers won't wish to use these techniques. It is for these reasons that this essay is an appendix to the text rather than one of its chapters.

FROM CONFLICT TO CONSENSUS: HOW TO GET THE MOST OUT OF THE WRITING COMMUNITY

Implicit in everything that's been said so far is the notion that thinking and writing are social acts. At first, this notion may contradict certain widely accepted stereotypes of writers and thinkers as solitary souls who retreat to cork-lined studies where they conjure great thoughts and works. To be sure, every writer at some point in the process requires solitude, but it seems equally true that writers and thinkers require periods of talk and social interchange before they retreat to solitude. Poets, novelists, scientists, philosophers, and technological innovators tend to belong to communities of peers with whom they share their ideas, theories, and work. In this section, we will try to provide you with some practical advice on how to get the most out of these sorts of communities in developing your writing skills.

Avoiding Bad Habits of Group Behavior

Among the first problems to be addressed by potential members of a learning community are the bad habits of group behavior that most of us fall into over time. While we use groups all the time to study and accomplish demanding tasks, we tend to do so spontaneously outside of classroom settings and thereby don't notice how or why some groups work well and others don't. Many of you, for example, have probably worked on ineffective committees that just didn't get the job done and wasted your time, or else got the job done because one or two tyrannical people dominated the group. Because of these sorts of experiences with committees, you may possess a healthy skepticism about the utility of groups in general. "A committee," according to some people, "is a sort of centipede. It has many legs but moves very slowly and possesses no brain."

At their worst, this indeed is how groups function. In particular, they have a tendency to fail in two opposite directions, failures which can be avoided only by conscious effect. Groups can lapse into "clonethink" and produce a safe, superficial consensus in which everyone agrees with the first opinion expressed in order to avoid conflict or to get on to something more interesting. At the other extreme is a phenomenon we'll call "egothink." In egothink, all members of the group go their own way and produce a collection of minority views which have nothing to do with each other and would be impossible to act on. Clonethinkers view their task as conformity to a norm; egothinkers see their task as safeguarding the autonomy of individual group members. Both fail to take other people and other ideas seriously.

Above all else a successful group must avoid either extreme by achieving unity out of diversity. Before consensus can be reached, a community of learners must pass through a period of creative conflict. Creative conflict results from an initial agreement to disagree respectfully with each other and to focus that disagreement on ideas, not people. The relationship among the members of a learning community is not so much interpersonal or impersonal as transpersonal or "beyond the personal." Each member is personally committed to the development of ideas and works to play whatever role is necessary to that development.

The Value of Group Work for Writers

Learning to work in groups, while valuable for all thinkers, is especially valuable for writers. One of the first advantages for writers is the potential conviviality of groups. If you can learn to trust the members of your group, then you can feel free to express "silly" ideas or to show them your roughest rough drafts without fear of embarrassment. Because we are basically social animals, we find it natural, pleasurable even, to deal with problems in groups. Proof of this fact can be found on any given morning in any given student union in the country. Around the room you will find many students working in groups. Math, engineering, and business majors will be solving problems together, comparing solutions and their ways of arriving at solutions. People from all curricula will be comparing their class notes and testing their understanding of concepts and terms by explaining them to each other and comparing their explanations. To be sure, their discussions will drift off the topic occasionally to encompass pressing social issues like what they're going to do next weekend, or why they like or dislike the class they're working on, but much of the work of college students seems to get done in convivial conversation over morning coffee. Why not ease into the rigors of writing in a similar fashion?

A second major advantage of working on writing in a group is that it provides a real and immediate audience for your ideas and work. Too often, when students write in a school setting they get caught up in the writing-for-teacher racket discussed at length elsewhere in the text. This practice, in that it causes you to oversimplify your notion of audience, can lead to bad writing habits. Little of the writing you will do outside of school will have so limited an audience, and even in school, as we suggested in Chapters 1 and 2, you need to have a complex sense of audience before you can get the most out of your writing.

There's danger, of course, in having several audiences consider your writing. Your peer audience well might respond differently to your writing than your instructor. You may feel misled if you are praised for something by a peer and then criticized for the same thing by your instructor. These things can and will happen, no matter how much time you spend developing universally accepted criteria for writing. Judgments are not facts which can simply be looked up. All judgments involve uncertainty, and students who are still learning the criteria for making judgments are going occasionally to apply those criteria differently from an instructor who has been working with them for years. But you should know too that two or more instructors might give you conflicting advice also, just as two or more doctors might give you different advice on what to do about the torn ligaments in your knee. (Once again, group work places you smack in the middle of the real world of competing ideas.) But through practice, fewer of these sorts of disagreements should occur. Moreover, in applying these criteria to each others' essays you are learning to become not simply better writers, but better critics of writing and better readers as well. In our view, the risks of misunderstanding are more than made up for by the gains in understanding of the process of writing, an understanding that comes from working in writing communities.

A third advantage to working in writing communities is closely related to the second advantage. The act of sharing your writing with other people helps you to get beyond the bounds of egocentrism which limit all writers. By egocentrism, we don't mean pride or stuck-upness; we mean the failure to consider the needs of your readers. Unless you share your writing with another person, your audience is always a "mythical group," a fiction or a theory which exists only in your head. You must always try to anticipate the problems others will have in reading your work, but until others actually read it and share their reactions to it with you, you can never be fully sure you have understood your audience's point of view. Until another reads your writing critically, you cannot be sure if there aren't patches of your paper in which you are talking to yourself.

FORMING WRITING COMMUNITIES: SKILLS AND ROLES

Given that there are advantages to working in groups, just how do we go about forming writing communities in the classroom? One's first decision is the size of the group. From our experience, the best groups consist of either five to seven people or simply two people. Groups of three to four tend to polarize and become divisive, while larger groups tend to be unmanageable. Because working in 5–7 person groups is quite different from working in pairs, we will discuss each of these different-sized groups in turn.

Working in Groups of Five to Seven People

In large groups, your communal goal should be to keep focused on your objective while at the same time considering the maximum number of viewpoints and concerns within the group. Because these two basic goals frequently conflict, you need some mechanisms for monitoring your progress. In particular, it is important that individual members of the group be assigned to perform specified tasks necessary to effective group functioning. (Some teachers assign "roles" to individual students, shifting the roles from day to day; other teachers let the groups themselves determine the roles of individuals.) That is, the group must recognize that it has two objectives at all times: the stated objectives of a given task and the objective of making the group work well. It is very easy to get so involved with the given task that you overlook the second objective, generally known as "group maintenance."

The first role is group leader. We hesitate to call people who fill this role "leaders" because we tend to sometimes think of leaders as know-it-alls who "take charge" and order people about. In classroom group work, however, being a group leader is a role you play, not a fixed part of your identity. Probably the term "coordinator" better describes what we expect of this person. The coordinator, above all else, focuses the group's actions toward agreed upon ends without limiting the freedom of any individual group member. It is an important function and group members should share the responsibility from task to task. Here is a list of things for the coordinator to do during a group discussion.

1. Insure that everyone understands and agrees on the objectives of any given task and on what sort of final product is expected of the group. (For example, a list of criteria, a brief written statement, oral response to a question, etc.)
2. Ask that the group set an agenda for completing the task and have some sense of how much time they will spend at each stage.

3. Look for signs of getting off the track and ask individual group members to clarify how their statements relate to agreed upon objectives.
4. Actively solicit everyone's contributions and take care that all viewpoints are listened to and that the group does not rush to incomplete judgment.
5. Try to determine when the task has been adequately accomplished.

In performing each of these functions, the coordinator must be concerned to turn criticisms and observations into questions. Instead of saying to one silent and bored-looking member of the group, "Hey, Gormley, you haven't said didley squat here so far; say something relevant or take a hike," the coordinator might ask, "Irwin, do you agree with what Beth just said about this paper being disorganized?" Remember, every action in nature is met with an equal and opposite reaction—commands tend to be met with resistance, questions with answers.

A second crucial role for well-functioning groups is that of recorder. The recorder's function is to provide the group with a record of their deliberations and to thereby allow them to measure their progress. It is particularly important that the recorder write down the agenda and the solution to the problem in precise form. Because the recorder must summarize the deliberations fairly precisely, he must ask for clarifications. In doing this, he insures that group members don't fall into the "ya know?" syndrome (a subset of clonethink) in which people assent to statements which are in fact cloudy to them. (Ya know?) At the completion of the task, the recorder should also ask if there are any significant remaining disagreements or unanswered questions. Finally, the recorder is responsible for reporting the group's solutions to the class as a whole.

If these two roles are conscientiously filled, the group should be able to identify and solve problems that temporarily keep it from functioning effectively. Maybe you are thinking that this sounds dumb. Whenever you've been in a group everyone has known if there were problems or not without coordinators or recorders. Too often, however, a troubled group may sense that it has a problem without being perfectly clear about the nature of the problem or the solution. Let's say you are in a group with Elwood Lunt, Jr., who is very opinionated and dominates the discussions (for a sample of Elwood's cognitive style, see his essay in Task 2 at the end of the Appendix). Group members may represent their problem privately to themselves with a statement like "Lunt's such a jerk nobody can work with him. He talks dumb constantly and none of the rest of us can get a word in." Rather than solve the problem, the rest of the group may focus its attention on punishing Lunt with ridicule and/or silence. While this may make you feel better, it does not solve your group's real problem, which is how to make the group work.

If Lunt is indeed bogging the group down by airing his opinions at great length, it is the coordinator's job to limit his dominance without excluding him. Because group members all realize that it is the group leader's "role" to handle such problems, the leader has a sort of "license" which allows her to deal directly with Lunt. Moreover, she also has the explicit responsibility to do so, so that each member is not forced to sit, silently seething and waiting for someone to do something. The coordinator can control Lunt in one of several ways: (1) by keeping to the agenda ("Thanks Elwood, hate to interrupt, but we're a bit behind schedule and we haven't heard from everyone on this point yet. Jack, shall we move on to you?"); (2) by simply asking Lunt to demonstrate how his remarks are relevant to the topic at hand ("That's real interesting, Elwood, that you got to see Sid Vicious in his last performance, but can you tell us how you see that relating to Melissa's point that a sense of humor is crucial to good teaching?"); or (3) by introducing more formal procedures such as asking group members to raise their hands and be called upon by the chair. While these procedures might not satisfy your blood lust, your secret desire to stuff Lunt into a Dempsey dumpster, they are more likely to let the group get its work done and perhaps, just maybe, to help Lunt become a better listener and participant.

The rest of the group, though they have no formally defined roles, have an equally important obligation to participate fully. To ensure full participation, group members can do several things. They can make sure that they know all the other group members by first names and use their names and a friendly manner in speaking with each other. They can practice listening procedures outlined in Carl Rogers' article "Communication: Its Blocking and Facilitation" (pp. 393–398), trying not to dissent or disagree without first restating the view with which they are taking issue. Most importantly, they can bring to the group as much information and as many alternative points of view as they can muster. The primary intellectual strength of learning communities, remember, is the ability to generate a more complex view of a subject. But this more complex view cannot emerge unless all individuals contribute their perspective.

One interactive task for writers which requires no elaborate procedures or any role playing is reading your essays aloud within the group. The only hard and fast rule for this procedure is that no one responds to any one essay until all have been read. This is often an effective last step before handing in any essay. It's a chance to share the fruits of your labor with others and to hear finished essays which you may have seen in the draft stages. Hearing everyone else's final draft can also help you get a clearer perspective on how your own work is progressing. Listening to the essays read can both reassure you that your work is on a par with other people's and challenge you to write up to the level of the best student writing in your group.

Many of you may find this process a bit frightening at first. But the cause of your fright is precisely the activity's value. In reading your work aloud you are taking responsibility for that work in a special way. Writing specialist Kenneth Bruffee, whose work on collaborative learning introduced us to many of the ideas in this chapter, likens the reading of papers aloud to reciting a vow, of saying "I do" in a marriage ceremony. You are taking public responsibility for your words, and there's no turning back. The word has become deed. As teachers, we can readily identify with your trepidation. We get the same queasy feeling before we walk into any classroom. The public statements we make in our classrooms and the responses to those statements are much more important to our sense of ourselves as teachers than anything else we do. In speaking with our classes, we are taking direct responsibility for the learning that goes on, committing our theories and plans and hopes to practice. Anyone who isn't at least a little nervous about reading an essay aloud or making public statements probably hasn't invested much in her words. Knowing that you will take public responsibility for your words is an incentive to make that investment, a more real and immediate incentive than a grade.

Working in Pairs

Working in pairs is another effective form of community learning. In our classes we use pairs at both the early draft and late draft stages of writing. At the early draft stage, it serves the very practical purpose of clarifying a student's sense of direction at the beginning of the writing process. The interaction best takes place in the form of pair interviews. When you first sit down to interview each other, each of you should have done a fair amount of exploratory writing and thinking about what you want to say in your essay and how you're going to say it. At the beginning of the interview, you should ask the interviewee to summarize the content of her intended paper for you. Don't settle for a one word reponse like "computers"; demand to know what the other person proposes to say about computers in a sentence or two. For example, "I'm going to discuss how a family should go about selecting the home computer that's right for them." The interviewer should write this and all other important responses down on paper.

Next, ask the interviewee who her audience is. You should ask why this proposed audience will be surprised by the writer's essay. What will they learn from reading it? How will they be changed? A typical response might be: "The media are filled with advertisements about how computers are fun and time-saving devices, but few people really get much use out of their computers. My paper will help them get more value out of their purchase." Interviewees should next explain what their audience can and cannot be expected to know about the subject. For instance, "They probably know that computers can help with planning budgets and learning French, but they probably don't know much about the programs which the different

companies have available for these purposes.' Next, you should ask if anyone might disagree with the position your interviewee takes in the paper:
"Someone might oppose buying a home computer on the grounds that they
will be cheaper and more powerful next year." At this point you should ask
the writer to talk you through the essay. What are you going to say first? What
next? and so on. This procedure helps the writer discover a form for the
essay. Finally, you should tell the interviewee anything you know about her
subject that might be useful to her. For example, "My aunt and uncle bought
one that was real cheap but couldn't do anything but play games." In sum,
the interviewer plays the role of the potential reader of the unwritten
paper, thereby helping the writer anticipate specific audience needs and
background.

There are a number of different ways of approaching the evaluation of
drafts in pairs. One practice that we've found helpful is simply to have
writers write a one-paragraph summary of their own draft, or to make a tree
diagram of it, and then give their drafts to another person to summarize or
diagram. In comparing summaries or tree diagrams, the writer can often
discover which, if any, of their essential ideas are simply not getting across.
If a major idea is not in the reader's summary or diagram, writer and reader
need to decide if it's due to a careless reading or to problems within the draft.
The nice thing about this method is that the criticism is given indirectly and
hence isn't as threatening to either party. At other times, your instructor
might also devise a checklist of features for you to consider.

SUMMARY

In this appendix, we have treated the writing community as a logical
extension of the reasonable individual discussed in Chapter 2. In particular,
we believe that creative conflict in groups leads to a heightened awareness of
contraries. A writing community is basically a mechanism for discovering
the similarities and differences among the viewpoints of the individual
group members and for helping thinkers move toward syntheses. By forcing
individuals to "unpack" or articulate their viewpoints to an audience of
peers, the writing community serves also to enhance people's ability to
communicate with each other, an ability which is directly transferable to the
act of writing. In turn, the writing community requires people to get into the
habit of developing their opinions into reasoned judgments and sharpens
their ability to recognize the differences between the two. Finally, in acting
out or externalizing reasonable thought processes, the writing community
allows people to see, literally, the *how* as well as the *what* of learning and
emphasizes learning-how-to-learn over assimilation of information.

For Class Discussion

1. As a group, consider the following quotation and then respond to the questions that follow: "In most college classrooms there is a reluctance to assume leadership. The norm for college students is to defer to someone else, to refuse to accept the position even if it is offered. There is actually a competition in humility and the most humble person usually ends up as the leader." (Philips, Peterson & Woods, *Group Discussion, A Practical Guide*, p. 126).
   a. Do you think this statement is true?
   b. On what evidence do you base your judgment of its truthfulness?
   c. As a group, prepare an opening sentence for a paragraph that would report your group's reaction to this quotation.

2. *A 3–4 Hour Group Project: Defining "Good Writing."* The problem we want you to address in this sequence of tasks is how to define and identify "good writing." This is a particularly crucial problem for young writers insofar as you can't begin to measure your growth as a writer until you have some notion of what you're aiming for. To be sure, it's no easy task defining good writing. In order for even experienced teachers to reach agreement on this subject, some preliminary discussions and no small amount of compromise is necessary. By the end of this task you will most certainly not have reached a universally acceptable definition of good writing. (It doesn't exist.) But you will have begun a dialogue with each other and your instructor on the subject. Moreover, you will have sketched out some principles to apply and modify as you go along and will have developed a vocabulary for sharing your views on writing with each other.

   For this exercise, we will give you a sequence of four tasks, some being homework and others being in-class group tasks. Please do the tasks in sequence.

Task 1 (homework): Preparing for the Group Discussion

Freewrite for 5 minutes on the question: "What is good writing?" After finishing your freewrite, read fictional student Lunt's essay below, and, based on the principles that Lunt seems to break, develop a tentative list of criteria for good writing.

Explanation

Before you come together with a group of people to advance your understanding and knowledge collectively, you first need to explore your own thoughts on the matter. Too often, groups collapse not because the members lack good will, but because they lack preparation. In order to discharge your responsibility as a good group member, you must therefore begin by doing your homework. By using a freewriting exercise, you focus your thinking on the topic, explore what you already know or feel about it, and begin framing questions and problems.

To help you establish a standard for good writing, we've produced below a model of bad writing by a fictional student, one Elwood P. Lunt, Jr. If you can figure out what's bad about Lunt's writing, then you can formulate the principles of good writing that he violates. Of course, *no* student of our acquaintance has ever written anything as bad as Lunt's essay. That's the virtue of this contrived piece. It's an easy target. In going over it critically, you may well find that Lunt violates principles of good writing you hadn't thought of in your freewrite. (We tried to assure that he violated as many as possible.) Thus, you should be sure to go back and modify your ideas from your freewrite accordingly.

A couple of important points to keep in mind here as you prepare to critique another person's work: (1) Remember the Principle of Charity. Try to look past the muddied prose to a point or intention that might be lurking in the background. Your critique should speak as much as possible to Lunt's failure to realize this intent. (2) Direct your critique to the prose, not the writer. Don't settle for "He just doesn't make sense," or "He's a dimwit." Ask yourself why he doesn't make sense and point to particular places where he doesn't make sense. In sum, give Lunt the same sort of reading you would like to get: compassionate and specific.

Good Writing and Today's Modern American Youth of America

*(A partial fulfillment of writing
in the course in which I am attending)*

In todays modern fast paced world computers make living a piece of cake. You can do a lot with computers which in former times took a lot of time and doing a lot of work. Airports for example. But there are no such things as a free lunch. People who think there is need to go to the Iron Curtain and take a look around, there are some computers which make you into just a number. Take 43 for example. Big Brother is everywhere and his little brother is you-know-what. I read once where Martin Snidder did not get paid for six months in *Newsweek*. The precious computer which people think is the dawn of a new civilization but which is in all reality a pig in a poke makes you into a number but can't even add right!

So what makes people think that they won't have to write just because they have had a computer looking over his shoulder I ask? "Garbage in and garbage out one philosopher said." Do you want to be garbage. I don't. That's why modern American fast paced youth must conquer this problem and writing is the answer to our dreams.

Especially good transitions are important and if they can't be done then don't try it! And don't forget grammar. My Dad Elwood P. Lunt Sr. hit the nail on the head; when he said grammar can make you sound like a jerk. Right on dad. So get on the bandwagon and write good and get rich with computers. Which you can make write right. And according to Websters dictionary which doesn't list good writing but does list them both in different places which makes it hard to figure out, good means not bad and writing means to fill in or cover which is not a bad cover.

Task 2 (in-class group work): Developing a Master List of Criteria

As a group, reach a consensus on at least 6 or 7 major problems with Lunt's essay. Then use that list to prepare a parallel list of criteria for good writing. Begin each item on your criteria list with the words, "A well written essay should ...." Please have your list ready in 30 minutes.

Explanation

Having been placed in small groups to discuss your critiques of Lunt's work, your goal is to reach consensus about what's wrong with Lunt's paper. (As opposed to a majority decision, in which more people agree than disagree, a consensus entails a solution that is generally acceptable to all members of the group.) After each group has completed its list, recorders should report each group's consensus to the class as a whole. Your instructor will facilitate a discussion leading to the class's "master list" of criteria.

Task 3 (homework): Applying Criteria to Student Essays

At home, consider the following four samples of student writing (this time they're real examples). Rank the essays "1" through "4" with one being the best and four the worst. Once you've done this, write a one-page rationale for your ranking. In your rationale, indicate which criterion for good writing you rank the highest and which you rank the lowest (for example, does "correct spelling" rank higher or lower than "grammatically correct sentences"? Does "quality of ideas" rank higher or lower than "organization"?)

Explanation

The essays reprinted below were all written in response to the "supporting reasons" assignment in Chapter 12 (Task 1 on pp.336–340). Before judging the essays, read over that assignment so you know what students were asked to do. Judge the essays on the basis of the criteria established in class.

Example A

"I think it's just a little bit behind the times," Mr. Anderson said of the two-room, 32-student Armington school near Belt, Montana. "The little red schoolhouse served its purpose, but it's seen its day." Many educators and laymen alike seem to share this viewpoint in the face of computerized teaching aids and specialized classes. There is the feeling that the rural elementary students are given the basics such as reading, math, science, english and history, but nothing extra such as computer skills and foreign languages to help them through high school, college and careers. In a world that's rapidly shrinking due to vastly improved technology in communication, this could be a serious detriment. Also questions such as "Can the rural elementary students compete academically, especially in the math and science fields which change so rapidly, with other students from large, urban schools?" frequently come up. Finally, it's believed that rural students are at a social disadvantage with not having the opportunity to interact at a multicultural level and to gain opinion diversification from several instructors. Despite these strong arguments, I feel that the small, rural grade schools can provide a quality education for Montana children for several reasons.

A quality education doesn't just mean learning how to read and write. Education also involves character building. First, the students of a small, rural grade school gain a special sense of community pride. They can see the active support of the community towards their school, and more importantly, towards themselves. The children want to return this with their best efforts. I remember our Fergus Grade School Christmas programs. Sure, every grade school has a Christmas program, but ours seemed to be small productions. We started work on our play and songs immediately after Thanksgiving. The Fergus Community Women's Club decorated the hall a few days before the program. When the big night arrived, the whole community turned out, even Mr. and Mrs. Schoenberger, an elderly couple. I, along with the other eleven students, were properly nervous as we performed our play, *A Charlie Brown Christmas*. As a finale, the whole community sang carols and exchanged gifts. One of the fathers even dressed up as Santa Claus. Everyone involved had a warm feeling down inside when they went home. Second, the students gain a strong sense of individuality and responsibility from attending a small, rural school. Being part of such a small school system, the students realize that they matter. Along with this, comes the realization that everyone has to work together to accomplish a task. There has to be both give and take. An example of this was our daily cleaning chores at Fergus Grade School. We would have to fold the flag, sweep the floor, etc. A big difference though, was that there was no janitor to clean up after us. If we didn't do our chores, the school didn't get cleaned.

My primary reason for supporting the small, rural grade schools over the larger urban schools is that the students do learn their subjects well and are allowed to work at their own pace. I am my own proof. I was the only member of my grade from the third to the eighth grade at Fergus Grade School. I relished the privilege of being able to work on two chapters of math, instead of one, especially if I enjoyed the subject. Upon graduation from the eighth grade, I attended St. Leo's High School in Lewistown. I maintained an "A" average throughout my four years there. I credit this to my being taught a solid core of fundamentals at Fergus Grade School. Also in the small, rural grade schools, the students have the advantage of being able to get the needed individualized help with basic comprehension problems which is so important in the primary years. With only ten to fifteen students, the teachers can spend fifteen minutes helping one student and not impair the other students' learning.

The issue of quality education from the small, rural grade schools relates to one of the problems at MSU today. There seems to be a great deficiency in math and reading skills. The students that are educated in the rural grade schools have that solid core which will serve them on into their careers. The strong sense of responsibility, individuality, and community pride gained from attending rural grade schools will shine through these students as adults. They will possess that inner strength and self-dependence, which when cultivated, will develop into leadership in careers, community responsibility and personal success.

Example B

The newly changed laws against drunk drivers has a lot of people thinking twice about drinking and driving. Driving while under the influence causes very severe accidents, often killing an individual. Will the harsher penalties on drunk drivers decrease accidents related to alcohol?

The law will protect innocent bistandards from possible injury from drunk drivers. Society looks down on individuals who drink and drive. Especially when someone is killed or injured from an alcohol related accident. Drinking really dulls a persons reflexes, possibly causing an accident.

Yes, drinking can cause a number of accidents but not all drivers that drink wreck their automobiles. Police officers will be cracking down but maybe too much.

Policemen will pull over students for almost no reason at all. Just to see if the driver is drinking or not. Policemen are really keeping a sharp lookout for drunk drivers on the week-ends. They pull over cars that break very minor traffic violations just for the sake of busting drunk drivers. Innocent bistandards are sometimes a victim of this abuse resulting in meaningless tickets. There should be just cause for an officer of the law to be able to pull a vehicle over just to check for booze.

The new laws are a good idea for safety reasons. Once the public realizes the severe punishment involved, they will think before driving while under the influence of alcohol. The laws will clean up the streets of drunk drivers and hopefully make them a lot safer.

Example C

It was a typical Saturday night in Bozeman for many people including me except for me this Saturday night turned out to be not quite so typical. I had just left the Molly Brown on my way to the Sundance, I had had a few drinks at the Molly so I was feeling pretty good and I was preparing to have a few more at the Sundance. I pulled out onto Main and saw that the light was yellow, figuring since I always go through lights when they are yellow, why shouldn't I now. The only difference this time was that I had been drinking because if I hadn't been drinking I would have checked for cops like I always do when I haven't been drinking. But this time good luck and the police were against me. I got pulled over and arrested for D.U.I. When I think back now about how scared I was when I got picked up I know that it will be a very long while before I get in a car with a person who has been drinking. This was a recent incident of mine that made me start to wonder whether "the new D.U.I. laws will cut down on drunk drivers and save lives?" Many people feel that the harsher and stricter laws are great when they are put into practice and are enforced. The major problem is when the police try to enforce them. There aren't enough policemen on the road to stop all of the drunk drivers so that is how they have problems enforcing the new laws. However, despite this argument I feel that the new D.U.I. laws will cut down on drunk drivers and save lives.

First, I think the new D.U.I. laws will really work because the police are enforcing them. Many people up until recently haven't really taken the D.U.I. laws seriously. You could get pulled over and many times talk your way out of it and end up with only a warning. And if you did get arrested the penalty wasn't usually very severe the first couple of times. That just isn't the case with the new laws and I think this might have an effect on the drunk drivers. People are finally starting to realize that the laws are seriously going to be enforced and aren't going to be nearly as easy to get out of as before. This will cause people to stop and think about what they are about to do. I can use myself as an example in this case because I know that now every time I start to drink I make sure that I am not going anywhere or if I am there is somebody there that is sober and not drinking. Another reason the new D.U.I. laws might help cut down the amount of drunk drivers could be that even though many people don't learn from other people's mistakes there are always the ones that do learn. These might not be many but it's still that many more that won't drink and drive. I know that this can happen from personal experience. A few weekends ago when I was pulled over for my

D.U.I., my best friend was in the car with me. She saw the cop arresting me (handcuffing me and all) and being put into the police car. She knew about me going to court and having to pay the fine and staying in jail. If anyone even mentions to her anything about getting in a car after she's been drinking or going in a car with anyone that has been drinking now, she tells them in no uncertain terms how stupid she thinks they are. Some lessons don't have to be learned the hard way.

My main reason for believing that the new D.U.I. laws will really work tho is because they really have teeth. The punishment for first, second, third etc. D.U.I. offenses have become very severe. This causes people to sit back and take a look at what they have done and if they can afford to have it happen again. For just your first offense D.U.I. you are fined anywhere from $100.00 to $500.00 dollars (usually about $300.00), your license is suspended for 6 months, you have to spend 24 hours in jail and you have to attend D.U.I. School 5 times over the next 5 weeks at a cost of $100.00 dollars to yourself. This is only for your first offense and this is enough to cause most people to start to think and figure out if it is really worth it or if it would be worth it to do it again. Most people after that kind of punishment can't afford either financially or emotionally to have to go through it again.

I think that this very definitely relates to the situation around Bozeman. Because Bozeman is a college town it probably has more people drinking and driving than many places. This gives the police a greater opportunity to put the laws into effect. In the last month I have known three people who have got D.U.I.'s. The day that I went to court there were about 20 people there. I was about the tenth person up and before me there were 6 people that were there for D.U.I.'s, two of them for second offenses and that was only half way through. This shows that the police really are arresting people for D.U.I.'s and making possibly an impact on the drunk drivers because people are finding out that the laws are really going to be enforced. And the people that have already been arrested and have to pay the fine etc. will probably be alot less likely to get in a car and drive after they've been drinking again.

Example D

Have you ever had to miss an important meeting because it was out of town and you had no way to get there? Have you ever woken up on a Sunday morning to find that you must walk downtown to church in below-freezing temperatures knowing that the wind will be biting at your face and body the entire way? These are just a couple of the things that have happened to me while being at college without a car. If I had my own car, it would be up to me whether to bring it to college or not. I would gladly pay for my own car, but my dad refuses to let me buy a used car because they're "undependable". The only other alternative is to buy a new car, but with my income I will probably never be able to afford one! I have had access to a vehicle for the entire four years that I have had my license.

We have three cars at home for two drivers. I can't help thinking about how much of a waste this is when I could be getting good use out of one of them here. My problem is that my parents claim that I would spend my time "running around" rather than studying. They think that having a car would give me a good excuse to "goof off". To them, a car is just a "distraction" to college. This may be true for some students, but for me having a car at college is important for a number of reasons.

First, having a car at college would give me the security of not having to walk everywhere. It's not bad on campus but walking downtown, especially at night, get's pretty scary. Like any college town, Bozeman has a moderate to high crime rate. In the first two months of school, there have already been reported rapes and assaults. Being a female, I am particularly vulnerable to these crimes. Having a car would help protect me because I could drive instead of walk. This would decrease my chances of being a victim of one of these crimes. A second reason that having a car at college is important is to let me prove to my parents that I am a responsible person. I have shown the desire to come to college and this demonstrates that I have the responsibility to keep up with my work and not fool around. I have proven that I can be trusted with a car. I have a clean driving record and I don't waste gas, which I pay for, on "cruising" or "looking for excitement". I feel that I have the good judgement to decide when a car is needed or when I could walk. Still another reason that having a car at college is important is for unexpected circumstances. Things like minor injuries which come up and must be handled by a doctor require transportation which isn't always provided by an ambulance. Since some of my friends and I aren't on the Student Health Care Plan, we must go downtown for emergencies. If something would happen to one of us, such as a freak accident in one of our intramural football games, we would have to find someone with a car. The extra time spent on finding a car could endanger the person's health. Regular doctor, dentist, and personal appointments also require the use of a vehicle because the places which I must go to are located off-campus. Other emergencies may come up during the year and I would hate to be stranded because I had no transportation.

But the most important reason for having a car at college is that I have many extra-curricular activities located off-campus and can't depend on others for rides. I am currently involved in the Swine project which has it's meetings at the Swine Center, off-campus. Although I have tried to make contacts for rides, I can't always find someone and have often had to miss important workshops. I will also be involved in the Beef and Sheep projects coming up during the winter and spring quarters. These also have their meetings at the Beef and Sheep Centers off-campus. Other activities include a job at one of the local banks downtown, skiing at Bridger Bowl, horsebackriding with friends out of town, and many other activities which come up during the year. I would like to be able to get places when I need to rather than having to find someone who is free and can take me where I need to go. I feel that I am missing out on many fun, as well as educational, activities because I can't find transportation.

The argument over having a car at college goes beyond a family disagreement. Many of my activities correspond to my course structure and help me with my curriculum. The Swine, Beef, and Sheep projects all help me in my hopes for a degree in Animal Health Technology. Having a car is directly related to my success in college because if I can't get to my extra-curricular activities, I can't expand my learning. Going to college shows that I have the maturity to be responsible for attending class and keeping up with the work. Letting me have a car at college is a way of showing me that I am trusted and can prove I am a responsible person. It is a way of letting me go.

Task 4 (in-class group work): Reaching Consensus on Ranking of Essays

Working again in small groups, reach consensus on your ranking of these four essays. Groups should report both their rankings and their justification for the rankings based on the criteria established in Task 2 or as currently modified by your group.

Explanation

Reforming with the same group you worked with earlier, reach consensus on how you rank the papers and why you rank them the way you do. Feel free to change the criteria you established earlier if they seem to need modification. Be careful in your discussions to distinguish between evaluation of writing quality and judgments about the personal beliefs of the writers. (In other words there is a crucial difference between saying "I don't like Pete's essay because I disagree with his ideas" and "I don't like Pete's essay because he didn't provide adequate support for his ideas.") As each group reports back the results of their deliberations to the class as a whole, the instructor will highlight discrepancies among the groups' decisions and collate the criteria as they emerge. If the instructor disagrees with the class consensus or wants to add items to the criteria, he or she might choose to make these things known now. By the end of this stage, everyone should have a list of criteria for good writing established by the class.

Task 5 (in-class group work): Comparing the Class's Criteria to Those of the Experts

Your instructor will distribute copies of evaluation criteria prepared by experts. In small groups, decide whether your criteria are similar to or significantly different from the experts' criteria. If they are different, prepare a defense of your criteria or decide to accept the experts' version. Recorders should report your group's consensus to the class as a whole.

Explanation

This task concludes the extended example of an "interactive classroom" in process. By now you should have a feel for the problem of evaluating essays as well as a sense of how the "conversation" about evaluation is conducted.

Index